Ethical Motivations

Kevin Alan Lee

LeTTers

Press

Vancouver

British Columbia

Canada

LeTTers.Press@gmail.com

Ethical Motivations

ISBN: 978-0-9937255-0-0 [Clothbound]

ISBN: 978-0-9937255-1-7 [Paperback]

ISBN: 978-0-9937255-2-4 [Electronic Book]

© Kevin Alan Lee

A.A., B.A.

2014

Table of Contents

Chapter 1	Introduction	7
Chapter 2	Nature of Man	31
Chapter 3	Intellect	62
Chapter 4	Emotional Centre	84
Chapter 5	Array of Principles	118
Chapter 6	Law of Hierarchy	150
Chapter 7	The Static Character	184
Chapter 8	The Dynamic Character	224
Chapter 9	The Formless Character	248
Chapter 10	Judgment	300
Chapter 11	Reciprocity	362
Chapter 12	The Newborn State	419
Chapter 13	Beauty	480

For My Family

Preface

"Ethical Motivations" outlines a system of ethics that is based both on the individual's actions, and the reasons that motivate his chosen actions. This is due to the fact that although two individuals may commit a similar act, the reasons that motivate this act may be inherently different. Hence, moral judgments must not be merely based on an individual's actions, but also the reasons that motivate him to act.

The individual's character is based entirely on his chosen actions. Yet, behind the individual's will to choose is a unique mindset. Every person's mind is comprised of three parts, but it is the interaction between these parts that essentially determines his character. Persons with a dynamic character possess a mindset that is governed by the law of hierarchy, while persons with a static character possess a mindset that is dominated by a single element of the mind.

The phenomenon of duty best illustrates an individual's primary motives. Individuals who accept their particular responsibilities do so because they are motivated by some kind of virtue. In contrast, individuals who refuse to take on their particular responsibilities do so because they are motivated by some personal vice. The difference between virtuous motives and vicious motives best demonstrates the difference between moral and immoral actions.

1   Introduction

OVER TWO THOUSAND YEARS AGO, a philosopher named Plato derived a theory concerning the human mind. According to him, the mind is an immaterial component in every human being. Many other thinkers also hold the belief that persons are comprised of an immaterial mind and a material body. This line of thinking is known as dualism. Some dualists define the immaterial component of the human being as the soul. Other philosophers hold the belief that there is no distinction between the human soul and the human mind. With respect to human character, the human soul may be defined as the combination of the individual's mind with his personal experiences.

Rene Descartes offers a compelling argument that all human beings possess both an immaterial mind and a material body. He does this by distinguishing the concept of a mind from the concept of a body. If both concepts are distinct from one another, then it follows that they may be perceived as two completely different substances. Descartes may be categorized as a dualism interactionist. He theorizes that the mind is not immediately affected by all parts of the body, but only by the brain. The connection between mind and body, then, occurs somewhere within the brain. In essence, every time the brain is in a specific state, it presents signals to the mind.

First, Descartes argues that, from time to time, he has been deceived by his senses. For example, objects that he perceives, from a long distance, appear to be smaller than they actually are. Moreover, he has been further deceived while asleep. For instance, while in a dreaming state, persons believe that they are present within a particular physical environment, while in actuality, they are asleep. Accordingly, persons believe that they are present within an environment that exists only within their imagination. Descartes then extends this circumstance by presenting the supposition that it is entirely possible that he could be in a similar dreaming state, even during times when he believes that he is awake within the actual physical world. In other words, he postulates the possibility that his entire physical existence is unreal, and that he has been present within a dreaming state for his entire life.

Instead of a world where God exists, his dreaming argument supposes that, instead, a malicious demon, which possesses the utmost power and cunning, exists and that this demon has been deceiving him about the existence of the material world. Therefore, the earth, the sky, and all external things are merely delusions of a dream. From the dreaming argument, Descartes then draws the conclusion that he can only be sure of at least one thing; namely that at least he, himself, exists. For, even if it is true that an evil demon is deceiving him about his existence within the physical world, something must exist, in the first place, to be deceived.

Descartes then comes to the conclusion that, with all certainty, the nature of his existence is purely that of a "thinking" thing. A thinking thing lacks extension and is, thus, immaterial. He reasons that if he truly exists within a pure dreamlike state, he still imagines and that his imagination is a faculty of thought. He is also a thing that doubts, understands, affirms, denies, wills, and experiences sensory perceptions. These are further modes of thought. Again, he comes to the conclusion that it is not possible for something to think, but not exist. The fact that one is thinking necessarily entails some kind of existence, and if his dreaming argument is true, then his entire existence may be utterly immaterial in nature.

It is possible to doubt, then, that the nature of his existence is based on physical properties. In the case that he merely exists within a dreaming state, he will be mistaken about his physical existence, and likewise, the belief that he is a man. Next, Descartes uses a piece of wax to define the concept of judgment, which illustrates the nature of the mind. Through his sensory perceptions, he lists the properties of a particular piece of wax that is before him. This object possesses a certain odour, it has a distinct colour, and it has some form of shape and size. Similarly, it is both hard and cold. Nonetheless, when this piece of wax is exposed to fire, it loses its odour, the residual taste is eliminated, it changes in colour, it loses its shape, and it increases in size. Moreover, it takes a liquid form and it is hot. Therefore, the properties that originally belonged to this piece of wax have changed, yet he still possesses the ability to identify this new physical substance as wax. How is this possible? Descartes argues that the faculty of judgment, within our minds, enables us to accomplish this task.

Essentially, our knowledge of this piece of wax does not come merely from what the eye sees, but also through the scrutiny of our minds. Descartes states, "if I look out of the window and see men crossing the square, as I just happen to have done, I normally say that I see the men themselves, just as I say that I see the wax". Nevertheless, all he truly sees, through his sensory perceptions, are hats and coats, and it is conceivably possible these individuals could just be mindless automatons. It is the faculty of judgment that enables him to further perceive these objects as men, and not something that just mimics the physical properties of a man. Therefore, physical objects are not perceived merely through the sense of sight or the sense of touch, but also by the intellect, and this enables them to be understood.

Sensory perceptions form a passive faculty that recognizes and receives ideas of sensible material objects. It is passive because the ideas in question are produced without consent and, on occasions, against the will. Therefore, we cannot avoid experiencing sensory perceptions of objects if they are present. Similarly, the ideas produced by physical objects are more lively and vivid in comparison to the impressions of those ideas contained within our memory.

According to Descartes' theory, if we clearly and distinctly understand one thing from another, this will make us certain that these things are truly distinct, and also that they are capable of being separated by God. Since he is a thinking thing that is not extended, and also since he experiences sensory perceptions through his body, which is an extended non-thinking thing, Descartes further concludes that he is distinct from his body and can exist without it.

We are justified in calling our bodies our own; however, we cannot separate ourselves from our bodies in the same manner that we can separate ourselves from other physical phenomena. Experiences of pain and pleasure come directly from our bodies. Nevertheless, Descartes argues that there is no connection between the tugging sensation, known as hunger, and our decision to take food. He also argues that there is no connection between the sensation of pain and the mental apprehension of distress that respectively results. Contrarily, he states that by the sensations of pain, hunger, and thirst that he, as a thinking thing, is closely conjoined with his body, in a sense that they form a kind of unit. Hence, sensations of hunger and thirst are not merely confused sensations, but are modes of thinking that arise from the union of the mind and body.

The fact that some sensations are agreeable, while others are not, seems to suggest that I, as a union of body and mind, possess the understanding that some physical bodies may either be beneficial or harmful to me. This kind of understanding occurs only, though, when our intellect has examined the matter. In fact, our sensory perceptions can mislead the individual who does not employ his intellect to analyze his sensations. For example, an individual may be deceived by the pleasant taste of some food, even though it may be tainted by some kind of poison. Without any examination from the intellect, the nature of man will simply urge him to choose any foods with a pleasant taste. In a similar manner, a man who suffers from dropsy will feel the sensation of thirst, even though the disease will be aggravated when his body ingests some form of drink. The body, then, may exhibit a disordered nature because it suffers from a dry throat, even though it does not require any liquids. The phenomenon of phantom limbs also illustrates his point. Some persons, who are missing a particular limb, will still experience sensations as if it was still attached to their body. Subsequently, while our sensory perceptions may sometimes mislead us, a mind is necessary to comprehend this.

  Descartes argues that while the body, by its nature is always divisible, the mind is utterly indivisible. This is due to the fact that as thinking things, we cannot distinguish any parts within ourselves. With respect to the faculties of willing, understanding, and sensory perception, it is a single mind that performs these intellectual tasks. As thinking things, we are single and complete. Likewise, as a union of body and mind, nothing will be taken away from the mind if some body part, like a foot, were cut off. In contrast, our physical bodies can be divided into parts, and this makes them divisible. He states that while we cannot conceive half of a mind, we can conceive half of a body. Logically then, we may recognize that the natures of mind and body are not only different, but in some way opposite of one another. The human body, then, is made up of a certain configuration of limbs, while the human mind is a pure substance. In essence, if the mind somehow changes, or if it has differing objects of understanding, different desires, or differing sensations, it does not become a different mind. The body, in contrast, loses its identity when there is a change in shape in some of its parts. Since the body is divisible, and the mind is indivisible, it is arguable that these are two entirely different things. From this line of reasoning, Descartes then draws the conclusion that while the body may easily perish, the mind does not perish and is immortal by its very nature.

    For a final point, Descartes states that we can understand ourselves without the faculties of imagination and sensory perception. Nonetheless, we cannot understand these faculties without being some kind of an intellectual substance. These faculties are modes of thought, which must be performed by some kind of thinking thing, or in other words, an immaterial mind. (Descartes)

    Descartes only raises doubt of the physical world to demonstrate that our knowledge of the mind is the most certain, and evident, of all possible objects of knowledge. Therefore, it is possible to doubt the existence of our physical bodies, but it is impossible to doubt the existence of our minds. It is a thought experiment that enables us to conceive the presence and nature of an immaterial mind.

The theory of dualism may best explain the true nature of all human beings. The existence of both material and immaterial entities should implicate the existence of the human mind. Thoughts are immaterial phenomena. Material objects, however, may be viewed by every person. Material entities are objects that are perceivable through the five human senses. In contrast, only I have access to my own thought processes. My thoughts are not perceivable by other persons, in the same manner that these individuals can perceive the colour of my eyes or the sound of my voice. My personal thoughts do not take on any kind of a material existence. If I perceive a teal coloured diamond, no other person can have access to this thought, unless I verbally communicate this thought to him. All persons possess the power to perceive other kinds of objects, which may or may not exist within our world, through their faculty of imagination. Yet, the only way that we can share these ideas is through some mode of communication.

Everything that we perceive in the world, like horses, flowers or rain clouds, exhibits some kind of a physical existence. Nonetheless, I can imagine some object with differing kinds of properties, like a unicorn, or think of new inventions that do not yet exist. This draws a real distinction between the material and immaterial. Material objects, like the space rocket, were created by human hands. Something material in nature was produced by something else that is also material in nature. In a similar fashion, my immaterial thoughts are produced by something that is also immaterial in nature. This, namely, is my mind.

Thoughts are essentially an extension of the mind because they cannot exist independent of a mind, in the same manner that a painting can exist outside of my body. My thoughts cannot be perceived by the senses of touch, taste, odour, sound, or sight. Likewise, as a purely physical being, I could not gain any kind of access to my personal thoughts, even through my own sensory perceptions. My thoughts are accessible only through my private and immaterial mind.

      All free souls possess an immaterial mind, simply because they possess a consciousness. When I touch a tree, it does not express the fact that it felt anything at all. However, if I were to poke an animal, or another person, that being will feel some kind of sensory sensation. Similarly, the fact that I can poke this animal, or touch this tree, implicates that I, myself, possess some kind of consciousness. My ability to act freely and independently suggests a higher form of consciousness, which may be classified as self-consciousness. Likewise, the fact that all sentient beings also express kinds of emotions seems to indicate a more complex form of self-consciousness. Conscious beings do not just merely experience physical sensations, but they are also social beings. The fact that my dog will experience a form of loss or pain, whenever I am away, implicates the fact that it possesses emotions that are not strictly affected by physical phenomena, as so much as psychological phenomena.

      Psychological phenomena are immaterial and also do not take on any kind of a physical existence. The feeling of loneliness cannot be perceived by any of the five senses, but only by my mind. Those who experience this psychological state may contemplate about seeking friendships with other persons. Therefore, emotions are immaterial entities that have a direct effect on our immaterial thought processes. This seems to indicate an interaction between elements within our consciousness. The idea of loneliness does not produce a direct effect on the physical body, in the same manner that it has on our state of mind. Therefore, self-consciousness must be something that extends beyond our ordinary definitions of a material existence. Self-consciousness, then, enables a life-force to transcend beyond a merely physical existence.

Further modes of thought include rational calculation, such as those performed within the fields of mathematics or science. Calculation applies theory with abstract concepts, which exist only within the mind of the operator. The imagination is a similar faculty that is not limited in the same manner that the physical world is limited. Objects within the physical world do not often change forms. However, through my imagination, I possess the ability to add or change a selection of attributes, within my mind, with respect to any given object that I perceive within the material world. Likewise, our memories form a detailed record of all of our past experiences within the physical world. Without this faculty, we would not possess the ability to relive or analyze past events that may have occurred during our personal history.

According to Plato, the mind consists of three parts. The first part is reason, which is the reflective element of the mind. Through the faculty of reason, human beings are able to acquire knowledge and think rationally. Cognitive elements like calculation, foresight, reflection and decision making are also made possible through reason. Likewise, reason is also necessary for wisdom and good judgment. Reason, according to Plato, masters the element of the mind linked to appetite.

    The second part of the mind is known as appetite. Through his irrational appetitive part, the individual will experience feelings of thirst and hunger. Urges or impulses, like lust or other forms of desires, are also created through appetite. In general, the appetite produces desires linked with indulgences, satisfaction, or pleasure. Plato holds the belief that reason masters appetite due to the fact that we can resist our urges or impulses exclusively through reason. For example, even though the individual possesses the appetite of thirst, he may rationally abstain from drinking, if he deems the possibility that drinking some specific substance will do more harm than good. Through reason, the individual desires kinds of drinks that are only beneficial for him, and not any kinds that may have a negative effect on his physical health.

    The third component, when translated into English, is known as the spirited or passionate part. This element causes persons to feel angry or indignant. Like appetite, it is also subordinate to reason. Nonetheless, appetite is subordinate to the element of spirit. Courage, determination and self-regard are other important elements of spirit. Through courage, the individual will be able to judge what he ought to fear and what he ought not to fear. Similarly, courage will enable the individual to judge what is correct and what is in accordance with established laws.

Plato believes that the individual will be self-disciplined when all three elements of his mind are in a friendly and harmonious agreement with each other. He will possess the attribute of justice if all three parts are performing their proper function. In fact, justice is not defined by external actions, but more appropriately by the man's inward self. The just man will not allow these elements to trespass on each other. Rather, he will keep all of these elements in tune, similar to the "notes of a scale". Contrarily, injustice occurs when there is a kind of civil war erupting between these three elements. Injustice, then, materializes when these three elements of the mind interfere with each other, and trespass on each other's functions. It may also occur when one element rebels against the whole to "get control when it has no business to do so", during occasions when its role is to be subordinate to the rightfully controlling element. When this occurs, the elements of the mind are confused, and this constitutes injustice, indiscipline, cowardice, ignorance and wickedness of all kinds.

Plato also theorizes that the state is further characterized through the human mind. Thus, justice within the state will be no different from justice within the individual. Conceptually, all states are essentially an extension of the human mind. He states, the "elements and traits that belong to a state must also exist in the individuals that compose it". (p.150) Accordingly, the state is also, in essence, comprised of three types of citizens.

The first class of citizens is the ruling class. Rulers have political authority and their function is to govern the state. The rulers must possess intelligence, they must be capable, and they must possess a genuine concern for their community. Likewise, they must devote their lives towards accomplishing what is in the best interests of their community, and they must never act against these interests. Integrity is also an important characteristic of the ruler. Those who lack it must be rejected as a possible ruler. Subsequently, the role of rulers of the state may be comparable to the role of reason in the mind. Rulers command the state, while reason commands the mind. Thus, Plato believes that rulers are analogous to the faculty of reason.

Auxiliaries form the second class of citizens who are responsible for military and police duties. These individuals must be high spirited. They must also possess speed, physical strength and a philosophical temperament. These individuals are soldiers whose main function is to protect the state. The auxiliaries will also aid rulers with the execution of their decisions. Within Plato's political philosophy, both classes must be educated at an early age, and at the highest levels of our education system. Plato draws a correlation between auxiliaries and the human spirit.

The final class is comprised of tradesmen. Tradesmen will perform occupations that are integral to our civilization. These occupations can include hunting, farming, cooking, shoemaking, and artistry. According to Plato, only tradesmen should possess the right to own private property, such as land, houses or money. This is due to his belief that wealth leads to corruption, and that the community as a whole does not suffer if this particular class of citizens becomes corrupt. Tradesmen may be comparable to the appetitive part of the mind. (Plato)

In theory, human character may also be viewed as an extension of the human mind. While the soul may be intrinsically viewed as immaterial, human character may be viewed as the materialization of the individual's soul. Hence, there is a causal relationship between the individual's soul and his character. In essence, the individual's soul will formulate his choices. The soul causes action, and the individual's actions determine his character. Character, then, is defined through the individual's actions, and every individual makes his choices through the elements of his soul. Accordingly, human character is, necessarily, a reflection of one's soul.

Nonetheless, it is always possible that the individual may make choices that will deviate from the true nature of his soul. In these cases, the reflection of an individual's character may be twisted or distorted. Through free will, persons possess the power to choose actions that may contradict the intrinsic nature of their soul. Hence, it is possible that a rational person may act in contrary to reason. Similarly, persons who have no sense of common reason may refrain from acting irrationally.

All human beings possess the power to choose, act, and to refrain from committing any forms of action. Actions that may be categorized as positive will provide some form of benefit to human civilization. In contrast, actions that may be viewed as negative will pose some kind of harm to our civilization. It is the difference between these two categories of action that defines human character. Consequently, at a rudimentary level, all persons may be identified as having either an ethical, or an immoral character.

Correspondingly, human character is always an extension of the individual's will. When an individual determines his choice, he is exercising his free will. When the individual acts on his choice, this behaviour defines his character. Therefore, human character is necessarily determined through individual choice, and therefore, through the freedom of the will.

In some cases, though, isolation will spark a differentiation gap between the individual's character and his soul. When this occurs, the individual's character does not represent a true extension of his soul. Through isolation and meditation, the individual will reflect upon any negative aspects that may surface through his character. He will then try to actively hide these elements, in an effort to bolster his character. This form of misconception demonstrates the individual's volition to actively hide elements of his soul, and it usually surfaces as a defence mechanism.

After some time, this lack of acceptance will grow into intolerance and then hostility. The individual may then disguise his soul, because he wants to hide elements that could be viewed as faulty or unappealing. In other cases, when the individual purposely misrepresents his soul, this may be done in an effort to trick or manipulate other persons.

In other individuals, there may be no clear distinction between their character and their soul. In these cases, the individual's character will always form a mirror image of his soul. Yet, the human intellect is fallible, and vulnerable to err. The intellect is responsible for gathering knowledge, and this knowledge has a direct effect on the individual's choices. In cases where the individual believes in falsehoods, these misconceptions may conflict with true forms of righteousness. When this occurs, the individual is liable to make choices that will contradict the basic essence of his soul.

Subsequently, human character can be a variable form of personal identity, while the human soul remains unchanging. Two parts of the soul may never change throughout the individual's entire lifetime. The human intellect is determined by nature. Likewise, the individual's emotional equilibrium also originates through the nature of his soul, which is granted to him at birth. On the other hand, the individual's array of principles, or spirit, will sometimes shift or be modified by age and first-hand experiences. These three elements of the soul, personified through choice, are the main defining elements of human character.

The intellect is one defining component in an individual's character. It is a component that is responsible for cognition. The scope of the individual's intellect will affect his acquisition of knowledge. Persons with a large scope will acquire a wide berth of knowledge throughout their entire lifetime. Individuals with a weaker intellect will fail to comprehend complex concepts and ideologies. The scope of the intellect usually remains fixed throughout the individual's life, though in some cases disease and injury may have negative effects on one or some of his faculties.

Emotion also has a role in determining the individual's character. On a universal spectrum, each individual will actively base his centre of emotions at some particular point. Persons with a high centre of emotions will be sensitive to many different forms of phenomena. Individuals with a low centre of emotions will exhibit no reactions in similar situations. Therefore, the individual's emotional equilibrium is essentially a fixed range of emotions that measures the trait reactivity in every individual. It is determined through a combination of natural factors, and the individual's personal value system.

The individual's array of principles is the final element that determines his character. The individual's array of principles is wholly based on free will, and is formulated primarily through his own personal ideals. It grows with knowledge, and is not determined by nature. Rather, it is a by-product of the interplay between the individual's intellect and centre of emotions.

For the majority of persons, components in their character are not easily alterable. Each part remains decisively constant, except for the individual's array of principles, which can only be affected by significant life experiences. Hence, the scope of an individual's intellect will never be truly altered, even in cases where there are physical changes transpiring within his brain. For instance, individuals with Alzheimer's disease are suffering from a degenerative condition. Nonetheless, while their memory may be deteriorating, the scope of their intellect will still remain constant. Therefore, only certain faculties will be affected by specific brain diseases, while the remaining faculties present within the intellect will remain unchanged.

Contrarily, a newborn's intellect will continue to expand, as his brain develops during adolescence. However, only the knowledge stored in his intellect will be affected by age, and not his ability to acquire knowledge. Also in this case, the scope of the individual's entire intellect will remain in a relatively fixed position, even when there are physical changes transpiring within his brain.

The individual's emotional equilibrium will also never change. However, it is based on something that is liable to change, which is the individual's personal value system. The individual's centre of emotions will be determined, in part, through his intellect. People will only react to phenomena that they understand. Concepts that subsist beyond the scope of the individual's intellect will rarely produce any emotional effects. Consequently, only forms of subjective, personal knowledge will have some type of effect over the individual's emotional expression.

Contrarily, the individual's array of principles can vary and change throughout his entire lifetime. The array of principles represents the individual's personal values and standard ethical code. It serves to guide the individual's everyday choices and behaviours. When the individual acquires knowledge, it will actively modify and reshape his array of principles. In structure, these changes may be mainly minor. Major changes will only come about if the individual experiences a form of extreme shock or trauma. In these cases, it is possible that the individual may replace an existing principle within his array with a newer and more practical maxim.

These are the three elements that define human character. Reason in the soul is produced by the intellect. Appetite will shape the individual's emotional equilibrium. The element of spirit may be comparable to an array of principles. Nonetheless, while the Platonist mind will never change, according to differing circumstances, change is possible with respect to the individual's intellect, emotional centre and array of principles. Indeed, some features of the soul are determined by nature. However, other elements are determined entirely through free will.

The three elements that define human character are also subject to the law of hierarchy. The law of hierarchy determines a natural relationship between the three components of the human mind. In theory, the law of hierarchy may be viewed as a constant continuum. While one element may govern a second element, this element will naturally govern a third element. Hence, the law of hierarchy may essentially be viewed as a kind of cycle.

In the law of hierarchy, there are two possible cycles. Within the ruling cycle, one of the components in human character controls another component. For example, in this cycle, intellect is the governing element over the individual's emotional centre. In contrast, in the regulated cycle, one component is subordinate to another component. Thus, in this cycle, the individual's emotional centre will govern his intellect. Both cycles of hierarchy are actualized by differing reasons in each and every individual. Similarly, both cycles are integral components that define the individual's character.

Fundamentally, there are three main subtypes of human character. The static character remains constant under all types of circumstances. These persons possess traits that are, for the most part, unchangeable. On the surface, such individuals may be viewed as inflexible. On the inside, however, individuals with a static character are motivated purely by the social aspects of power and control.

The dynamic character is a second subtype of human character. A dynamic character changes under differing conditions. Persons with a dynamic character may be viewed as truth-seeking, yet non-antagonistic. They value peaceful modes of interaction over aggression. On the inside, individuals with a dynamic character are motivated by affection and fraternity.

The third subtype of human character is known as the formless character. Persons with a formless character exhibit both static and dynamic characteristics. Under certain circumstances, these individuals may be viewed as hostile. On other occasions, these individuals may be viewed as sociable. In both instances, the individual is motivated by differing reasons. Regarding the first stereotype, the individual is mainly motivated by intolerance. Within the second stereotype, the individual is motivated towards gaining forms of social acceptance. While all formless characters seem to exhibit a similar temperament, the reasons that motivate each individual will usually be wholly private and unique.

The human mind is comprised of an intellect, an emotional centre, and a culmination of spirit. Human beings, in essence, are a conjunction of an immaterial mind with a physical body. Seemingly, within the physical world we cannot exist outside of our physical bodies. Our existence on Earth is grounded firmly through a physical nature. Nevertheless, the immaterial mind also seems to be an important element regarding the true nature of all human beings.

Free will probably represents the best proof that we possess an immaterial soul. Through free will, I possess an unlimited ability to choose between two alternatives. This ability is unlimited because it is not restrained by any physical object in the world. The will to choose is totally dependent on the mind of each individual.

Introduction

Everything in nature is limited by the laws of physics. For example, I cannot will myself to fly because of the nature of my physical body. Nonetheless, the natural liberty within the will is limitless. Through consciousness, I possess the ability to reflect upon my choices. With this level of awareness, I then possess the ability to analyze my mistakes, and choose differently at future times. Therefore, since I possess an independent ability to act or refrain from action, within an infinite amount of situations, this entails the fact that I am not a kind of being that is wholly limited by my physical existence. I am not a mindless automaton that cannot extend beyond its physical nature, in the same manner as that of a robot who cannot make choices that contradict his programming. The fact that the will is never constrained suggests the fact that I am a kind of being that is not purely based on a physical or material existence.

I can choose to quench my thirst by drinking this bottle of juice, this cup of coffee, this glass of wine, or I can refrain from drinking anything. Subsequently, the materialization of every person's will results in uniqueness and individuality. Individuality, itself, additionally implicates the existence of an immaterial soul. Every human being is identified by a unique persona, which possesses a unique history of personal experiences.

Nonetheless, a well-known problem within the dualist philosophy is based on the interaction between mind and body. What is the mechanism that enables the interaction between these two kinds of substances? Well, if there does exist immaterial entities within our universe, this should, necessarily, indicate that there are forces in nature that are not observable by the human senses. Hence, the mechanism behind mind and body interaction should simply be another kind of unobservable entity.

    A second problem is the vulnerability of the mind. If the mind is truly a different substance from the body, why is it vulnerable to diseases within the brain? The faculties of the mind are utilized in the quest for knowledge and understanding. With regard to Alzheimer's disease, the patient's capacity to access his memories will steadily decrease. In patients with bipolar disorder, their emotions will shift from moments of elation and happiness to states of deep hopelessness and depression. Yet, all other faculties of the mind will remain in these patients. Hence, a single injury only negatively affects one capacity, while all other faculties remain constant within the mind. Accordingly, only the quest for truth within the physical world will be impoverished in patients that suffer from a mental disease, while, at the same time, their unique personal identity remains intact. Illness within the brain affects knowledge, but not identity. The major core of each patient's unique persona will still remain, despite the fact that they have lost some faculty. Therefore, mental diseases simply indicate that the immaterial mind may be affected by events within the physical world, while the individual's soul, which is the culmination of the individual's mind and his personal experiences, remains perpetual, unceasing and persistent.

With respect to character, one may question as to whether the individual's choices are fully dependent on his soul? In theory, there is a necessary link between the individual's soul and his actions, and likewise, there is a necessary link between the individual's actions and his character. Now the problem of free will comes into play. Is the individual's character wholly determined through his soul? Or is it possible that the individual's character may misrepresent his soul? In actuality, the individual's soul mainly serves as a blueprint for his character. All of the elements in an individual's soul are in a constant state of flux. Accordingly, while the individual's character is defined entirely through his actions, he still possesses the power to choose actions that will contradict the true nature of his soul. In other words, the element of free will makes it possible for an individual to choose acts that will deviate from the true nature of his soul.

The theory of human character will conjoin the free will and deterministic philosophies together. Human beings have no role in determining the entire nature of their soul. It is a wonder that is created through the will of God. Nonetheless, God has also empowered human beings with a free will. When persons exercise their will, they will create a materialization of their soul known as human character. Therefore, with respect to character, every individual is fully accountable and responsible for all of his personal actions and behaviour.

2 Nature of Man

HAVE YOU EVER ASKED the question "What is existence"? To exist may simply be the opposite of nothingness. In other words, existence may simply be defined as being something. How about the question "What am I"? I do possess the ability to perceive substances, such as those observed within the physical world. I also possess the ability to interact within this world. Perhaps, I am something that possesses both abilities to perceive and to act.

To exist as a human, then, could be to exist as an entity that possesses both powers to act and perceive. My own existence, and thus my actions and perceptions, are personal experiences that are unique to myself. This element should also be a defining component in human existence. Therefore, to exist as a human being means to exist as an autonomous and distinct individual.

The latter questions may inevitably lead the next question, "What is it to exist or be alive"? The answer to these questions can be simple or complicated, depending on who is pondering the subject. When the individual experiences a form of "surreal" or "elevated" self-awareness, the question of what is life, or more importantly, what is life as a human being may become more complicated.

When we look at a tree, do we deem this as a form of life? This tree requires elements like sunlight, nutrients and water to survive, which is for the most part, a defining attribute common among all forms of life. We may, then, define it as something that is alive. Nonetheless, forms of plant species possess no physical forms of freedom whatsoever, and they also exhibit no forms of consciousness. What attributes they do possess is the ability to grow in a distinctive fashion, and reproduce. Therefore, they are a kind of life-force that produces an aura. Intrinsically, they embody a kind of spirit.

What about animals? Animals possess a corporeal body, they require nourishment, and they also reproduce. Animals are a more complicated form of life, though, when compared to forms of vegetation. Animals possess the ability to control their corporeal body, and are mobile within their environment. Trees always exist within a fixed position. Subsequently, animals possess a form of liberty in relation to their physical existence.

Thus, in comparison to forms of vegetation, animals are free spirits. All animals in the wild possess differing kinds of bodies, so their modes of mobility will also differ. In addition, they all exhibit a form of consciousness, and subsequently, they demonstrate some degree of intelligence. The majority of animals also possess a rudimentary ability to communicate. Nonetheless, they do not possess the ability to communicate complex concepts.

Accordingly, we should be able to conclude that all animals possess some kind of a mind. The decisions carried out by their mind will depend on the knowledge that they have obtained, and the scope of their brain to understand phenomena. However, they are driven by their appetites, and they mainly think instinctively. Instincts are pre-programmed, while reason requires orderly thought. Subsequently, their actions are aligned towards their natural predispositions. They also lack a higher degree of self-awareness that humans possess, regarding our actions and the personal reflections of our actions. Therefore, from one point of view, they may lack sophistication. In essence, their limited intellect allows them to live with nature, but not command it. Wild animals possess only a limited ability to act in contrary to their instincts, so they lack the intellectual faculties necessary for living a lifestyle that extends beyond primeval survival.

The gift of existence is common among all forms of life, and it is the most basic element in all forms of life. As we examine other forms of life, our definition of human life will successively increase. Indeed, human existence is much more intricate than other forms of life. There are many differences between other forms of life and human beings. Human beings possess the ability to invent. The scope of our faculties of reason and deduction are exemplified through our knowledge gained through science. Regarding our analytical skills, we have the ability to observe the laws of physics, and this is largely unknown to all other known forms of life.

Accordingly, humans possess a powerfully innate form of intelligence known as the intellect. Therefore, in comparison to the wild animal, we are intelligent, free spirits. Through farming, we possess the ability to foster new forms of life. Through the greenhouse effect and nuclear weapons, we also possess the power to destroy life. Our power to destroy the entire physical world, through nuclear weapons, makes us the rulers of nature. We possess the ability to manipulate our environment to a much greater extent than any wild animal. No sea creature in the ocean, nor wild animal in the jungle possesses an equivalent amount of power over his natural environment. This power also forces us to recognize the concept of responsibility.

Animals are a higher form of life in comparison to vegetation because they possess the power of free movement, and essentially liberty. Our intelligence is what differentiates us from the common animal. We possess the ability to create culture, conventions, and subsequently, civil society. We further possess the ability to make choices according to reason. These choices could act in contrary to our instincts. We also have a greater faculty of awareness. This is evident in the creation of art. All forms of music, theatre, and poetry demonstrate the vast human nature in the realm of complex emotions. Through self-awareness, we can analyze both nature and ourselves, which is an ability that seems to be absent in the wild animal.

To exist as an animal is to live hand in hand within nature's wilderness. To exist as a human is to live in a culturally and technologically advanced society. Through the power of our intellect, we are able to calm our appetites and act according to what is civilized. The creation of government and law instill maxims regarding both moral and ethical forms of behaviour. Our ability to design continually improves our standard of living. Culture is a further attribute that demonstrates the diverse human ability to socialize.

When I carefully scrutinize this discovery, I will gain further insight regarding the basic element of my nature. In comparison to the wild animal, humans possess a higher class of intelligence. When comparing wild animals to forms of vegetation, animals possess freedom. Subsequently, the only thing that is common among all forms of life is the fact that all forms of life will possess a kind of spirit. The very basic essence of all life, then, is spirit.

The difference between a subjective existence and an objective existence is also an important element within our definition of life. Entities that possess a subjective existence have the ability to both perceive and control what they perceive. A subjective existence, then, requires some kind of consciousness. Likewise, only forms of life can exist subjectively. In contrast, every physical object in the world possesses an objective existence. Phenomenon, then, that possess an objective existence can be perceived through one of the five human senses. Rocks exist within the physical world, and thus they exist objectively. Nonetheless, it is impossible to conclude that these objects possess the ability to act or perceive. Rocks do not grow, and thus, they do not intrinsically change. Likewise, they do not exhibit a consciousness, so they do not experience any kinds of a subjective existence. Their existence differs from that of all forms of life. When we look at this forest spotted owl, we observe that it acts in a fully independent and autonomous fashion. This differentiates objects with a subjective existence from those with a merely objective existence. Subsequently, our definition of life should also include this latter element.

Human intelligence is also exemplified through our ability to communicate and utilize language. We use language to communicate the immaterial thoughts within our mind. Our ability to speak also proves that we have an immaterial mind, since words basically represent private ideas. We make an effort to communicate a specific thought within our mind, but we cannot know if other persons will acquire the exact concept that exists within our own frame of mind. Some words could potentially represent exact concepts, while other words may be gross misrepresentations within the listener's mind. Ineffective modes of communication will inevitably lead to misunderstandings. As a consequence, our ability to articulate complex thoughts differentiates us from all wild animals. These beings only possess the ability to communicate through simple and less precise noises and gestures.

It is possible that some animals may possess a form of reason and awareness. Nevertheless, their social interactions remain basic, in comparison to the complex nature of human socialization. In comparison to the amoeba, I possess the additional attributes of both freedom and intelligence. When I analyze my nature, I will find that my freedom, intelligence and spirit are non-material attributes. These attributes are then materialized by my body, but are not defining elements of my body. These are elements that define the most basic components of my mind.

Hence, my body must be connected to something that accounts for my individual experiences and autonomous existence. This entity is my soul. Only my soul has access to both the ideas produced by my mind, and the sensory perceptions that I experience through my physical body. My ideas and sensory perceptions can only be accessed by own soul. No individual can enter my mind and perceive that idea which I currently perceive at this moment. Likewise, you can never know if what you perceive is what I perceive through an absolute and complete likeness.

This is due to the fact that my ideas do not have an objective or physical existence within our world. They cannot be perceived objectively by differing persons, like any ordinary physical object. They exist purely as immaterial entities. We can, for example, view this same table that is present right in front of us. However, you can never, knowingly, perceive this table with the exact likeness of my own personal sensory perception of it. If I were slightly colour blind, I would perceive this table as cardinal, while in your own eyes, you would view it as scarlet. We both see the colour red, but our ideas still differ. You do not possess the power to enter into my mind and view my subjective perception. In fact, it may be entirely impossible for you to ever perceive this table, in the exact likeness as my own unique perception. This makes my experiences essentially my own, and likewise your experiences solely your own.

Thus, our souls are independent, yet closed entities. I cannot wander from my body to my neighbour's body and perceive the world through his sensations. I only know my own sensations, and thus, my soul must be connected to something that is similarly independent and detached. This is namely my body. My perceptions are immaterial, like my mind; nevertheless, my soul can only establish a link to my own bodily sensations and not anyone else's. This makes all of my immaterial thoughts strictly my own. However, I can communicate my personal thoughts and ideas through language. Language, then, is the association of my personal thoughts with verbal constants. I also possess the power to draw a sketch of something that I have invented within my imagination. When I achieve this, my private ideas will then become public. Yet, this is the maximum possible exposure, with respect to my private ideas. Accordingly, my idea first exists as an immaterial entity, and then it becomes materialized through my physical body. This materialization will then transform into another subjective idea, within the mind of those persons who perceive it.

When I examine myself more intimately, I will come to realize that I am something that has control over a physical body. Attributes like the colour of my skin, my height, and my weight will differ from other human beings around the world, and accordingly, when we take my facial features into account, my physical appearance will be mainly unique. Similarly, all other person's physical appearances will also possess unique attributes, and this enables us to identify differing individuals, at least from a physical perspective.

After I look at myself in the mirror, I will see a unique physical body. I also realize that I have full control over this body. At this point, I may now ask if this, then, is the definition of life. That is, is life defined as being something with a corporeal body? The answer to this question should be no. Indeed, a mountain does possess a physical body, though no person will deem a mountain as something that is alive. A form of life necessarily possesses the ability to grow and reproduce. Therefore, the definition of life must have elements that reach beyond a purely physical existence.

However, I want to know what "I" am. I want to know what it is to be alive and I want to know what life is. Seemingly, I have exclusive control over this body, and no one else controls it. I, thus, possess a physical existence, but is my existence limited solely to a physical one? I possess the ability to think and imagine, and this enables me to think about my future. My imagination is seemingly limitless, because I can imagine more than one possible future. In the physical world, I have but one true corporeal existence, but through my thoughts I can envision multiple kinds of possible futures.

When I seize my imagination and focus on these dreams, does this mean that I can travel to the future? It is possible to travel to the past, through my faculty of memory, and therefore my imagination could serve a similar purpose. Subsequently, through my thought processes, I possess the ability to travel through time, and this suggests that my thoughts transcend both space and time. I can exist, then, according to a physical, corporeal body within the natural world, while in addition, I can focus on a world that is based purely on the power of my thoughts. It may be most rational to include both worlds, when I define the true nature of my being. This leads me to believe that I possess both a material body and an immaterial mind.

Nevertheless, some persons could question why I would separate myself from the corporeal object that I would seemingly have total control over. When I view myself as something other than a corporeal life form, I am taking into account the fact that I can view myself through an objective, as opposed to a merely subjective, perspective. Thus, because of my ability to view the world through a perspective that extends beyond my physical sensory perceptions, I will come to realize that my mind is something that can extend beyond the realm of the natural, material world. That is, because I have the ability to view the world not merely through my physical body, but also through my thoughts, I will come to understand that I am a life form that is more complicated than a being that is solely limited to a physical existence.

In this case, the definition of life, or more specifically, my essential existence is some phenomenon that can transcend physical sensory perceptions. Since I can perceive both a non-material and a physical world, I must be something that is more powerful than a simple corporeal life form. I am an entity that can see, smell, hear, taste and touch physical objects in our material world. Nevertheless, my mind allows me view another possible world that exists beyond my ordinary sensory experiences. These additional immaterial perceptions seem to suggest that my life is not restricted merely to a physical environment.

According to some persons, the concept of life may be more narrowly limited. Through science, the acquisition of knowledge is limited to what is observable in the physical world. However, what we deem as knowledge should not be limited solely to what is discoverable through science. It would be naive to limit the concept of life based purely on what is physically observable on the planet Earth.

As a consequence, isn't it possible that I exist only as a brain in a vat, and am deceived about the fact that I possess a material body? This supposition makes the concept of doubt comprehendible, and doubt motivates persons to seek the truth. If it is possible that I am truly a brain in a vat, it is equally possible that an immaterial world exists in conjunction with our physical world, because if I can doubt the material, what truly exists must be solely the immaterial. Atheists doubt the existence of an immaterial world, but the brain in a vat scenario provides all individuals with an equivalent form of doubt regarding our material world. If I am a brain in a vat, then my entire physical existence, as I know it, is false. We all possess ideas of what could be, but also of what is. Anything could be, but there is only one true reality, and this is what is.

One may also ask, is it possible for me to perceive without action? Technically, the answer to this question is yes. For example, when I am asleep in my bed and dreaming, I do perceive an environment with other forms of life. Similarly, when I am staring at the stars while imagining my possible future, my physical body is in a state of rest. Hence, the ability to perceive, at least in humans, may be the most central gift to our existence. The most important attribute linked to existence is the ability to perceive the universe, in a manner that is entirely unique to myself.

We all have three modes of perception. We may view the physical world through the senses, we may analyze our sensory perceptions through the intellect, and we may perceive nothingness if, for example, we are present in a state of deep sleep. As a perceiving being, I have no choice in this matter. I am an entity that perceives, and I can be nothing else. However, I have the ability to focus my perceptions at will, from sensory perceptions to ideations within the intellect, and this suggests that I have a mind that is wholly powerful. However, when I perceive nothing, because I am entering into a state of deep slumber, I possess no awareness of my true physical state.

When I close my eyes to sleep at night, all I perceive is darkness, or nothingness. When I then enter into an REM state, I will perceive a world based purely on my imagination. This seems to indicate that my body is not necessary for my ability to perceive. All that is necessary is my immaterial mind. When I waken, I will perceive the real physical world, again, through my five senses. My senses provide me with an additional mode of perception. Through my body, I can now perceive the physical world. However, the one element that is essential for the totality of all of my perceptions is strictly my immaterial mind.

The dreaming argument demonstrates the fact that our minds are conjoined with a physical body. Before I fall asleep at night, I am resting comfortably within my bed at home. However, when I eventually enter into a dreaming state, I will perceive an entirely new physical environment. Then when I awake, my consciousness returns its focus back into my physical body, and I find that I am present within the same bed, in the same home.

In fact, my body has not changed the slightest bit from the period before I entered into a dreaming state, until after I have actually woken from this dreaming state. Yet, my mind continues to perceive differing environments, while I am asleep. After I have left the dreaming state, my mind then seems to reunite with the same body, which remains constant. Then, I will also perceive a similarly constant reality again, through my senses, due essentially to the fact that I am conjoined to the same physical body. The fact that both my mind and body remains constant, in this reality, indicates that my personal identity has never changed. As such, what I am, intrinsically, must be a mind that is conjoined with a unique physical body.

The fact that I have control over a physical body seems to implicate the fact that life as a human being will most definitely be based within some type of physical environment. However, my imagination allows me to exist within a mental reality, with no true physical components. When I am asleep at night dreaming, I will perceive a world that is comprised purely of non-physical elements. The persons that I perceive in my dream are not actually physically present. The environment that I am seeing through my eyes is not truly through my sense of sight. The fact that I am in this environment, interacting with other persons is false, at least from a physical perspective. Accordingly, the power of my mind to create an entirely new non-material world seems to suggest the fact that existence, or life as a person in particular, can never be limited solely to a physical existence.

    The power of my mind to daydream, while I am actually awake within the physical world, also implicates the fact that existence as a person is not limited to purely a physical existence. I can ignore my physical environment at will, or I can focus my attention back on to myself as something that has control over a physical body. I can perceive the world, not only through my own eyes, but also through my mind, which has the ability to analyze what I currently perceive through my sensory perceptions. I can switch my perspective of the world between my imagination, to my physical reality purely at will. Then, when I become aware of my latter actions, I will be further utilizing my faculty of self-awareness. As a form of life, my mind can produce thoughts that surpass the purely physical world, which I know strictly through my five senses.

When in a woken state, my body is an essential part of my nature, because of the fact that I have total control over it. The fact that I seemingly existed in another environment, during my dreams, may be classified as a purely immaterial existence. This environment is purely immaterial in nature. Accordingly, through my dreams, I possess the power to exist in world that is not limited by any physical boundaries. The world in my dreams is not governed by the laws of physics, nor any other laws that may be relevant within the physical world. I, at least conceptually, can exist in an immaterial world due to the power of my mind. My immaterial mind enables me to transcend my physical existence, and this indicates that there is more to life than a purely material existence. It implicates that my true nature must also include the realm of the immaterial.

Concerning the mind, human thought may truly face no limitations. The individual can conceive thoughts, and expand on his thoughts with very few observable restrictions. The human body, on the other hand, is finite and more restricted. My ability to mentally control a physical object is limited to the operation of my body. When I exercise my will, I have the ability to move my hand. However, I cannot move other physical objects solely through my immaterial mind. If I want to move an object, my mind will have to send a signal to my corporeal body, which will then enable me to move an object through my hand. Therefore, the power of my soul can only have a direct effect on my own physical body.

When the individual exercises his will over his body, this is defined as behaviour. At any given moment, I may lift my index finger, if I so desire. Similarly, I may lift my ring finger at any given moment, if I choose to do this. This power of my soul, over my physical body, is known as free will. At any given moment, I can move any limb of my body, according to my personal volitions.

On the other hand, the individual has no power to choose the attributes of his physical body. From the best of our knowledge, no individual has the ability to choose his sex, ethnic background, or place of birth. Our physical bodies have already been determined, according to some power beyond our personal control. Hence, the nature of man may be defined by components that belong to contradictory paradigms. Can both free will and determinism exist? When we examine the nature of man, the answer to this question may be a yes.

Hence, human existence is comprised of elements from opposing theories. It is true that many of the individual's personal characteristics are determined by nature. However, the element of free will is also a defining feature in human existence. Persons do not have the power to choose their body, but they do possess the power to control their body. As a result, the ideology of responsibility is also a defining feature of mankind.

Human beings are responsible for their actions, and their actions will define their character. Thus, it is possible that a highly revered individual may commit a crime, and likewise, it is possible for a criminal to abstain from criminal behaviour. In both cases, the individual will exhibit a characteristic that may be inconsistent with his true nature. The element of free will enables persons to exhibit character traits that contradict any seemingly established personal characteristics. Accordingly, every individual is fully responsible for his character, and likewise, human character is determined by the will of the individual.

When I experience a moment of surreal awareness, and I ask myself about the true nature of life, I will be examining what existence means to me. I am an entity that has total control over a physical body. I can experience feelings of hunger and pain because of my body. However, my mind enables me to reason, deduce, and remember. These are faculties that, otherwise, do not exist within our physical world. When I remember what I ate last weekend, this is an operation that exists only within my mind. Subsequently, the fact that I have a mind must imply the notion that life as a human being, or at least my life as a human being, is complicated, but still symmetrical.

Every individual has the power to conceive immaterial thoughts, and also to experience physical pleasures through each of his five senses. These elements form the truest essence of mankind. My soul has the ability conceive thoughts within the mind. Moreover, I am an entity that perceives, and through the power of self-consciousness, I am fully aware of the fact that I am a being that perceives. Also through this power, I can view my existence as something that is conjoined with a physical body. My soul has the further ability to control this physical, corporeal body. Therefore, the boundary of my existence is based both on an immaterial soul, and a physical body.

My ability to control the motion of my body seems to indicate that some link exists between my soul and body. The exact mechanism behind this connection remains unknown though. Wireless technology may provide an analogy that illustrates this mechanism. When I play with a remote controlled car, I possess control over its movements. Just because I cannot perceive this connection through my sensory perceptions doesn't prove the notion that no connection exists. In theory, the brain could act as a hub, or controller, between my mind and body.

My body defines me as something that perceives the world through the five senses. However, my body is limited physically, or is finite, and this also puts a limit on my sensory perceptions. Through my imagination and other faculties, I find that my thoughts are not restricted, nor limited, to a similar degree.

Therefore, the scope of our intellect has the potential to be greater than the scope of our bodily experiences. Our ability to imagine, create and invent distinguishes us from the random animal. We create "man-made" objects, like homes, clothing, forms of transportation, and forms of technology. This is what differentiates human beings from all other species. Our intelligence reaches far beyond the common animal's intellect. It is our intelligence that defines how we exist. Thus, multifaceted intelligence is a sole characteristic found only in humans.

By its very nature, the immaterial must exist beyond the realm of human sensory perception. By its definition, it is without physical properties or substance. Hence, the link between the immaterial mind and body may also exist as something that is beyond the realm of sensory perception. Nonetheless, some kind of link must exist. As physical beings, it may be impossible to discover the true nature of the link between the material and the immaterial. It may not even be comprehendible within our minds.

My ability to think may not be infinite, but it does not face the same constraints that are imposed on my body. I perceive the world, through my body; however, I know that there are other phenomena in the universe, like other planets, that exist beyond the realm of what I can perceive. My senses are limited. Through the power of my mind, I can at least entertain various thoughts as to what exists beyond my personal sensory perceptions. Through my imagination, I can perceive a unique range of differing possible worlds that could exist within our universe. Accordingly, the totality of the universe does exist beyond the realm of any individual's personal sensory perceptions.

When my existence is conjoined to a physical body, this also indicates that uniqueness is an important attribute of existence. Thus, I do not only perceive the universe in a unique manner, but my actions within the physical world are also unique. In the physical world, my existence is individual and subjective. This entails the fact that what

I perceive and how I act are entirely dependent on myself, or in other words, my free will.

The fact that I possess a free will indicates the truth that existence is a kind of gift, where my experiences are personal, and belong to no one else. Existence, itself, is wonder that is realized because of my own unique perceptions of the world, and the fact that my perceptions are wholly personal. To exist, then, is not simply to act and perceive, but to control how you act and what you perceive. This may be the closest definition of true existence.

Now that I have established the fact that I am a complex physical and intellectual entity, is it possible for me to narrow my definition of existence? My mind allows me to control my physical body at will. If I so desire, I can move any one of my limbs at will, in the same manner that a puppeteer controls his puppet. Likewise, with my mind, I can spend the whole day gazing at one of the colours in the rainbow that appears before me. Life, as I know it, may be more accurately defined as a kind of independent wonder. My subjective existence, then, is that of a powerfully liberated spirit.

This makes liberty the most basic element of my immaterial soul. I could direct my attention towards the physical world, or I can withdraw my attention away from reality onto my imagination. Within my imagination, I am free to think at will, and this ability is not constrained by any entity. When I perceive the physical world, when I imagine, or when I perceive my own bare existence, this is entirely under my own control and will. To possess the ability to direct my perceptions onto differing modes of thought demonstrates the vast power of my mind.

If I wish to utilize my faculty of reason, I possess the ability to do so, purely and wholly in an autonomous fashion. However, there are many things that I do not understand about our world, and this indicates the finite nature of my mind. I also possess the intellectual ability to analyze and compare two distinct mannerisms. After I have discovered the best alternative, I will choose according to my volitions, and this is an exercise of my will. My will does not seem to be constrained by anything. I will always possess the ability to act or refrain from action. My will, then, is unconstrained, and this could also be a defining element of my nature. What I am, now, is something that perceives, something that thinks, and something that freely chooses a mode of action.

Our higher intellect allows us both to destroy nature, or make it flourish. Therefore, the power of our will places upon us a sense of responsibility that differentiates us from all other forms of life on Earth. The degree of responsibility that each individual assumes, though, may at times be difficult to recognize and assess. Some agents possess an ever increasing degree of responsibility as they grow older during their adult years, while others will continually lose a certain degree of social and personal responsibility. While it may be easy to recognize a sense of responsibility in other persons, recognizing one's own personal responsibility may be more difficult. A limited degree of self-awareness hinders persons from assessing their actions from an objective perspective.

In fact, it is easy to assess and judge the actions of other persons, but not our own. This lack of a higher consciousness may be a common attribute among all human beings. The fact that some persons possess a firm grasp, with respect to a higher form of consciousness, seems to imply the possible existence of yet an even higher form of consciousness that exists somewhere else in nature. Nonetheless, when we view our physical world, we perceive no other forms of life that possess a higher form of consciousness than ours. Consequently, a higher form of consciousness, then, must exist somewhere beyond our physical world. Most persons recognize this entity as God.

Different conceptions of happiness also enable individuals to enter into a higher state of consciousness. When it is a sunny day, we become happy, and our consciousness will rise in an automatic fashion. Likewise, when my girlfriend gives me a kiss, I will enter into a kind of euphoria, and this also raises my consciousness. Therefore, emotional states have a direct impact on our ability of self-consciousness.

The mind has a fundamental nature that cannot be viewed through human eyes. It may be a substance that has a nature that is beyond human understanding and perception. If deaf or blind persons have no idea of that human sense, then it is conceivable that those, who do not possess a disability, could similarly lack some kind of sense. A person who was born blind cannot view the beauty found within our natural world, but this does not mean that no forms of beauty exist, or that there is nothing to see.

If we do possess an immaterial mind, a good question would be to ask why it is limited by brain injury or disease. The human body, and our physical existence, enables us to perceive the wonders that exist within a material world. Our physical world is finite, and likewise the human body is also a vessel that is finite. As a consequence, the human will is the only element within us that is infinite. Our spirit remains free, while our intellect is limited. The differences, then, between our finite mind and potentially infinite spirit demonstrates the power of free will. The power of the will faces no limitations, except those imposed by the souls who exercise it.

Nonetheless, why would an individual's memory processes be impeded by a physical brain problem, if our mind is truly of an immaterial nature? When the individual exhibits problems with his spinal cord, he may lose the ability to use his legs. While the individual's soul may not be constrained within the immaterial world, within the physical world only his will remains unconstrained. This demonstrates the power of the will over both the mind and the body. While my mind may be susceptible to disease, and my body vulnerable to injury, the power of my will over my mind and body never ceases. Since the power of my will never changes, this indicates that the nature of my existence is always independent, and that the choices that I may make are entirely my own responsibility. As a consequence, it does not face any forms of interference from anything else within our universe, including God.

Brain diseases do not prove the notion that the immaterial mind does not exist. The existence of brain diseases only demonstrates that the scope of our ability to carry out our will is restricted by our bodies, within the physical world. When the brain takes damage, our mind will become increasingly more limited. Specific brain diseases will affect a single faculty within the intellect, or a specific range of emotions. However, the individual's array of principles, or spirit, remains mainly intact. The existence of mental disabilities only demonstrates that our minds are as vulnerable as our bodies, and that they face the potential to be incomplete. All souls, then, are capable of experiencing some form of loss.

Yet, the individual's spirit is not vulnerable to any physical brain impediments. The individual's spirit can only be directly affected by other spirits. Successively, our will is always free. No matter what kind of intellect we are born with, we will still always possess an unbounded ability to choose. As a consequence, this seems to indicate that the most basic essence of our soul lies in our ability to choose. The blind man has lost the ability to see, while the Alzheimer's patient has lost his ability to remember. The schizophrenia patient views a world that is symptomatically different from reality. However, all three individuals still possess a free will, and the ability to independently choose. The mind may be directly affected by an assortment of phenomena, but the will faces no such impediments. It is the only unrestricted faculty of the human soul.

Mental illnesses are similar to physical illnesses due to the fact that both kinds of ailments will hinder some specific part of the body.

Subsequently, illnesses, in general, will affect the complete functioning of one's body. Persons who lack a range of faculties will lack completeness, similar to persons who have lost the ability to use their legs. Therefore, the existence of illness merely demonstrates that both the mind and body possesses the potential to be incomplete. As a result, the concept of completeness may be wholly significant to human existence, since it will lead to the best possible life.

Dependence, then, may be a defining feature within human civilization. Babies who are born into this world, necessarily, depend on their parents for their physical survival. In a similar manner, when a baby becomes an adult, he will still depend on other persons for his spiritual survival. Indeed, spiritual dependence is what motivates persons to acquire forms of friendships, of all differing degrees. Therefore, persons who are entirely healthy will also possess the potential to be incomplete.

The drive to be complete motivates civilized behaviour within the individual. Accordingly, the dependent nature of our spirit only serves to reinforce the importance of each and every individual to his community. When one individual becomes affected with an illness, this does have some impact on our society. His society, in response, will then become motivated to cure that illness. As a consequence, the quest for completeness may not be merely based on a spiritual level, but on a communal level as well.

Indeed, illness is a part of living within a material world. Nonetheless, even though illness detracts from our experiences within the material world, it may have an opposing positive effect that expands the totality of experiences available to mankind. Consider the individual who suffers from a thought disorder. This person may believe in an extremely radical notion, such as the notion that his true personal identity is that of a world saviour. Since the average mentally healthy person holds no such belief, the latter delusion marks a kind of experience that is only available to persons who are suffering from paranoid schizophrenia. In turn, this unique experience will also produce a unique kind of emotional experience in the individual, as a direct consequence.

In the case of the emotional states experienced by the individual with schizophrenia, this facet of humanity, alone, seems to indicate that there may be no true limit, regarding our emotional experiences. If the person who suffers from some kind of mental illness experiences a unique emotional state, then this seems to indicate that the experiencing of our emotions depend entirely on our personal experiences.

Since it is possible to lose some faculty, like the sense of sight or the faculty of memory, this could further indicate the possibility that there exists an infinite amount of wonders, which exist beyond our natural sensory perceptions, that we have yet to experience. In actuality, the Alzheimer's patient will have lost the ability to access his most important memories. In this case, there does exist forms of immaterial wonders that cannot be perceived by this particular individual, due directly to some material aspect within his brain, and thus, the physical nature of his body.

Physical vulnerabilities characteristic of human life indicates the fact that a loss of wonders will affect our soul. Loss is a part of the physical world, however, it may not be a factor within an immaterial world. The physical world is limited, by nature, while the immaterial world faces no similar constraints. If there is no loss of wonders within the immaterial world, then there could exist many more unique wonders to experience, that we had no access to within our material existence.

The material world, then, is full of constraints, while the immaterial world will lack these particular constraints. The immaterial world differs from the physical world according to the maxim that all forms of life are not bounded by any physical constraints. In the immaterial world, our soul is unbounded and is confined by no physical object. Perhaps, life as a human being could be limited to life in our physical world. However, the question as to whether we still exist after our life in the physical world will challenge this definition. In death, our life as a physical being in the physical world will have ended. Nonetheless, in many cases, our non-material spirit will still exist within the physical world. The person who invented the wheel could be viewed as having a spirit that still exists on Earth. His ideas and imagination are still being utilized by future generations, for possibly an infinite amount of time. In this case, his spirit still remains, even though his physical existence may have ended years ago.

All forms of loss within the physical world emphasize the importance of the effects of wonders on our emotions and way of life. If I suffer from a physical disability, my freedom will be affected. If I suffer from a brain injury, my intelligence will become affected. More specifically, certain mental illnesses may negate specific faculties that I possess. Yet, my soul, in its totality, still remains the same. Therefore, none of these ailments can hamper the rest of my soul. No matter what happens to my body, my soul will always remain intact and unequivocal. This seems to indicate a kind of invulnerability within the soul. There is no object in the physical world that possesses the power to destroy my soul, in an equivalent manner to my body. Therefore, it is possible that the soul still exists, even after the physical death of our bodies. The invulnerable aspect of my soul could enable it to transcend a mere existence within our physical world. The invulnerability of my soul could indicate that it exists independent of what happens to my body.

Accordingly, the body may be finite so that it can provide our souls with a kind of experience within a world that possesses finite, material properties. Our material existence grants us with the ability to interact with other physical objects, within a material world. If no persons possessed the sense of taste, then there would be no meaningful differences between a honeysuckle and a honeydew. Moreover, when we view another person who has lost his memory, we will then come to value our own ability to utilize this faculty. When there is death in the material world, we will then ponder about the wonder of existence within an immaterial world. Subsequently, our physical lifespan may be finite so that we may experience other kinds of wonders that exist solely within a purely immaterial world. The most important wonder of all, with all certainty, will be the phenomenon of existence, as opposed to nothingness or non-existence.

In fact, every person has experienced the feeling of nothingness. When I become dizzy, I experience troubles while I am trying to focus my attention back onto the real world. In this state, my attention will continue to shift from nothingness, back onto the physical world. What caused my dizziness will be due to some malfunction within my body. As a consequence, I necessarily need a fully functioning body to properly perceive the wonders that exist within the physical world.

The human body cannot function without nourishment, and it cannot survive without oxygen. However, forms of nourishment and the air we breathe are physical objects that do not exist within an immaterial environment. Human life may be limited by physical constraints so that we may experience kinds of physical wonders, essentially through our five senses. Yet, when the brain is affected by some disease, this is no different from losing the sense of sight or sound. The human body is the materialization of our soul, which enables us to perceive material forms of wonders. Its vulnerability demonstrates a possible lack of completeness within our souls. It is restricted, physically, to reflect the fact that we all exist as independent entities. However, illness demonstrates that we are also dependent entities as well.

Every person is spiritually free. No individual lacks a free will. Yet, loss within the physical world also illustrates the fact that we are emotional beings. Thus, physical vulnerabilities implicate both psychological and emotional vulnerabilities, and these are elements that define our values, ideals and culture. Subsequently, loss within the physical world will always mirror loss within the soul, pertaining to the many wonders that exist within our universe.

The nature of human existence is based on the conjoining of a body with a soul. In our physical universe, a material body is wholly necessary for all modes of action. In a similar fashion, an immaterial mind is wholly necessary for all modes of perception. Indeed, we cannot travel with absolute freedom within the physical world, because of the laws of physics imposed on our bodies. It is restricted, physically, to enable us to interact with other forms of physical wonders. On the other hand, our mind faces no similar restrictions. This enables us to perceive the multitude of differing forms of wonders that may exist beyond the physical nature of our universe.

Therefore, the physical nature of our bodies enables us to perceive material kinds of wonders. Yet, its finite nature further demonstrates the possible existence of other kinds of wonders, which have yet to be perceived by the individual. The existence of illness demonstrates the fact that there does exist kinds of wonders in our world, which may not be perceivable by the lone individual. Therefore, the immaterial world may possess types of wonders that cannot be perceived within the strict confines of a physical world.

Consequently, while our physical freedom may be restricted within the physical world, our immaterial freedom, based on the will, faces no bounds. Do persons exist in an immaterial world after their physical existence on Earth? No one knows the answer to this question. However, I do know that my mind is an immaterial object, which allows me to exist in a world that is defined beyond the confines of the material world. The differences between the material and immaterial, then, indicate that while there are laws imposed on us physically, there exist no conceivable laws that restrict our immaterial existence, or in other words, our souls. Even though certain faculties of the mind may be finite, our soul in its entirety, nonetheless, remains invulnerable and limitless.

To exist is a true marvel. When we reflect upon ourselves, we will realize the fact that life is a wonder that cannot be easily explained. What is human existence? To live as a human is to exist as an intelligent, free spirit. We have freedom because we possess control over a corporeal body. We have intelligence because we are able to surpass our natural instincts through reason and morality. Likewise, our spirit is an element of our lives that is granted an unbounded form of personal autonomy.

3 Intellect

THE HUMAN INTELLECT is the part of the mind that is utilized to acquire knowledge. The individual's level of intelligence depends solely on his intellect. The intellect is not easily alterable, and it mainly remains constant throughout an individual's life. Moreover, the individual's intellect is determined entirely by nature. No person possesses the power to increase his intellect, and likewise, in most cases, the individual's intellect will never decline. When the intellect is functioning properly, objective knowledge will be gained. Objective knowledge consists of the truths about the world discovered through research, in addition to forms of common knowledge that are known by all persons. In contrast, when the intellect fails, falsehoods will become subjective knowledge within the individual. Subjective knowledge consists of beliefs that are classified as knowledge, even though they are unverified, and therefore could be false. Thus, the knowledge gathered through the intellect may be subject to change, when it acquires false truths or understandings. Moreover, the truth values of the subjective knowledge stored within an individual's intellect may vary by differing degrees.

The human intellect performs the main functions of analysis, comprehension, and deduction. To accomplish these tasks, it employs many differing faculties. During the operation of analysis, the intellect compares one idea within the mind to another. The faculties of memory and judgment are required for this operation. The operation of comprehension combines ideas within the mind together, in order to gather knowledge and an understanding of a specific phenomenon. The faculties of cognition and intuition are pivotal for this operation. The last operation of deduction applies ideals on the knowledge gained through the operation of comprehension, which results in the acquisition of foresight and the mastery of knowledge. The faculties of reason and imagination are utilized in this operation.

During the operation of analysis, the intellect will examine and differentiate one idea from another. At least one of the ideas in question is stored within the individual's faculty of memory. Both ideas are then brought into focus, within the intellect. For example, the individual may be contemplating about choosing a religion. Within his intellect, he will then focus on the possible choices available to him. After this recollection phase, the faculty of judgment is then employed. Through this faculty, the intellect will then examine and come to favour one idea over another, according to the main purpose of the operation. The individual, then, makes a choice according to which idea is most similar to his personal values, desires and beliefs, in addition to that idea which personally benefits him the most.

The most basic faculty of the intellect is memory. All animals in the wild demonstrate that they possess this faculty. When we perceive an object within the physical world through our sensory perceptions, our intellect will automatically store this perception within the faculty of memory. All of our experiences are stored within our memories, even those perceptions that were gathered during a dreaming state. Our ability to access these memories, though, will vary from individual to individual.

Persons with a powerful faculty of memory will possess an extraordinary ability to differentiate two distinct models or ideas. Their analytical skills enable them to comprehend kinds of information gathered solely through their personal experiences. However, some of these persons may often ignore all of their other faculties, as they mainly rely on this faculty for the gaining of all forms of knowledge. This results in the acquisition of subjective knowledge.

In contrast, persons who possess a limited faculty of memory will demonstrate poor analytical skills. Their ability of analysis, then, will be rudimentary, and this greatly affects their acquisition of knowledge. In the majority of cases, individuals with a poor memory will struggle during their educational pursuits. During social interactions, however, they may demonstrate a higher level of functioning memory. This indicates that these individuals still possess the most essential analytical skills necessary for building friendships and other kinds of relationships within a community-based environment.

The faculty of judgment functions as a kind of decision-maker that depends on the freedom of the will. It is correctly employed only if it possesses the kind of freedom that exists within our wills. Similarly, its correct employment also requires both objective and subjective knowledge. It requires objective knowledge so that the decision it subsequently comes to does not pose any kind of harm to any forms of life within the physical world. It requires subjective knowledge so that the decision made does not pose any kind of threat to the individual decision maker. Hence, the correct utilization of the faculty of judgment should not only benefit the decision maker, but it should also cause no kind of harm against the general public.

In contrast, the incorrect utilization of the faculty of judgment occurs when the actor does not possess the power to freely choose, and is thus under a kind of coercion. When the individual does not possess the power to autonomously focus on any ideas of his choosing, he will then be focusing on the private ideas of an individual who is external to him. The decisions he makes will, subsequently, reflect a lower utilization of the will. Accordingly, this reflects upon a form of judgment that the actor would not have made if he were free. The decisions he makes, then, are not truly his own, but are the decisions of some authority figure, who is primarily responsible for that act of coercion.

The operation of comprehension differs from the operation of analysis, in that the intellect is not comparing and differentiating two distinct ideas. Rather, it is joining one idea with another. During this operation, the intellect is focused on a base idea and is adding subsidiary ideas, known as properties, to that base idea. For example, when considering our galaxy, we add properties to this base idea to gain a more thorough understanding of this concept. Ideas such as stars, comets, and planets with rings may be properties that we can add to the concept of our galaxy, so that we can understand what this term actually means. Therefore, when the intellect comprehends, it joins individual ideas to a general concept, and this results in a more developed and sophisticated concept.

Cognition is the most important faculty of the intellect. Through this faculty, we possess the ability to view a base idea and process it into a more specific idea. Thus, while many base ideas are perceived through sensory experience, the faculty of cognition draws focus onto one of these ideas, and inspects it thoroughly. Through cognition, the individual possesses the ability to analyze all of his base ideas, and order them into subtypes. Next, he will choose a specific idea within one of these classes, and examine all of its pieces. After this process is complete, one particular property of a base idea will then be chosen, and the intellect will further examine all of its components. This process will be repeated indefinitely, and hence, this is the essential process of the faculty of cognition. After all of the properties of a base idea are thoroughly examined, the intellect will then draw connections between these properties to that base idea, and this is the nature of understanding. The faculty of cognition, then, draws relationships of all kinds between distinct ideas and their properties, and this enables us to grasp a greater understanding of what was once an unknown and solitary idea.

The opposite of cognition is ignorance. Ignorance demonstrates a particular lack of awareness regarding some base idea or category of base ideas. Persons who are witless may not lack the faculty of cognition. The intellect mainly becomes illiterate when it does not employ the faculty of cognition. Hence, an idea perceived through the senses only becomes a kind of knowledge when the actor focuses and directs his attention towards that idea, and examines it. The degree of knowledge obtained, however, does depend on other faculties of the intellect. The faculty of memory is sometimes necessary within some instances of cognition. Therefore, comprehension is an increasingly more complex operation within the intellect.

The faculty of intuition is also utilized by the intellect during the operation of comprehension. Intuition may be viewed as a more advanced and complicated faculty when compared to the common animal's faculty of instinct. In comparison to instinct, intuition requires not merely habitual impulses, but also a natural ability to make an assembly between ideas that, on the surface, seem to lack any forms of an association. Therefore, a proper faculty of judgment is required for intuition. Forms of intuition are usually based on previous life experiences. When the intellect employs the faculty of intuition, it draws a weak association between some base idea and some specific idea. The attributes added to that base idea, then, have not been proven with entire certainty. Nonetheless, when this weak link is established, the intellect does possess some objective reason for the basis of this connection. The faculty of intuition draws on a kind of knowledge that appears to be certain, during cases where there is an insufficient amount of evidence, or ideas, that will prove that it is certain.

Instinct is a lower form of intuition that is the main driving force behind the common animal. When human beings act according to their instincts, they do not act according to any forms of knowledge. Essentially, their actions are driven by primitive, uncultured impulses. Within nature's environment, the wild animal relies on its instincts primarily for its survival. However, the size of its intellect is much more limited, in comparison to any human being. Therefore, any individual who acts according to his natural born instincts is ignoring the potential power that could exist within his intellect. His actions could be just, but these actions will stem mainly from his subjective knowledge. Hence, persons who mainly rely on their instincts will usually act unjustly, due to the complex cultural nature that defines human civilization. Instinctive knowledge only belongs within the wilderness of nature, as it has no place within any communal environment that values peaceful and cooperative relationships.

Deduction is the most powerful operation of the intellect. Through deduction, we examine relationships among ideas based on the principle of cause and effect. Within the intellect, this operation links ideas together, where one idea will provide a necessary foundation behind another idea. Contrariwise, also through this operation, the intellect associates one idea as the result of another idea. The most common application of this operation may be found in mathematics, or the sciences. In the subject of engineering, the operation of deduction enables us to create and invent new forms of technologies. Within the subject of medicine, this operation grants us with the ability to treat and possibly cure many forms of disease. The faculty of reason is the primary building block behind any processes of deduction. On the other hand, the faculty of imagination, when utilized with reason, may be the most powerful faculty known to all of mankind.

Rational thinking differentiates human beings from all other species. Through the faculty of reason, we possess the ability to draw permanent correlations between a primary and a secondary idea. Therefore, reason provides a cause behind every effect. Through reason, we possess the ability to conceive abstract laws that are always true, within our physical world. For example, understanding the laws of gravity enables us to create forms of technology necessary for space travel. From a cultured perspective, possessing a rational frame of mind also enables us to act logically, and thus, create communities based on the principle of cooperation. Conversely, without this faculty, our actions would digress into habits based on instinct, where no kinds of civilized communities could exist. Our faculty of reason, then, provides us with the power to sort our ideas according to an orderly and sensible system of thought.

Without the faculty of reason, the human mind would be sentenced into a permanent state of chaos. No ordered cities would exist, nor any kinds of cooperative tribes. Human civilization, as a whole, would never come into existence because we would possess no kinds of technology, and also because the element of culture would have never been born. Moreover, the concept of a family system would be sporadic, and a solitary existence would become common. Our faculty of reason provides us with a rational frame of mind, and this grants us with a way of life that is primarily based on the principle of a peaceful coexistence. If all human minds were irrational, we would lack any ability to determine our future, and contrariwise, our lives would be mainly determined by nature.

Our faculty of imagination is also necessary during the process of deduction. Through deduction, we analyze a primary idea and then we compute some correlation that results in a secondary idea. During the process of deliberation, a primary idea exists within the intellect. A secondary idea depends on the proper calculation of that primary idea, and thus, it exists only after this calculation is made. When the intellect does employ the operation of deduction, the result could either be true or false. In the case that it is false, the result could essentially represent anything. In the case that it is true, the secondary idea still primarily exists as a subjective thought within the mind of the perceiver. Accordingly, since the individual has no knowledge of what will result after he employs the operation of deduction, this secondary idea is primarily formulated through his imagination. It is only after someone has verified that this secondary idea is entirely true, in which case, it may then take the form as an objective piece of knowledge.

Therefore, the calculation made on a primary idea could yield a correct result, or a faulty result. A correct result will only exist after the intellect has made a proper deduction. Therefore, since the process of deduction is liable to err, an incorrect secondary idea will be mainly a product of the individual's imagination. In contrast, a correct secondary idea will also be first conceived through the individual's imagination, but its existence is wholly dependent on the primary idea and a sound deduction. Logically, then, the existence of a secondary idea may either partially or entirely depend on the individual's imagination.

Similarly, the imagination is used when the latter process is reversed. Consider the invention of the airplane. Within one engineer's mind, this kind of machine would only need a single set of wings to fly. Another engineer has started calculations on a model based on a biplane, while yet another engineer has imagined a plane that possesses three sets of wings. However, a working airplane still did not exist at this time. Subsequently, it must have first existed within the mind of the engineer who was successful enough to conceive a working model. Consequently, deduction is an operation that can also be properly realized when the calculation process is made through the reverse order. In other words, the engineer may have first imagined an end result as his primary idea, and then he may have made the necessary calculations to create a functioning product.

On the other hand, the faculty of imagination may also be improperly utilized, and this results in the decline of human existence. The utilization of our imaginations results in ideas that are newly conceived and understood. However, the topics contemplated within our imaginations may truly be limitless. I possess the power to both contemplate about heaven or hell. If I focus on goodness, I will imagine God, angels, and utopia. When I focus on the evils that exist within our world, I can imagine an infinite amount of punishments and condemnations. All persons possess an unbounded will to imagine, however, possessing the ability to control the focus of our imaginations can sometimes be difficult.

Other individuals will lack the ability to release the power of their imagination. When this occurs, the individual essentially lacks control over the most powerful faculty of his intellect. The individual, then, will have lost the ability to realize his strengths, and he will have lost the ability to conceive his possible potential. Without an unlimited scope of imagination, the individual will be doomed to a mere existence based on dire, privation and destitution.

Similar to its faculties, the intellect, as a whole, may also be misused. When this occurs, criminal acts will usually result. In general, individuals may possess either a high level of rationale, or a low level of rationale. The individual's level of rationale, in great part, determines his intelligence. The focus of one's emotional centre also demonstrates intelligence. Nonetheless, the rational intellect is the major component behind all forms of knowledge, intelligence and insight.

Individuals with a low rationale will often misuse, or fail to use their intellect. When they are faced with a state of ignorance, they will often abandon any kinds of rational thoughts, and will then enter into the intellectual state of frustration. In moments where they lack understanding, these individuals will often compare themselves with other persons who possess a higher level of rationale. This compounds their feelings of anger which essentially motivates their next actions, based on criminal forms of behaviour.

Most criminals that possess a low level of rationale are con artists. These individuals apply their intellect for crimes based on flimflam and fraud. Deception is a major idea that is exploited by these individuals. These criminals will disguise themselves as honest, law-abiding citizens. They do not focus their crimes on any specific targets. In the general public, only those persons who are unsuspecting will be swindled by their schemes. The con artist is mainly motivated by some form of material or monetary gain. He is responsible for the most cunning fabrications and deceptions.

On a higher criminal level, deviants also avail the methods used by con artists. These criminals acquire forms of legitimate employment to manipulate others for their personal benefit. Deviants will acquire positions within all realms of employment. There are deviants who are employed within high levels of the public sector, and even high levels of our health-care system. These individuals are known as white collar criminals. Some of them seek wealth and material gain. Other deviants are motivated by personal aims, which do not involve any forms of economic gain.

Other kinds of deviants commit cowardly crimes like animal abuse. These individuals will usually try to maintain their innocence, and do not take any forms of responsibility for their acts. By hurting innocent animals, these deviants are motivated to inflict harm on those who are sympathetic to forms of wild life. This makes their crimes extremely calculated, deliberate, and premeditated.

Another form of deviance pertains to individuals who are known as fence sitters. These individuals remain objective and neutral in the face of any kinds of dispute. After a specific dispute is settled, these deviants will abandon their neutrality and support those individuals who are the actual winners of the dispute. These persons are extremely conniving and without scruples. They are motivated by the authority granted, by the winners of a dispute, over those individuals who may be the losers of a given dispute.

The last kind of intellectual criminal is rare, yet most destructive. The tyrant is a deceiver until he achieves full political authority over a nation-state. Before he is granted power, he will demonstrate a charismatic persona. After he is granted political authority, though, he will exercise his power according to his own personal volitions. He primarily seeks conformity over the citizens that he rules. Those who do not conform will be punished according to his sole discretion. Accordingly, any persons who challenge his self-righteousness or authority will be penalized and branded as outcasts.

These criminals are examples of individuals who possess an intellectually dominant personality. That is, these persons mainly exercise their intellect during the bulk of their social interactions, and they largely ignore the other two elements of their mind. The reason for this may be based on their childhood, where they mainly succeeded in attaining their personal goals through the sole utilization of the intellect. Therefore, these individuals rely on their intellect, exclusively, to achieve their personal goals. Comparatively, while their intellect remains in a process of development throughout their entire life, their emotions and spirit remain neglected and undeveloped. During their adult years, these individuals will develop the habit of utilizing their intellect, as a means of achieving social dominance, during all kinds of differing social circumstances.

In general, the intellectual deviant is motivated by a superiority complex. They are egoists who subscribe to the impression of survival of the fittest. They are decidedly self-centred, they lack access to a full range of emotions, and accordingly, they place no value on emotional states. With respect to their spirit, they do not value any kinds of universal principles. Essentially, they do not recognize common social values because they believe in the concept of individuality, where every person may avail any types of means to achieve forms of personal contentment. Regarding personal identity, this criminal is narcissistic and only acts civil towards those persons who are subservient to his rule, and those who fundamentally act according to his bidding.

When utilized correctly, the intellect is responsible for the human ability to surpass nature. Through the intellect, we have saved innocent lives because of our theoretical invention of science. The paradigm of science is based on all operations within the intellect. Through experimentation, we analyze compounds in nature and this also leads to our comprehension of the natural world. Through deduction, we take the knowledge that we have gained, turn it into a universal principle, and then apply it among all relevant cases. Some persons define the nature of science as a method based on observation and prediction. A better definition, perhaps, may be based on the ideal that true science utilizes the entire intellect in the quest for knowledge of our physical world.

To illustrate this, consider the grizzly, which crosses an open field and stumbles onto a river bank. Upon finding this source of water, he also finds an abundance of fish. The grizzly, then, will store this particular location within his memory, so that he may retrace his steps when his hunger has returned. Now, consider the professional fisherman who discovers this area on the same river, but is looking for a particular kind of fish. This fisherman is not looking for any ordinary sockeye. Actually, he is looking to catch a shark. Through personal experience, and the experiences of other catchers, this fisherman knows that sharks do not swim within narrow streams, and that their natural habitat is located within the oceans. The fisherman then uses the experiences of professionals before him, which is empirical knowledge, and then he comes to the conclusion that he will not find any sharks within this particular stream. This deduction is based on his faculty of reason. Since he knows that sharks only swim in the ocean, the fisherman uses both experience and reason to come to the conclusion that he should fish elsewhere for his daily meal.

    The concept of science, then, is similar to this scenario. Through medical science, human beings, alone, possess the power to treat and cure natural diseases. First, research specialists observe the particular physical ailments present in sick bodies. Next, they experiment with differing kinds of compounds in an effort to correct these ailments. Upon discovering the specific element that will relieve a specific ailment, they gain medical knowledge. Then through reason, we apply this treatment to all patients who suffer from the same ailment. Since the makeup of all human bodies remains relatively similar, we deduce that this particular treatment will not only work on the subjects within the experimentation phase, but it will also work on all other persons. We have evidence that this treatment is effective on a group of subjects, and rationalize the fact that this treatment will also work at a universal level.

    Empirically, our ability to communicate is also gained through experience. In the beginning, we must observe and remember all twenty-six letters of the alphabet. Next, we must remember the sounds associated with every letter, and likewise, we must memorize the spelling of words. Then, we must learn how to pronounce every specific word, and relate it with a particular meaning. Communication, then, is mainly employed through our faculty of memory.

Rationally, we possess an innate ability to communicate. Human beings differ from the wild animal because we possess the intellectual ability to communicate complex thoughts, and thus we possess the faculty of language. After I have associated concepts with words, I will require instruction based on the laws of syntax and grammar. To communicate my ideas, I am free to combine many differing words as I see fit. However, if I use any random combination of words to communicate, my efforts may lose its efficacy, or it may not be effective at all. Thus, I must use the laws of grammar as a standard mode of communication, and this stems from our ability to use reason. Therefore, with respect to our faculty of language, we must employ both operations of analysis and comprehension to communicate effectively.

Art is a further human ability that marks the exchange of ideas. In the creation of all kinds of art, the artist employs the operation of analysis. Firstly, he examines some aspect of human nature. Then he creates his craft based on his own subjective, personal analysis. His faculty of judgment, thus, is employed as he views something in nature, and creates his own representation of that idea. In perceiving the creations of the artisan, the individual also employs the intellectual operation of analysis. While viewing this new creation, the individual compares the idea materialized by the artisan with his own ideas based on the same phenomenon. Then, he uses his faculty of judgment and compares the likeness between these two individual conceptions of the same phenomenon, and this determines the unique value regarding that particular piece of art.

In the cases of both our scientific discoveries, and our ability to communicate, laws are necessary for any kind of knowledge. Accordingly, reason is a necessary component within all forms of knowledge. It is only through our faculty of reason that we possess the ability to understand laws, and other concepts based on cause and effect. However, to observe these laws, we also require experience. Within the field of science, the laws of physics are integral to our knowledge of nature and the world as a whole. Regarding language, the laws of grammar are essential for effective forms of communication. Without the laws of physics, our world would not be governed by some kind of constant, and this would impact our ability to understand the material world. Without the laws of grammar, our speech would be fragmented and imprecise, and thus, extremely futile.

Consciousness also requires an intellect, and it is a mode of the operation of analysis. Simply, consciousness is a subjective awareness that one is alive. Yet, it is also a state of mind. Self-consciousness is an intellectual act where the individual directs his focus and attention onto himself. This is a unique state of mind that may be viewed as a higher level of consciousness. For some individuals, self-consciousness is a common and recurrent intellectual state. For others, entering into a state of reflection may be infrequent and rare.

Moreover, there are also kinds of consciousness based on the material and immaterial worlds. These intellectual states are two further levels of consciousness. Consciousness of the purely physical world is the lowest form of awareness. Persons who are conscious of the purely physical possess an awareness of only their physical environment. Conversely, consciousness of the purely immaterial, or spiritual, is the highest form of consciousness. These individuals possess an awareness not only of their own spiritual nature, but also of others. They also conceive ideologies related to heaven and God.

Most human beings possess a consciousness of both the physical and the immaterial world. Only these individuals possess the power to obtain an awareness of the purely immaterial. Therefore, persons whose consciousness is limited to the physical world cannot grasp the purely spiritual, because they possess no foundational idea of the immaterial world.

No persons possess the power to choose our physical bodies, and thus, our bodies are granted to us by nature. If we did possess the power to choose our bodies, no individual would pick a body that is vulnerable to illness or disease. As a result, our bodies constitute an exceedingly minor element of our identity. Focusing on our physical attributes will often be misleading. Hence, those persons who achieve a consciousness of both the physical and the spiritual realms possess a much firmer grasp within the area of personal identity. Those who possess a strong awareness of both levels of consciousness will also be empowered with the virtue of empathy. This makes them capable of making good and sound judgments. Likewise, these persons have been granted an exceptional ability to focus on the abstract, and they will view the world without any kinds of bias or pre-conceived judgments.

To illustrate the differences between these two levels of consciousness, consider the following scenario. If an animal in the wild, perhaps a fawn, were to encounter a human being, it would act mainly according to its instincts. This animal is only aware of the physical presence of another kind of animal. On the other hand, consider this individual's domesticated pet. When this pet encounters the individual, it possesses more than a simple awareness of the physical, as it identifies and also possesses an awareness of the spiritual. Within the pet's frame of mind, his owner is more than just another physical being. As his owner, the pet perceives his owner's spiritual nature, and this motivates him to reciprocate the ideals of affection and loyalty. Nonetheless, if this pet were to encounter some stranger, it may lack the ability to perceive the spiritual, and it will then return to its instinctive habits.

This, furthermore, demonstrates the power and importance of our faculty of memory. Every animal in nature demonstrates that it possesses this faculty. Every animal needs to remember where its feeding grounds are located, in conjunction to where its home is located. Social animals also need to remember the spiritual nature of other members that belong to their pack. As a consequence, memory may be the sole faculty of the intellect necessary for survival, within the material world.

The scope of an individual's intellect is granted to him by nature, and it usually remains constant for his entire life. In a small minority of cases though, it is possible that the individual's intellect may be altered. Physical head injuries may disrupt processes of cognition. Chemical imbalances can also modify an individual's intellectual faculties, which will in turn disrupt his comprehension. Subsequently, these conditions will affect the individual's ability to think rationally or objectively. When this occurs, the intellect will affect the individual's character, in so far as it reduces his ability function. His intellect is, thus, reduced in a manner that will compromise his effectiveness in areas of employment, and in some cases, general social interactions.

Lastly, in comparing the categories of rationalism and empiricism, we must consider the concepts of a priori and a posteriori truths. A priori truths exist prior to experience. We know that "the heroic do what is good" as a rational truth. A posteriori truths, contrarily, can only be known through experience. Our knowledge that there is a low field of gravity on the moon is gained only through experience. For it is entirely possible that other moons within our universe could possess a high field of gravity. Accordingly, while our bodies are necessary for empirical truths, only our minds are required for rational truths. This makes human knowledge extremely complex, yet constructive. It is the power of our intellect that differentiates us from the common animal.

Likewise, it is the power of our intellect that enables us to become the rulers of our natural world.

4   Emotional Centre

EVERY HUMAN BEING experiences some set of emotions. However, the specific emotions and the specific circumstances connected to them will vary on an individual basis. Some persons may be manic, while others may be stoic. The individual's core of emotional expression will be initially based on some point in between these two extremes. At the beginning, this core, or the intensity of an individual's emotional expression, is granted to him by nature. No individual possesses the power to alter the range of feelings that he experiences through the emotional element of his soul.

However, the individual does possess the power to direct his core of emotions towards a specific target. The individual's emotional centre will be directed towards the object of his love. Thus, while the individual does not possess the power to moderate his emotional experiences, he does possess the power to direct his core of emotions towards those objects which he values the most. The individual's emotional being is, thus, comprised of two halves. The first half, known as the core, is the range and intensity of his emotional experiences, which is initially determined by nature. The other half is his emotional centre, which is entirely determined according to his personal volitions.

The individual's emotional centre will be situated at the median point, with respect to the range of his emotional expression. He centres his emotions towards that object which is the primary element of his concerns. This object could be physical, for example, such as a concern towards other human beings. Nonetheless, this object may also be ideological, for instance, such as an apprehension towards self-conceit. The target of the individual's emotional centre will cause the most passionate feelings or emotional experiences, while that object which is its complete opposite will generate few experiences of emotion.

Experience is a necessary component that expands one's core of emotions. Therefore, some persons who lack specific life experiences will not experience certain kinds of emotions. For example, persons who have never served within a military institution will not experience a similar form of a post-traumatic stress disorder that some soldiers will suffer from. Likewise, experience is necessary for the experiencing of emotions on the opposite ends of the emotional spectrum. For instance, persons who have won the top prize in a lottery will experience a form of elation that is reserved for princes and princesses.

In both cases, the individual's emotional centre will still remain at the same point, though the range of his emotional expression will increase. Hence, through unique experiences, the individual will experience a higher range of emotional feelings. Life experiences, then, deeply affect the individual's core of emotions. On the other hand, the individual's centre of emotions will deeply affect his perspective and interpretation of all life events.

When the individual values extrinsic phenomena, his emotional experiences will be limited and superficial. The differences between extrinsic and intrinsic phenomena relates to the worth of some component to human civilization. Extrinsic phenomena are inessential for a well-lived life. Forms of material wealth are often perceived to have more value than they actually produce. Appearances based on the concept of vanity are also trivial and artificial. Individuals with an insignificant centre of emotions are shallow, and thus will value elements that are extrinsic to a prosperous civilization.

The most common individuals who possess an insignificant centre of emotions are known as bullies. Their acts of physical aggression are fuelled by their emotional feelings of anger. These criminals are haunted by an inferiority complex that may be based on a variety of elements. Some bullies are unhappy with their appearances, either physically or spiritually. Other bullies become irritated do to their inabilities within the realm of intellectual sophistication. Accordingly, the stereotypical bully lacks a number of intellectual faculties, which results in his inability to comprehend complex concepts and ideals.

The victims of the bully are usually chosen because of their inclinations towards peaceful modes of conduct. No bully ever picks persons who are either aggressive in nature, or similarly bent on some form of revenge. Thus, the bully mainly picks victims who will not retaliate through forms of physical aggression. This demonstrates his true cowardice. By choosing targets that are inclined towards the peaceful resolution of all forms of disputes, the bully hides his feelings of anger and aggressive tendencies from the general public. He demonstrates that he can act civil, but only to those persons who are the object of his personal fears. In essence, he justly lacks pride and self-righteousness.

Arsonists are also a kind of bully, however their feelings of anger may be bottled, and subsequently, more intense. Also similar to the bully, the arsonist hides his feelings of rage from the general public, because he is motivated to commit his acts of terror in an anonymous fashion. However, he differs from the bully in that he does feel pride and self-satisfaction in relation to his criminal acts. In the act of setting fires, the arsonist is releasing feelings of anger that he holds towards his community or the public in general. He believes that the feelings of fear that he wants to produce will satisfy the personal injustices that have been committed against him.

Nihilists are individuals who are similar to terrorists, but they are motivated by personal, and thus, non-political reasons. Some nihilists are recruited by terrorists to complete actual acts of violence. Other nihilists work alone, because their reasons for committing acts of violence are private and exclusive. In some cases, this criminal may claim some kind of political motivation behind his acts of violence. Nevertheless, his claims are phony and are meant to rationalize his criminal acts within the eyes of the public. The nihilist is primarily motivated by the emotion of hatred, and he believes that he has been wronged by some group within his community. In his acts of violence, he is seeking revenge for all of the wrongdoings, that in his mind, he has come across, due to the wealth or prospering status of some minority group.

Serial murderers are different from nihilists with respect to their emotional states and motivations for committing a criminal act. These criminals do commit murders for personal reasons. However, serial murderers seek self-gratification as opposed to revenge. Lust and sexual gratification usually motivates this criminal. In other cases, these criminals murder others to compensate for their own personal deficiencies, which are also usually sexual in nature. These individuals are extreme egoists who exhibit no kind of regard towards other persons. They experience emotions based on inadequacies, and after they have committed a criminal act, they feel that they have fulfilled their inadequacies. Nonetheless, after some time, their original emotional state returns and then they will re-enter into a mental state of insufficiency. This element is what drives them to become multiple reoffenders.

The serial murderer usually feels entirely justified with respect to his criminal acts, because he is an egoist. Therefore, at times, he will feel that he has committed no wrongdoing. This makes his mind-set extremely unstable and irrational. Contrarily, when entering into a public domain, he does not exhibit any irrational tendencies. This enables him to commit multiple offences before he faces our justice system.

Subsequently, the serial murderer actively camouflages himself within the public realm, which reflects upon the notion that he views his criminal lifestyle as a kind of game. Within the public realm, the serial murderer disguises himself and acts as if he does not possess any of his particular inadequacies. He interacts with other persons as if he were innocent of any wrongdoing. Strategically, then, he exhibits a kind of multiple personality to hide the true nature of his disposition. Every time he has fooled another person, regarding his true disposition, he gains momentum and believes that he has won that particular confrontation, comparatively to a kind of battle. Similarly, every time he commits any wrongdoing without getting caught, he will gain further momentum. This illustrates the fact that all serial murderers will learn more about their craft as they commit more instances of deception and wrongdoing. The serial murderer, then, is a progressive criminal who develops more proficiency as he commits multiple offences, based on trickery and other forms of deviant behaviour.

All persons who possess an insignificant centre of emotions will experience pessimistic kinds of emotions for their entire life span. Pessimism is a constant and continual negative outlook on life, where the individual focuses on all of the evils and immorality present within our natural world. It is a kind of mindset where the individual lacks an awareness regarding positive experiences, even when he is engaged in a pleasant activity. Therefore, the pessimistic outlook dominates the totality of these individual's experiences, which results in social encounters based on conflict and antipathy.

Anger is the most common emotion displayed by the pessimistic. It is a heightened emotion because it can potentially dictate the individual's state of mind. Many different elements in our natural world can cause emotions of anger. Persons can become angry because of their relationships with other persons, because of certain concepts or ideals, or even because of the unequal distribution of wealth. The experience of rage brings out an instinctual nature within the individual. Persons who experience extreme forms of anger will often lose a rational state of mind, and they will, therefore, act with haste. This classifies the emotion of anger as a form of motivational force behind immoral acts and behaviour.

The feeling of agitation is a lessened emotion that is essentially a kind of anger, though it is experienced on a much lesser scale when compared to anger. Persons who become agitated will focus their thoughts on a particular characteristic found within other individuals. For example, the individual may become agitated with persons who do not reciprocate a form of respect. In this case, the individual experiences a less severe degree of anger that is focused on a highly specific element within another person's character.

The emotion of annoyance is a lesser kind of agitation, and thus, a lesser degree of anger. Persons who experience this emotion focus these negative feelings towards a specific action carried out by an individual. Nonetheless, these feelings are controllable reactions. In contrast, feelings of anger and agitation usually erupt within the individual in a rapid and uncontrollable fashion. Hence, feelings of annoyance form a type of anger that can be ignored, dismissed or forgotten, according to the will of the perceiver.

Hatred is another kind of heightened emotion. Those who experience this emotion on a frequent basis will direct these feelings towards some group of persons. Comparatively, those who experience this emotion on an occasional basis will direct these feelings towards a single individual. Feelings of angst originate through the many kinds of dissimilarities observable between the differing personal characteristics found within each unique individual. The objects of hatred are those persons who are perceived to possess specific characteristics that are either worthless or valueless. This emotion also often motivates criminal forms of behaviour. Individuals who feel hatred on a regular and recurrent basis will often resort to criminal forms of behaviour as a coping mechanism, which may or may not address the negative frame of mind produced through this consuming emotion.

Contempt is a lower form of hatred that is directed towards principles or ideologies. Persons who experience this emotion are unsatisfied with certain cultural factors. Forms of contempt may be directed towards the justice system, governmental policies, or the workplace. The emotion of contempt mainly motivates kinds of behaviour, comparable to peaceful protests. When peaceful protests are conducted due to some form of injustice, the pursuit for social justice remains as the primary motivation behind these types of acts. However, when this peace is broken or neglected, the individual will then be guilty of a form of criminal behaviour. At times, this emotion could motivate destructive forms of behaviour that are not directed towards any specific persons, but towards a specific institute in general.

As a lesser degree of contempt, irritation is another kind of consuming emotion where the individual loses a rational frame of mind. In comparison to hatred, however, the emotion of irritation is directed towards the actions of another individual. Similarly, the emotion of hatred also holds a greater control over the individual's frame of mind. Irritation, then, is a kind of hatred that is sporadic and brief. It is a short-term emotion, where the perceiver possesses the ability to return into a more rational frame of mind after a relatively little amount of time.

The emotion of destructiveness is caused by all forms of hatred. Persons who become wasteful will actively create forms of chaos within some kind of ordered system. These systems may be political, communal, or familial. Usual forms of destruction take some kind of physical shape. Other kinds are ideological in nature, and thus more subtle. When the individual becomes consumed with destructiveness, he will lack the ability to use any forms of reason. Consequently, he cannot but feel a form of hysteria towards that target which is the object of his hate.

The emotion of fear is also a kind of heightened emotion. Persons who experience fear hold the belief that their lives are threatened in one manner or another. Some individuals will then take measures in effort to defend themselves. Other individuals will cower upon facing their personal fears. Animals in nature often become hostile when they fear either their own or their children's safety. Therefore, fear is a very common emotion experienced within the animal kingdom.

Intimidation is a lower kind of fear directed towards those who are perceived to possess more positive characteristics, in comparison to oneself. Physical strength is often an important characteristic, though intellectual strength could also intimidate those who are of a weaker nature. However, since all persons possess differing degrees of diverse characteristics, feelings of intimidation are often held by individuals who are of a younger age, or those who lack a sufficient amount of life experiences.

Suspiciousness is a kind of fear directed towards no specific individual. Persons who do experience this emotion will be frightened by some group of persons or some general category of persons. Therefore, these individuals usually discriminate against persons of a particular ethnicity, or persons who belong to other forms of stereotypes. Regarding the individual's fears, it is usually justified. These individuals expect to be engaged in some kind of hostile encounter with individuals that belong to a particular stereotype, and when these events do transpire, the individual will possess enough reasons to continue and maintain his feelings of caution.

Confusion is a heightened emotion that is related to the individual's intellect. Those persons who lack the ability to carry out some operation within their intellect will often enter into the emotional state of confusion. When this occurs, their intellectual aptitude becomes exasperated, they become overwhelmed, and they will then become easily distracted. Furthermore, the emotion of confusion usually leads to the experiencing of apathy and weariness. When persons enter into this condition, their rational knowledge pertaining to civil society becomes impoverished, and they will remit back into an instinctual state of mind.

The emotion of jealousy often follows the emotion of confusion. Individuals who experience this emotion place a high value on all forms of material elements, such as wealth or beauty. Those individuals who possess more kinds of wealth will usually be the objects of jealousy. Furthermore, those who experience this emotion will place little value on their own lives. Urges of competitiveness, then, subsequently arise within these individuals. They believe that their life could be better if they possessed certain forms of material wealth. However, in truth, even when these individuals acquire some kind of material wealth, their jealous urges will return. This is due to the fact that they will still continue the habit of belittling the value of their own lives, regardless of any new forms of wealth that they do manage to acquire.

Greed is a similar to jealousy. However, this emotion is mainly directed towards currency. Those who are greedy are often dishonest, and some commit crimes in an effort to gain more wealth. Greed is often a compulsive emotion that becomes a primary driving force behind many individual's immoral acts. These persons view material wealth as the sole and exclusive component to a prosperous life. Therefore, they will often neglect other kinds of responsibilities, such as family duties or other forms of obligations towards their community.

Carelessness is an emotion experienced by persons who are primarily motivated by self-interest. These individuals only focus on their own wellbeing, while lacking any forms of concern towards other persons. In some cases, individuals who experience carelessness will use other persons as instruments in their quest to achieve their personal goals. However, these individuals are also highly susceptible to being used by other persons. This is due to the fact that they are primarily oriented towards accomplishing their personal goals. Hence, they impose no forms of limitations on their actions, so long as they hold the belief that these actions will bring them closer to completing their personal objective.

The emotion of boredom results after the individual becomes ignored. When the individual enters into a prolonged state of listlessness, he will then adopt immoral methods of behaviour for a source of pleasure. This leads to forms of premeditated crimes. Likewise, the emotion of boredom usually leads to a state of permanent isolation, since persons who experience this emotion usually lack the social skills necessary to acquire relationships, and other kinds of friendships.

Anxiety is a heightened emotion based on feelings of nervousness or worry. The objects of anxiety may be anything in nature. One may lack feelings of comfort towards his public image, or towards his test scores during a final exam. Through life experiences, all forms of pressure may be addressed and then conquered. In other individuals, though, feelings of anxiety will continually persist and consume their frame of mind, even during the most mundane life events.

Guilt is a specific form of anxiety directed towards the individual's immoral behaviour. Immoral forms of behaviour can include criminal acts, or other forms of abuse. Only individuals who experience this emotion will seek forgiveness for their actions. However, degrees of guilt are purely subjective, and are dependent on the guilty party's life perspective. Accordingly, some major forms of abuse will appear to be minor within the guilty individual's frame of mind. When the apology under shadows the crime, forms of forgiveness can never be fairly or justly granted.

Apprehensiveness is the most common emotion that follows the emotion of guilt. Individuals become apprehensive because they fear possible forms of revenge or social justice that may be imposed on them. These individuals may not admit the fact that they committed a specific criminal act, however on a personal level, they are aware of the fact that they are guilty of some crime. Consequently, these individuals remain in a state of uneasiness if they are aware of the fact that forms of justice or revenge are imminent. Within their frame of mind, persons who are apprehensive will continue to contemplate about possible forms of punishment associated with their crime, to better prepare themselves for the time when forms of social justice become actualized.

Another emotion that follows guilt is embarrassment. When the individual is guilty of some wrongdoing, and when he values his public image, feelings of embarrassment will evolve. Some of these persons will only experience feelings humiliation when they are actually caught for their transgressions, while others experience feelings of humiliation necessarily. Nonetheless, some criminals do not place any kinds of value upon their public persona. These individuals will not experience feelings of embarrassment, and on the contrary, they may experience feelings of pride with respect to their wrongdoings. As a result, only criminals who actually value other persons within their community will potentially experience feelings of embarrassment.

Impatience is an emotion that follows the emotion of anxiety. Those who are impatient experience an elevated feeling of anxiety. Their feelings of impatience are usually directed towards persons they view as incompetent. Nevertheless, the origins of this emotion are usually based on the individual's own personal incompetence. Therefore, these individuals deal with their own stupidity by externalizing this attribute onto other persons. In essence, they view other persons as incompetent as a means to direct their focus away from their own personal flaws.

The emotion of panic may sometimes follow emotions of impatience. Individuals who experience feelings of panic are also experiencing an elevated form of anxiety. Nonetheless, this emotion usually surfaces in a consistent, yet sporadic fashion. Therefore, persons who experience this emotion are quite liable to re-experience it for the remainder of their lives. Moreover, these individuals will always have room for feelings of hesitation, during all kinds of social situations.

Burden is a form of anxiety directed towards other persons. These individuals feel that they are being used whenever they are assigned with some form of responsibility. As a consequence, they will never acknowledge any forms of responsibility. The only kind of responsibility that they do possess pertains solely to their own well-being. Any forms of responsibility outside of this scope will be considered to be superfluous. Subsequently, rather than acknowledging any forms of responsibility, these individuals will experience emotions of burden instead.

Persons direct their feelings of anxiety towards that object which possesses the power to cause feelings of agony. Feelings of agony may come about through either physical pain or mental anguish. No individual wishes to experience feelings of agony. However, feelings of agony arise in the individual without warning. The emotion of agony has a necessary causal relationship with the emotion of anxiety. When the individual becomes overwhelmed with feelings of anxiety, the emotional state of agony will subsequently evolve.

Sorrow is the final heightened emotion that usually follows feelings of agony. However, the individual will enter into a state of sorrow because he is the direct cause of some form of emotional anguish. Therefore, this emotion can mark the development of moral forms of behaviour. Nonetheless, in most cases, this development is usually stunted. Instead of actually developing a moral core, persons who remain in a state of sorrow may just limit their immoral acts. Therefore, this emotion does serve as a learning tool, but the scope of this learning may often be narrow or slight.

The emotion of despair commonly follows emotions of sorrow. When the individual lacks the ability to learn from his mistakes, these feelings will subsequently arise. Those who experience despair will lack all forms of hope. This indicates the reality that the majority of their personal problems will never be solved. In an equal fashion, the current physical environment that these individuals are subjected to will also never change. Despair, then, marks a kind of spiritual existence that will never evolve, while contrarily, it marks the process of de-evolution.

Misery is an emotion that follows despair. Those who experience misery will remain in an impoverished state for an indefinite period of time. Persons who experience misery also often experience this emotion in isolation. These individuals will lack forms of friendships, and any other kinds of positive relationships with other persons. Likewise, these individuals will usually be at odds with other persons, which enhance their feelings of discontentment. The emotion of misery, then, may be the worst possible emotion experienced by those individuals who possess an insignificant centre of emotions.

On the contrary, individuals with a significant centre of emotions will mainly experience optimistic emotions for the remainder of their lives. Optimism is a frame of mind where the individual perceives all of the forms of goodness that exists in our world. Those who are optimistic believe in an infinite amount of possible wonders that may be present within our universe. This leads to friendships, and the emotions of caring and love. They are a class of individuals who directly oppose persons with a pessimistic outlook.

Happiness is a heightened emotion, whose direct opposite may be either sorrow, or anger. Those who are lucky enough to experience this emotion focus on all of the forms of beauty that are available within the natural world. We perceive the beauty in our world through each of the five senses. However, happiness is also a state of mind. Those who experience this emotion do realize that, in addition to pleasure, there also exist forms of pain within our world. Subsequently, persons who experience happiness mainly focus on the positive aspects in life, and they also have the ability to filter out forms of negativity that are simultaneously present within our natural world.

Joyfulness is a kind of happiness generated through the wonder of existence. Persons who experience this emotion are happy with their existence. Therefore, persons who do not value their own lives will never experience this emotion. Joy may also be an emotion that is generated because of the existence of other persons. These persons add value to the individual's life, which results in the shared emotion of joyfulness.

Subsequently, persons experience joy when they value the gift of life, in general. They mainly focus on the gift of existence, while everything else within our natural world may be of a secondary importance.

The emotion of cheerfulness is experienced because of an individual's relationships with other persons. The individual becomes cheerful whenever he receives acts of kindness. Cheerfulness, then, is an emotion linked to the positive reactions relative to an individual's social relationships. When alone, feelings of cheerfulness will gradually fade. Therefore, it is a short lived emotion. Yet, the existence of other types of wonders may also provide a source for cheerfulness. Similarly, when these wonders are no longer perceived, the emotion of cheerfulness will subside. Accordingly, the experiencing of this emotion remains entirely dependent upon the perceptions of wonders that exist within the individual's frame of mind.

Delight is a form of happiness directed towards non-essential elements within an individual's life. The individual will experience this emotion, for example, when he gains forms of material wealth. Something as simple as a fashionable form of clothing may also cause delight within the individual. Other kinds of delight may result when the individual is eating a meal, listening to a piece of music, or watching a unique form of art. Therefore, delight is an emotion where the individual develops an appreciation towards the materials that have been created, for all of mankind.

Love is a heightened emotion that directly opposes hatred. When the individual experiences the emotion of love, he will draw an unbreakable tie with some other person. When both persons experience the emotion of love together, they will be actively creating a reciprocal relationship with each other. This relationship may be based on infrequent contact, such as an acquaintance, or daily contact, such as a marriage. The intensity of love experienced, at times, may determine the frequency of contact that exists between two persons. Nonetheless, the existence of long distance relationships may also be based on the highest kind of love. Subsequently, the emotion of love has many different degrees, and it is also present in many differing kinds of circumstances.

Compassion is a strong mode of love directed towards the imperfections found within other persons. In feelings of compassion, the individual empathizes with other persons, in the manner of viewing the world through his subject's perspective. He then gains a kind of understanding that allows him to relate with the unique experiences of this person. In the creation of this kind of relation, he develops sympathy, and this enables him to provide some form of counsel. The individual who often experiences forms of compassion will then develop this habit, and this enables him to help a range of other persons when they are most in need.

The emotion of resolve is a feeling of love that exists purely between life partners. The individual who experiences this emotion wishes to secure the most deep felt needs of his lifetime partner. The most common form of a life partner is based within a marriage. However, a lifetime partner may also subsist within other forms of relationships. Parent-child relationships, relationships between siblings, and other kinds of friendships may cause feelings of resolve within the individual. All that is necessary for the experiencing of this emotion are kinds of relationships based on thoughtfulness, tolerance, and respect.

Peacefulness is the most common form of love possessed by those who are optimistic. Those who experience this emotion do not easily succumb to feelings of hatred. It is an emotion felt by persons who are at one with all of the aspects present within our natural world. Therefore, these individuals accept elements of both goodness and evil, essentially because both elements are naturally occurring within our physical world. When evil does occur, pessimistic emotions such as anger and hate will naturally evolve within the individual. Nonetheless, persons who experience the emotion of peacefulness possess a rare ability to address these forms of negative emotions, in favour of the emotion of peace. These individuals, then, possess the ability to not be consumed with feelings of anger or hate, which dominates those persons who never experience this emotional state.

Courage is a heightened emotion marked by a lack of fear. Those who are courageous do still possess some degree of fear, particularly when they are engaged in new kinds of circumstances. However, these individuals possess the ability to ignore and then dissolve these fears both quickly and coherently. The resulting emotion is courage. No evil doers experience the emotion of courage. This is due to the fact that they commit evils primarily because of their personal fears. Courageous persons, on the other hand, replace their emotions of fear with nothingness. In so doing, they may then enter into a variety of situations through their emotions of courage, in contrary to the emotion of fear.

Capability is an emotion that follows the emotion of courage. Persons who experience this emotion experience feelings of both confidence and adequacy. These individuals do not shed their personal responsibilities. On the contrary, these individuals embrace their obligations and duties. Likewise, these individuals are honest, such as in cases where they must honour forms of contracts. Capability is also a feeling of success found in individuals who have fulfilled their inborn, or natural abilities.

Certainty is an emotion that is similar to the emotion of capability. Nonetheless, while capability reflects upon both mental and physical abilities, the emotion of certainty only reflects upon the perceiver's state of mind. Those who are certain do not possess any kinds of doubt regarding a specific piece of knowledge. This emotion then motivates the individual to act with assurance and discretion. All in all, this emotion provides the individual with a state of mind that is both stable and impregnable.

Eagerness is the lowest form of courage. Persons who experience this emotion will usually lack feelings of confidence. Nonetheless, these individuals are entirely willing to accept new forms of responsibilities, and likewise, they make every effort to fulfill their newly acquired duties. Persons who experience this emotion may or may not possess the natural capacities necessary for fulfilling new kinds of responsibilities. However, these individuals do exhibit the volition to complete any forms of assignments that may be granted to them.

The emotion of determination is a heightened emotion based entirely on the human will. Its direct opposite could be the emotion of confusion. Persons who experience determination either do not acknowledge the existence of obstacles, or they will surpass these obstacles, with respect to any given situation. Determination is a powerful emotion that is responsible for the human ability to surpass the boundaries of nature. The fields of architecture, engineering, and medicine will continue to advance and progress due to individuals who embrace this emotion. Therefore, determination is an emotion that motivates the human intellect.

The emotion of inspiration arises in perceivers who view other human beings that are motivated by great forms of determination. It is an emotion that both produces and is produced by the emotion of determination. When the individual feels inspired, he will then utilize his faculty of imagination. Next, he will perceive his own unique ideas, in relation to the ideas that have inspired him. This results in both cultural and technological advancements. Hence, both determination and inspiration provides the mindset necessary for the continual progression of our civilization.

Hopefulness is another emotion that is produced through the emotion of determination. Persons who experience some form of loss will inevitably enter into a state of sadness. Their emotions of sadness may be relieved if they believe that their loss will not be permanent. Subsequently, it is the pensiveness of other persons, who are motivated to make the individual's loss temporary that causes and creates feelings of hopefulness. This marks the power of the emotion of determination. When one individual is determined to help another, this creates hope in favour of grief. The emotion of hopefulness grants all individuals with a mode of escape from their personal feelings of grief.

Gratefulness follows both hopefulness in the individual, and determination in those individuals who are providing some form of aid. Some individuals may be successful in their efforts to provide aid. Others may not be successful. However, the emotion of gratefulness persistently arises in persons who are the recipients of these kinds of efforts. Persons who have managed to exchange feelings of grief, or worry, with feelings of hope will always experience feelings of relief. At times, the emotion of gratefulness also generates feelings of determination within the individual, which motivates him to additionally provide a similar kind of aid for other persons.

Glory is a heightened emotion that is only experienced by those who experience the emotion of determination. As an emotion, glory represents the highest form of happiness, as it relates to some particular kind of power, or achievement. Persons who experience glory have achieved something that is rare, unique and useful. Hence, these kinds of feelings may also be rare. When the individual does experience glory, he possesses a great power that is both special and exceptional.

Feelings of exhilaration are directed towards that which is magnificent. This emotion may be directed towards physical beauty, or spiritual beauty. Persons who experience a kind of fascination in relation to a physical beauty will demonstrate a kind of affection towards it. Likewise, persons who become fascinated with a kind of spiritual beauty will value it. The emotion of exhilaration, then, is an emotion directed towards some instance of the sublime found either within nature, or another individual.

The emotion of excitement is similar to the emotion of exhilaration. However, this emotion is limited, in that it is only directed towards objects of significance. Accordingly, these objects may be characterized with a lesser kind of magnificence. Likewise, excitement is more frequently experienced in comparison to the emotion of exhilaration. Even animals in the wild demonstrate forms of excitement. The common nature of this emotion makes it a defining element in all forms of life that possess a consciousness.

Feelings of expectance are found in persons who are waiting for some kind of good fate or fortune. This fortune may be due to luck, or it may also be due to hard work. In some cases, these individuals possess a general idea regarding their good fate. In other cases, the individual may experience feelings of excitement towards something that is unknown. Subsequently, emotions of great expectations are based on feelings of gladness or joy towards one possible future, within the mind of the beholder.

Surprise is an emotion that also requires some form of understanding within the intellect. People who experience this emotion possess feelings of exhilaration that are directed towards some unexpected event. On the other hand, feelings of excitement may be directed towards some kind of expected event. Accordingly, this makes the emotion of surprise a much rarer form of excitement.

Gracefulness is the last kind of heightened emotion. Only individuals who belong to a certain class of citizens will experience it. The emotion of gracefulness requires acts of politeness and respect. Persons who consistently demonstrate forms of respect will experience this emotion as a direct result. This is due to the fact that many individuals, such as those persons who possess a criminal nature, do not deserve the same level of respect that should be granted to those who possess a peaceful nature. Accordingly, the individual experiences grace because he does not act with, nor sustain, an ill will towards those persons who are guilty of transgressions. Gracefulness, then, is a rare emotion felt only by those who possess the purest spiritual existence, who address experiences with transgressions through acts of dignity.

The emotion of pleasantness is only experienced by persons with a nonviolent nature. Individuals who experience this emotion will never use methods of aggression to solve their disputes. Accordingly, they are more inclined to act with forgiveness, as opposed to being at odds with some person. Therefore, persons who possess a violent nature will never experience this emotion. Only acts of intrinsic forgiveness will cause emotions of pleasantness within the individual.

Liveliness is an emotion demonstrated by persons who are charmed by all of the forms of wonders that exist within our world. These individuals place a high value on their own existence, as well as the existence of all other persons who are a part of their social circle. Persons who are lively have made peace with all of the imperfections that may be found within their personal relationships. They are energetic and view the gift of life with enthusiasm. Further characteristics associated with liveliness are a lack of fear, anxiety and distress.

A third class of emotions may also be found within human nature. Complex emotions mark a category of emotions experienced by persons who possess a significant centre of emotions. When these persons come into contact with persons who possess an insignificant centre of emotions, complex emotions will subsequently arise. Therefore, complex emotions mark a category of negative emotions that may be experienced by persons with a significant centre of emotions. This category of emotions does not shift the individual's centre of emotions. Rather, complex emotions merely extend the range of an individual's core of emotions beyond the realm of goodness, into the darker aspects that may be found in persons that possess an insignificant centre of emotions.

The first level of anger observed in persons with a significant centre of emotions is based on the emotion of indifference. Primarily, when an innocent individual encounters evil, he believes in the mind-set that no person possesses the power to pass judgment over other persons. However, when he encounters a higher form of evil, known as hate, he does realize that all individuals are capable of judgment. After the individual realizes the differences between the love in his heart, and the existence of hatred in other kinds of persons, forming some kind of a judgment becomes an easier task. He will then enter into a state of indifference in relation to all persons who actively materialize the emotion of hate. In essence, the individual has reversed the love that he holds towards all persons, and has adopted feelings of disappointment with respect to the class of individuals who are mainly responsible for producing feelings of hate.

In a subsequent fashion, the emotion of disgust is produced after one experiences the emotion of indifference. Disgust is directed towards that object which initializes feelings of anger within the subject. When the individual views similar instances of hate, carried out by more than one individual, his indifference will elevate into disgust. Indifference, then, is directed towards single individuals, while loathing is directed towards a group of individuals who may be guilty of a same evil, or a same crime.

Emotions of obnoxiousness form the second level of anger that arises in persons with a significant centre of emotions. When the individual realizes that emotions of hate and anger are not merely emotional states, but are also modes of actions, he will experience emotions of obnoxiousness as a direct result. When the individual extends his emotions through action, obnoxious acts serve to challenge the actions of hate and anger carried out by other persons. By acting through feelings of obnoxiousness, the individual is essentially defending the targets of hatred. Subsequently, he is exercising the unlimited freedom in his will to neutralize the concepts of hate that exist in some persons.

The final level of anger is based on the emotion of hostility. Persons experience the emotion of hostility when acts of hatred do not cease or desist. Their feelings of obnoxiousness then heighten to the degree of hostility. Emotions of hostility usually motivate acts of opposition. In time, the individual's hostility will elevate into a permanent antagonistic state of mind directed towards those persons who were first responsible for expressing emotions of hate. This, then, elevates into a conceptual war where enemies, and in some instances, groups of enemies are born.

Hand in hand with hostility, the emotion of concern is experienced by persons with a significant centre of emotions. While these individuals direct their hostility towards the origins of evil, they are simultaneously directing emotions of concern towards the victims of that specific occurrence of evil. Feelings of concern, thus, are not merely focused towards the spiritual well-being of persons, but are also directed towards the physical safety of those persons. The emotion of concern is a higher form of caring where specific actions are taken to ensure the well-being of victims of evil.

The emotion of concern marks the beginning of emotions of sadness. Negative events such as disease or death are a natural occurrence within our physical world. Therefore, when the targets of our concern experience some kind of negative event, emotions of sadness will naturally arise. Both emotions of happiness and sadness, then, are inevitable results of the emotion of concern. Nonetheless, forms of caring are necessary for the emotion of happiness, while emotions of sadness may be experienced by all persons, even those who exhibit no kinds of caring or concern.

Following any kinds of hostile acts, the individual could experience feelings of remorse. Remorse is an emotion felt by those persons who are responsible for some kind of evil doing. Not all criminals, who are guilty of committing evils, will experience remorse though. The emotion of remorse is only felt by persons who possess some kind ethical, value system. When one commits degrees of hostility that are unwarranted, and when this individual possesses some kind of value system, he will then enter into a state of remorse. The emotion of remorse is only felt by actors who are guilty of some kind of injustice. Thus, if the individual's acts of hostility are just in nature, he will not experience any emotions based on remorse.

Individuals who experience remorse will subsequently possess feelings of shame. The emotion of shame is directed towards a hostile act that later produces feelings of regret within the actor. Hence, feelings of shame reflect upon the learning process that some persons gain when they are guilty of committing hostile acts. After the individual experiences the emotion of shame, he will become motivated to refrain from committing any similar acts during future times. Therefore, the emotion of shame reflects upon the actor's realization that he has acted dishonourably. True forms of shame will motivate the individual to act morally within similar types of circumstances.

The emotion of pride is the direct opposite of the emotion of shame. When the individual is responsible for an inglorious act, he may either learn from his experiences or continue to act in a shameful way. Subsequently, all persons are liable to commit errors. However, when these individuals learn from their immoral ways, this marks the establishment of emotions of pride. Individuals who have both learned from their mistakes and continue to act in an honourable manner can experience emotions of pride as a consequential result. This is due to the fact that under similar circumstances, one individual may act honourably, while another individual may act dishonourably. Emotions of pride result due to honourable forms of behaviour, because it was entirely possible that the individual could have chosen to act dishonourably.

Regarding those persons who possess an insignificant centre of emotions, these individuals rarely experience optimistic emotions, due to the nature of their desires. In essence, their ability to acquire forms of material wealth may be minute. Likewise, their pursuit towards acquiring forms of physical beauty or respectable appearances also face complications. Accordingly, these persons only experience optimistic emotions when they come into contact with persons who possess a significant centre of emotions. When the latter kinds of persons possess some kind of influence over the former, they will possess the power to share their ideas of happiness and optimism.

Therefore, emotions are contagious. For example, the emotion of hate causes enemies. When one individual does not tolerate another, a conflict will necessarily ensue. Contrarily, the emotion of love produces relationships. When one individual holds a high esteem for another person, this kind of love will be reciprocated. Subsequently, our emotional states are also deeply affected by the emotional states of other persons.

Emotions are mental states that embody our responses to life events. Positive life events will produce feelings of optimism, while negative life events will produce feelings of pessimism. The object within our centre of emotions determines the intensity and effects of differing life events upon our soul. Therefore, the individual's centre of emotions is the most essential element that defines who he is, as an emotional kind of being.

Persons with an insignificant centre of emotions will be sensitive to phenomena that are extrinsic to a prosperous life. Elements like material possessions and vanity have a limited importance in the realm of human civilization. Yet, some individuals are quite selfish with their material wealth. These individuals believe in the notion that those who are wealthy may be of a higher status than those who are poverty stricken. Thus, vain individuals who acquire riches may discriminate against the poor, essentially because they are perceived to be inferior persons. Individuals who are motivated by the vice of vanity will associate material wealth with prestige, and they will inevitably shun those persons who may be lacking in terms of material wealth and other forms of status symbols.

Contrarily, individuals with a significant centre of emotions will be largely affected by intrinsic phenomena. Elements such as spiritual life forces are important to our civilization. This makes elements, such as caring relationships, highly valued. As a result, these individuals would rather spend their material wealth not merely for their own benefit, but also for the benefit of other members within their community.

Nevertheless, similar to the intellect, physical problems within the brain could affect the individual's emotional states. A brain disease like depressive disorder can change the range and intensity of the individual's emotional states and feelings. This indicates a natural vulnerability present within the individual's core of emotions. After the individual is treated for his disorder, his core of emotions will reset back into its original position.

On the contrary, the individual's centre of emotions is not as vulnerable as his core of emotions. When he values some object within the universe, no brain disease possesses the power to alter this freedom. This further demonstrates the limitless nature of our will. Nevertheless, the individual may redirect his emotional centre because of his experiences. This is due to the fact that the object of one's emotional centre is mainly determined by his intellect. These occasions are rare, however. The individual will mainly direct his emotional centre towards that object which he has pondered most about, and thus, that object which he understands the most.

The most basic emotions experienced by all forms of living animals are happiness and sadness. Laughter is a reactionary form of expression that demonstrates feelings of delight. However, only human beings possess the ability, or capacity, to laugh. Therefore, laughter is a unique form of happiness which demonstrates that human beings possess the greatest range of emotions available to all of the species of life that may be found within the natural world. Nonetheless, not everything that brings delight to the individual is humorous. Likewise, laughter is not a deliberate act. Humour is a particular feeling of joy that causes a kind of reaction that is, essentially, beyond the individual's realm of control.

Similarly, sadness associated with the reaction of crying is also solely observed within the human species. No wild animal in the world possesses the ability to cry. Accordingly, this further indicates that human beings are granted with a greater core of emotions, in comparison to the core of emotions present within the common animal. A greater range of emotional feelings entails a greater range of experiences, in general. This, then, also makes human life much more intricate when compared to the wild animal. Within the optimistic person's point of view, a greater range of emotional states also necessitates a greater quality of life.

In theory, the individual's emotional experiences may be the key component linked to a successful life. The intellect determines our intelligence quotient; however, our emotional centre determines our outlook on life. Emotions are reactionary feelings and mental states. As such, we would never experience feelings of happiness or love without this element of our soul.

5   Array of Principles

THE INDIVIDUAL'S SPIRIT is analogous to his array of principles. Therefore, the individual's spirit is the immaterial culmination of a specific system of values or principles. The individual's system of principles embodies a major part of his life-force. Principles are rules that will guide the individual's everyday behaviour. They are internal beliefs, which either justify or restrict some form of action. Both the intellect and the individual's centre of emotions are necessary for the development of a certain principle. Primarily, when the individual experiences some kind of emotional state, he must then employ his intellect to understand the proper causes behind that specific emotional state. After the operation of comprehension is complete, the individual may then acquire a new principle, or refine his personal system of values.

In theory, the individual's array of principles will guide his daily actions. When this is true, the array must also then guide the individual's intellect. When it is employed, the intellect will be responsible for the actions that produce an emotional response within a spectator. When this spectator analyzes and comprehends his emotional response, his emotional response may either be optimistic or pessimistic. The spectator then acquires some kind of principle based on the essence of his emotional response.

For example, a nurse may provide a more gentle and sympathetic mode of care for an exceptionally sick kid. The child recognizes his nurse's actions, and he then becomes exceedingly grateful. After this emotional response, this child recovers and starts a charity designated towards helping other children who suffer from his particular ailment. Spiritually, because of his experiences, the child develops feelings of compassion towards his peers. He then secures the belief that all healthy persons should also help others who are sick and in need of care. Accordingly, this is how all individuals acquire their personal values and principles.

Therefore, all of the individual's principles depend on some form of interaction between his emotions and his intellect. Persons may learn and acquire new principles, they may substitute older principles with more advanced principles, and they may also rid themselves of impractical principles. Subsequently, values may be acquired, replaced or lost. Nonetheless, the individual's array of principles does not change easily, because it is partly based on knowledge. However, in comparison, this part of the individual's mind changes more easily than his emotional centre.

The individual's array of principles is not determined by nature. Rather, each principle is freely chosen. Principles are mainly procured through life experiences. Therefore, our array of principles is a belief system that is dependent on our personal experiences. Nonetheless, there are determined aspects within every person's life that has influence over his experiences. Our place of birth, for example, will determine our cultural experiences. If an individual is born within a highly religious community, it is likely that he will adopt some religious principles. Likewise, our gender has some bearing over the principles we adopt. The male body is physically larger than the female body, so correspondingly, some males may adopt the principle that "might is right". On the other hand, most females lack the aggressive tendencies commonly attributed to males, and accordingly, they may hold the belief that "the pen is mightier than the sword". Therefore, the guiding principle in a male dominated society would be based upon a kind of physical justice, while in a world comprised equally of both males and females, the principle of peaceful co-relationships may be a dominating principle.

Every individual secures his principles through both positive and negative life experiences. A specific principle may be learned at any point in an individual's life. Since all persons also possess the ability to remove a principle from their array, no principles are absolute. A single principle cannot be abided by in every type of circumstance, because there may exist an equally moral principle that guides an opposite form behaviour. The individual's array of principles merely serves as a precept that guides his actions and everyday behaviour. For example, the individual may possess the principle of generosity, which is solely directed towards his family members and friends. Nevertheless, if a major natural disaster were to suddenly occur, he may experience feelings of compassion, and thus he may provide further forms of aid towards this particular cause. Accordingly, the individual applies every principle within his array according to each unique condition or circumstance. Universal principles are quite rare, and depend highly on the emotions experienced by each unique person. Accordingly, if this person did not experience feelings of compassion, his principle of generosity would be more rigid and exclusive.

Some individuals adopt a system of personal values and beliefs based solely on their own personal well-being. Other persons are more altruistic in nature, and thus, they adopt principles according to the well-being of their society. The former group of persons may be known as narcissists, while the latter group of persons may be known as nobles. Instead of adopting the principle self-sufficiency, the noble will adopt the principle of fraternity, and accordingly, he will provide forms of aid towards persons he considers are his friends. Hence, the principles adopted by nobles directly oppose the selfish principles adopted by the narcissist.

Poor principles lead to the birth of an evil soul. The most narcissistic principles are embraced by the terrorist. Terrorists disagree with a certain political policy implemented by some state. However, instead of a peaceful protest, or leaving his society in favour of a more just nation-state, these individuals murder innocent civilians as their form of protest. In actuality, a differing culture may coincide with the terrorist's personal value system. Therefore, he also possesses the further option to leave his community, and freely enter into this other community.

The terrorist essentially believes in some kind of other political system, while utilizing violence as a means to achieve change. Therefore, the terrorist places higher value on his personal beliefs over innocent human lives. In essence, he believes in principles that precede the well-being of those whom these principles were intended to protect. Objectively, then, the narcissist usually possesses a value system that is comprised of conflicting beliefs. Forms of irrational and contradictory behaviour, then, may be commonly observed within most narcissists.

Extremists are, categorically, similar to terrorists. However, these individuals will use less lethal means to carry out their political message. For the most part, extremists resort to vandalism and the destruction of property. There are some extremists, though, who become violent once they have been intermingled within a large group of protestors. This shields their identity, which allows them to commit acts of violence through a veil of anonymity. On the whole, extremists differ from the average protestor in that they will not impose any limits pertaining to unlawful forms of behaviour. These individuals lack principles based on peaceful action, and this makes the extremist a criminal.

Some persons are known as attention seekers. These persons will commit immoral kinds of acts, but not criminal acts. Therefore, these individuals understand the laws that govern their community, and will commit acts that are similar in nature to a criminal act. However, the severity of their actions does not warrant criminal arrest or prosecution. These persons are mimicking criminal forms of behaviour in an effort to receive attention. For example, some women seek pregnancy exclusively to maintain a relationship with another person. These individuals do not care for the wellbeing of their child, and accordingly, they may be guilty of a form of negligence. Nevertheless, the severity of their negligence is not high enough to warrant forms of criminal justice. In this case, the woman is seeking attention from other persons through an immoral manner, and this escapes the grasp of our current justice system.

Men may also be guilty of attention seeking. Some individuals do not believe in the legalization of abortion. In order to gain attention, regarding their personal beliefs, these individuals may then resort to violence by killing doctors who specialize in that particular operation. These individuals could be viewed as extremists. However, most extremists hold their protests within a large group of individuals. In contrast, the abortion killer works alone, and is guilty of a much more severe crime.

Gangsters form another category of criminals who adopt a poor value system. Within these individual's frame of mind, making money, or more specifically economic success, is more valuable than human life. Although most gangsters focus on one specific criminal enterprise, as whole these individuals are guilty of a wide range of crimes. The crime of murder, within the gangster's frame of mind, may be based on revenge, but more often than not these individuals commit the crime of murder to further their economic development. In fact, most of the crimes the gangster commits are directly related to his economic well-being. Therefore, the majority of gangsters are principled criminals, in that they abide by the laws of the underworld, which focuses solely on illegal commerce and unlawful industries.

Corrupt politicians differ from regular politicians because of their narcissistic ways. Primarily, these individuals will manipulate the general public, during times of election. The principles they propose are merely observations of important ethical principles that are valued by the general public. Hence, these individuals possess great analytical capabilities. Once they have identified the common ground shared by all of their constituents, they will propose some kind of policy that will enhance these interests of the general public. Nonetheless, when they actually gain power, they will backslide their mindset into their narcissistic ways. The policies that corrupt politicians do create will only be in the interests of a specific minority group. This minority group will share a similar kind of temperament with the corrupt politician. Accordingly, these individuals have manipulated the general public, and the policies that these individuals do create will not reflect the general will. In the creation of specific unjust policies, the corrupt politician will experience a feeling of power, and this is a partial motivating factor behind his fraudulent behaviour. In essence, the corrupt politician materializes any forms of public policies that feed his desire for greater communal power. All of the policies implemented by the corrupt politician are principles which merely encompass his personal system of beliefs. At best, these policies will benefit only a small minority group, and thus, will always be quite contrary to the will of the general public.

There are many differing kinds of principles that reflect the general will. Nobles begin to comprehend these principles when they use their intellect to examine their own emotional centre. Primarily, nobles will examine the most common emotions of optimism that they experience, on a personal level. Then after they have analyzed these feelings through the intellect, they create a particular principle that reflects upon their emotional experiences. Therefore, all forms of principles are acquired through life experiences.

Personal principles serve to guide the individual's behaviour during common relationships, and everyday circumstances. Probably the most important personal principle is that of respect. There are many differing degrees of respect. The highest level of respect is directed towards God. Persons who are religious exhibit this form of respect. Our definitions of God may differ, and this is evident in the many different kinds of religion that remain prevalent within our world. However, the level of our regard for God still remains equivalent among all religions. Therefore, all truly religious persons develop a similar principle of respect.

Self-respect is the next level of respect. Persons who possess self-respect will also naturally demonstrate respect towards other persons. This is due to the fact that persons, who lack self-respect, focus on their own inadequacies and thus, by nature, will focus on all other forms of inadequacies that may exist within our world. Therefore, self-respect leads to a form of acceptance directed towards all forms of life in general, which, unfortunately, many persons lack.

Next to the principle of respect is the principle of toleration. Persons who acquire this principle demonstrate a form of regard towards all human beings. Similarly, toleration is also directed towards all of the spirits that exist within our natural world. Persons who are tolerant value all forms of life, and thus, they do not tolerate that which destroys forms of life. Thus, hand in hand with the principle of toleration is intolerance, which is directed towards persons who actively destroy any forms of beauty within our natural world.

Honesty is a principle that places value on the truth, over falsehoods. When the individual is lied to, he may experience a pessimistic emotion like anger. After he analyzes this experience, and since he possesses altruistic characteristics, he realizes that he does not want to cause this emotional state in other persons. In turn, he then develops the principle of honesty, where he avoids telling falsehoods in a general manner.

Certain principles may be realized through the realm of friendships. The principle of understanding is an extension of toleration. Persons who tolerate others will gain an understanding with respect to another individual's spiritual nature. Understanding is the next natural step for persons who appreciate the many differing kinds of spirits that are present within our natural world. Therefore, the principle of understanding is not merely directed towards the unique spiritual nature of other human beings, but it is also directed towards the totality of nature and the other kinds of spirits that roam within it.

Following the principle of understanding is the principle of trust. Trust is the first element that serves as a building block in the relationship between two distinct individuals. After a mutual form of understanding is achieved, the principle of trust serves to safeguard this exchange of knowledge. Once a friendship built on trust is established, this relationship will further develop in a natural fashion. Moreover, without the principle of trust, no individual could establish nor sustain a mutually beneficial relationship with another person.

Dependability is an important principle acquired by persons who enter into relationships with other persons. It is a principle that turns strangers into friends. No human being is entirely independent, and similarly, every human being possesses some level of dependency. Those who are dependable will fulfill another person's needs. They will also depend on these persons to fulfill their own needs. The principle of dependability may be the most integral component within all forms of timeless relationships. It is a necessary spiritual component that is reciprocated within all forms of true friendships.

Subsequently, the principle of fraternity may only be actualized after a high level of dependability has been established between two persons. This principle marks a kind of relationship that may be comparable to a marriage between two individuals. There is something about marriage that makes it both rare, yet inclusive. Accordingly, individuals who acquire this principle will treat their closest friends as another form of life partner. It is like entering into a band of brothers, even though there may be no technical familial relations.

Similar to the principle of fraternity is the principle of devotion. However, while a fraternity exists between friends, forms of devotion exist between intimate spiritual or life partners. When the individual discovers this principle, he will essentially devote his life to the duty of making his life partner happy. Devotion, then, is a kind of selfless passion that exists between two partners. In an act of devotion, the individual will put his partner's needs above his own. This demonstrates a form of commitment that is also rare, yet extremely powerful.

Loyalty is a principle that follows acts of devotion or fraternity. The concept of loyalty only exists within the highest forms of relationships. It marks a kind of love that is both unwavering and infinite. Nonetheless, forms of loyalty may dissipate within abusive relationships. Only dogs remain loyal to their abusive masters. Therefore, the principle of loyalty is a much more complicated subject, within a human being's frame of mind, because it is based on the totality of elements that define any given relationship.

The principle of commitment may be directed towards two kinds of objects. First of all, the individual may commit himself to other persons. When this occurs, the individual will be actively maintaining some form of social relationship. In other cases, forms of commitment may be directed towards areas of employment. Many committed individuals possess a particular idea that they believe would benefit their entire society. When committed, the individual will demonstrate a strong form of perseverance towards materializing his personal goals. In general, those who persevere always act according to moral forms of behaviour. Therefore, even during the most difficult of circumstances, when the individual is plagued with forms of immoral behaviour from other persons, those who truly persevere will remain consistently ethical with respect to their decision making process and modes of action. In contrast, persons who become consumed with adversity will never achieve success, with respect to their personal goals. Individuals who characteristically persevere will never succumb to any forms of adversity. Therefore, the principle of commitment is exemplified in individuals who dedicate the totality of their efforts towards some meaningful purpose.

The principle of sympathy is actualized in all forms of love. When the individual is sentimental, he demonstrates a type of caring that is extraordinary and not easy to come by. Those who are sympathetic do not merely accept the flaws of another individual, but they also cherish these flaws. Indeed, the scope of every person's intellect is limited by nature. However, those who are sympathetic will recognize this attribute in other persons, and they also hope that their partners will do the same. After this occurs, the element of consideration will be established. Therefore, all who are sympathetic place a high value on their social relationships, because they do not take any of their established friendships for granted. When the sympathetic comprehend the feelings of other persons, they will benefit from a spiritual perspective. Essentially, the sympathetic agent places value on his partner's own personal perspective of the world. The receivers of this sentiment will then inherit a greater understanding of both their own selves, and the natural world. This may further result in the dissolution of many of both individual's personal fears.

Curiosity is a principle that stimulates all kinds of growth. When directed towards other individuals, it inspires spiritual growth. For example, many persons have wondered what it is like to be superman. As a consequence, the individual will contemplate and then understand concepts like sacrifice and justice. Nonetheless, curiosity may also be directed towards the natural world. Through the principle of curiosity, scientific inquiries within the subjects of chemistry and biology were born. Therefore, the principle of curiosity stimulates both cultural and scientific growth.

The principle of paternity, or maternity, applies to all of those who are married with children. However, many persons who are involved in the process of procreation rid themselves of their responsibilities, in favour of their own personal pleasures. In contrast, most animals within the wilderness possess paternal or maternal instincts. Therefore, parental care is a kind of responsibility that is usually implicit.

Individuals do possess parental instincts, yet the forms of care we offer to our children ranges well beyond mere basic survival. We want our children to be educated, and thus cultured. With these two elements, our children will not merely survive within the physical world, but they will also thrive within it.

Adoration is a form of love that is directed towards the wonders present within the human soul. When we adore another person, we recognize and greatly value the irreplaceable elements that are present within his life-force. In this act, we may then secure this spiritual element and apply it through our own unique perspective. In essence, the principle of adoration empowers us to both observe a distinct principle and add it into our own array.

The principle of benevolence is a form of kindness that is directed towards all living spirits. Persons who are benevolent will pose no harm to any forms of life. Rather, these persons will encourage the power of freedom that exists in all forms of spirits. Benevolence is an act of kindness between one individual and another. It is exchanged without any expectations of reciprocity. Rather, those who are benevolent possess a nature that is both giving and thoughtful. The principle of benevolence is important when sustaining a positive relationship with other persons. Those who are conniving possess characteristics that directly oppose benevolence. Hence, these individuals are, necessarily, sustaining a negative type of relationship with other persons. Objectively, those who are benevolent are giving persons, while those who are conniving will expect other persons to be giving.

Generosity is a second principle based on the concept of giving. However, it differs from benevolence in that it is a form of kindness based on material need. Therefore, those who are generous are willing to share their material wealth with other persons. Individuals who are generous do not conceive their monetary wealth as a status symbol. Rather, these individuals are giving because they value another person's happiness over their own. Accordingly, those persons who possess the principle of generosity may work towards acquiring a material fortune not for their own sakes, but for the sake of providing for another person. Instead of monetary elements, those who are generous could also provide a service. Therefore, the principle of generosity encourages acts of provision between two individuals. Those who abide by the principle of generosity demonstrate a highly unselfish nature.

The principle of responsibility pertains to every citizen within a society. Forms of responsible behaviour may be based on the concept of harm. Those who are responsible ensure that all of their personal actions do not harm another living being. Hence, individuals who do pose some form of harm to other kinds of life are not acting responsibly. Whenever this occurs, other persons must take a higher form of responsibility, to ensure that abusive individuals will not commit any further transgressions. Therefore, the state essentially assumes the abusive individual's responsibility by taking away his liberty to act in a free and independent manner.

The principle of obedience pertains to both criminal and civil law, which are critical for any kinds of social order. In the just state, civilians will exercise this principle freely, while in a tyrannical state, civilians will exercise this principle due to personal fears of prosecution. Therefore, in some societies, civil obedience is practiced as a personal liberty, while in others it is practiced due to coercion. The main difference between these two states comes down to the difference between legitimate rule and illegitimate political authority. Within a legitimate political state, obeying the laws established is pivotal for a well-lived life. Those who disobey the laws of their community will face forms of either physical or social justice. For example, forms of physical justice are based on concepts like incarceration, while forms of social justice are based on concepts like reputation. Persons who obey established laws will never face these predicaments. As a result, the principle of obedience is commonly practiced by all persons who do not commit any forms of criminal acts.

Citizens also possess an obligation to their state. This obligation is based on the principle of service. All able persons must necessarily contribute something towards their society. Persons who adopt the principle of service believe that it is necessary to contribute something positive towards their society. The kinds of services that an individual may contribute depend wholly on his imagination. Some kinds of services are necessary for our survival. Other kinds of services improve our quality of life. For example, the individual who turns a big piece of bamboo into a pan flute is responsible for a creative and unique contribution.

Individuals who do not adopt the principle of service may simply wish to reap the benefits of the services that may be provided within their community. These individuals believe in the notion that they are entitled to social services, even though they, themselves, do not contribute any kinds of services within their community. Other individuals who are motivated by greed will attain material forms of wealth, while they systematically reject any forms of a legitimate means to acquire their goal. Accordingly, the latter individuals do not truly take on the principle of service.

The principle of creativity is adopted by persons who are passionate about human culture. Creativity is a guiding principle behind all new instances of art. Some forms of artwork are embraced by the general public, while other kinds of art may receive less attention. However, the principle of creativity is the primary building block behind both examples. There exist no true bounds that limit the creative mind. Hence, all creative persons take the risk of creating works that may not be embraced by the general public. In the latter cases, forms of unique creativity may still deserve the recognition of being innovations within the imagination.

Appreciation is a principle where the individual recognizes the efforts of other persons who have made a difference in his life. Individuals who are appreciative have a positive outlook, which is necessary for feelings of gratitude. They also value life as a miracle, in itself, in addition to valuing all of the possible fruits of existence. Likewise, they do not take any forms of happiness for granted. The act of appreciation is not merely a form of recognition, in relation to services provided by other persons. It entails a full understanding with respect to the importance of the concept of service. Those who appreciate other persons recognize the fact that the services that they have received are not implicit, but are mainly acts of kindness and benevolence. Those who lack the principle of appreciation do not value the miracle of life and they are never satisfied with any intrinsic forms of happiness. This makes them prone to criminal behaviour.

With respect to the public realm, humanitarianism is a defining principle where forms of sympathy are exchanged between groups of persons. Through this principle, one community will acknowledge the fact that another community may be in need. Accordingly, forms of aid, between distinct communities, result due to the principle of humanitarianism. Without this principle, forms of collaboration would not exist, within the political level. Therefore, humanitarianism is a defining characteristic of human nature based on the concepts of cooperation and insight.

Unity is a principle that results due to the principle of humanitarianism. After acts of insight and cooperation, a kind of bond will be established between two communities. Unity is a kind of bond that can never be broken. It is a kind of relationship that is stronger than any kind of economic tie. The principle of unity is based on a friendship between distinct nations. It focuses not merely on material forms of cooperation, but also on the acceptance of the immaterial attributes that define an entire nation's culture.

The principle of equality is a social perspective that opposes all concepts of discrimination. Hence, it is a political principle that recognizes every form of life as both unique, and valuable. Those who do not believe in equality hold firm notions based on superiority and inferiority. Forms of inferiority may be based on extrinsic physical elements, such as an individual's ethnicity, gender, sexual orientation, health, spiritual characteristics, or nationality. However, the principle of equality negates all of the latter forms of discrimination. On a personal level, those persons who possess the principle of respect will also, necessarily, recognize the principle of equality.

Persons who develop the principle of goodwill recognize the most important cultural values that define any given community. Individuals will then promote their values within their community, in contrary to those individuals who are inclined to oppose them. Subsequently, goodwill is the active continuance of communal moral values. These morals are shared by all persons that contribute some kind of service within their community. As a result, through goodwill, the individual may also recognize and depend on the abilities of his neighbours. When this occurs, all forms of conceptual hardships will be dealt with, not on an individual basis, but through a communal basis. Goodwill can also exist between persons who live within distinct communities. The latter occurrence marks the beginning of a form of cultural exchange, where significant pieces of knowledge will then be interchanged.

The principle of leadership is acquired by persons who have the ability to secure some kind of foresight regarding our natural world. This foresight is both visionary and extraordinary. Persons who have foresight possess the ability to address and solve any potential problems before they actually surface. Hence, true leaders will guide other persons towards something that is both new and beneficial. The content of this foresight could be based on any industry that exists within our physical world. Accordingly, the best leaders provide a form of common focus, which serves to advance some distinct aspect or element within our civilization.

The principle of bravery is procured by individuals who willingly confront forms of evil. When the individual challenges evil, he is acting in the best interests of his society. He is also actively protecting innocent persons within his community. Accordingly, those who acquire bravery will take the form of a kind of hero, based in the realm of social justice. The kinds of evil addressed through social justice may vary. Most kinds of evil are based on some instance of discrimination. More dangerous forms of evil are based on some form of physical harm. The brave will challenge kinds of evil that he thoroughly understands. This knowledge will be based on the interplay between his intellect and array of principles. Hence, as there are many forms of evil, there also exist many kinds of bravery.

Sensibility is a principle that recognizes rational thinking as the most powerful form of argument. In contrast, forms of understanding based on an individual's belief system are sometimes mistakenly deemed to be forms of knowledge. In reality, beliefs are unconfirmed forms of deduction, while forms of reason are confirmed forms of knowledge, based on deduction. Hence, the principle of sensibility materializes a kind of hierarchy where reason is placed in a higher regard, in comparison to any individual's distinctive belief system.

The principle of conscientiousness guides the individual's everyday decision making process. All individuals possess the ability to choose. However, conscientiousness necessarily entails rational choice. Those who are conscientious possess a firm grasp over their moral values, and they make choices according to these principles. Thus, persons who are conscientious possess a clear understanding over their array of principles, and they make choices in relation to these moral principles. The materialization of an individual's spirit is an integral part of an evolving community.

The principle of courtesy is based upon acts of politeness, which is a kind of protocol based on proper and correct forms of mannerisms. Therefore, persons who are courteous belong to a class of persons who demonstrate a well-mannered demeanour. Those who adopt the principle of courtesy also demonstrate a form of understanding and gentleness within their social interactions. Courtesy is manner of action that further encourages peaceful relations among all human beings. Those who act without courtesy demonstrate deficiencies regarding important social interaction skills, and they also do not value the virtue of peace. Consequently, the principle of courtesy is essential to lasting interactions between acquaintances, and it also reflects upon the individual's characteristics of humbleness, grace and modesty.

Fairness is a principle where an individual's subjective experiences are considered, during processes of judgment. It is an important principle that negates all forms of personal bias. Through this principle, the actions of an individual are being judged, in relation to his life experiences. When every factor has been considered, the individual will have been judged fairly. The principle of fairness usually reflects upon our feelings of compassion. When we feel compassion for another human being, we will consider all of the factors that led to his choice of action. As compassionate persons, we will then provide aid to those who are facing various kinds of diversity, essentially because we care about their wellbeing. In so doing, we take into consideration the individual's subjective experiences as a primary causal factor behind his actions.

Objectivity is a necessary principle utilized by individuals who enter into new social situations. Persons who remain objective will avoid forms of dispute with strangers, whose personal value system may be unknown. Therefore, impartiality is a social principle that provides unique individuals, who possess differing value systems, with the ability to converse and understand one another. Objectivity also enables the individual to solve forms of conflict based on only the most necessary and relevant forms of evidence. On the other hand, persons who continually remain subjective are liable to enter into numerous amounts of quarrels and disputes. When the agent views the world objectively, he will not consider any forms of personal bias or private opinion, but this form of insight is not easily accessible, nor obtained.

The principle of discernment is only adopted by individuals who possess the principle of objectivity. Discernment is the ability to compare one's own value system with the value systems of other persons. In so doing, the individual will gather knowledge of whether a relationship can be maintained with such persons. Likewise, through discernment, he will also gain knowledge of the types of personality traits, where possible disagreements may arise. Therefore, discernment is necessary in the creation of healthy relationships, where one's value system remains similar to the value system of another person. This principle is acquired through the combination of wisdom and life experience. Individuals who gain this principle are knowledgeable of right and wrong, and of moral and immoral action. This makes them capable judges of the differences between beauty and imitative appearances.

Discretion is another principle that persons must adopt when entering into newer social circumstances. Persons who are discrete possess the ability to maintain an objective perspective when forms of conflict arise. In maintaining an objective perspective, the individual then actively adopts a neutral role within a particular instance of conflict. This limits the further escalation of aggression, within any given dispute. Accordingly, this action prevents the build-up of feelings of anger and hostility. Even when angry, the discrete will promote peaceful forms of behaviour as the most proper mode of action. Discretion, hence, is a powerful principle that potentially addresses forms of conflict with a peaceful resolution. Persons who are discrete rarely exhibit any forms of anger or aggressive behaviour. It is a principle that is possessed by persons who possess a firm control over their temperament.

The principle of restraint only pertains to situations of hostility. When some individual becomes fuelled with aggression, it may be a natural reaction to become overcome with an equivalent degree of belligerence. Nonetheless, in the majority of cases, the utilization of self-control may be the best possible mode of action. Individuals who utilize restraint demonstrate a form of control over their behaviour, while persons who become belligerent demonstrate a lack of control over their behaviour. Accordingly, the principle of restraint marks a major difference between civilized behaviour and irrational action.

Discipline is a principle that is similar to the principle of restraint. Nonetheless, while restraint pertains to action, discipline pertains to the individual's thought processes. Accordingly, persons who are disciplined possess the power to negate their pessimistic thoughts through the power of their mind. Through discipline, the individual will never be entirely consumed with feelings of anger or hatred. These individuals possess the ability to control their natural impulses, with respect to negative emotions. In essence, they hold the view that anything that is not essential to life is inessential. Similarly, that which is essential to life is regarded as precious. This prevents the possibility of over-indulgence and self-pity. Total self-control is the primary ideal materialized by those who are disciplined. The disciplined are effective and efficient with their choices of action, and this enables them to deal with the most direct and relevant issues, whenever any problems may arise. This makes discipline both a difficult and a rarely acquired principle. It is gained through experience and our personal understanding of our experiences.

Humility is a principle exhibited by the champion. Some champions are capable of grand achievements, even as teenagers. Hence, humility is a principle that is adopted by champions so that they can share their glory with other persons. This then stimulates the imagination of other individuals, who may be characterized as dreamers. In a subsequent fashion, the principle of humility encourages a particular kind of world that consists of multiple champions and forms of glory. When this occurs, a further link between champions and all other individuals will be established, which serves to strengthen a community as a whole.

The principle of diversity places value on differing forms of characteristics. Persons who adopt this principle experience an appreciation towards all possible forms of wonders that are present within our universe. Instead of fearing possible sources of wonder, diversity enables the individual to embrace all unique forms of beauty. The principle of diversity also enhances our choices and the exercising of our free will. One day I will have huckleberries, while the next day I will choose vanilla ice cream. These are the kinds of benefits that are made available through this principle. In contrast, those who do not value diversity will usually be guilty of a vast range of bigotry and discriminatory behaviour.

The principle of flexibility is necessary in a world that is full of diversity. Diversity enables choice within the physical world, while the principle of flexibility opens our perceptions to even more kinds of diversity. As such, persons who are flexible are not stubborn in either their manners or decision making. Persons who are flexible do not adopt a stern stance on any single issue. These individuals are open to new lines of thinking, and therefore new kinds of experiences. Accordingly, possessing the ability to adapt to new situations enables the individual to perceive the world through another person's perspective. Furthermore, individuals who are flexible will recognize the need for creative solutions, when more conservative means are no longer effective.

The principle of vigour is acquired by persons who have found comfort regarding their personal imperfections. Many persons do not accept their personal imperfections, and this leads to violent and abusive behaviour. However, vigour promotes confidence in the individual, whenever he is morally correct. Those who are vigorous place the highest amount of importance on ethical forms of behaviour. They also shun all forms of abuse. Persons who demonstrate vigour understand all of the imperfections that are present within our material world, yet they do not allow these obstacles to hold them back. Accordingly, persons who adopt this principle demonstrate a form of maturity, in that they are able to recognize all of the unique forms of beauty that exist within our world. This makes them natural born leaders.

Faith is a principle that relates to the unknown. All persons possess feelings of intuition. However, when these persons come into contact with the concept of doubt, feelings of intuition may be downgraded into feelings of belief. Faith is a kind of belief that is based on the individual's intuition, in conjunction with feelings of doubt. Moreover, it is a more powerful feeling of confidence, in comparison to intuition. Even though the individual recognizes the fact that his feelings of intuition could be wrong, he understands that the doubt associated with his particular belief may be based on an extremely weak premise. This, then, enables the individual to have faith, or a stronger form of intuition regarding the unknown. Accordingly, the principle of faith is based on the belief that there are phenomena that do exist, which surpass our current understanding of the physical universe.

With respect to the negative principles held by narcissists, there exists no such thing. Narcissists mainly act according to the principle of self-interest. However, the principle of self-interest is an ethical principle. All persons should seek a personally fulfilling life because existence is a miracle in itself. Likewise, if no individual sought a fulfilling life, the gift of life would no longer be a gift. Those who are incapable of achieving a fulfilling life will, instead, experience a life full of pain.

Nonetheless, the difference between narcissists and nobles is based on the fact that the narcissist does not acquire any principles other than that of self-interest, while the noble does consecutively acquire other forms of principles throughout his entire lifetime. Accordingly, the narcissist does not secure negative principles throughout his lifetime. He is merely lacking with respect to all other forms of ethical principles.

For example, the individual who continually tells lies does not adopt the principle of dishonesty. Objectively, he merely lacks the principle of honesty. In fact, there is no such thing as a negative type of principle, like dishonesty. Principles provide a layout with respect to moral forms of behaviour. Hence, all evil doers are lacking with respect to their spirit, because they lack a sufficient amount principles that are necessary for positive social interactions within a community based setting.

All narcissists lack a sufficient amount of principles, within their array, necessary for moral forms of behaviour. However, these individuals do hold something in common with their peers. Namely, every narcissist holds the principle of self-interest. This may not necessarily make two narcissists friends. Nonetheless, it does provide a building block for a kind of relationship based on criminal forms of behaviour. As such, principled criminals are most likely to commit their crimes in groups.

With respect to most bank robberies, this is usually a premeditated crime. Therefore, these felons have both planned and prepared for the crime that they intend to commit. Likewise, they share a similar form of greed, which essentially makes them compatible with each other. Nonetheless, bank robbers threaten innocent individuals during their premeditated crimes. When we compare the bank robber to the gangster, these two kinds of felons are both motivated by greed. However, with respect to the gangster, these criminals rarely harm innocent individuals. On occasions when this does occur, this usually occurs as a mishap, as their violent crimes are mainly planned and directed towards other gangsters. Hence, their criminal enterprise is usually directed towards willing participants.

What differentiates these two kinds of criminals is based on the principle of respect. The bank robber, who is willing to harm innocent persons, lacks a form of regard towards the common civilian. Contrarily, the majority of gangsters will not intentionally harm an innocent civilian. Their criminal activity is mainly directed towards their peers and freely willing consumers. As a consequence, the gangster does possess some degree of respect. Essentially, the gangster does not harm the common civilian because of his respect for the innocent. Accordingly, while the bank robber lacks the principle of respect, the gangster does possess some level of respect that is directed towards the common and innocent civilian.

A similar norm applies to the terrorist. In producing some form of harm towards the innocent civilian, the terrorist lacks the principle of restraint. This is due to the fact that the terrorist will place no kinds of limitations on the means that he uses to accomplish his goals. When the terrorist joins a particular cell, his acquaintances will also share something in common with him. Namely, they will also lack the principle of restraint.

In comparison, the corrupt politician utilizes legitimate means to materialize his political views. The corrupt politician does not commit any crimes, similar to a terrorist, yet most will become tyrants after they have achieved power. This individual, then, lacks the principle of discipline, since he will utilize his power essentially to cope with his internalized feelings of anger. The political policies he does implement are based on his need to control a particular segment within his society, which he perceives may be the direct cause of his feelings of anger. These particular policies will only appeal to persons who hold a similar kind of perception, and thus, these individuals will also gain a feeling of control similar to that experienced by the corrupt politician.

Within the mind of the extremist, some particular principle outweighs all other kinds of principles. For example, environmentalists, known as tree huggers, value the principle of diversity over the principle of flexibility. Thus, while these individuals value the diverse nature of plant species, they lack a perspective based on human values. For human civilization is based on our ability to modify nature according to our concepts of need, relative to our personal habitat. Accordingly, the tree hugger possesses a stringent frame of mind that is lacking, with respect to the realm of an objective perspective.

The attention seeker also possesses a stubborn frame of mind. These kinds of individuals will prey on innocent individuals through immoral forms of behaviour, in an effort to achieve some form of consideration from other persons. However, all immoral forms of behaviour are due to a lack of the principle of responsibility. Individuals who possess this principle maintain some form of responsibility over their actions and behaviours. Those who do not maintain any forms of responsibility attribute the cause of their actions to another source. Essentially, the attention seeker uses immoral means in an effort to become the subject of another person's thoughts, while in principle, he does not acknowledge the fact that he has created some kind of victim through this process. A lack of responsibility enables all kinds of attention seekers to hold a morally free conscience, while they simultaneously act in immoral ways.

All principles are acquired through emotional experiences. These emotional experiences can either be positive or negative. When the individual later analyzes and deliberates about his experiences, he procures a specific principle through a kind of reverse deduction. In essence, the individual adopts a moral principle to cause feelings of a similar positive emotion in other persons. Accordingly, principles guide the individual's behaviour, which inevitably causes a positive effect on other persons. Contrarily, all persons who act immorally are simply lacking some element, with respect to their array of principles.

Hence, the individual forms his array of principles through a wholly autonomous fashion. The individual's array is not determined by nature. Rather, each principle within an individual's array is freely chosen and adopted. The array of principles reflects upon an individual's moral beliefs and value system. As the individual matures, he will inherit newer principles, and in some cases he may replace out-dated principles with more modern principles. For example, children who are well mannered may, at some future date, replace the principle of politeness with the principle of courtesy. Correspondingly, the particular principles within an individual's array demonstrate intellectual development, spiritual growth, and social maturation. Individuals with a bare array of principles do not demonstrate any forms of social development, and they have not matured in a manner consistent with the average human being.

6   Law of Hierarchy

WITH RESPECT TO THE HUMAN MIND, the three elements of an individual's intellect, emotional centre, and array of principles are governed by a law of hierarchy. The law of hierarchy illustrates an interconnectedness that exists between all three elements. Primarily, these elements interact with each other through a kind of system based on affect and effect. Within this system, there are two possible cycles. The first cycle is known as the ruling cycle. Elements in the mind that are engaged in the ruling cycle hold the power to affect another element. The second possible cycle is the regulated cycle. Within the regulated cycle, elements in the mind are subject to the effects of another element. Therefore, within the ruling cycle one element governs another element, while within the regulated cycle one element is subordinate to another element.

Within the ruling cycle, the individual's intellect governs his emotional centre. Therefore, the intellect possesses a kind of power over the individual's emotional experiences. More specifically, the intellect possesses the power to modify or even negate some of the individual's possible emotional responses. To illustrate this, consider the crying baby.

When a newborn has come into this world, his primary emotional state is evident through his acts of crying. After some time, as the newborn grows into a baby, he gains life experience. Through his life experiences, the baby's intellect also starts to grow, as he gains more understanding of the natural world. Consequently, through his intellect, this baby will possess a greater power over his emotional experiences, and he will, thus, enter into a state of tears in a progressively less frequent manner. As the baby experiences other modes of communication, through language and sign language, his intellect further grows and possesses more control over his states of sadness. When he grows into a toddler, he gains more experiences and new abilities, like the ability to walk. Consequently, through the stimulation of the intellect, this toddler eventually gains the ability to moderate his feelings of sadness. Essentially, because his intellect has grown, the toddler has gained more control over his crying states, and in comparison to his first years as a baby, he will enter into a crying state in a much less frequent manner.

Therefore, when the individual gains knowledge through the intellect, he will gain more control over the specific elements that cause his emotional states. In other words, through understanding and comprehension, the individual gains more power over his emotional states. This power is exemplified in his ability to control and modify his emotional centre. When the individual matures, he gains more knowledge of the physical world through experience. With the addition of more knowledge, the individual then gains the ability to draw a distinction between significant phenomena and insignificant phenomena. His intellect then acts as a kind of filter, which focuses more on things of importance, in addition to ignoring phenomena of less importance. Consequently, through the understanding of the intellect, the individual gains more power over his centre of emotions.

Also through the intellect, the individual develops his faculty of reason. Rational modes of thinking also have an effect over the individual's emotional states. Through reason, we all possess the power to organize our thought processes. Accordingly, when we think rationally, we sometimes attribute a specific cause behind some kind of effect. In so doing, we recognize that some specific circumstance may have been unavoidable. Hence, through reason, we understand that some events occur, within the material world, beyond our sphere of control. For example, if some person were to pass away on his one hundred and first birthday, we rationalize through our intellect that he experienced longevity. Through this rationalization, then, we possess some control over our feelings of sadness. In another case, if we see a forest fire that was caused due to a lightning strike, we come to the understanding through our intellect that this natural disaster occurred beyond anyone's control. In so doing, we are able to come to terms with the destructiveness and the loss of life that ensued because of some happenstance.

On a further note, our rational thinking processes may also cause us to enter into emotional states. When we react, we enter into a specific emotional state because of our understanding of the natural world. For example, suppose we are travelling through the savannah and we witness a large group of lions who are hunting a wild boar. After that pack of lions has killed their prey, through our faculty of reason, we deduce that this boar is experiencing pain, even though it may not be explicitly expressing these feelings. Through this deduction, then, we will experience forms of sympathy towards that particular creature. Nevertheless, we know that carnivores naturally exist within wild. Accordingly, through our faculty of reason, we may view our natural environment as a crazy, yet beautiful world.

Regarding our emotional centre, this element of our soul governs our array of principles. Our array of principles is a combination of a belief and value system that guides our everyday actions. Yet, how we come to value a particular thing in the world comes directly from our emotional experiences. For example, consider a system of religious beliefs. Those who are religious value the concept of God, and accordingly, they possess a faith in His existence. Other persons, who are not religious, place no value on the concept of God, and subsequently they lack the principle of faith. Therefore, our values towards a fatherlike creator leads to a certain system of beliefs, which depending on one's conception of God, may include the principles of tolerance, diversity, and equality.

Our emotional centre is also responsible for the creation of a well-ordered, cooperative community. When we value the work of other persons within our community, we will eventually come to value the principle of service. Those who, subsequently, acquire the principle of service will want to contribute something back to their community. Accordingly, all well-ordered, cooperative communities are based on the exchange of services between common citizens. If no individuals valued services from other persons no markets would exist, and in addition, there would be no forms of a cooperative community. In contrast, human existence would be reduced to a lonely and solitary existence.

In a subsequent fashion, within the ruling cycle, the individual's array of principles will govern his intellect. This is evident in the formation of all kinds of relationships. For example, persons who adopt the principle of devotion will act with care and gentleness towards their life partner. Primarily, the individual carries out his acts of passion and intimacy simply because he is devoted to her. Therefore, the principle of devotion serves to guide his personal thoughts and actions, within this particular circumstance.

In another circumstance, consider the principle of respect. The lowest form of respect is self-respect. Persons who adopt the principle of self-respect demonstrate a form of unconditional self-love. In other words, these individuals value the totality of both their spiritual and physical life-force. Their behaviour is never self-destructive because they value their subjective existence. Similarly, they also value their personal perspective on life itself. Accordingly, these persons will then create friendships with other persons who share a similar perspective on life. This common perspective, in addition to the principle of self-respect, leads to a higher form of respect towards the individual's peers. Consequently, self-respect leads to a respect for one's peers, and this leads to the creation of friendships. Accordingly, the principle of self-respect is responsible for actions based on kindness and a form of regard towards other persons.

On the contrary, within the regulated cycle, the direction of the governing process between the three elements of the mind will be reversed. Hence, within this cycle, the individual's array of principles will be subordinate to his intellect. When the intellect governs the individual's spirit, this marks the creation of a balanced array of principles. Instead of the individual's emotional centre, the intellect serves to directly affect the nature of his spirit. When the individual possesses both a greater quality and quantity of knowledge within a specific field, he will usually come to adopt the principle of leadership. This is due to the fact that the intellect is responsible for all forms of intuition and creation within our physical world. For example, consider the individual who has heard a reciting of Shakespeare for the first time. This person will have a greater grasp on the concept of love, in comparison to those persons who have never read any forms of poetry. Therefore, persons who understand the works of Shakespeare will understand more degrees of love. This enables these individuals to have a higher quantity of relationships within their community, which makes them, from an intrinsic perspective, natural leaders. Rationally, then, the individual adopts the principle of leadership, because he has secured a social position that will enable him to spread and demonstrate more kinds of love, and this, in turn, benefits his entire society.

A second example where the intellect governs an individual's spirit may be based on the principle of sensibility. Individuals who employ their faculty of reason will eventually come to view the world through a kind of logical perceptive. This perspective is based on the concepts of reason, and order. Individuals who gain some kind of understanding of our world, through their faculty of reason, will eventually acquire this particular habit. As his base of knowledge grows, the individual will then come to rely on his faculty of reason. Consequently, when the individual employs his faculty of reason on a continual and recurrent basis, he will have acquired the principle of sensibility.

When the individual's array of principles governs his emotional centre, this represents a form of control where he experiences less forms of reactivity within similar circumstances. Accordingly, individuals who adopt the principle of discipline possess the potential to moderate or modify their personal feelings based on pessimistic emotions. For example, when the individual witnesses a physical altercation, his feelings of anger could motivate him to join in and take some role within this confrontation. However, individuals who possess the principle of discipline will actively moderate their feelings of anger. In these cases, instead of taking part in a physical altercation, the individual will try to resolve this dispute according to a peaceful manner. The principle of discipline, then, modifies the individual's feelings of anger into feelings of grace.

A second example may be based on the principle of service. When the individual receives some kind of gift, he may react emotionally through a grateful manner. However, if this individual possesses the principle of service, his emotional reaction may be elevated into a form of inspiration. Essentially, within the individual's frame of mind, he not only appreciates the gift that he has been given, but he also wants to return this gift to another person. The principle of service turns feelings of appreciation into feelings of inspiration, which motivates the individual to return the gift that he has received to arouse feelings of gratefulness in another person.

Lastly, within the regulated cycle, the individual's emotional centre will have a similar kind of influence over his intellect. This is exemplified through the emotion of determination. When the individual experiences the emotion of determination, he is highly motivated to create something that is beneficial to human civilization. For example, the individual who perceives some form of suffering may first experience feelings of compassion, which change into feelings of determination because he feels obligated to relieve this suffering. The individual, then, may be determined to either become a doctor so that he may treat instances of suffering, or become a scientist so that he may cure a particular kind of disease. In this case, the individual's emotion of determination motivates him to acquire knowledge within some specific field or subject matter.

Emotions of courage may also have an impact over the individual's intellect. The emotion of courage leads to a kind of action that will correct some form of evil. It is the most evident motivational factor behind individuals who serve within the military, or police. Firemen will also fit into this category. Through their emotions of courage, these individuals will inherently sacrifice their own lives to save the innocent. With respect to persons who serve in the military, these individuals will correct some form of evil that exists on a world-wide scale. Policemen correct forms of evil that exist within distinct communities. Likewise, firemen provide all kinds of aid, mainly on an individual or domestic level. Accordingly, their emotions of courage motivate them to provide a form of chivalrous aid, even during cases when their own personal safety may be jeopardized as a direct result.

The law of hierarchy reflects upon a kind of harmony that exists within the individual's soul. If the soul is engaged in the ruling cycle, it is actively gaining particular characteristics, which will define an individual's character and persona. Hence, when the individual's intellect is ruling his emotional centre, he is selectively modifying its target from a general to a more specific material or immaterial object. Similarly, when his emotional centre is adding to his array of principles, he will come to value a particular instance of moral behaviour. Then, when his array of principles guides his intellect, he will think and deliberate in accordance with his moral beliefs.

In contrast, when the soul is engaged in the regulated cycle, it is determining its place within the natural world. Thus, when the individual's array of principles is regulated by his intellect, he will gain a kind of value that, in comparison to the ruling cycle, is more unique and difficult to obtain. This is due to the fact that while most persons share a generally similar core of emotions, the scope of every person's intellect will vary, quite widely, on an individual basis. Therefore, since persons possess differing degrees of knowledge, the principles that they do acquire, through the intellect, will also differ according to various degrees.

Further, when the individual's array of principles regulates his centre of emotions, his emotional experiences will increase on a qualitative basis. This is due to the fact that spirit leads to friendships, and distinct relationships will further lead to distinct experiences. Accordingly, spirit results in an elevated form of life experiences, within the domain of friendships and other kinds of personal relationships.

Finally, when the emotional centre regulates the intellect, the individual will focus all of his energy and efforts towards that object which he values the most. This results in a unique form of contribution by the individual, which he realizes through the motives of love and devotion. Consequently, the individual's distinct contribution, within his community, also distinguishes himself from his peers.

The differences between the three elements of an individual's mind will also provide him with a unique life-force. Indeed, the scope of an individual's intellect, the content in his array of principles, and the target of his emotional centre will be entirely distinct. Likewise, the interaction between these three elements, within his soul, may also vary on a unique basis. Accordingly, not only will the individual's physical character differ from all other persons, but so will his immaterial life-force.

On a further note, the law of hierarchy also exists outside of the human soul. A kind of hierarchy exists in nature which demonstrates a form of order present among all species of life. On the planet Earth, human beings serve as the main ruling species. We are more powerful than any other species of life because we possess the capacity to duplicate and thus create new instances of life within our ecosystem, through the method of farming. We also possess the ability to destroy forms of life within our ecosystem, through the method of hunting. Further, we possess the power to destroy entire ecosystems, in a variety of different ways. First, if we overhunt a single species, this will disrupt the food chain, which in turn will cause the destruction of an entire ecosystem. If we wish to speed up this process, the utilization of nuclear weapons can also effectively extinguish an entire ecosystem. Therefore, our ability to manipulate our natural environment makes us the most powerful species of life in our world.

With respect to the natural law of hierarchy, a single species of life governs its ecosystem. It mainly ranks a governing species of life, according to its place within the food chain. When we examine the oceans, it is the orca that rules this particular environment. Similarly, when we examine the wilderness, it is the lion that reigns supreme. Correspondingly, no other species of life possesses the raw and intrinsic power necessary to either hunt or destroy a ruling species, essentially because a ruling species is at the top of its food chain. In a similar fashion, no other species of life, within a particular ecosystem, can contend with the ruling species' power over its environment. On the contrary, a ruling species should, conceivably, possess enough power to hunt all other species of life that habituate its particular ecosystem. This, then, is the basic definition of a ruling species.

On a grander scale, man is responsible for governing the Earth, and all of the ecosystems that subsist within it. We rule our planet because we possess the power to eliminate the entire orca species, through overhunting. We possess a similar power over the wilderness. The power of man to rule the Earth is due solely to the power of our intelligence. It is through our intelligence where we gain the powers to either create, or destroy. As the intelligence of man increases, so will our powers over the natural environment. Therefore, intelligence may be rightfully correlated with power.

Nevertheless, while we govern the Earth, our continued existence, at the same time, is still limited by our physical environment. Thus, while man governs nature, he is also, at the same time, governed by it. Our natural environment could be viewed as a complex, yet ordered system. Indeed, we could not exist without the warmth from our sun, and we also could not exist without the differing forms of nourishment that are present in nature. The same principle applies to the orca, which cannot survive in an environment beyond the boundaries of the ocean, and also to the lion which could not survive outside of the savannah, for example, within a desert-like environment. Accordingly, while we are the governing species of our planet, what governs the universe, in its entirety, must be something that possesses more intrinsic powers than any human being.

This governing entity must, at the very least, possess all of the kinds of powers that are present within our universe. For when we examine life on Earth, every category of life is based on a natural law of hierarchy. Flowers represent a kind of spirit, while animals possess both a kind of spirit, in addition to liberty. Humans possess all of these attributes, though we are also empowered with intelligence. According to the natural law of hierarchy, the governing entity of the universe must, at the very least, possess liberty, a spirit, and intelligence.

We all refer to the governing entity of our universe as God. As the ruler of our universe, God must possess all of the qualities that are present in all other kinds of life. Therefore, since human beings possess the power to both create and destroy, we may also attribute God with these powers. Further, when we examine the average human being, we observe his will to be unbounded and unlimited. Hence, the will of God must also be correspondingly unbounded. Lastly, when we examine the differences in intelligence between man and the wild animal, this difference is vast. A similarity is also apparent between the wild animal and plant life. Thus, in accordance with the natural law of hierarchy, the difference in intelligence between God and man should be equally as vast.

Due to his intelligence, the creator of our universe subsequently possesses an immensely higher quality and quantity of powers that may be possessed by any human being. Moreover, if we perceive our universe to be physically limitless, then we may rightfully attribute its creator with an infinite amount of power. Therefore, the limitless physical nature of our universe entails the probability that God is an omnipotent life-force. Inversely, power also reflects upon intelligence. Thus, any entity which possesses an infinite amount of power will also necessarily possess an infinite amount of intelligence.

Indeed, human beings possess all forms of knowledge possessed by any animal found in nature. Subsequently, the governing life-force of any world necessarily possesses the most innate kind of intelligence. With respect to our universe, this makes its ruler all-knowing. Certainly, the ruler of our universe must possess the knowledge possessed by any creature, within the entire cosmos. Through the natural law of hierarchy, then, we may deduce that God possesses more knowledge than all of the ruling forms of life, in any world within the universe, as a totality. This, furthermore, makes Him omniscient. In addition, if the universe is truly limitless, then there will also be no limits on the kinds of life that may exist within it. Since all forms of life possess some kind of spirit, God's spirit must also be limitless.

With respect to the natural law of hierarchy, we understand God to possess the characteristics of omnipotence, omniscience, and that He is also spiritually limitless. Additionally, through this law, we will view our universe to possess a kind of order and harmony that exists within each person's soul. Within our natural world, there exist two categories of life forms. Both categories are forms of life that could not survive, if there were no true forms of order present within our universe.

A basic form of life is any single bodied organism that requires nourishment for its continued existence. All single instances of vegetation, wild animals, or individual human beings are classified as a basic form of life. Within the bodies of basic forms of life, there exists a kind of ordered, interconnected system. Within this system, every individual part is necessary for the life-form's continued existence. For example, in human beings, oxygen is breathed in through the lungs, which oxygenates the blood vessels. The heart then pumps these blood vessels throughout the individual's body. Furthermore, the individual's brain stem is also necessary for the act of breathing. Accordingly, this particular system, among others, is required for the continued survival of any human being. If we negated, or took out, any single element within this system, the system would not work. Thereby, each component within this system is wholly necessary for the individual's survival.

The existence of oxygen seems to be necessary for the survival of most forms of life. In other cases, such as plant species, carbon dioxide may, instead, be necessary for its survival. Nonetheless, in both cases, if our world ran out of either gas, some species of life would not continue to subsist. Therefore, every form of life relies on a form of environmental system, where it would not survive should any single component within this system were to be similarly negated, or lost. Ecosystems form an environmental system of independent parts that work interdependently.

This leads us to the definition of sophisticated forms of life. Sophisticated forms of life also exist due to a similar kind of ordered system. Its definition may be similar to the definition of an ecosystem. Therefore, a sophisticated form of life is comprised of many diverse species of life, where these species interact with each other through a systematic fashion. Consider the ocean, which is comprised of a multifaceted, yet ordered food chain. Mammals, such as the orca, feed on all kinds of smaller fish. These smaller species of fish feed on forms of plankton, which, in turn, feed on kinds of algae. The continued existence of this ecosystem is entirely dependent on a balanced food chain. If we were to eliminate enough species of life within this ecosystem, it would then lose its harmony and balance, and every form of life within it may eventually die out, and become extinct. Therefore, a sophisticated form of life is similar to a basic form of life in that its continued existence depends highly on a balanced and ordered system. This system is based on interactions between basic forms of life. With respect to a basic form of life, if we were to take away any single organ, such as its heart, lungs or brain, it could not exist. In a similar fashion, a sophisticated form of life necessarily requires all of the species within its food chain for its incessant survival.

When we examine each individual ecosystem, it continues to exist due to a perfect balance, with respect to the differing species of life that reside within it. All ecosystems are a sophisticated form of life because there exists a kind of regularity and order among all of the basic forms of life that are found within them. As a consequence, our solar system may also be categorized as a sophisticated form of life. It is true that human beings rule the entire globe. However, our continued survival also depends on elements that exist outside of the Earth. Every form of life, on Earth, requires heat from the sun. In addition, our survival is also dependent on the element of gravity. Therefore, our solar system may be classified as a sophisticated form of life because all forms of life that reside within it cannot exist without a precisely ordered planetary system. Our solar system is a perfectly balanced and harmonious system, based not on random or chaotic elements, but on the concept of order.

First, all forms of life require water. Next, forms of life require heat. The Earth is at a perfect distance away from the sun, which provides the necessary range of heat that enables forms of life to subsist and survive. It is neither too hot, nor too cold on the planet Earth. Correspondingly, the combination of the Earth's oceans and heat from the sun provides the means for delivering the necessary amounts of water to forms of life, within inland ecosystems. Vegetation then provides oxygen, which is necessary for other classes of life. Hence, the Earth embodies a perfectly balanced system of order which enables the continued survival of all forms of life. As an ecosystem, if one of these elements were to be taken away, then in time, no forms of life on Earth would continue to exist.

Essentially, this system of order, within our solar system, is based both on the existence of the sun, in conjunction with its particular distance from the planet Earth. When we examine our solar system, there exists a perfect balance among the planetary bodies, which is necessary to sustain all forms of life on our planet. This balance is based on a relationship of regularity, regarding distance, between the sun and our planet. If we were to move our planet relative to a position near Venus or Mars, then no forms of life on Earth would continue to exist. Likewise, if we were to take out the element of our sun, then life on Earth would also cease to exist. Accordingly, our solar system is an ecosystem because all of the forms of planetary life, within it, depend on the constants of heat and light that are granted to it by way of the sun.

Even if no other forms of life exist beyond our solar system, the universe, as a whole, can still be categorized as a sophisticated form of life. This is due to the fact that our solar system cannot be truly separated from the universe as a whole. Our solar system is merely a small division within the universe, in its entirety. The universe contains many galaxies, and within a single galaxy there exists many differing kinds of solar systems. Logically, we may deduce that since there is life on Earth, there also exists life within our universe. Further, if we negate the conceptual boundaries that define our solar system, we may, instead, conceive the entire universe as the key ordered ecosystem responsible for sustaining life on Earth, and thus consider it as a sophisticated form of life. In other words, when we extend the conceptual boundaries of our solar system to encompass the entire cosmos, the universe, instead, becomes the principal ordered ecosystem that supports life on our planet.

In fact, our solar system is not restricted by any kinds of physical boundaries or constraints. It is a small component of the entire universe as a whole, in the same manner that a drop of salt water is a part of the ocean. Accordingly, we may justly conclude that whatever rules our solar system must be the same entity that rules the entire universe. This entity, however, is not man. All human beings still exist as a basic form of life within a sophisticated universe. Hence, since our existence is governed by our solar system, we cannot be the rulers of the universe.

As such, according to the natural law of hierarchy, there exists some higher form of life that governs the totality of the physical universe. That which rules the universe can only be the designer of this ordered system, who is namely God. Essentially, our universe is an ecosystem that continues to exist due to a system based on order. It is an ordered system because it continues to support and maintain all forms of life on Earth.

Indeed, without the elements of balance and harmony among its parts, all of the species of life within our universe would have died long ago, as a short-lived anomaly. Yet, there are many different species of life on Earth that continue to both flourish and reproduce. This makes our universe a sophisticated form of life, since it is a kind of environment that sustains life on Earth. We know that it is a perfectly balanced ecosystem because, even though it may not have an infinite life span, every form of life on Earth still continues to flourish and exist, nonetheless.

In direct opposition to the theory of creation, based on an intelligent and ordered design, is the big bang theory. According to this theory, the beginnings of all forms of life, within the universe, began with a few small molecules. At the birth of our universe, only molecules of matter and anti-matter existed. By pure chance, the molecules of matter outnumbered the molecules of antimatter, and since these two elements cancel each other out, only a few molecules of matter remained. These molecules of matter then, subsequently, began to join together.

After this possible conceptual origin of the universe came the big bang. In essence, the material universe was born due to a tiny ball of energy that first exploded, and then expanded in a rapid fashion. It is through this explosion, and its subsequent cooling, that is proposed to be responsible for the general evolution of our physical universe. The explosion itself has been estimated to occur at a time of approximately 13 billion years into our history. Furthermore, according to many scientists, the universe is still expanding at present times.

By the big bang theory, I would like to include all possible theories of the origin of our universe that does not include God as its creator. For even if we were entirely certain that the big bang theory is true, it is possible that God may have been responsible for the creation of molecules of matter and anti-matter, or for the explosion itself. In fact, the big bang theory only provides a possible explanation regarding the evolution of the universe. It does not provide an explanation of how any forms of energy, or molecules, came into existence. Hence, if we just assume the notion that molecules of matter and anti-matter merely existed, without providing any explanation of how they came into existence, the same assumption could be applied to the existence of God. Hence, since it is possible that God may have been responsible for the initial big bang, my concept of the big bang theory includes all other possible scientific theories of creation and evolution that do not include God as its original creator.

In opposition to the theory of the big bang, is the law of reproduction. According to this law, every instance of life comes into existence due to a previous generation of life. Furthermore, within this law, the next generation of life can only possess the properties that are to be found within its parent, and nothing more. For example, when we view the natural world, we observe that a tiger cannot produce offspring with a chimpanzee, nor can a snake mate with a rat. All forms of life are limited, in the sense that they must mate with a similar species of life. Indeed, no forms of life, within our natural world, can create offspring with an entirely new set of physiological and biological traits. Therefore, no forms of life possess the ability to create a new species of life during the mating process. All forms of life are restricted, in the sense that they can only reproduce new forms of life that belong to their own categorical species.

According to the law of reproduction, two persons with an equivalent ethnic background cannot create a child with a differing ethnic background. Equally, animals cannot produce offspring with an entirely new nature. Rather, all forms of offspring represent a kind of hybrid with respect to the physical properties of their parents. Therefore, according to the law of reproduction, no new instances of life are ever created as a random accident. Life must create life. In accordance with this law, our universe, as a sophisticated form of life, also could not have been created by a random accident. Rather it must have been created by some form of intelligence that possesses all of the properties, of all forms of life that may be present within the entire cosmos. The creator of all life, then, must be both a complex and a powerful form of life.

A child can only possess the physical properties found within his parent. However, a ball of energy does not possess any properties that may be found in any differing species of life. Moreover, no forms of life on Earth possess the natural capacity to produce an explosion of energy, similar to that of the big bang. Therefore, all new instances of life do not come into existence merely through some random process, and likewise, the birth of a newer generation of life requires some uniform and ordered system that directly contradicts any kinds of a random process.

Concepts like the will to survive, which all animals possess, also implicate the probability that forms of life were created by something that possesses some kind of intelligence. Hence, according to the law of reproduction, non-material entities like free will and the immaterial mind suggests that forms of life must have been created by an entity that also possesses these non-material attributes. The big bang could have created a physical world, but it cannot account for the existence of any kinds of immaterial phenomena.

Within the entire globe, all forms of life are governed by the law of reproduction. On the other hand, the big bang theory suggests the notion that our entire universe was created purely by chance. Moreover, within this theory, there are no forms of intelligent order that governs our universe, which implicates the notion that our ordered universe essentially evolved through a chaotic process.

Yet, forms of energy are not a kind of life, and neither are single molecules of matter. The properties found in life, including the immaterial mind, may be much more complex in nature. Indeed, the complex systematic nature found in all forms of life, and our universe in general, cannot continue to subsist within a purely chaotic, or orderless, system. Additionally, forms of life cannot be created by something that lacks the intrinsic properties found within them. The big bang theory proposes the notion that something evolved from nothing.

The law of reproduction favours the position that, from an equally layman's perspective, something could not have evolved from nothing. When we view the nature of all forms of life on Earth, we observe a natural order where new forms of life only come into existence due to a previous life-force. We also understand, through science, that no kinds of life have ever come into existence due to an explosion of energy. The bulk of our knowledge of nature comes from our scientific observations of life on Earth. Accordingly, there exists no evidence which suggests that new forms of life could have ever been born outside of a parental system of order. Rationally, then, the law of reproduction should remain as the most prevailing theory of creation, with regard to all of the forms of life that exist within the entire universe. What we know about the creation of life on Earth should extend to the universe as a whole, until we find evidence that suggests the contrary.

Hence, all forms of life must have been born due to a parental generation of life. The diverse nature of all forms of life on Earth seems to implicate that the creator of life, within our universe, possesses an infinite amount of properties. As a consequence, the law of reproduction implicates an intelligent design theory, regarding our universe. It further substantiates a kind of order observed within the law of hierarchy. Within the natural law of hierarchy, there exists a form of order among basic forms of life, within every ecosystem. This opposes the notion that our universe is a chaotic system. For within the big bang theory, there may not exist a sense of regularity or order within our universe. All forms of life have evolved purely by chance. Yet, if this were true, then some kind of new species of life on Earth should also possess the potential to evolve from a pair of crystal rocks or a bolt of lightning, and this makes the fundamental creation of life sporadic and without any kinds of regularity.

However, we do observe kinds of order and regularity pertaining to life on Earth, in both laws of natural hierarchy and reproduction. Sensibly, it is conceivable to extend our concept of order, with respect to life on Earth, towards everything else that exists within our universe. The universe, as a sophisticated form of life, must also be governed by a kind of natural order. If the law of reproduction does pertain to the entire universe, then all forms of life within it must have been born due to a previous generation of life, and this parent must contain all of the properties observable within every instance of life. Only an entity that is spiritually limitless could be the parent of all forms of life within our universe, and this entity must further possess the unlimited omnipotence and omniscience we observe in God.

When we view and conceive of the vast amounts of spirits present on our planet, we have no reason to discount either the laws of natural hierarchy or reproduction. Indeed, every ecosystem is ruled by a specific species of life, and every form of life has come into existence because of a parental generation. We have never observed any kinds of life that may have evolved due to any other possible cause. Nonetheless, what the big bang theory does offer us is a theory of creation based on the observable, physical properties of the universe. It offers us a theory of creation based solely upon the material aspects in nature that may be perceivable through the five human senses.

Undeniably, God does not reveal Himself to us through a physical nature. He exists immaterially. Nonetheless, just because we cannot perceive something through our senses doesn't necessitate the notion that some entity cannot exist. Consider dark matter. Dark matter represents a kind of matter that cannot be perceived through the human senses. Nevertheless, many scientists have compelling reasons to believe in its existence. Within the minds of other persons, the same may be true with respect to the existence of God.

Since we do not physically perceive God, many persons would be more inclined to believe in a theory of evolution. However, this line of reasoning cannot provide a firm justification against the existence of God. When we examine the intelligence of marine species, it is utterly impossible for them to possess the knowledge that humans rule the earth. These forms of life only have forms of knowledge that are limited by their particular ecosystem. Nevertheless, even though they may lack certain forms of knowledge regarding the natural world, this does not entail the fact that humans do not rule the Earth and that there may be no other kinds of life that could exist outside of their oceanic environment. Rationally, our knowledge of the physical universe may be equally as limited. This paves the way for the existence of God as the ruler of our universe, and also as the creator of all forms of life that exist within it.

If the big bang theory is true, then all forms of life within our universe were not created due to a higher purpose, in the mind of God. Rather, all forms of life were created merely by random chance. Any kinds of worlds could have evolved through the big bang and every world that exists did evolve through an explosion of energy. Our universe was not created by any forms of an intelligent design, and thus, it is a kind of system that lacks order. Instead, our universe is mainly a chaotic system. Likewise, all forms of life also exist as a random anomaly. Everything in our universe exists without reason, and without any forms of regularity. There is no ruler of the universe, and there is nothing that governs our universe. Since all possible worlds could have evolved, it is equally possible that no forms of life would have ever evolved. Thus, without an intelligent creator, the universe is expanding without any system of order or regularity. However, if this were true, how is it possible that there do exist laws which govern our planet?

All forms of scientific discoveries reflect upon certain laws that remain constant in our world. The laws of physics do have bearing over all material objects in our world. The natural law of hierarchy and the law of reproduction also reflect upon species of life found within our planet. Accordingly, we must ask how a system, based on this kind of order, could be created by something that lacks order. A universe without order is not bounded by any kinds of laws. Theoretically, it should continue to remain and persist as a chaotic system.

Logically, a chaotic system cannot produce a harmonious system, because harmony requires regularity, but regularity is the direct opposite of randomness. In fact, it is highly unlikely that the order found within our ecosystems came into being purely through chance. It is possible that randomness could have created our world, but the concept of randomness cannot sustain our world. A harmonious system necessarily depends on constants, and a form of regularity between these constants, for its continued existence.

Subsequently, if the universe is truly expanding, then it is necessarily creating newer types of solar systems. However, since life continues to persist on Earth, the universe is also simultaneously supporting life within our solar system. This would seem to indicate that the universe is expanding in an orderly fashion. More specifically, this would seem to indicate that the expansion of the universe is further guided by some set of laws, which actively sustains all forms of life on Earth. Accordingly, this directly contradicts the notion that our universe is evolving through some random and lawless process.

Comparatively, all ecosystems on Earth, like the oceans or rainforests, also possess the potential to expand and grow. Nonetheless, only forms of life possess the capability to reproduce. This indicates that our universe is a sophisticated form of life. Yet, forms of sophisticated life continue to exist due to a complex interaction amongst all of its parts. Therefore, it is highly unlikely that a random system could both create and maintain a highly intricate and complex system of order, which is the very essence of a sophisticated form of life. Sophisticated forms of life do need a source of constant sustenance that is similarly observable among basic forms of life. Therefore, if life on Earth continues to subsist, then the universe itself must be the source of its constant sustenance, and this makes the universe a highly ordered system.

Without a form of regularity and harmony among elements within our universe, no kinds of life, either basic or sophisticated, would continue to exist. Every form of life, on Earth, continues to exist because it is an intricate part of a complex, yet ordered system. With respect to life on our planet, it depends on the constant of gravity. Without gravity, there would be no life on Earth. In a similar manner, if our oceans were to suddenly dry up, then all forms of marine life would become extinct. Our oceans continue to exist due to a harmonious and ordered system that could be unique to our planet. Without a perfect relationship between the sun and Earth, the oceans would cease to exist. Similarly, without a harmonious relationship between our solar system and the universe, our solar system itself would cease to exist.

The laws of gravity may be the most essential element that regulates our universe. Without this constant, the universe would expand in a chaotic fashion, and no ordered solar system would ever be born. Accordingly, since we are able to deduce that the laws of gravity both govern our solar system, and the universe as a whole, there does exist some kind of regularity within the cosmos. The laws of gravity implicate a form of order and regularity within our universe, and this implicates an intelligent theory of design. It also rightly opposes the concept of a random and chaotic system.

A well-ordered system does implicate an intelligent design. Similar to a finely crafted marine watch, all ecosystems would cease to function if one of its parts were defective. Humans possess the power to disrupt this system unintentionally, through greenhouse gases or the destruction of the ozone layer. This indicates that a lack of harmony amongst parts within an ecosystem easily possesses the potential to destroy it. Ecosystems, thus, are extremely fragile, and only continue to exist due to a firmly established system of order.

Therefore, if all forms of life were truly created at random, due to the big bang, then all other elements within our universe would also be created in an anomalous fashion. Nevertheless, because all forms of life on Earth require a sophisticated and balanced ecosystem for their survival, life within our universe would not continue to exist if all of the elements within it were also not perfectly balanced. Accordingly, while a chaotic system could possibly create forms of life, it cannot sustain any forms of life. A harmonious and ordered system seems to depend on an intelligent design, which must essentially be the will of God.

A universe without God would be like a community without laws or government. There would be no forms of an ordered system, only lawless chaos. Likewise, a chaotic system has no intrinsic potential to sustain any kind of interdependencies among differing species of life. If the big bang theory is true, then all forms of life and the universe, itself, have no true purpose. Our universe is essentially a random accident, and life has no higher meaning above our physical existence.

The big bang theory also implicates the notion that survival is directly correlated with the fittest species of life. However, the concept of survival of the fittest may not actually be a true property of our material world. The possible extinction of any species of life within the wild does seem to indicate that only the strongest forms of life will naturally maintain their own survival. Yet, the concept of the food chain seems to indicate that all forms of life will depend on the survival of other forms of life, for their own continued survival. Therefore, the element of interdependence, within all ecological systems, seems to indicate a kind of equality, among all inclusive forms of life. Accordingly, survival of the fittest species may not be relevant within any type of ecosystem, since every species of life depends on the existence of another species of life, for its main source of nourishment. If there does exist some kind of equality among differing categories of life, this would make the concept of survival of the fittest highly ludicrous.

Accordingly, every form of life depends on the existence of some other form of life, for its own existence. We may then conclude that with respect to the life span of our universe, God is responsible for its continued existence. No other known source possesses the intrinsic power to sustain a system of order that may be infinite in nature. As a result, this further entails the possibility that God must be the sole cause of our universe. Likewise, through observation and science, we possess the knowledge that every form of life does, indeed, have a parent.

Yet, we cannot apply the law of reproduction to God, simply because we have limited knowledge regarding His properties. He transcends our knowledge of the universe because of His immense power to create. Accordingly, we require experience within the immaterial world to gain more knowledge of Him. We do, however, possess sensory access to the known physical universe, and this is how we are able to extrapolate the laws of physics, natural hierarchy and reproduction.

When we combine the laws of natural hierarchy and reproduction together, the only rational conclusion we may deduce is based on the idea that God exists and that He is the creator of our universe. This makes Him the king of both the physical universe and the spiritual world. Only through an intelligent design can there be a form of harmony present within our universe. Furthermore, only an ordered system may potentially preserve and nourish all physical forms of life, for an indefinite period of time.

Yet, we can only speak and pray to God through our thoughts, as we do not perceive Him through any of the five senses. He, then, mainly exists within the immaterial world. In essence, the immaterial world does not seem to be bounded by the laws of physics. Conceivably, all other constants found within the physical universe, in all probability, also do not govern the immaterial world. Therefore, God is not governed by His environment in the same manner that forms of life on Earth are bounded by their particular ecosystem. This makes Him the supreme governing body of the universe.

God, at the very least, exists spiritually. We know that unique persons, within diverse communities around the world, possess a similar and basic idea of God. Therefore, His immaterial existence is flowing within our thoughts. Whether He exists materially, there may be more evidence to support this supposition than the contrary. Nonetheless, if we do possess an immaterial mind, then the existence of an immaterial universe will be highly plausible. Likewise, if an immaterial world exists, our beliefs regarding the existence of God will be wholly justified.

Thus, God exists somewhere beyond our physical universe, which is the immaterial world. Since He is all knowing, He understands both the male and female genders. This makes Him essentially genderless, at least to the extent that He is neither male nor female, but an immense spirit that embodies both genders. As the creator of our universe, He possesses every quality observable in all forms of life. Only a Godlike figure possesses the power to provide, maintain, and sustain some sense of order within the entire universe. Yet, since He exists within the immaterial world, He is not limited by any laws which may govern our material world. This makes Him infinite and limitless. Hence, we may characterize God as an unlimited, intelligent free spirit. We believe that God exists within the immaterial world due to the existence of our immaterial souls, in combination with the law of reproduction. However, this does not mean that God could not exist within our physical world, if He so desired. We lack sufficient knowledge of the immaterial world, and thus, can only come to the conclusion that God is its ruler. Since He exists beyond the physical world, we also cannot apply any laws of physics to His existence. This entails the fact that He possesses a truly unlimited amount of power. Our ability to possess some idea of Him, even though He does not physically reveal Himself to us, does demonstrate the enormity of His powers.

7   The Static Character

THE LAW OF HIERARCHY indicates a kind of harmonious relationship between the three elements that define an individual's soul. Nonetheless, some persons possess a dominant personality, where one element of their soul governs the other two. In these individuals, there are no kinds of an interrelationship present among the elements within their soul, and thus, they do not recognize either the ruling or the regulated cycles that pertain to the law of hierarchy. Hence, there are no forms of order present within these individuals' soul, based on this particular law. In actuality, during the bulk of their social interactions, one element mainly determines the majority of their actions. Therefore, their personality remains mainly unchanging, obstinate and tenacious. These individuals are known to possess a static character.

The static character bases his social interactions, for the most part, on either the power of his intellect, his emotional experiences, or his spiritual awareness. Persons who possess an intellectually dominant personality may be mainly guilty of intellectual crimes. Likewise, those who are highly emotional may be guilty of emotional crimes, while those who are spiritually authoritative may be guilty of crimes based on a lack of principles. Not all those who possess a static character will commit technical criminal acts. Nonetheless, they will be guilty of transgressions within their social sphere, and this indicates that they have the potential to raise their acts of abuse to a criminal level.

Every person that possesses a static character is primarily motivated to gain some kind of social authority. In general, the static character interacts with other persons according to a constant, non-changing formula, based on the dominating element in his soul. The reason why he continually seeks power and respect is usually based on an inferiority complex. In essence, the static character views imperfect character traits as human weaknesses. He is somewhat consistent in the fact that he also views his own personal imperfections as potential weaknesses. After he possesses a conception of his own personal imperfections, he will then prey on the innocent, in an effort to bolster his self-esteem. In actuality, the static character habitually focuses on personal weaknesses, both in him and in all other persons. As a consequence, he believes that he can effectively mask his natural imperfections after he gains some form of social authority over another person.

Within the static character's frame of mind, whenever he has a negative effect on another human being, he possesses some form of power. Furthermore, when he possesses power over another individual, this may be the epitome of his life. This line of reasoning is what drives the static character towards his life-time pursuit for power. In fact, the static character believes that a life without power has no intrinsic meaning. Hence, life without power is a useless life. Therefore, when the individual possesses no forms of authority over another individual, life is mundane and worthless. Accordingly, while power implicates importance, a lack of power implicates impotence. This rationale is both a defining feature and a concrete mindset among all persons who possess a static character.

Nonetheless, the static character is careful when he chooses his victims, essentially because he fears any possible forms of retribution. Hence, the targets of his abuse will pose no kinds of threat to him. Therefore, all static characters take into consideration their own personal fears when choosing a potential victim. His victims are usually innocent in nature, because it is likely that they will not challenge his immoral acts of abuse. The imperfect character traits that he focuses on can include stupidity, foolishness, or social oddity.

The static character relies on a constant element within his soul because he lacks balance and order at an internal level. In some instances, he may have failed to develop the other two elements of his soul, during his lifetime. In other cases, the static character may ignore the other two elements of his soul because he has learned that he profits the highest possible degree of social authority through this repetitive form of behaviour. In addition, the static character may view the other components of his soul as potential weaknesses, regarding his particular personality. Therefore, he develops a static character because he has not achieved the qualitative level of power and respect that he so desires.

Accordingly, the static character necessarily lacks social maturity. He will become angry when he does not achieve any forms of respect. Next, he will enter into a constant state of competition with other persons, including other static characters, until his struggle for power and authority is resolved.

In general, the female static character is overly concerned with outward appearances. The kind of social authority that these individuals seek will be based mainly on the element of beauty. These individuals gain a feeling of power over other persons when they are deemed as beautiful. However, the beauty that they seek is physical in nature, and it usually does not involve any spiritual elements. When these individuals are not recognized as beautiful, this motivates them to perform actions based on forms of abuse or revenge. Essentially, these individuals will adopt a discriminatory attitude towards some kind of social minority, due solely to their physical unattractiveness. When they are successful at belittling another individual, they will gain some degree of power, which is their original and primary goal. After gaining this form of social authority, they will then experience feelings of satisfaction. Accordingly, when these individuals are not successful in acquiring forms of social authority through their physical beauty, they will resort to forms of discrimination in an effort to gain a nearly equivalent feeling of authority.

The male static character usually does not seek to be recognized as a physically attractive person. Mainly, he seeks the power to control the actions of other persons, which results as a form of spiritual authority.

During his social interactions, he seeks a form of authority, comparable to that of a dictator. When persons challenge his authority, he will then resort to some form of abuse against these persons. In his mind, true forms of respect will only result when he has total power over another individual's thoughts and behaviour. Accordingly, when individuals do not submit themselves to the static character's demands, he holds the feeling that he is being disrespected in some manner. Within his frame of mind, forms of social respect are mainly equivalent to some level of control over another person's will. Therefore, the male static character seeks to be respected in a Godlike manner, where he possesses total control over the conduct and deeds of another person.

The static character acts in a rigid and repetitive manner because he has learned that he is most successful in his acquisition of social authority, when he acts with a dominant personality. Since the elements of his soul are not harmonious, he, in turn, seeks to produce an equivalent amount of lawlessness within his community. Moreover, his relentless pursuit for authority entails the fact that he does not believe in the principle of equality. In fact, inequality is a major driving force behind his behaviour. No static characters want to exist as an equal human being. Hence, to simply exist is not enough for the static character. The static character does not appreciate any forms of life, as an equal citizen. He rejects any kinds of lifestyles based on equality, in favour of some grander life based on power and control. Therefore, the "good life", in the mind of the static character, is one where he possesses any forms of authority over another human being.

Indeed, the static character is a social creature, in so far as he fears that he will be labelled into a lower social class. In actuality, he seeks to be revered, and he fears anything that may be contrary to this social status. Nevertheless, the static character is not bounded by any ethical laws, and he often becomes abusive. The static character will lie, swindle, cheat and defraud other persons in an effort to gain social authority. For that reason, we may question the notion about whether the static character is truly free. In so far as every static character possesses the power of choice, he is free. However, the static character's obsessive desire for power will limit his ability to make ethical choices. Therefore, the static character's true freedom revolves around the concept of authority and nothing else. As a result, the static character cannot experience any other wonders that are present within our natural world, and this limits his spiritual growth. The static character lacks freedom with respect to his spiritual growth, and this negatively impacts his impending social development.

The static character is also hampered by a limited intellect. He functions almost entirely through his faculty of memory, while his ability to become self-aware may be comparable to a juvenile's ability to become self-conscious. His inability may be based on two dimensions. Firstly, the static character may purposely enter into a form of "tunnel vision", in which he is actively ignoring his own personal imperfections.

In other cases, the static character may simply lack the intellectual faculties that are necessary for entering into a prolonged self-conscious, or analytical, state.

A lack of freedom can also occur when the static character is ruled by his emotional centre. Every action taken by this individual will primarily fulfill his insignificant centre of emotions. In return for a pleasurable emotional state, the static character often ignores any knowledge that may be stored within his intellect. Accordingly, this process may be responsible for a decrease within his array of principles. In essence, because of his insignificant centre of emotions, the static character may view the general citizen as a monotonous individual. Through his commitment to acquire material possessions, the static character may often neglect his social relationships. When this occurs, he will take his established relationships for granted, and this eventually destroys any bonds that he may have established. In a subsequent fashion, his quest for authority will then fall short.

This, then, is a kind of paradoxical state of mind that eventually evolves into a state of confusion. When the static character lacks the ability to choose between either gaining social authority or satisfying his insignificant centre of emotions, he is essentially gambling on the fact that he will acquire both feats through a simultaneous fashion. Actually, the static character experiences a sense of entitlement with respect to both matters. Nonetheless, in cases where he does not acquire both elements, he will enter into the preliminary stages of a psychological breakdown, where rash and irrational forms of action may follow.

This breakdown marks the beginning stages of the static character's gambling habit. In essence, the static character is always gambling on the fact that persons will automatically accept his immoral forms of behaviour. While he is picking his potential victims, he is also gambling on the fact that these individuals will not seek any forms of formal justice or personal revenge. Hence, the static character is always betting on the fact that his victims are intrinsically passive and peaceful. In these cases, he holds the personal belief that he will be safe from all forms of retribution.

In a similar manner, whenever the static character commits a crime, he is always gambling on the possibility that he will never be caught nor punished for his crime. When he commits multiple offences, his state of mind may be similar to the state of mind possessed by persons who are clinically addicted to the act of gambling. The static character is always aware of the fact that he may be punished for his offences. However, he is always gambling on the fact that he can either outwit policing authorities, or find a possible loophole, which enables him to escape the grasp of our justice system.

The static character's single-minded pursuit for power not only limits his freedom, but also his social status. In his quest for authority, the static character will reveal his steadfast nature, and this limits his ability to act in any other manner. Yet, no other kinds of persons will continue an irrational pursuit for social authority. Within the realm of politics, the individual's pursuit for power may be justified, because he seeks the authority to make the best decisions for his people. Nonetheless, in all other kinds of circumstances, the average citizen will not seek a form of authority, simply because social power will be irrelevant within his specific social environment.

When the static character does achieve success during his acts of discrimination against a social minority, he will then gain a false sense of superiority. Due to these feelings of power, he will then enter into a warring state with any other persons who may contest his authority. Subsequently, the static character will be born due to the concepts of competition and envy. When he loses a competition for some form of social authority, he will be consumed with envy. As a consequence, this jealousy motivates all of his immoral acts and behaviours.

In fact, when he views another individual who is flourishing, the static character almost always enters into a state of jealousy. Therefore, while the static character is primarily motivated to gain social authority, more specifically, he is motivated to gain the particular kind of social authority possessed by those persons who are the objects of his envy. Persons who are flourishing, within the static character's point of view, are individuals who are engaged in relationships based on love and brotherhood. He is jealous of the fact that the innocent are loved and blessed with a multitude of social connections. The static character then becomes envious, because he ultimately becomes aware of the fact that he lacks these basic necessities of life. If he does achieve a form of brotherhood or mutual respect, his persistent quest for authority will usually impede the development of these social relationships. In contrast, when he does not acquire these life basics, he will usually resort to aggression or violence as a typical response.

When he is unsuccessful in attaining social authority, his next actions will be motivated by feelings of revenge. This is due to the fact that he envies those persons who do possess a legitimate kind of social authority. This authority may be in the public sphere, as in the case of a just politician, or within the private sphere, as in the case of a loving parent. Since he lacks authority, he will refocus his attention back onto his inferiority complex. Firstly, he will experience feelings of anger, due to his poor problem solving skills. Then, feelings of incompetence will usually lead to a state of anger within the static character. Next, he will essentially become destructive, within either the public or private spheres, depending on where he seeks a form of authority.

His problematic perspective on life then fuels his aggressive tendencies, essentially because he envies the good life experienced by the common civilian. He will continue to act aggressively until he attains a definite form of authority over those persons who are the specific objects of his jealousy and envy. Through this destructive behaviour, the static character wishes to disrupt all forms of order, in favour of chaos and disorder. The overwhelming feelings of anger experienced by all static characters will eventually turn them into a kind of bully. However, in cases where acts of abuse are mainly based on psychological or emotional factors, the general public may not realize his actual state of mind.

Every static character wishes to be admired by the general public. Therefore, after he is publicly acknowledged as a kind of bully, he will then become hindered with more personal problems, based on his social reputation. Accordingly, when the general public perceives him through a negative frame of mind, this will mark the beginning of his downfall, with respect to his quest towards achieving any higher forms of social respect.

The static character becomes abusive due to two main reasons. Firstly, he lacks a sufficient amount of self-control over his emotions of anger. If he possesses a low level of rationale, he will then resort to forms of violence in order to relieve his negative emotional states. Secondly, he also becomes abusive when he realizes that he possesses no form of power or authority over other individuals. During both moments, his frame of mind naturally progresses into a heightened state of self-awareness. While in this state, he will focus on his personal imperfections, which stimulates his inferiority complex. Furthermore, when he enters into these mental states, he does acquire the awareness that his behaviour towards other persons have lacked civility. If the static character is a criminal, during these moments, he will then comprehend that his acts of abuse are criminal in nature. Therefore, the static character does possess the ability to realize that his acts of abuse are immoral. Nonetheless, his incessant drive for authority will circumvent any feelings of guilt, and correspondingly, he will continue his particular acts of abuse.

When his personal problems begin to compound, the static character will then enter into an extreme state of agitation. As a consequence, he will be less concerned with the feelings of other persons, due to his agitated frame of mind. Then, he will exploit any weaknesses that he perceives in other persons, to relieve his feelings of aggravated agitation. In essence, the static character becomes easily agitated due his limited psyche. His understanding of the world, and of civil social interactions, will be affected by his limited ability to use reason. Indeed, rational thinking is a key element that distinguishes civilized behaviour from animal instincts. It is the most essential part of the intellect that differentiates human culture from the natural state of wilderness.

Subsequently, raw animal instincts are what fuel all forms of abusive behaviour. The static character experiences feelings of disrespect when he is denied social authority, and thus, he relies on forms of abuse to reciprocate his feelings of emptiness onto other persons. When the static character resorts to acts of revenge, he has usually entered into a state of desperation. Accordingly, when desperate, the only feelings of happiness experienced by the static character will be based solely on the level of pain that he has inflicted on other persons. This results in an artificial sense of power over his victims. It is this sense of power which drives the static character to inflict some form of pain on a clearly innocent victim, who may have no relation to him whatsoever. When unsuccessful in this pursuit, though, he will have lost the last forms of authority that he has possessed over any persons.

After the static character has lost all forms of respect within his community, he may direct his aggressive tendencies towards acts of animal abuse. At this stage, animals become an easier target within the mind of the static character. This is based on the fact that animals possess a limited ability to communicate, and thus, they cannot report any transgressions to a policing authority. The concept of an easy target enables the static character to exercise a form of authority, through violence, without any threats of justice or retribution.

In a subsequent fashion, when he is in the presence of persons who are bent on vengeance, the static character will moderate his aggressive tendencies into a more passive state of mind. During these circumstances, the static character demonstrates both his cowardice and his inferiority, in relation to the persons that he fears. In addition, he usually lacks the awareness that he possesses these latter character traits. This would seem to indicate that the static character both wishes to be feared, and that he is also governed by it.

After anger, fear is the second dominant emotion that haunts the static character. In actuality, his feelings of fear motivate him to inflict feelings of fear in other persons. Within the static character's frame of mind, he wishes to mirror his feelings of fear onto the common civilian, in order to address his present state of inferiority. After an innocent civilian experiences an equivalent mirror-image, related to his personal feelings of fear, the static character may then accept and come to terms with his original mental state.

The static character often justifies his acts of abuse due to the fact that he was experiencing feelings of anger. Actually, it is often the case that many static characters lack the ability to control their emotional states. The ability to moderate one's pessimistic emotions can be a difficult course of action. Nonetheless, a lack of control over one's emotional state does not provide any individual with a justifiable liberty to utilize acts of abuse. Indeed, all individuals still possess the liberty to act freely, even when entering into a state of overwhelming rage. Therefore, while our emotional states do provide a reason for certain forms of action, they do not hold a form of absolute power and control over the agent's subsequent behaviour.

The majority of static characters lack an ability to consciously enter into a heightened state of self-awareness, which indicates that they mainly act instinctively. Primarily, he mainly enters into a state of surreal awareness after his failed attempts to achieve power. When this occurs, he then seems to focus and direct his energy and attention towards his personal failures. He only experiences feelings of shame during moments where he actually realizes and possesses an awareness regarding his personal failures.

Furthermore, the static character does not comprehend the concept of mutual respect. Primarily, he demands grandiose amounts of respect from other persons, even when he does not reciprocate feelings of respect towards other persons. This marks the beginning of his social isolation and alienation from the rest of his community.

When one static character starts a relationship with another, both persons will enter into a contest, based on a struggle for power. This contest will end only when one individual submits himself to the other person's authority. Accordingly, comradery is not an ideal that the static character subscribes to. The relationship between two static characters will continue to be based on some kind of power struggle, which sometimes results in mutual feelings of loathe and hate. Since every static character wishes to become a tyrant, there are no relationships between two static characters that do not involve interactions based on the elements of dominance and submission.

However, if the latter kind of relationship is never established, the two individuals involved will wage a psychological war with each other for an indefinite period of time. Within this war, both static characters will evolve into a form of slave, who is governed by his specific and uncontrollable emotional states. Accordingly, the combination of anger and feelings of inferiority will usually be the centre point within this feud. At its core, both individuals will engage in a battle in an effort to make the other person feel inferior in some manner. After this occurs, a savage war for dominance will then ensue. Moreover, in time, their psychological acts of abuse may escalate into acts of physical abuse.

In actuality, victory within this war can only be achieved when one opponent submits himself to the other person's authority. In its aftermath, the winner of this war will be the person who has fostered the utmost degree of anger within his opponent.

In other cases, the static character will seek to establish a collective between himself and other persons who possess a similar temperament. Within this collective, all parties involved will equally possess some form of a dominant personality. Nonetheless, the static character always seeks power within all of his relationships. Therefore, during these friendly interactions, the static characters involved may hold some kind of contest to determine who should rightfully possess the most authority. The leader of this collective is determined by the individual who wins these contests, and likewise, the individual who possesses the most authority over all of the other members of this particular group.

In cases where a static character does achieve social authority over another individual, these kinds of arrangements do not form a true relationship based on love and tolerance. Rather, these kinds of relationships are based on the concept of convenience. In essence, this relationship takes the kind of form where one static individual's needs are satisfied by the other. Therefore, the relationship between two static characters is formed due to their inability to independently acquire their own desperate needs. The individual who fulfills a quantitatively greater amount of his partner's dependencies will eventually assume leadership. On the whole, most static collectives resemble a corrupt criminal organization, where static individuals join together mainly so that each member will have a better chance to both pursue and acquire their wicked self-interests.

When the static character achieves some form of social authority within his collective, his next priority will be directed towards gaining a form of sexual gratification. This is due to the fact that the authority that he seeks needs to be characteristically absolute in nature. These urges, in most cases, may not be technical sexual acts. The actions that he commands may be merely representational in nature, according to the degree of power that he requires within his sexual fantasies. Likewise, these commands are given mainly in order to test the loyalty of those persons who are members of his collective. In essence, the static leader will command persons within his collective to serve his personal whims. Those who do serve his personal whims will be recognized, and thus, will gain a form of social authority and respect within that particular collective.

Persons who do not serve his personal whims will be demoted, according to a kind of rank within the collective, based on authority. This demotion will essentially be based on a position where the lowest ranked persons will receive the lowest amounts of respect, within the collective as a whole.

In cases where a static leader perceives a loss of personal authority over a member of his collective, he will further enter into a state of extreme agitation. Within his own psyche, he perceives a loss of personal authority as a major form of disrespect. His next course of action will be based on some form of competition with that individual. In effect, he does not want to lose the upper hand that he had previously possessed over this individual. Thus, he does not want an equal standing, nor does he want to become subordinate to this individual. Within this competition, he will usually not abide by any forms of rules. In an effort not to be outdone by the other individual, the static leader will disregard any forms of established rules, to regain his upper hand. Essentially, the static character will resort to cheating to ensure his victory within this personal competition.

Since he requires a form of absolute power over everyone within his collective, those persons who wish to maintain their membership within it must continue to comply with all of his requests. Nonetheless, these individuals may not be satisfied, themselves, with the amount of respect that they are granted within their collective. Next, when the static leader faces rejection from these individuals, he will then evolve into a kind of bully. Furthermore, when his demands become too outrageous, this will spark strife and discontent among those who are positioned at the lowest ranks within his collective. After this occurs, the static leader will then have lost some degree of authority over his collective, where some of the parties involved may purposely disobey their leader. A form of civil war, then, may possibly ensue, where leadership within the collective may be challenged and contested. One possible result, within this war, will be based on the formation of a new collective, based on new leadership. The other possible result may cause anarchy and disorder within the collective, which will serve to slowly disband the entire collective as a whole.

In most cases, the civil war sparked between two static characters will last for an indeterminate amount of time. In fact, whenever there exists some form of ignorance between two static characters, there will also exist a sense of mistrust. When the static character eventually becomes guilty of some form of abusive behaviour, his criminal acts will usually be focused towards the objects of his ignorance. In essence, the static character also utilizes acts of abuse in an effort to understand the habits of his enemy. He is motivated to gain this type of understanding so that he may acquire his desired social authority over that person.

In turn, his enemy will usually plot a form of response, based on the concepts of vengeance and retaliation. Yet, when the original abuser receives his due, he will not experience any feelings based on sorrow or remorse. In actuality, he will measure the amount of abuse that he has received, and respond with actions that will also be based on the concept of revenge. In these cases, an indefinite and cyclic exchange of abusive behaviours will be the main focal point in the minds of both individuals, and this will consume their entire purpose and reason for existence.

In a community comprised of static characters exclusively, there will exist no forms of cooperation, due to this kind of continuous struggle for power. In the end, this potential community, which could have been built through good intentions, will falter because of the fact that each static character will disengage in any forms of cooperative relationships, essentially so that he may acquire his own personal interests.

In his relationships with peaceful individuals, the static character will mimic some aspect that he perceives within the dynamic character, to gain a form of trust. He mimics the specific kinds of behaviours that will enable him to acquire forms of friendships and respect. After this trust is achieved, though, the static character will revert back into his authoritative style of behaviour. In actual fact, the static character learns his authoritative methods entirely through experience, which could either be his own or through another static character's mindset. He may then conduct experiments with peaceful individuals to understand which forms of authoritative behaviours are most effective. Accordingly, he seldom learns through reason or cognition. This suggests the probability that he acquires knowledge exclusively through his faculty of memory.

When interacting with a dynamic character, a similar struggle for power may ensue. During his interactions with a dynamic character, the static character will utilize some method of abuse so that his victim will experience a harsh mental state that may be equivalent to his own personal experiences. If the static character achieves some form of dominance over the dynamic character, he will enter into a state of personal self-concord. Nevertheless, since the static character possesses an insignificant centre of emotions, a state of anger will eventually replace his state of internal accord. In essence, the static character will re-enter into a form of cyclic behaviour, where he will pursue higher forms of social authority. Actually, he is never content with any forms of authority that he may already possess. Since he is limited and can never achieve an infinite amount of authority, he may be motivated to make other persons, within his community, experience a similar form of unrest.

Unfortunately, the dynamic character must possess life experiences to understand the true internal nature of the static character. Nonetheless, it is possible for him to also gain knowledge through the experiences of other persons within his social circle. Experience always leads to knowledge, yet reason and deduction also prepares the individual for any mishaps that may originate through the static character.

Due to his continuous quest for authority, the static character mainly seeks appeasement from a community of persons with a dynamic character, in exchange for any kinds of a peaceful coexistence. If he is unsuccessful with this pursuit, he will be motivated to acquire power in some other manner. Not all static characters will utilize violence to achieve social authority, yet the potential to become physically abusive remains in all of them, nonetheless.

In actuality, all static characters are hedonistic. Their hedonistic behaviour usually begins during childhood, and it becomes amplified as they grow older. Within their frame of mind, all forms of action that maximize their own personal pleasures are morally correct. Therefore, the concept of hedonism provides the static character with a reasonable excuse to abuse other persons. Hedonism also provides all criminals with a reason to commit criminal acts. Those who are hedonistic will not waver when they cause suffering in other persons, should these actions bring them pleasure. Accordingly, self-interest is the main driving force behind all hedonists.

Static characters are similar to each other in that they all depend on some variation of hedonism, for their source of happiness and pleasure. Nonetheless, not all persons with a static character will break any formal laws established by our justice system. Some will only rely on forms of psychological or emotional abuse, as a means to acquire their personal pleasure. Hence, these individuals do not commit crimes that are punishable within our society. Rather, they commit crimes against the human spirit. Through his hedonistic ways, the static character will work against the principles of cooperation and mutual benefit, whenever it is the case that these actions will provide him with some form of authority or pleasure.

In fact, the static character's tools for personal success mainly stem through some form of abuse. All variations of physical, mental, and emotional abuse causes suffering, and this enables the static character to acquire some form of an authoritative perspective. In the beginning, the static character will compete for intellectual superiority with another individual. When he believes that he is intellectually superior, he will expect some form of authority over his competitor. Nevertheless, when he does not gain the authority that he desires, this is where he will resort to some form of intellectual, or psychological, abuse which subsequently enables him to demonstrate his intellectual prowess.

If this particular contest results in a loss or stalemate, the static character may then resort to some form of emotional abuse. He focuses on emotional vulnerabilities essentially to gain a form of control over his competitor's state of mind. If he wins this contest, he will then declare himself as the superior being, due to the fact that he is less vulnerable to any forms of emotional attacks. However, if he loses any forms of emotional control over his competitor, he may, as a last resort, utilize forms of physical abuse, in an effort to recuperate the control that he once possessed through his acts of emotional abuse.

At this stage, the static character will utilize his physical superiority to gain some form of authority. Yet, not all static characters will resort to acts of physical abuse, because these are kinds of acts that are punishable by our justice system. Only those individuals who lack the minutest scruples will abuse other persons through a physical manner. Static characters who are culpable of physical abuse must be recognized as the most dangerous offenders known to mankind.

Some static characters resort to forms of physical abuse out of desperation, as psychologically, they hold the belief that they are inferior to their peers. Acts of physical abuse are intended to satisfy the static character's need for authority, yet when these kinds of actions do not satisfy his ego, his acts of abuse will escalate in terms of severity. First, it begins with minor forms of aggression, based on inflicting some kind of physical pain on his victim. Next, he may intend to inflict some kind of permanent damage, through his acts of physical abuse. In time, when he is not satisfied with the level of control that he possesses through his physical transgressions, the last stage will result in a loss of life. Only those individuals who experience the highest levels of frustration will be capable of murder. Likewise, only those persons who are not successful in relieving their feelings of frustration, through a single instance of murder, will be capable of committing multiple instances of this offence.

The severity of forms of physical abuse carried out by the static character will depend solely on his ego, and his need for social respect. After he achieves a form of dominance over another individual, he will rely on forms of physical abuse, essentially as the easiest means that will enable him to accomplish his personal goals. A lack of authority also motivates feelings of vengeance within the static character. Hence, any persons who reject his authority could potentially be the victims of physical forms of retaliation, based on the concept of revenge. Accordingly, the most common motivation behind the violent acts of all static characters is based on their need for social respect.

During many interactions, an individual will be abused to the point where he experiences a similarly harsh experience, within the static character's personal history. This is a main objective within the static character's frame of mind, as he wants to try to learn from his victim, so that he can better cope with his own personal feelings of frustration, at some future time. Accordingly, most static characters lack the ability to manage their imperfections, and when this occurs, they automatically enter into a state of frustration. When other person's perceive his frustrations, the static character then enters into a state of indignation. Actually, every human being possesses the capacity to experience emotions of extreme anger, yet the static character loses awareness of this fact, whenever he enters into that particular mental state. He then fears the possibility that he will become a lifetime victim to his own feelings of anger. In his effort to defend himself, he will then try to affect all persons within a particular social circle, with the same degree of rage that he experiences on a continual basis. Subsequently, resentment is another key motive that drives the totality of the static character's behaviour.

On the whole, persons with a static character are also nihilists. The static character usually rejects all forms of morality because of his quest for more physical pleasures. Accordingly, although some static characters appear to be religious, intrinsically they do not follow the moral principles that define any given religion. Those who appear to be religious will only consider passages, within a religious text, that exclusively promote some type of personal benefit. Since they only follow specific passages, they ignore the majority of other moral principles that may be stressed within a certain religion. In turn, they may also eventually deny the existence of God. This may be due to two reasons. First, when the static character denies the existence of God, he seeks to disrupt the order that may be produced by any given religion. Secondly, the static character denies the existence of God essentially to promote his own potential to acquire a paralleled form of authority.

Gaining power and authority acts like an illicit drug with the static character's frame of mind. His quest for authority begins with small gains within the family setting. After he has discovered a successful formula of action within the private sphere, he will use the same set of actions, within the public sphere, to gain similar forms of social authority. However, when he is not granted power within the public sphere, his dishonest acts will spiral towards an increasing degree of immorality. The only limits that he does impose on his immoral forms of behaviour depend solely on the ethical principles that he has managed to grasp during his early childhood.

Even though the static character may be unscrupulous in matters of ethical and moral behaviour, he still, surprisingly enough, cares about how other persons view him and how they subsequently judge his character. Accordingly, some static characters essentially possess two personas. One persona truly reflects the nature of his soul, while the other persona is fundamentally a misrepresentation of his soul. In fact, the static character's public persona usually does not clearly reveal his feelings of anger and hatred towards some person, or group of individuals. He adopts a public persona in an effort to mask his pessimistic emotions, and this enables him to function within his society according to the stereotype of that of a regular or ordinary civilian.

This is how serial killers are able to commit multiple offences. During their childhood, the serial killer has not acquired any values towards other forms of life. When his authoritative behaviour becomes rejected by other persons, he will then develop a form of grudge. In time, his feelings of anger will accumulate, and since he has lacked all forms of spiritual development, he will be capable of committing the most gruesome crimes. This is the worst case scenario in relation to the static character. These individuals are bounded by no moral virtues. Moreover, these individuals will stop at nothing to achieve the power and control that they desire.

In the majority of cases, persons who are personally acquainted with this type of criminal will not suspect that he is guilty of any crime. It takes multiple instances of this crime before policing authorities can gain enough evidence, which will enable them to focus their investigation towards the true perpetrator. Consequently, the serial killer places importance on his public persona. Essentially, he has learned to hide his feelings of anger to the point where he possesses the ability to "blend himself in" within the general public. On the surface, he portrays the image that he is just another innocent, law-abiding citizen. Nevertheless, during private times, his feelings of anger overwhelm him. Accordingly, even the most vulgar criminals can look innocent within the public setting. Those who appear to be guiltless can be guilty of the most senseless crimes.

The most hardened static character feels no sense of remorse after he hurts another form of life. He will only appear to be remorseful after he is judged to be responsible for his crimes. Hence, the criminal only communicates feelings of sorrow to evoke feelings of mercy from the general public. Similarly, he only expresses remorse before he is punished for his crimes, merely to lessen the degree of his punishment. After his punishment is complete, he may also act remorseful to take on the role as a rehabilitated criminal. He knows that if the general public perceives him as someone who is likely to reoffend, he will have lost all potential to be respected within his community. In essence, then, the static character uses feelings of remorse as a tool that will enable him to enter into a higher social class, where he will subsequently gain some degree of respect. Thus, he uses remorse mainly to further his primary motive in life.

The latter individual is the gravest criminal who possesses very few fears. This is due to the fact that feelings of fear will deter most forms of criminal behaviour. Fears of retribution or incarceration are the only things that limit the static character from materializing the lawless feelings that reside within his psyche. He only picks innocent victims, whom he does not fear, during his quest for power and control. Accordingly, this is how the gravest criminals are born into our society. When he successfully gains some form of control over another individual, he will then develop some understanding that may negate his intrinsic personal fears. His intrinsic fears will return, though, after the general public establishes a concrete understanding regarding the true nature of his soul.

This static character also loves havoc and mayhem, because he feels more powerful whenever any forms of social disorder occur.

Within a democratic society, the static character usually does not challenge the principles that define this kind of political system. He merely seeks an extremist account of democratic principles to further his own personal cause. In general, the static character usually wishes to abolish principles that provide aid to some social minority group. When he is not successful in this undertaking, he will merely seek to disrupt the order within a well-functioning or harmonious political system. Both modes of action provide the static character with an intensified feeling of authority, which is what primarily motivates him to enter into the realm of politics.

Static characters who become political protestors are motivated to create a disunited society by abandoning their society's political system, in favour of an opposing kind of system. Within a democratic society, the protestor will advocate for reforms based on an unreasonable welfare state. Likewise, within a communist society, the protestor seeks liberation from policies that, only in the mind of persons with a static character, are grave injustices within the realm of individualistic freedoms. Therefore, the static protestor also adopts an extremist political stance, not for the betterment of his society, but merely because he wishes to gain political authority within his society.

Actually, the existence of checks and balances, within any given political system, is necessary for the best possible community. Many ethicists also push for conflicting political interests within their society. However, ethicists seek to provide order within their society, while the static character's motives are aimed towards the creation of a disordered society. These motivations differentiate persons with a static personality from all other persons within their community.

In a static character's frame of mind, the flaws he observes within a particular political system will directly conflict with the core values that are implemented by his society. Consequently, the static character seeks to create an aggressive opposition against common moral values. When successful, the static character will be responsible for the creation of policies that do not truly benefit his society. After this occurs, the property of disunity will be attributed to a society's political system, and this enables the static character to potentially acquire higher degrees of authority within his society. These additional policies may seemingly be beneficial, while in actuality, they merely extend the power and control of the static character over his community.

Some static characters hold the belief that they lack forms of liberty, essentially because their immaterial soul is confined within a material body. In these instances, the static character remains in a constant state of derangement, due solely to his physical and material attributes. He is unhappy with his physical beauty, or he may be unhappy with other kinds of defects that he perceives in himself. When this person views the world, it is through a state of immeasurable anger. In essence, he holds the belief that the nature of his material body limits his ability to gain any forms of authority. When he does not possess any kinds of authority, he then views himself to belong to a lower-class. As a consequence, he will then spend some time contemplating about an act of suicide. In his mind, the latter choice of action may be the only solution that will enable him to free himself from his limited physical existence.

After a prolonged period of meditation, the static character will eventually come to realize that persons who do commit suicide do so because of their personal weaknesses. Accordingly, since his main objective in life is to gain authority, he reasons that an act of suicide will reveal his personal weaknesses to other persons, which, in turn, will hinder, impede and essentially dissolve the last remnants of his quest for social authority. Instead, he then develops into a kind of bully who utilizes psychological, emotional or physical kinds of abuse. He attacks the weaknesses he perceives in other persons essentially to rationalize the fact that, within his own mind, other persons also possess forms of personal weaknesses that are comparable to his own. Hence, he believes that, through the act of bullying, he is actively increasing his social class from that of a weak individual, into one that possesses a negative form of power over other persons, which is based mainly on the concepts of fear and intimidation.

Even when the bully comes to realize that his negative power is actually superficial, he becomes hardened and will never stop his immoral behaviour. The superficial power that he experiences is greater than no forms of social authority at all. Therefore, this power also provides him with a false sense of security, which enables him to perceive himself as a person without any weaknesses. It is only the case when he faces justice for his forms of abuse when he actually realizes that he has decreased his social status to an even lower standard. Since the bully's acts of abuse are based on thoughts of desperation, his latter feelings will merely escalate and become compounded.

After the bully begins to realize that he possesses no true forms of authority, he may raise his level of abuse over other victims. Nonetheless, this marks a second episode related to his suicidal frame of mind. In effect, the static character eventually develops the awareness that he will gain no forms of social authority through his criminal acts. Due to his desperation, he then wishes to reinforce, within his own personal frame of mind, the notion that his criminal behaviour is both rational and justified. Subsequently, this enables him to rationalize the conception that he is truly a respectable member within his community. However, through his final act of desperation, he will permanently sequester himself from the rest of his peers.

In time, the level of abuse actualized by the majority of static characters will decrease, essentially due to the fact that they will be present in a total state of isolation. Feelings of loneliness, then, motivate them to seek a form of sympathy and forgiveness from the victims of their abuse. Indeed, social maturation plays a large role in this respect. The state of total isolation that he enters into grants the static character with the opportunity to reflect upon his actions and interactions with other persons. Nonetheless, he still does not experience any feelings of shame related to his acts of abuse. He only experiences feelings of regret, pertaining not to his abusive behaviour in general, but due solely to the consequences that will follow after he commits his acts of abuse. These feelings of regret only surface after the static character has faced some form of social justice within his community. Nonetheless, the static character still utilizes his feelings of guilt as a kind of tool. He expresses feelings of regret solely because he wants to be given another chance to re-enter his social sphere, which will subsequently cure his social isolation.

Hence, the static character also experiences no sense of shame when committing his criminal acts. When the average civilian is responsible for some form of transgression, he will naturally experience feelings of shame. If he hurts another individual, he may potentially experience a prolonged mental state of shame, until he has been forgiven. Nevertheless, most persons with a static character will lack all forms of a conscience. Some even lack the ability to perceive the differences between moral and immoral forms of behaviour. Others act ethically only during circumstances when they are granted a form of social authority.

After he enters into a state of desperation, the static character may eventually recognize the ruling cycle, pertaining to the law of hierarchy. At this stage, the bully will take responsibility for his acts of abuse, and he will seemingly accept the fact that he rightfully belongs to a lower social class. However, after some time where he has peacefully interacted with other persons, he will revert back into his original character. This usually occurs when he faces the regulated cycle of the law of hierarchy. In fact, he will abandon the law of hierarchy when it stops serving his personal needs for social contact.

In actuality, the static character's dominant persona usually remains constant throughout his entire life span. Therefore, if he subjugates himself and enters some collective, this usually occurs as a temporary act of desperation. Isolation causes loneliness, and this motivates him to grant some form of authority to the leader of an established collective. During these cases, the static character will acknowledge his flaws, related to his problem solving skills. He does this in the hope that he will receive a form of aid from the leader of this collective. However, after his specific problems are resolved, he may leave the collective to establish his own personal collective.

Indeed, the static character is a slave to his insecurities. Whenever his insecurities may be challenged, he will adopt an aggressive stance, in an effort to protect his personal vulnerabilities. Therefore, the static character lacks the virtue of courage, since he does not truly address his personal insecurities or fears. He also lacks the virtue of pacifism, due to the fact that he cannot control his emotions of anger. When this occurs, the true nature of the static character's personality will become apparent, and likewise, what specifically motivates him will become clearer, from the general public's perspective.

Therefore, the static character's thirst for power will usually override any other of his motivating desires. He is neither insightful, nor does he contribute anything positive towards his community. Within his society, he will look for flaws within the political and justice systems, in his effort to achieve authority. Nevertheless, the flaws that he discovers are never productive, but are always counterproductive. Indeed, he will possess more respect within a chaotic community, as opposed to an ordered and highly functional community.

Thus, the static character wishes for devastation and loss within his community, so that he may take advantage of another person's misfortune. In these cases, he will be successful in gaining the social authority that he seeks. Nonetheless, since he does not subscribe to the principle of equality, this attribute, alone, will mark the creation of his downfall. Through his perverted egotistical perspective, the static character will, by accident, exhibit his true limitations. The concept of higher and lower social classes will actually be materialized after the static character reveals his true personal ideologies. However, he will fail in his attempt to gain membership within a higher social class, because he will, unintentionally, reveal that his personal nature truly belongs to that of a lower social class.

The static character's lack of belief in the principle of equality will actually compound his original feelings of inferiority. Therefore, in this case, his lack of morals will actually work against his efforts to acquire some form of social respect. After this occurs, he will finally become personally aware of his total alienation from the entire general public.

When the static character eventually realizes and accepts his social status, feelings of anger will ultimately replace his motivation for power. At this stage, his feelings of anger may spiral into an uncontrollable state, and thus, he will then adopt the concept of revenge as his primary motivation in life. When this occurs, the static character will be, even more so, negating any forms of liberty or freedom that he may have previously possessed. Likewise, because he is consumed with vengeance, any of his antecedent personal characteristics will have been lost. If he chooses to commit criminal acts, he will have evolved into a formal enemy of the general public, and he will then be subject to the principles of justice that exist within every community.

Whether the static character ever recovers from this agitated personal state of anger depends on each individual situation. If he fails to control his emotions of anger, his emotional state may elevate into a constant and continual state of hatred. He may then shun all forms of conventions or laws that have been established within his particular community. Most persons who act upon their feelings of hatred will enter into the lowest possible social class, as they will be rejected by all other upstanding citizens that belong to our entire civilization.

After the static character enters into a state of hatred, he will threaten the general public through acts of terrorism, against some specific group of civilians. To achieve his goal, he will not be bounded by any forms of common principles. Rather, fear is the main weapon that is used by this individual. It is through inciting the emotion of fear where the static character regains a form of social authority.

In addition, the static character will also come to realize that his imperfections, based on anger and hate, are actually his greatest traits, since it is through these kinds of vices where he will gain the kind of social authority that is rare, yet, within his frame of mind, still acceptable. Nevertheless, within the public realm, he will seek to hide these personal imperfections, essentially so that he may be perceived to be an ordinary citizen, which enables him to freely enter into a communal environment. On the contrary, he also realizes that his personal weaknesses could still provide an avenue of attack, from other static characters. This would lead to his subjugation, instead of a position with authority. Therefore, he is motivated to resort to some form of terrorism, both for the purpose of gaining authority and also for the purpose of self-defence from other persons who may be seeking a similar form of authority over him.

In other instances, the static character will cause mischief in an effort to amuse himself. These instances occur when the static character possesses no hope to achieve any other forms of social authority. Instead of waiting for his lifetime to expire, the static character will pass the time by engaging in activities that will cure his personal feelings of boredom and isolation. His only true friend may be another individual who possesses a similar mental state. If he achieves this feat, he will finally discover some form of personal comfort. In most cases he does not, however, because of his inability to form compromises with other persons.

Yet, the drive for authority still remains in all static characters. When one static character achieves authority over another, this relationship is not usually permanent. The subordinate individual is mainly motivated to learn how to gain forms of authority, and subsequently, mimic his master. In time, when he gains the opportunity to achieve a higher form of social authority, he will then betray his master. The static character will then leave his master, to find a subordinate of his own. An indefinite cycle of betrayal then ensues, where one static character both achieves and then loses a form of authority over his peer.

An act of betrayal will cause deep feelings of animosity between two static characters. This animosity results in a permanent state of enmity between these individuals. A continual feud will ensue whenever they come into contact with one another. Nonetheless, within their rationale, this war will not end after their physical existence. In essence, the same battle of wits will continue after their physical deaths. Therefore, an astral war will result, where both individuals will continue to compete for the highest forms of respect, and the status of a monarch.

Successively, the static character's end goal is to suppress life. He possesses the constant fear that he will be outdone within his lifetime. When he is outdone, he will seek revenge. In these cases, the static character experiences no true intrinsic forms of happiness. He is motivated first by anger, then by jealousy, and when he lacks the ability to gain some form of happiness, he will seek to reduce the feelings of happiness in other persons, either through insult or physical injury.

His life will be devoid from all forms of happiness, essentially because of his unsuccessful quest for power and control.

The static character places the utmost importance on his public image. He values physical appearances due to his belief that those who possess physical beauty should be privileged within their society, and that they also deserve special treatment. Nonetheless, the static character acts instinctively, according to his dominant personality trait. Similar to a species of wildlife, he will not consider alternative modes of action that may differ from his particular paradigm of behaviour. He merely acts and reacts.

When both isolated and bored, the static character loses a form of confidence, related to his ultimate claim for authority over other individuals. He will only regain this confidence if he finds another person that will submit to his authority. Every static character desires social authority because of his inferiority complex. The static character believes that the possession of social authority will camouflage his personal imperfections, into a kind of perfection. However, the static character is highly intolerant, with respect to his personal imperfections. Therefore, the static character faces a constant internal struggle, as his struggle to tolerate his own imperfections may essentially govern his entire demeanour. A lack of ability to tolerate one's own imperfections is an intrinsic, yet hidden motivation with every static character's frame of mind. Initially, the static character directs his will towards gaining some form of social authority. When he is denied such authority, he will utilize forms of abuse, be it physical, psychological or emotional, in an effort to gain the power that he failed to acquire during times of peace. Consequently, anger is a primary emotion that motivates all of his violent acts. In essence, the static character will use violence as his only means for obtaining a form of respect from other persons. Yet, those who hurt other persons deserve no forms of admiration. As a consequence, when he is not granted this form of recognition, he will redirect his will towards the specific actions that will generate feelings of anger or disgust, in those individuals who failed to show him any kinds of respect. After this continuous cycle of abuse, he will seek appeasement in return for a form of peaceful coexistence. Even if this were to be granted, due to his endless and continual pursuit for social authority, the life of the static character will still be destined to be a life filled with personal wars and conflict. Only through the activation of social justice will the static character realize that his fits of abuse are incompatible with a civil society. Following the aftermath, he is fated to experience a lifetime of solitude and isolation.

8   The Dynamic Character

SIMILAR TO THE STATIC CHARACTER, persons who possess a dynamic character also possess a dominant personality trait. Hence, these kinds of individuals will mainly rely on either their intellect, centre of emotions, or array of principles during their interactions with other persons. Nonetheless, the dynamic character differs from the static character in that his dominant personality trait does not reign supreme over the other two elements of his mind. In essence, the dynamic character acknowledges the law of hierarchy, in that there does exist a form of unison between all three elements in his soul. During social interactions, it is this form of harmony that governs the relationship between two dynamic characters.

In other words, when the static character interacts with other individuals, he will mainly utilize either his intellect, emotional centre, or array of principles, depending on which element is the dominating element of his mind. Nevertheless, the dynamic character utilizes all three elements of his soul, during the bulk of his social interactions, even though he also possesses a dominant personality trait. In his relationships, it is the harmony produced through the law of hierarchy that governs his interactions with other persons.

The dynamic character is not motivated to gain any forms of social authority in his interactions with other persons. Rather, he utilizes the law of hierarchy in an effort to maturate and evolve his personal identity. The dynamic character is primarily motivated to gain both the truth, and affection. With respect to the truth, the dynamic character seeks a greater understanding of our physical universe. With respect to affection, he seeks to be both the producer and the receiver of differing kinds of love. When we combine knowledge with passion, the dynamic character's end goal is to work towards some form of goodness. Subsequently, rectitude is mainly achieved when two individuals interact with each other through a dynamic fashion.

The dynamic character utilizes the law of hierarchy, during his social interactions, to both teach and also to learn from other individuals. The specific act depends on the cycle that is being utilized. If the individual is utilizing the ruling cycle in his interactions, he will usually be taking the role as a teacher. Likewise, if the individual is interacting by way of the regulated cycle, he will usually be taking on the role as a learner. Thus, the specific act that each individual is responsible for, when conducting interactions through the law of hierarchy, determines his role as either a teacher or a learner.

In other cases, the interactions between two individuals will be based solely on a single element of the mind. For instance, both persons may be solely utilizing their intellect during a particular conversation. Within this conversation, neither individual will utilize either his centre of emotions or array of principles. In these cases, there may be two possible circumstances. Either both individuals are engaged in a peaceful and cooperative interaction, or contrarily, they are engaged in a hostile and competitive battle of the wits.

If these individuals are interacting through a peaceful method, then both persons will take on the roles of both a teacher and a learner. Thus, under this particular circumstance, the interaction between two intellects will essentially become an exchange of knowledge. Likewise, when two persons are freely exchanging knowledge with each other, they are necessarily interacting through a cooperative manner.

In direct opposition, it is possible that two individuals, who are solely basing their interactions through the intellect, may be communicating in a hostile manner. In essence, the battle of the intellects reflects upon a competition of wits. The individual who possesses more knowledge, within his intellect, will win this competition. In theory, the individual who has won this competition will have achieved a kind of dominance over the other individual.

It is also possible that two individuals may be interacting with each other solely through their respective emotional centres. Whenever this occurs, this specific interaction will always be based on feelings of love. Actually, the concept of love is both an action and an emotion. People who interact with each other solely through their feelings and emotions are simultaneously discovering personal vulnerabilities in their partner, and they are also revealing their own. This exchange of knowledge only occurs between two individuals who have built a relationship through feelings of comfort, and the principle of trust. Therefore, when two individuals interact with each other solely through their centre of emotions, each person is gaining more knowledge, with respect to the intrinsic makeup of his partner's soul.

A social interaction may also be based solely on each individual's array of principles. When this occurs, both individuals are actively engaged in an exchange of spirit. With respect to spirit, each individual possesses a unique set of values, both on a qualitative and a quantitative level. Therefore, unique individuals will possess a differing set of principles, and each principle within this set will vary according to some kind of degree. For example, some individual may experience feelings of compassion, but due to his age and lack of experience, he may lack a similar degree of compassion towards children. He may only develop stronger feelings of compassion towards children after he marries and has children of his own. Accordingly, an exchange of spirit is based on the same basic model. When two individuals interact with each other solely through a spiritual manner, both persons will attain a higher spiritual awareness that may be based on a qualitative level, a quantitative level, or both.

Even when engaged in a mutual exchange, whether it is based on intellectual, emotional or spiritual knowledge, the dynamic character will still end his interactions through the law of hierarchy. This is what makes him dynamic. In actuality, through this latter act, the dynamic character is mainly expressing his gratitude towards a pleasant experience. If he is expressing gratitude through the ruling cycle, he is communicating a form of indebted gratitude. For example, in an exchange of emotional knowledge, the individual would be expressing gratitude through an intellectual nature. On the other hand, if he is expressing gratitude through the regulated cycle, he will be doing so through a spiritual manner. In this latter instance, he is communicating a form of sincere gratitude. The differences between these two forms of gratitude are slight. Yet, any forms of gratitude indicate that the individual has enjoyed this particular interaction, and that he will be looking forward towards similar exchanges of knowledge at some future time.

Therefore, the dynamic character always recognizes the law of hierarchy. He is different from the static character in that he is always evolving, and subsequently, he rarely portrays a rigid or stubborn attitude during his interactions with other persons. The dynamic character also recognizes the fact that every soul is unique, and that every circumstance is different. He additionally recognizes the fact that many forms of knowledge are both subjective and relative. Knowledge, within a subjective perspective, is anything that the individual believes is true. Therefore, in his quest to acquire subjective knowledge, the dynamic character is always motivated by the virtue of empathy.

Subjective knowledge is gained through the combination of experience, and the operations within the intellect that transforms the individual's physical experiences into immaterial ideas. Even under an exact representation of physical circumstances, two individual's personal experiences will remain unique. For instance, within the same classroom, every student physically perceives the same lecture. Nonetheless, within each student's mind, a distinct set of ideas will be successively produced. This may be due to the unique nature of each student's intellect. One student may possess a relatively short attention span, while another student may possess the ability to focus on his professor's entire lecture. Similarly, forms of misunderstandings will also be unique to each individual. A third student may experience confusion during the beginning of the lecture, while a fourth student may not comprehend the final point of the lecture. This phenomenon is what makes subjective knowledge, within each individual's frame of mind, exclusive and entirely unique.

Within the law of hierarchy, the ruling cycle denotes knowledge and truth finding. Accordingly, when a learner uses the ruling cycle as a response to some specific interaction, he is acknowledging a concrete form of understanding, pertaining to the details within a specific conversation. On the other hand, if he responds through the regulated cycle, he may be indicating the fact that he requires further clarification, with respect to the topic of a specific conversation. Accordingly, the interactions between two dynamic characters are always based on a mode of communication that is governed by the law of hierarchy.

In the teacher's frame of mind, a ruling response, within a particular conversation, is mainly used to convey a specific idea within the learner's psyche. The teacher will then continue to utilize the ruling method, until the learner grasps the point of their conversation. When the learner does acknowledge a certain degree of understanding, the just teacher will then utilize a regulated form of response, specifically to acknowledge the latter fact. The dynamic interactions between two individuals merely materialize the emotions of compassion within the teacher, and the act of comprehension within the learner.

The main purpose of the law of hierarchy, within specific social interactions, is not to create a division of classes. Rather, it is used to indicate a specific degree of understanding, relevant to the topic at hand. Persons become dynamic whenever they understand and then utilize new forms of knowledge. This is quite evident in all dynamic learners. However, the teacher is also dynamic, in the case of his personal experiences. When the teacher encounters new students, he will have completed a form of mentorship that enables him to grow not intellectually, but through a spiritual manner.

Reason is the primary intellectual component that connects two dynamic characters together. Initially, each individual possesses subjective knowledge, in that his form of knowledge is based on his personal point of view. For example, consider the person who suffers from dyslexia. Whenever I perceive the letter "R", it is in its truest form. However, when the individual with dyslexia perceives this letter, he may see "Я" instead. This illustrates the definition of subjective knowledge. Subjective knowledge is based on the kinds of information that the individual believes is true, even though this information may be entirely false. In contrast, objective knowledge is based on forms of subjective knowledge that have been confirmed by another individual, because a similar or equivalent idea exists within this other person's intellect.

When two individuals meet and exchange their subjective knowledge, and they possess ideas that are consistent with one another, objective knowledge may be potentially produced. Fundamentally, objective knowledge marks a kind of knowledge that, at the very least, has some rational truth. This is due to the fact that every person exercises a unique and distinct focus, with respect to his faculty of imagination. Coincidences are always possible, yet when two distinct individuals possess a highly equivalent idea within their intellect, we must consider the fact that this common idea was produced by some feature within the physical world, as opposed to being solely created through the individual's imagination. Accordingly, we must distinguish the source of our common ideas in order to evaluate its truth value.

In the case where two dynamic characters have coincidently imagined the same idea, it is possible that this idea may then be false. In order to evaluate its truth value, these individuals must discover some kind of evidence, found within our material world, to corroborate their shared idea. If they do produce some form of concrete evidence that substantiates their claims, then this idea is essentially true, and it can then be considered to be a form of objective knowledge.

Therefore, every piece of objective knowledge is necessarily true, because it has been proven to be true. Contrarily, some forms of subjective knowledge are liable to be false, since it originates through a biased perspective. Indeed, when two persons share a similar idea that is false, their common opinion must also be considered as subjective knowledge. Therefore, it is entirely possible that an entire class of citizens may be mistaken about a common ideology that has yet to be proven true.

At this point, one may ask how it is possible to transform forms of personal subjective knowledge into concrete forms of objective knowledge. The answer to this question lies solely in our faculty of reason. Subjective knowledge is based solely on private concepts and sensations. Consider the sensation of taste. Is it possible for any individual to describe the difference between the Kona and Arabica coffee bean? Sure, I may voice the fact that one bean may have a stronger taste, while the other may provide a more powerful aroma. Nevertheless, can I describe this taste, or communicate this aroma? The ability to describe what coffee actually tastes like lies well beyond our intrinsic powers. Yet, the dynamic character does not consider any of these kinds of limitations when he interacts with another individual. He merely makes due with the intellectual faculties that he does possess, and this provides him with a strong enough backing, which enables him to discover the truth.

In fact, there is no way for me to know, with one hundred percent certainty, that my sensation of coffee is exactly similar to my partner's sensation. I merely view the feelings of pleasure that my partner experiences, and I come to the realization that my personal experiences are essentially the same. This form of awareness is produced through the operation of deduction, which can only be generated through my faculty of reason. Thus, it is through my faculty of reason, alone, where my subjective knowledge of coffee changes into a form of objective knowledge.

When I view that my partner experiences similar feelings of enjoyment, I will, by nature, also assume that his particular experience is similar to my own. For that reason, when there is an agreement of feelings between two or more parties, our instances of subjective knowledge usually turns into objective knowledge. Nonetheless, when we interact with a third party, it is possible that this individual's subjective knowledge may be inconsistent with ours. In this case, there is a lack of agreement between this individual's experiences, in comparison to our own. During this interaction, three possibilities may result. First, it may be the case that the subjective knowledge that I share with my partner is truly correct, in which case we will enter into the role of a teacher. Secondly, it may be the case that the other individual's subjective knowledge is correct, in which case we will enter into the role as a learner. Thirdly, it may be the case that our subjective knowledge and the other individual's subjective knowledge are both objectively incorrect. In the latter case, all three of us will essentially become students who seek the objective truths that we failed to comprehend through our own merit.

Accordingly, even though my partner and I believed that we had discovered an objective truth, when this knowledge conflicts with another person's subjective knowledge, we must entertain the possibility that our agreed knowledge could be false. This is the essential lifestyle of the dynamic character. We interact with our peers in an effort to discover the objective truths that govern our physical world. All of our subjective knowledge remains unverified, until this knowledge is agreed upon on a universal basis. Likewise, any forms of objective knowledge that may be held by some kind of collective principally turns into a belief, if this knowledge is not commonly verified on a universal basis.

The main problem relevant to objective knowledge is based on the difficulties that may be faced when an individual is trying to obtain the objective truth. The ignorant person will mainly possess subjective knowledge that conflicts with the objective truths that may be established within any given community. In actuality, all forms of objective knowledge are dependent on the individual's faculty of reason. Hence, those persons who lack a rational frame of mind will never be able to discover the many objective truths that exist in our world. This is due to the fact that any degree of collaboration and mutual aid depends on the rational faculties of each individual, who is a member of a specific social circle. Without reason, there are no forms of "joint efforts" nor are there any forms of "common goals". In a collective of irrational persons, their interactions will be primarily based on their self-serving motivations.

Another problem may be based on a persistent lack of agreement between two feasible theories of knowledge. Within any given community, there may be divisions, within the populous, who believe in conflicting theories of knowledge. In some cases, we must rely on those who are most knowledgeable within some specific subject matter. In other words, we must rely on those who have legitimately become experts within a precise field of interest. It is possible that only ten percent of the population may be experts, within any given field, who endorse a specific theory. The other ninety percent of the population may be laymen, who believe in a conflicting theory. Through our faculty of judgment, it may be most rational to assume that the experts are the most dependable community of persons who have knowledge of the objective truth, even though they are a minority group. After we judge the credentials of both groups, the most rational decision we may take may be to believe in those persons who possess the most personal experiences, relevant to the particular topic at hand.

Indeed, when forms of subjective knowledge are tainted with personal bias and self-interest, this form of knowledge usually results in a misunderstanding. Actually, many persons make the mistake of turning their assumptions into what they personally believe is objective knowledge. When the individual stubbornly remains within his subjective viewpoint, his subjective knowledge will be highly vulnerable to criticism. Persons may only grasp the objective truths that exist in our world, when they perceive the world through an evolving frame of mind. Through the method of dynamics, the character will continue to develop and work towards discovering those objective truths, many of which may be, at present times, currently unknown to man.

In addition to gaining the objective truths that may be found within our world, the dynamic character is also motivated by feelings of affection. The birth of affection comes about through the will to understand another person's subjective experiences. When this application of the will becomes reciprocated, a form of friendship will then be established. In fact, there is no way to confirm that my experience with the Kona bean is precisely equivalent to my partner's personal experience. Ideologically, the only unequivocal way that I may gain this understanding would be based on the possibility where I could leave my body and enter into my partner's body, through an exchange of our souls. Nonetheless, I do not possess this kind of intrinsic power, and thus, I must rely on my faculty of language to gain a qualitatively lower degree of this kind of understanding.

What motivates me to understand the subjective experiences of my partner can only come about through the emotion of love. In theory, it is possible that my sensation of the Kona bean may be entirely different from another person's sensation. However, I must ask myself what intrinsically motivates me to gain this objective truth? When I travel to the coffee shop, do I really care to experience the sensations of any ordinary stranger? I would expect that the majority of persons would agree with me, in that my answer to this question would be no. Yet, there does exist that kind of motivation in me, when I focus on those individuals who have gained membership into my own personal social circle.

I am motivated to gain an understanding of my partner's subjective experiences, essentially because of my feelings of affection. When I experience specific instances of pleasure, I wish that my partner will experience an equivalent form of pleasure. Similarly, if my partner experiences discomfort, I want to understand the source of this discomfort. This is due my sympathetic spirit. I am motivated to understand my partner's subjective knowledge simply because I want to gain a more detailed understanding, regarding the true nature of her immaterial soul.

However, the partner that I do choose can never be any mere outsider. I am not motivated to understand the spiritual existence of any recluse that I may meet on the street. In fact, the nature of my partner's soul will always be quite complex. My partner will possess some kind of dominating element within her soul. To discover this knowledge, I will first require the virtue of patience, in addition to a wealth of time. Yet, since my physical lifespan is finite, I do not possess an unlimited amount of time to gain experiences within our material world. This factor motivates me to shorten my social circle, essentially because it may be impossible to gather a true and concrete spiritual understanding of the entire general public.

When I discover the dominating element of my partner's soul, I will be in the position to gain a more in depth understanding, with respect to the unique form of harmony that exists within her soul. The three elements of her soul will be governed by the law of hierarchy. Nevertheless, the nature of this relationship will vary on an individual basis. In one set of circumstances, my partner may utilize the ruling cycle during her dynamic interactions. In another, she will use the regulated cycle. My ability to understand the harmony, within her soul, will most definitely take some amount of time. This kind of understanding can only be acquired through our dynamic interactions.

Thus, dynamic interactions mainly provide the individual with an understanding, with respect to the nature of another person's subjective knowledge. In some cases, this will result in the acquisition of objective knowledge. In other cases, this will result in a sympathetic exchange of subjective knowledge. Yet, a form of mutual respect is always necessary before two individuals decide to exchange their subjective knowledge. This respect is gathered through a preliminary judgment of character, and it continues through experiences of admiration.

In its simplest form, knowledge is based on the individual's perspective of the world. When we compare the knowledge obtained by the common civilian, in comparison to the knowledge acquired by a quietly observing crow, the most fundamental discrepancies remain in their unique perspectives. Even if this crow could articulate a particular perspective of our natural world, its subjective knowledge may be false within the perspective of the common citizen. This is why a great deal of human knowledge remains subjective. Both this particular crow and the common civilian perceive the world through a differing point of view. In theory, persons with differing forms of subjective knowledge may rigidly retain their false beliefs, because their perspective of the natural world remains entirely constant. In all likelihood, these particular individuals may never attain a degree of objective knowledge that will possess the potential to change their particular standpoint.

Accordingly, subjective knowledge only becomes downgraded into either a belief, or a misunderstanding, within the mind of the dynamic character. It is through his dynamic interactions with other persons where he gains an understanding that his particular perspective of the world differs from that of other persons. As a consequence, the objective truth will remain as a mystery in the minds of persons who are isolated from established social networks, or entire communities. Since he is motivated by his quest to gain both knowledge and affection, the dynamic character always seeks to gain membership within differing forms of networks and communities.

When the dynamic character seeks to enter into a particular social network, he is mainly motivated by the emotion of pride. With respect to differing nations around the world, every country possesses a unique culture that is established through differing moral values. When the individual chooses to visit a specific country, he is not merely observing the forms of natural beauty that may be present within a particular society. Actually, many differing nations possess similar environmental features, such as mountains, beaches, or a particular climate type. Within the dynamic character's frame of mind, the location that he chooses to visit will also be based on the robust cultural elements that define it. Accordingly, the dynamic character's motive to gain subjective knowledge, of a specific culture, also plays a role in his choice.

Similar to nations, differing social networks are also established by persons who possess the same core values. Therefore, the dynamic character chooses a particular network, or community, essentially because of its cultural properties. The main factor that determines his choice is based on the similarities between his own core values and the values of a particular group. The dynamic character chooses groups based on similar values because he wishes to develop certain elements, within his soul, that have thus far remained undeveloped. Common values serve to bind two distinct individuals together, because of the fact that all human beings are social creatures. When two individuals pursue common goals, it may be highly difficult for one person to commit a transgression against the other. As a consequence, the dynamic character continually matures and develops through these particular social interactions. The culture he chooses will provide him with the opportunity to develop some specific element within his soul, according to his own particular volitions.

Thus, when he seeks to learn new cultural elements, the dynamic character will be motivated by emotions of pride. The dynamic character must first possess a form of self-love in relation to his soul, in order to properly develop it. Contrarily, individuals who do not possess this kind of self-love will never seek to improve, nor cultivate their soul. Persons who loathe the intrinsic nature of their soul may never form a bond with those persons who possess a similar spiritual nature. Therefore, the establishment of thriving communities, which possess distinct cultures, are produced through the elements of pride, within all of its members. Through his choosing, the dynamic character is both motivated by pride, and he also wishes to acquire a unique form of pride that exists within some other culture.

Subsequently, self-love provides the fundamental foundation behind all forms of friendships. Individuals who experience the emotion of pride will naturally relate to other persons who possess comparable personal characteristics. This relationship will continue to grow and evolve in cases where both individuals discover more spiritual similarities with each other. In the qualitatively highest forms of friendships, the individual will not only gain an understanding of his partner's intrinsic soul, but he will additionally gain forms of objective knowledge, whenever his personal subjective knowledge resembles his partner's subjective knowledge. Likewise, if the individual is lacking knowledge in a particular subject matter, he will gain forms of subjective knowledge that have been attained by his partner. In essence, then, all friendships are based on an exchange of knowledge. Nevertheless, mutual feelings of affection are primarily necessary before any exchange of knowledge takes place.

During the highest forms of partnerships, the dynamic character may be motivated to live an even greater life. Both individuals may wish to further their feelings of affection towards the care of a child. The first attribute of this greater life comes in the form of a newer kind of social dynamic. In caring for a child, the individual is essentially taking on a newer social role, in the form of a responsible caretaker. The dynamic character always takes responsibility over his children, essentially due to the fact that he is the physical cause of their existence. Yet, when he fails as a caretaker, this usually reflects upon his limited intellect, and the finite scope of his intrinsic spirit.

The second attribute of this greater life comes in the form of providing a greater life for another individual. When the caretaker improves upon the parenting skills of his father, he is essentially providing a qualitatively higher standard of living for the next generation. The dynamic character then furthers his feelings of pride, due solely to the feelings of satisfaction that he attains when he is successful in this undertaking. Essentially, he takes pride in the fact that he has created a better world for his children, in comparison to the world that he lived in throughout his childhood.

In his effort to discover the objective truth, the dynamic character will exhibit sympathy towards the subjective knowledge of other individuals. This is due to the fact that he learns through both his own experiences, and the experiences of other persons. Accordingly, the dynamic character's ability to become sympathetic reflects upon the fact that he gathers knowledge through the paradigm of reason. It is through his faculty of reason where the dynamic character will realize that the experiences of other persons could be relevant to his own. During the majority of his social interactions, the faculty of reason remains as the most dominating element behind his continuous acquisition of more knowledge.

Contrarily, when interacting with a static character, the dynamic character learns mainly through these specific experiences. Within these interactions, both parties will demonstrate problems while utilizing their faculty of cognition. Fundamentally, this faculty will remain underutilized during the bulk of their social interactions. Thus, when comparing the subjective knowledge attained by a static character, the dynamic character will usually come to realize many inconsistencies. This phenomenon illustrates the fact that the static character acquires subjective knowledge through a completely divergent mindset.

In fact, it is possible that the mindset of many static characters will elude comprehension. No dynamic characters will express conceit, nor will any dynamic character adopt the vice of vanity. Hence, no dynamic character will pass judgement on other persons, based solely on either their physical appearances or imperfections. The discriminatory mindset possessed by the static character illustrates the fact that his actions are never motivated by any forms of virtue. Rather, the static character is fundamentally motivated by some form of vice.

In contrast, the dynamic character mainly views personal imperfections as a form of beauty. Within his frame of mind, an individual's personal imperfections denote uniqueness, which distinguishes two individuals who may be born with similar physical attributes. In fact, the concept of individuality could not exist without our personal imperfections. A community comprised entirely of perfect beings would lack a substantial degree of individuality. Within this theoretical community, every person would also lack the quality of being distinct. Hence, within this community, no dynamic character would possess the motivation to understand another person's subjective experiences, simply because this kind of knowledge would essentially be repetitive and unenlightening.

In addition to knowledge and affection, the dynamic character also values certain worldly elements that constitute his chosen environment. Imagine the case that I am entering into retirement. I see an ad in the newspaper, where there is an island for sale. If I sell all of my assets, I will have enough funds to purchase this island, and live securely on it for the duration of my life. We will call this habitat Yoshi's island.

Actually, Yoshi's island does not, as of yet, have a physical existence. It only exists within my personal thoughts. If you were to enter into this circumstance, how would you envision this island? Where is its location? In my mind, it would exist somewhere in the Caribbean, where there is plenty of sunshine. However, instead of the tropics, perhaps you would prefer an island within the temperate zones, where all four seasons take their turn. In a similar fashion, some persons may choose an area near the Arctic or Antarctic, where there is an abundance of snow.

The next question we must address will be based on the material properties found within Yoshi's island. Does it possess a multitude of trees? What kind of trees? In my mind, I would prefer all kinds of trees that bear fruit. Yet, some persons may prefer a rainforest, with a large beach and a range of mountains. Furthermore, we must also consider what kinds of wildlife will be present within this habitat. I imagine an island filled with an assortment of birds and a few champion equestrian horses. Perhaps other individuals may prefer an island filled purely with dogs and cats.

The last question, though, is of most importance. Imagine an island solely comprised of your loved ones. Who are these people? In my mind, I would like to share this habitat with my life partner. Nonetheless, some persons would also include their parents, and others would include their children. Equally, some persons would include their siblings and close friends. The answer to this question essentially reflects upon the main function of our centre of emotions. It is through our emotions where we come to understand what we truly value in our lives. It is through our emotional centre where we define the specific properties that encompass Yoshi's island. Our distinct definition of Yoshi's island contains all of the material phenomena that may be found on our planet, which we particularly value the most.

Everything on Yoshi's island are things on Earth that you cannot live without. From my perspective, I cannot live without sunshine, sweet fruit, and my wife. However, within your perspective, Yoshi's island will differ with respect to location, size, and clan. Accordingly, every person's conception of Yoshi's island basically represents some form of utopia, in relation to our physical existence. Without any single element, our physical existence on Earth would be incomplete.

Yoshi's island simply represents all possible kinds of worldly phenomena that are of utmost importance within the mind of a dynamic character. The dynamic character's basic and essential identity stems through all of the objects that exist on Yoshi's island. Dynamic characters that are complete will be intrinsically happy. Those who are incomplete will experience intervals of happiness, throughout their physical lifespan. The size of Yoshi's island also has some bearing over the dynamic character's feelings of happiness. Its size depends exclusively on its makeup. A larger island will be comprised of more properties and features, while a smaller island will be comprised of fewer elements. Persons with an idea of a larger island are likely to experience more instances of happiness, on a quantitative level. In contrast, those who imagine a smaller island are more likely to experience higher forms of happiness, on a qualitative level.

One's conception of Yoshi's island reflects upon the individual's most valued elements, as it pertains to his physical existence. Nonetheless, what the dynamic character may not realize is the fact that he may also be a member of another dynamic character's conception of Yoshi's island. Therefore, the dynamic character, himself, will be a valued element within some other person's concept of Yoshi's island. Theoretically, if the individual were to expand his concept of Yoshi's island to include the conceptions of other persons with a dynamic character, who are related to him through this kind of membership, the island will multiply to an ever increasing size. When all of these properties are recognized, Yoshi's island could, in theory, encompass almost every instance of life that exists on the planet Earth.

Hence, it is through reason where the concept of cooperation is born. In turn, the concept of cooperation spawns friendships. Friendships, furthermore, provide the basis for civil society. Therefore, human civilization, as a whole, has been built upon our faculty of reason. Our civilization is the creation of rational human beings. Between rational persons, the law of hierarchy provides a blueprint for collaborative forms of action. Through this law, the dynamic character maintains a mindful attitude, and he reciprocates acts of love.

In a similar fashion, self-love also leads to companionships, and companionships lead to the acquisition of objective knowledge. After the dynamic character has reached a certain level of maturity, he will enter into his community as a responsible agent. Strictly under these circumstances will he utilize the objective knowledge that he has acquired thus far. In the end, he will be rewarded with intimacy, and a higher form of awareness.

9   The Formless Character

MOST PERSONS POSSESS only a single dominant personality trait. With respect to the formless character, these individuals will possess either two dominant personality traits, or they may lack a dominant personality trait altogether, where all three elements of their soul are utilized in an equivalent fashion. Spiritually, there is only a single dominating personality trait that defines every person's soul. Nevertheless, the individual's character is primarily defined through his actions. When we add free will as an intrinsic property of every soul, it is possible that the individual may contemplate and then act on choices that may be inconsistent with the true nature of his soul. Accordingly, it is through free will which enables the individual to negate the dominating element of his soul, in favour of a more balanced character. Individuals who possess the ability to adopt and utilize a second, or third, dominant personality trait should be properly characterized as having a formless character.

Individuals who possess a formless character do not appear to fit into the stereotype of either a static or dynamic character. Essentially, the formless static character will sometimes appear to possess a dynamic character, while the formless dynamic character will sometimes appear to possess a static character. It is this deviation between the individual's character and his soul that marks the birth of a formless character. Every formless character originally demonstrates either a static or dynamic character, during the early stages of his life. Subsequently, the acquisition of objective knowledge and major life experiences are wholly necessary in the development of a formless character.

Static characters that develop a formless character deviate from their habitual routines, while utilizing acts of mimicry in order to disguise the true nature of their souls. Actually, the static character is quite ignorant, and usually demonstrates a lack of understanding with respect to his less dominant personality traits. However, after his lack of success in the realm of acquiring social authority, the static character may then analyze his previous interactions with other persons. In an effort to become more successful, he may actively develop a second aspect of his soul.

For example, consider a hostile interaction between two static characters. One individual possesses a dominant intellect, while the other person possesses a dominant centre of emotions. Since, according to the law of hierarchy, the intellect governs the emotional centre, the static character who possesses a dominant intellect will win the bulk of their contests. The individual with a dominant centre of emotions may then analyze these particular interactions, so that he will be better prepared for any future altercations. Accordingly, he may eventually come to realize the fact that the intellect naturally governs the centre of emotions. As a consequence, he will then develop the intellectual part of his soul, primarily as a means of self-defence. After he has accomplished this feat, he will have acquired the means to protect himself from any further attacks against his intellect.

Nonetheless, in cases where the static character possesses two dominant personality traits, he may still be vulnerable to attack, with respect to the third element of his soul. For instance, the individual who possesses an underdeveloped array of principles may be susceptible to attack, with respect to a principle that he may lack. For that reason, the static character that lacks the principle of respect may, himself, become the object of disrespect. Other static characters may lack the principle of service. In these cases, their expectations to receive the most common or basic services may be denied. Likewise, individuals who lack the principle of humility may be automatically perceived to belong to a lower class. Consequently, the static character that lacks many forms of principled values will be vulnerable to attack, in relation to his distinct moral insufficiencies.

Other static characters may possess an underdeveloped intellect. These individuals are vulnerable to attack, in relation to their subjective and objective knowledge. Primarily, their belief system in relation to both forms of knowledge may be easily undermined. Similar to those who are lacking in spirit, this static character will be vulnerable to attack according to the deficiencies that he possesses within his intellect.

Those who lack the faculty of reason will also lack the ability to utilize logic, in their quest for objective knowledge. Furthermore, they will also experience troubles when conducting the operation of deduction. Other static characters may lack the faculty of cognition. These persons will experience problems while trying to acquire various forms of objective knowledge. The static character may also lack the faculty of judgment. These individuals lack a coherent understanding with respect to the spiritual nature of other persons. In the majority of these cases, this kind of static character may be guilty of underestimating the degree of power or authority that many other persons possess. Therefore, static characters with an underdeveloped intellect will fail to comprehend basic truths that may be commonly known within the general public.

    The last possible weakness of the static character may be exemplified in his underdeveloped emotional centre. These static characters have failed to develop emotions of resolve. Subsequently, these individuals will fail to establish any kinds of relationships based on the elements of devotion and trust. Some may maintain relationships based on convenience, in order to alleviate their mental states of boredom. Other static characters may lack emotions of courage. In these cases, the individual will moderate his natural tendencies and submit himself to some authority figure, due solely to his personal fears. These individuals will moderate their actions only during cases where they are overwhelmed by their subjective fears. In all other situations, the static character will study and then act upon the fears of other persons.

This is usually done in an effort to balance his inferior attributes with feelings of power or control.

Lastly, this kind of static character may further lack emotions of gracefulness. Under these circumstances, the individual will usually succumb to his feelings of anger. Correspondingly, he will possess the tendency to materialize his feelings of aggression, whenever he experiences challenges of any nature. The static character who does not develop his emotional centre will be destined to live a kind of life where he lacks a certain degree of freedom, because the majority of his actions are ultimately governed by his negative emotional states.

In general, the static formless character possesses an advantage, in his contests to gain a kind of tiered control over the average static character. This is due to the fact that the static character will never possess the ability to gain power or authority through his undeveloped character traits. Similarly, the static formless character will possess an additional dominant spiritual element, and this increases his possible avenues of attack.

These are reasons why the static character will develop another element of his soul. Basically, the main motivation behind his spiritual development remains in the fact that all static characters are, by their own liberty, mainly hostile individuals. During their hostile interactions, the static character, who possesses a single dominant spiritual element, will be vulnerable to attack by way of his two other underdeveloped spiritual elements. As a direct consequence, this static character will be motivated to develop that spiritual element which is most exposed to avenues of attack. This will make him a more arduous force during arguments and other forms of hostile interactions. In the development of the second aspect of his soul, he inherently possesses a greater ability to defend himself from the hostile actions of another static character.

Now consider the static character who develops both passive elements of his soul. For example, the individual who possesses both a dominant intellect and emotional centre may then wish to develop his array of principles. Nonetheless, we must ask what his primary motivations are under this circumstance. Is the static formless character developing the final aspect of his soul for the similar motive of self-defence? In his hostile interactions, the static formless character possesses two dominant and reliable elements of his soul. However, does he need a third dominant element to win his confrontations? Actually, a high majority, of both static and dynamic characters, cannot develop a second element of their soul. The majority of these persons lack the intrinsic ability to become formless. If this is the case, then it should also be true that the formless static character will also win an overall greater amount of his battles and contests. Thus, the individual who possesses two dominant elements will have already addressed the main reason why he loses his personal battles. Theoretically, since he is now winning more battles of aggression, there should be an ulterior motive behind the massive amounts of time that he spends, in the development of the third element of his soul. He has already addressed the feelings of anger that he experiences whenever he loses a contest. Yet, it is highly probable that he has neglected his feelings of jealousy. Accordingly, the static formless character who chooses to develop the final element of his soul may be addressing his feelings of envy.

In particular, the static character will always envy the power and authority that may be possessed by another living being. When he views his own particular position within his society, he may not value any of its particular qualities. Therefore, in the development of the final element of his soul, the static character has basically lost value in every object that he possesses. In this case, the static formless character comes to value some quality of life possessed by another person. This motivates him to develop the final element of his soul, essentially because he believes that it is this third element that will successively grant him the object of his envy. Hence, the static formless character's primary motivation to develop the final element of his soul changes, from defending himself from potential attacks, to acquiring the riches possessed by another human being. Nevertheless, the price that this particular formless static character pays amounts to a loss of value regarding all other kinds of riches, which he may subsequently possess.

When consumed with envy, these cases usually come about when the static character lacks a form of "self" tolerance or self-respect. Nevertheless, these motives, will for the most part, be hidden from public view. That is, the public may view the formless character's actions as chaotic, but they will not have full access to the specific motivations behind his actions. This is due to the fact that he will employ differing personality traits, in an effort to mask the true reasons behind his chaotic behaviour. In essence, the formless static character exhibits a chaotic personality to hide his true motivations, and this enables him to defend himself from possible avenues of attack.

Even though these particular individuals possess the ability to become formless, they still lack a coherent understanding of the law of hierarchy. Therefore, as opposed to having a friendly and respectful demeanour, they will usually reveal a commanding presence. This shortcoming limits their ability to become dynamic, and it also simultaneously demonstrates signs of their original character. Thus, at a subconscious level, the static formless character may still exhibit his primary motive to acquire social authority. Generally, those who utilize the dominating element of their soul, during all forms of circumstances, are categorized as persons who possess a static character. On the other hand, the formless static character will not demonstrate a single dominating tendency, even during circumstances when certain acts of compliance are customary, within their particular community.

Therefore, the static formless character demonstrates a limited ability to interact with other persons through a dynamic fashion. In fact, his intrinsic ability to become formless comes solely from his interactions with a dynamic character. Therefore, static characters who become formless are quite observant, and they utilize their faculty of memory to repeat their observations of the dynamic character. Nonetheless, this form of repetition illustrates the extent, or magnitude, regarding the static formless character's understanding of the law of hierarchy. Even though they may have developed a second or third aspect of their soul, these individuals will still exhibit static tendencies, during times when they come into contact with newer cultures and experiences.

When the static character becomes formless, he will mimic the dynamic character's common, everyday mannerisms, because of the fact that he lacks the virtue of courage. During occasions when he is granted the social authority that he seeks, he is mainly good mannered during his social conducts. In time, however, his dominant behavioural tendencies will return. During these times, when he is not granted social authority, he will then become defensive. Accordingly, similar to all static characters, he will continue his egocentric tendencies until he has acquired the social authority that he seeks.

As a result, the static formless character will always lack a certain degree of modesty. Those who are capable of amassing great fortunes are never humble. These individuals will also utilize their fortunes to prey on the weaknesses of the innocent. Moreover, since he has learned how to mislead persons during the majority of his lifespan, the formless static character will have knowledge of the most effective methods that will grant him some form of success. He will, then, gain more confidence in his ability to become formless.

Within the public realm, the static formless character will mimic dynamic mannerisms. In particular, he may exhibit differing character traits during each unique situation. Therefore, within distinct relationships, he sometimes demonstrates a unique persona. However, he is limited with respect to his understanding of dynamic relationships. The static character does not comprehend any ideals related to dynamic interactions. He merely demonstrates a differing persona within each unique circumstance. Each persona is similar in the fact that he pursues some degree of social authority. Moreover, within the private realm, his courses of action may revert back to his original dominating spiritual element.

      Hence, during social occasions, he will demonstrate another kind of persona. The face he reveals is less specific in nature, and more general, in terms of temperament. Thus, he will moderate all three elements of his soul so that he may be perceived to possess a kind of neutral demeanour. In so doing, he only reveals his static characteristics in a timely, yet subtle fashion. This form of restraint prompts him to choose a specific person to confide in. The confidant he chooses will be the individual who is most likely to understand and accept his static character traits. However, even if this individual is trustworthy, the formless static character will still have started a chain of events that will expose the true nature of his character. In an effort to acquire more forms of friendships, the static formless character will, in due course, choose more individuals to confide in. This event marks the beginning of his transition back from a formless character, to a purely static character. Fundamentally, he will gradually abandon the habit of acting with temperance, during all social circumstances. In more time, his static tendencies will slowly override his neutral demeanour, and his true character will then be observable within the public realm.

When the static formless character does find a trustworthy confidant, a power struggle will eventually ensue, and this marks the beginning of a lifetime feud. Within the static character's frame of mind, all social interactions may be comparable to a game of thrones. The winner of this game gains power and authority. Nevertheless, the formless static character only plays this particular game with other static characters, so that his public appearance will remain formless. If he plays this game with a dynamic individual, he will have lost his formless appearance, at least within the eyes of his opponent.

During these interactions, the static formless character does not want to lose his personal upper hand. Accordingly, if his confidant becomes hostile, he will exploit the weaknesses that he perceives in this individual, in an effort to maintain his authority. Within the public realm, this relationship may seem to be normal, yet in private, the static character will take any advantage that may be given to him. Accordingly, the static formless character's thirst for domination and power will, still, inevitably reveal his true spiritual nature.

Nonetheless, if no such person is available, he will continue to exhibit a neutral demeanour, and this enables him to remain formless for a period of time. Accordingly, while in the eyes of the public, he does not conform to any single personality. Rather, he exhibits more than one kind of mannerism, in a kind of systematic fashion. Through the eyes of God, his character could be viewed as chaotic. He is extremely devious, as he employs a form of mimicry in an effort to acquire social contacts. His ability to mimic other persons comes from his painstaking observations. He will also use the method of trial and error, to gain forms of cultural understanding. All in all, this individual wishes to blend in within the general population.

This kind of formless static character prides himself in his ability to be viewed, not as a criminal, but as an upstanding citizen. Since he resembles the common citizen, he will not be the topic of any conversations, because of the fact that he remains out of public view. Likewise, since he possesses no true friendships, his intrinsic spiritual nature will continue to be masked. Throughout his lifespan, he has mastered the concepts of deviation and manipulation. Moreover, since he remains formless, he possesses the potential to calculate a precise strike towards the core values of any given society. Yet, after some time, when his acts of deception are discovered, he will lose the upper hand. This is what he fears the most.

On the other side of the spectrum, the dynamic formless character lacks symmetry, in relation to his actions and behaviour. He is primarily motivated by a level of fury, which subsequently inflicts fear in other persons. This fear comes about due to his immanent potential to act through a vengeful manner. Accordingly, when he does enter into an angry state, he will exhibit a static personality, since the emotion of anger scarcely changes in terms of intensity, or its intended target. During these circumstances, when he takes on the additional personal attribute of anger, this causes him to lose his dynamic characteristics. Hence, his actions will not be regulated by any principles related to the law of hierarchy, and this makes him to appear to have an unbalanced character.

When the dynamic character becomes formless, he is also motivated by emotions of resentment. However, his experiences with anger usually do not pertain to any lost competitions with other persons. When the dynamic character experiences emotions of anger, it is usually related to some loss involving entities that belong to his conception of Yoshi's island. Therefore, he develops a further element of his soul in an effort to protect those persons whom he values the most. The specific spiritual element that he chooses to develop is not related to any forms of a personal loss, regarding any single contest. Rather, the dynamic formless character chooses to develop that element of his soul which he believes will safeguard and protect the totality of individuals, whom he ponders about the most. Hence, the dynamic character is motivated to become formless for two main reasons. Firstly, he wants to protect other persons, who may be the potential victims of abuse from a static character. Yet, secondly, the dynamic character also wishes enlighten his life partners with newer forms of spiritual affection.

During specific circumstances, when the dynamic character takes on the additional attribute of anger, this fundamentally changes his personal identity. In fact, all dynamic individuals will strive towards developing their intrinsic character through the most peaceful means. However, when the dynamic character personally witnesses forms of injustice, he will be motivated to materialize his own personal conception of justice. This, conceivably, makes him a keeper of justice. His idea of justice takes on two major forms. First of all, the dynamic character wishes to confront abusive individuals with a form of social justice. Under this circumstance, he will develop the particular element of his soul that will enable him to realize this form of justice. For example, if his life partner possesses a dominant centre of emotions, he may choose to develop his intellect in an effort to provide safety and a form of protection for this individual. On the other hand, he may also choose to develop his array of principles, so that he will possess the ability to console his partner. Therefore, the dynamic character's choice to develop a second element in his soul depends greatly on the kind of social justice, which he values the most.

With two dominating spiritual elements, the dynamic formless character will usually win his confrontations with the average static character. As a keeper, he will also usually achieve victory in his battles with a formless static character. This is due to the fact that he possesses more objective knowledge than any static formless character. Recall the fact that the static character becomes formless, essentially to defend himself from the attacks of other static characters. In contrast, the dynamic character becomes formless to defend those persons who are members of his social network. This wider scope of concern, exhibited by the dynamic character, entails a higher form of social awareness. In fact, every dynamic character possesses unique forms of subjective knowledge. However, in order to become the most effective keeper, he must also hold an understanding with respect to the subjective knowledge possessed by those persons who are members of his personal social network.

Therefore, the dynamic formless character possesses many differing forms of subjective knowledge, in addition to forms of objective knowledge, while the static formless character is mainly limited by his own distinctive subjective knowledge. The higher awareness and greater spirit possessed by our keepers, alone, empowers them to win the majority of their conflicts with all other persons who possess a static formless character. A higher base of knowledge enables the keeper to address and solve his conflicts through many diverging means. Likewise, his greater spirit provides him with a form of knowledge regarding social truths, which all static characters lack. In essence, the static formless character only possesses enough knowledge to solely defend himself from avenues of attack. This simply results in a stalemate, whenever he is engaged in conflicts with other static characters.

The goal of every keeper is to understand the subjective knowledge obtained by his life partners. After this type of knowledge is attained, it is at this point where he can then properly defend all of the members of his social circle. Nonetheless, some keepers wish to reciprocate the feelings of affection that they have acquired throughout their life span. This embodies a further conception of justice held by all keepers. In addition to defending the members of his social circle, the keeper also wants to encourage growth and vitality among all of these individuals. This is a concept of justice that is not based on punishing persons for their wrongdoings. In actuality, this is a concept of justice that encourages stronger relationships, based on the reciprocation of benevolent acts. Therefore, this type of keeper fills both roles of protector and provider, within his respective social network.

As a key protector, the keeper does not, necessarily, need to develop the third element of his soul. However, if he does cultivate the final element of his soul, he does this in an effort to fill the role as a shepherd. Therefore, while the static formless character develops the final element of his soul due to feelings of envy, the dynamic formless character develops this final element due to feelings of kindness. In other words, while the former individual wishes to receive, the latter individual is motivated to give. When the keeper is successful in developing the final element of his soul, he will be responsible for producing many of the wonders that exist, within our physical world. While many forms of wonders may be taken for granted by the average person, these miracles remain as wonders, nonetheless. In actuality, the most brilliant form of wonder, that is taken for granted by many persons, is the wonder of love. Love can be an act that escapes our comprehension, and it can also be an emotional state that eludes awareness, within the eyes of its perceiver.

Accordingly, the shepherd's basic liberty is not limited by any single desire. In some cases, he will be motivated to perform acts of reciprocity, while in other cases he will be motivated to perform acts of justice. Accordingly, these kinds of keepers are empowered with two possible modes action, whenever they come into contact with any forms of injustice. In both cases, they may resemble a kind of constrictor, in that they possess the ability to change their physical form at will. Accordingly, the formless dynamic character never reveals his true intentions, until he decides that it is the right time to change from a passive state into a protective state.

All keepers uphold the law of hierarchy, and their ability to become dynamic usually weakens the mind of the static character. However, when the dynamic formless character exhibits feelings of anger, this causes him to cease being dynamic. Therefore, whenever he experiences negative emotions, he usually demonstrates static characteristics. Nonetheless, all true keepers possess the ability to moderate and control the level of intensity, in relation to their feelings of anger. This, then, enables the keeper to remain somewhat dynamic, but it mainly grants him with the power to acquire the attribute of formlessness. The true formless dynamic character possesses the ability to focus his all of his negative emotions towards a single or specific object. Therefore, when the dynamic character evolves into a formless character, he demonstrates a unique and rare characteristic that serves to differentiate him from the common static character.

In fact, every static character intrinsically fears the volatile nature of the formless dynamic character. When he becomes formless, the dynamic character's dominant characteristic will usually take a backseat to the other two. This unpredictability makes him especially feared among the minds of static characters who are guilty of grave delinquencies and injustices. Similarly, when he enters into a fraternity, he will join a clan that is as formidable and intimidating as the fighting Sioux. Therefore, the dynamic character's transformation into a formless character is primarily motivated by the virtue of courage. After this transition, he will have addressed his personal fears, and this demonstrates his true valiance.

The differences between the formless dynamic and static characters may be subtle on the surface, yet cosmic in spirit. The dynamic character evolves into a formless character whenever he centres his behaviour through the emotional state of anger. Contrarily, the static character becomes formless whenever he shields his fits of anger. Hence, while the acquisition of anger makes the dynamic character formless, concealing emotions of anger primarily makes the static character formless.

The formless static character also mainly relies on his personal instincts, even though the reason behind developing a second aspect of his soul may be somewhat rational. Accordingly, he rarely uses reason, while he mainly relies on his personal predispositions during the bulk of his social interactions. On the other hand, the formless dynamic character resembles a kind of dark angel. In effect, he will utilize both instinctive and rational forms of behaviour, depending on the specific social circumstance. While the static formless character stops at nothing in his pursuit towards gaining his own self-interests, the dynamic formless character is primarily motivated to carry out the will of the general public.

With respect to their similarities, both kinds of formless characters may be viewed as a kind of mixed-double, where their personas will vary between a kindly husky to an untamed wolf. Nevertheless, during the development of their alternating form, both characters will experience troubles during the process of assimilation. This is due to the immense ideological differences between the static and dynamic characters. Under most circumstances, the common individual will lack a clear understanding of the opposite persona.

Within the eyes of the innocent, the static formless character will take on the role as a responsible caretaker, and this enables him to maintain some level of social authority. All the while, his reasons to fulfill the role as a caretaker are due to some ulterior motive. Accordingly, when the static formless character is perceived to possess a dynamic personality, he will have achieved success in his acts of deception.

Therefore, the static formless character does not take on the form of a shabby, barefooted man. Within the public realm, he will appear to possess a persona that may be similar to the common civilian. This enables him to interact with other persons within his community through a seemingly peaceful demeanour. Nevertheless, whenever he interacts with persons in our society who may be vulnerable, he will almost always be guilty of a form of entrapment. Except instead of using a legal form of prosecution, the static formless character seeks a form of social disparagement. In essence, the static formless character will oppress and coerce the innocent, in his effort to gain a higher social status.

In these instances, the static formless character possesses enough familiarity to pressure an innocent person into committing some form of transgression. After this is accomplished, he will then possess a plenitude of knowledge that could, in theory, ruin the reputation of this innocent civilian. The power to manipulate the innocent comes directly from his ability to become formless. His ability to appear dynamic will enable him to form a sense of trust, among those individuals who lack a sufficient amount of life experiences. The static formless character will then threaten the innocent with acts of neglect and betrayal, in an effort to sustain his social status over these particular individuals.

His true cowardice is revealed in the fact that he never tries to manipulate those individuals who are less vulnerable within our society. Indeed, while the courageous possess fewer fears than the average citizen, the coward possesses more fears than the average citizen. Therefore, while he may portray a dynamic persona towards one category of individuals, he only demonstrates malicious intents towards those persons who may be most susceptible to his acts of subjugation and persecution.

As he ages, though, the static formless character will become increasingly unhappy with his social status. Since he still possesses static tendencies, he lacks the inherent ability to become truly dynamic, and thus, he lacks the ability to establish genuine and lasting relationships with other persons. Likewise, all forms of relationships that he may have previously acquired will eventually dissolve and dissipate. In these cases, he will, in a subsequent fashion, enter into a state of seclusion. After he loses all of his personal contacts, the static formless character will then have become insignificant within the minds of all other persons who may belong to his community.

Psychologically, the static formless character cannot withstand this particular condition. In an effort to regain some form of regard, he will then commit some kind of transgression, in a purposeful manner. Within his rationale, he would rather be remembered as a kind of social misfit, as opposed to being forgotten almost entirely. In other words, the static formless character would rather be remembered, albeit through a negative perspective, as opposed to being forgotten altogether. This illustrates an act of desperation on the part of the static formless character, in relation to his need for some kind of attention or consideration from other persons.

Through this form of attention, the static formless character stands to benefit from some kind of higher regard, at least through the minds of other static characters. Even though he may be viewed as a social misfit, the static formless character still holds the belief that he belongs to a higher class of persons, in comparison to the average static character. This is due to his ability to remain formless for some period of time. Essentially, he recognizes the fact that, even though he may be currently perceived as an outsider, he still remains as an object of thought within the mind of other persons. Due to the fact that he still receives some form of consideration, he then concludes that his social status ranks higher than that of the average static character. He also holds the belief that rather than being entirely rejected by his society, he has still retained some degree of membership within his community, and that he is merely perceived to be something similar to that of a highly eccentric citizen.

Consequently, the static character also becomes formless because he fears loneliness. In essence, he has not received the amount of attention that he has sought throughout his childhood and adolescence. He may then develop a second spiritual element of his soul, in an effort to have a dynamic relationship with some other person. Therefore, this individual understands that he possesses a static character, and he is also aware of the fact that he does not want to establish any forms of relationships with other static characters. In essence, he develops a further spiritual element in order to disguise his static nature, and this will enable him to enter into his community as an upstanding citizen. Nonetheless, those static formless characters who are guilty of crimes against humanity, in the form of some kind of abuse, will inevitably re-enter into their previous state of seclusion. Similar to the average static character, these persons will be doomed to face their worst fears, which is the possible fate of entering into a state of total and utter isolation.

Actually, the greatest possible evil originates through a breed of a formless character. These individuals are guilty of the greatest evils, because their victim usually does not realize that he is being wronged, until the crime is actually committed. Likewise, only this type of formless character is capable of unbridled malice.

In view of that, the third kind of formless character may be known as a psychopath. The psychopath is born due to the elements of boredom and the virulent means that he utilizes which will enable him to alleviate this boredom. He will become violent whenever he feels that he has become victimized by some other person within his society. Yet, all of his psychopathic behaviour will be mainly motivated by his obsessive need for some type of social recognition.

The psychopath is inherently evil. For the most part, he is exclusively motivated by an inferiority complex. This inferiority complex may be based on either one of two dimensions. The first dimension is based on a materialistic inferiority, where he lacks the kinds of wealth that are necessary to acquire the material possessions that he desires. The second dimension may be based on a social inferiority, where he lacks the forms of caring relationships that he desires. Due to his feelings of inferiority, the psychopath will abuse innocent victims, who may have no relation to him, in an effort to impose his feelings of emptiness and desperation onto another individual.

The psychopath's inferiority complex will remain with him for the duration of his life, and this leads to feelings of increasing inward aggression. During his maturation process, he will realize that his actions are mainly antisocial, and that he lacks any forms of a moral compass. Through this form of awareness, the psychopath will then develop a form of hatred towards his intrinsic spiritual nature, essentially because he realizes the fact that he will never acquire the riches that he desired during his childhood. In other words, the psychopath develops a form of self-loathing, essentially due to the awareness that he will never acquire the kinds of material wealth that he so desires.

As his feelings of inward aggression compound, the psychopath will then look for a person to victimize. He will abuse another individual in an effort to release the brunt of his inward aggression. Within his frame of mind, he believes that this will address and cure his feelings of self-loathing. The act of victimizing another individual will also provide the psychopath with a feeling of control, and a sensation of power. Yet, the original problem will still remain, and the psychopath will continue to experience emotions of self-hatred, because of the fact that he still lacks any forms of material wealth.

Therefore, his self-loathing will continue to multiply, and this eventually leads to thoughts of brutality, in the form of murder. Actually, psychopaths still possess a definite understanding, in relation to moral and immoral forms of behaviour. However, his constantly increasing inward aggression, and the feelings of authority that he experiences while abusing other forms of life will both motivate him to become progressively more violent. In time, the psychopath will disregard all forms of moral behaviour, and this enables him to commit the capital crime of murder.

Within his mind, killing another individual may be the most exhilarating form of experience possible. However, the feelings of authority that he experiences will only relieve his inferiority complex temporarily. A serial killer will then be born, in cases where the psychopath's feelings of inferiority return on a constant and continual basis. Within the serial killer's frame of mind, only the act of murder will relieve his recurrent feelings of inferiority. The act of murder may then be viewed as a necessary mode of action that serves as a kind of personal therapy, which temporarily treats his feelings of lowliness and subordination.

Psychopaths will always pursue authority over the average static character, while the average criminal will usually submit himself to a psychopath. This relationship is established on the fact that psychopaths always contemplate about social evils, while the average criminal will periodically enjoy forms of luxury that may exist within his society. Therefore, static criminals differ from psychopaths because the ordinary criminal may be accustomed with the comforts and amenities that exist within a cooperative community.

On the contrary, those psychopaths who do possess monetary wealth still do not value a comfortable and luxurious way of life. This is due to a continual negative predisposition, where psychopaths who do possess material wealth will, in subsequent fashion, then focus on their lack of social relationships and friendships with other persons.

The bulk of the psychopath's built up anger comes from the constant reliving of his painful memories. In the majority of cases, he will lack the ability to focus on anything else besides his painful memories. Yet, the psychopath also lacks the volition to change these natural tendencies. His built up anger further develops due to his inability to establish true kinds of friendships. In his relationships with other static characters, the psychopath will either get into an altercation, or he will form a kind of hierarchal relationship with this individual. The leader of this particular group will be mainly determined either by intellectual knowledge or life experiences, relative to antisocial forms of behaviour.

However, psychopaths are usually alone when they commit the crime of murder, and very few seek an accomplice to aid them with their premeditated crimes. Those who do manage to find an accomplice will share some kind of a similar dark or haunting memory with this individual. With a common background established, both individuals will mutually benefit from their premeditated crimes.

With respect to an accomplice, the psychopath will usually choose a submissive individual. Hence, in the majority of cases, this will be a common static criminal, and not another psychopath. In the common criminal's frame of mind, he becomes a psychopath's accomplice primarily because he is motivated to relieve his feelings of boredom. Yet, in his relationships with the common criminal, the psychopath's frame of mind may be quite paradoxical. On the one hand, the psychopath seeks friendships to cure his feelings of isolation. As an observer, he recognizes the fact that all social relationships are based on a form of love. However, the psychopath lacks an ability to maintain any friendships, essentially because he does not value any forms of life. Hence, the psychopath, himself, is mainly responsible for his state of continued isolation. Indeed, he becomes jealous whenever he views a healthy relationship between two dynamic characters, and this fuels the feelings of anger and hatred that he holds towards all other forms of life.

He possesses a paradoxical state of mind essentially because he seeks relationships with other persons, based on the principle of affection, even though he himself is incapable of reciprocating or returning any sentiments of love. His mind is also paradoxical in the sense that even though the psychopath himself does not value any forms of life, he will become enraged with persons who do not particularly value his gestures of friendship. Accordingly, while the psychopath demonstrates no forms of regard towards other persons within his social sphere, he expects these individuals to express some form of regard towards himself.

The psychopath becomes deeply affected by his lack of friendships, and consequently, his social isolation. In time, when he becomes permanently isolated, this will mark the beginning stages of his criminal behaviour, where he premeditatedly plans forms of transgressions against the innocent. When he enters into the planning stages of his criminal outbursts, the psychopath revels about committing the most destruction, within his community, through the method of some horrific evil. He chooses innocent victims who are unknown to him, instead of those static enemies who are known to him, essentially because of his fear of retribution. Probably the only thing that a psychopath truly fears is being the victim of another psychopath.

In actuality, the psychopath lacks the ability to establish any forms of peer to peer relationships. During their youth, they may initiate confrontations with other children. In time, since they desire social contacts, they will then mimic moral forms of behaviour, in an effort to fulfill these desires. After this occurs, the psychopath will come to realize that his natural demeanour is mainly antisocial, and that he cannot establish any forms of true relationships without mimicking the forms of moral behaviour that he observes in other persons.

As a result, psychopaths adopt at least one kind of stereotypical identity, which enables them to deceive other persons through the concept of a red herring. For the most part, they are looking to fool other persons, in an effort to disguise their true spiritual nature. With respect to his intrinsic spiritual nature, the psychopath lacks any experiences with a common or normal human socialization process. He studies books, movies, music, and the demeanours of persons with a dynamic character in an effort to educate himself on the subject of basic human socialization tendencies. Those who are particularly successful with their studies will adopt multiple stereotypes, where they will utilize differing stereotypes, depending on the social or environmental circumstances. Likewise, they will also utilize divergent stereotypes depending on what they want to achieve. Accordingly, distinct social settings may demand a differing persona or a differing personal identity.

In order to test the validity of his adopted persona, the psychopath will commit some form of a minor misconduct. He will then observe the reactions of other persons to see if his stereotypical persona still remains as an effective disguise. If his disguise becomes compromised, then persons within his social circle will recognize his true nature, and then he will most likely be condemned within the public setting. However, if the latter event does not occur, the psychopath will gain confidence in his ability to camouflage his true identity from other persons within his community. On a similar note, the average formless static character will also create forms of distractions, though this is done in an effort to disguise his true personal weaknesses. Hence, the reason behind these actions will also be similar to a kind of camouflage. Moreover, the formless static character learns this technique from the sociopath, but he is less skilled in its application.

During his early childhood, the psychopath naturally explores forms of antisocial behaviour, without really having any awareness that his acts are immoral. His feelings of anger usually begin to erupt after he is punished for his antisocial behaviour. This may be due to the fact that the psychopath believes that, within his own mind, his actions are both natural and innocent.

After he experiments with actions that disrupt some form of social order, the psychopath will then begin to discover the feelings of power and control that may be associated with such actions. Next, during his adolescence, the psychopath may then commit some criminal act, in an effort to test his community's justice system. The reactions of persons within his social network, in addition to policing professionals, provide the psychopath with some kind of indication, related to the severity of his offence. Within his mindset, the psychopath wants to know how persons will regard him after he commits a criminal act. It is probable that persons within his social circle may regard him as an immature adolescent, who lacks life experience. On the other end of the spectrum, it may also be possible that persons will regard him as a deeply troubled youth. At this point, the psychopath will also be able to make a further assessment as to whether other persons have accepted his adopted stereotypical persona. All of these factors provide the psychopath with knowledge pertaining to his public identity, or in other words, knowledge of how the general public will perceive him.

Consequently, all psychopaths develop their malicious psychological tendencies throughout their childhood. As children, they are afforded with the freedom to experiment with acts of evil, through the method of trial and error. During this stage of their lives, psychopaths learn mainly through experience alone. When they go unpunished for their malicious intents, they will learn methods that will enable them to become formless throughout their adulthood. Therefore, the psychopath develops throughout his childhood, during occasions when he discovers new methods to commit acts of malice without facing any forms of repercussions.

All psychopaths also seem to be influenced by other tyrants, or other psychopaths, who are infamous for their evil doings. Therefore, all psychopaths will continue to evolve, with respect to their evil intents. Nevertheless, when the psychopath eventually comes to the realization that his natural tendencies are basically antisocial in nature, he may then conceive thoughts related to his inferiority complex. This then leads to thoughts of suicide. Yet, after he contemplates these thoughts, he will become further enraged with his community. This is due solely to his belief that his inferiority complex comes about directly because of the presumptuous and insolent nature of his society. He then holds the belief that his community is ultimately responsible for his suicidal thoughts, since they are mainly responsible for his feelings of inferiority.

Hence, all forms of moral behaviour from the psychopath are due solely to acts of mimicry, and they are not characteristic of his true spiritual nature. The psychopath's ability to moderate his emotional state of anger also enables him to disguise himself, so that he will essentially blend in within the rest of his community. When successful, the psychopath's true identity will be hidden after his stereotypical character becomes accepted by the general public. This makes all psychopaths opportunists. As opportunists, psychopaths will utilize all of the resources that they possess, like material wealth or relationships with other persons, in order to further their personal goals. Therefore, the psychopath's stereotypical identity provides him with enough tools to enable him to remain formless, before he commits any crimes of abuse.

In fact, the psychopath's true nature will remain hidden until he deems it necessary to unleash all of his built up anger and hatred. As he bottles up all of his rage, the psychopath will usually choose to release his tensions towards an unsuspecting target. Subsequently, he only chooses to abuse innocent individuals, who in his mind, will never retaliate. Similar to the bully, the best opportunity for the psychopath comes about when he personally perceives another individual as an "easy target". Therefore, the psychopath does possess a fear of retribution, and this is why he chooses his victims very carefully.

Regarding his public identity, there are three main possibilities. First of all, the general public may accept his adopted stereotype, in which case the psychopath will continue with his successful role playing. Secondly, the public may scorn his stereotype. Under these circumstances, the psychopath may then adopt another kind of stereotypical persona. The third possibility may be based on the chance that he has failed in his efforts to fool the general public. In this case, the general public will view him as he is, and his public identity will be that of a psychopath. When this occurs, the psychopath will usually regress back into his natural tendencies, in which cases he will subsequently abandon his stereotypical persona. Furthermore, this state of affairs will serve to compound his feelings of internal rage, since he will be ultimately viewed as an outcast within his community.

The psychopath develops a formless character by nature. These individuals realize, at a very early age, that antisocial behaviour is not tolerated within their respective community. As a consequence, they develop their other two spiritual traits in an effort to disguise their antisocial tendencies. However, the psychopath differs from other formless characters in that he will permanently mask his original dominant spiritual trait. Therefore, the psychopath may justify some particular action on one day, and then justify an opposite form of action the next day, without acknowledging the fact that these two actions are inconsistent with one another. Accordingly, he believes in the righteous liberty of the will, over responsible modes of action and accountable forms of behaviour.

Therefore, there exists no system of checks and balances that govern the psychopath's behaviour. Similar to the static character, the psychopath is motivated to create disorder within some specific system of order. However, there exists a major difference between the primary motivations behind these two kinds of individuals. In essence, the static character creates chaos and disorder due to the motive of retaliation. He believes that he has been wronged by another individual, and he is motivated to wrong this individual to a similar degree, in an effort to even out his losses.

In actuality, the static character wishes to create chaos because of his feelings of anger. As a direct consequence, the average static character may be guilty of similar copycat crimes, which are committed by the psychopath, to further extend a state of chaos. Nonetheless, he becomes abusive mainly as a reaction to some given event. Within his mindset, he feels that he has been personally wronged and he wishes to produce an equivalent feeling within his opponent. Moreover, when the static character becomes angry, he has also lost a sense of happiness. He is further motivated to make his opponent experience a similar fate. As a consequence, the static character believes that he has been mistreated, and he abuses his opponent because he is motivated by the concept of vengeance. Therefore, the static character is always bent on some form of revenge.

With respect to the static character, his feelings of revenge come about directly from his feelings of anger. Therefore, when the static character abuses another individual, he is in a reactive state of mind. In other words, the static character, is to some degree, abusing other persons due to his personal emotional states.

Nonetheless, the psychopath does not act on feelings of revenge, directly after he enters into an emotional state of anger. Contrarily, the psychopath is primarily motivated by the concept of malice. From a psychological perspective, these individuals will suppress their feelings of anger from public view. Then, through a calculated frame of mind, they will choose a victim purely at will. The psychopath does not wish to even out his losses against his opponent. He is motivated to spread hatred and contempt throughout his entire community. Hence, the psychopath acts mainly in a premeditated fashion and he is meticulous when choosing his potential victim.

The psychopath, then, is proactive in his forms of abuse. He does not become abusive to produce an equivalent form of anger within his opponent. Rather, he becomes abusive in order to produce a sense of happiness in himself. Therefore, he is rarely motivated to gain some form of revenge. Through his abusive behaviour, the psychopath does not wish to reduce his opponent's ego. His malicious intents are designed to boost his own personal ego. This is what differ actions from reactions. Accordingly, while acts of vengeance are intended to produce negative feelings within another individual, acts of malice are intended to heighten feelings of power within the abuser.

Therefore, in layman's terms, the static character becomes abusive in order to bring someone down. During occasions of conflict, the static character becomes angry because he believes that he has been lowered, in terms of social class. As a consequence, he is driven to make his enemy experience a similar fate. Contrarily, the psychopath becomes abusive, mainly so that he will gain the upper hand. Within his frame of mind, he believes that his acts of abuse will essentially raise him, in terms of social class. Accordingly, the reasons, or intent, behind their abusive acts is what differentiates the common static character from the psychopath.

The psychopath, then, possesses a higher level of self-control, in comparison to the average static character. In addition, the premeditated aspects associated with the psychopath makes him more dangerous than the average criminal. Likewise, his malicious intents make him more unpredictable than the common criminal. The psychopath possesses the ability to pause, reflect, and then plan a premeditated crime. This latter element makes the psychopath the most dangerous form of criminal. He will not lash out at other individuals through his fits of anger. Rather, he is cold and deliberate in the choosing of his specific acts of abuse.

Even so, psychopaths demonstrate a similar loss of control over their temperament, during occasions when their feelings of anger elevate into feelings of hatred. Actually, the static character lacks the ability to control his feelings of anger, yet he does possess enough self-control to moderate his emotional states of hatred. Conversely, the psychopath does not possess the ability to control his feelings of hatred, though he does possess the ability to moderate his emotions of anger. This variance in emotional control also differentiates the static character from the psychopath.

The heinous nature of the psychopath seems to be born after he comes into contact with another psychopath, sociopath or dysfunctional person, whether this is a family member or acquaintance. Nevertheless, all psychopaths lack any forms of true bonds or relationships, because they do not value other persons. The psychopath only grasps relationships based on authority and subjugation, because of his inferiority complex. Similar to the static character, the psychopath always seeks social authority. Therefore, whenever he is in a position where he lacks social authority, this particular relationship will eventually disperse.

The psychopath may become physically violent, if he is in a position of authority and loses it, within any given relationship. In contrast, within the same situation, the sociopath will utilize either psychological or emotional forms of abuse. The average static character may also resort to some form of abuse in this situation as well. However, the main differences are, again, based on the fact that the static character abuses persons due to his reactions, while psychopaths and sociopaths become abusive proactively.

In terms of their intellect, psychopaths may be conceivably viewed as an evolved static character. The psychopath possesses all of the tendencies that the average static character may possess. However, they are evolved in terms of their evil intent. As the static character reacts through his feelings of anger and rage, the psychopath will carefully plan his acts of retribution. Both individuals lack the ability to moderate certain negative emotions. Yet, overall, the psychopath demonstrates more moderation and control over the totality of his other negative emotional states.

Like all static characters, the psychopath suffers from a limited intellect, except for his faculty of memory. Furthermore, like all bullies, the psychopath's acts of abuse originate through his negative emotional states. However, the psychopath potentially goes on to commit acts of murder, in order to cover up his painful memories of the past. This form of criminal evolution enables the psychopath to boast to the static criminal, in relation to his psychopathological behaviour. He boasts about his crimes primarily to establish some form of authority over these "lesser" criminals. In addition, the psychopath is motivated to relive his criminality as an ad hoc cure, with regard to the painful memories of inferiority that he has experienced during his personal history.

On the other hand, the average static character may be known for his wrong doings, but if he cares about his reputation, he will actively limit his behaviour according to some of the established laws and social conventions that exist within his community. Actually, the average criminal wishes for some degree of a positive social image, because he wishes to live a luxurious life within a communal setting. Nevertheless, the psychopath possesses no such desire. The psychopath is always motivated to abuse other persons, in an effort to attain some degree of social authority, and this is the only element that will address his particular inferiority complex. Similarly, the psychopath also wishes to create havoc and devastation within his community, because of the fact that he has faced some type of social rejection during his lifespan. This social rejection usually originates through some personal or sexual relationship, where the psychopath's inferiority complex has both surfaced, and subsequently, become exposed.

The best definition of a psychopath may be based on his uncanny ability to hide the true nature of his essence, which is mainly antisocial, through the creation of a publicly accepted persona. Likewise, the psychopath rarely reacts through his emotions of anger. Contrarily, he is mainly proactive, in that he possesses the ability to repress his emotions. He then releases his feelings of anger in a calculated and premeditated fashion, at a time of his own choosing, through the motive of ill will and spite.

Therefore, the main difference between the static character and the psychopath is based on the fact that the former commits acts of abuse because of his personal emotional states, while the latter mainly represses his emotional states, as he pre-emptively causes malice and harm in a thought-out fashion. A third kind of individual also demonstrates psychopathological tendencies, even though he possesses a sense of self-interest. Due to his self-interest, this individual will impose a limit regarding the crimes that he may commit against other persons. Hence, these individuals will not commit the crime of murder. These types of individuals should be more properly deemed as sociopaths. The sociopath actually cares about his outward appearances and how other persons perceive him. Since he demonstrates a limited degree of value towards human life, the sociopath will impose limits on his behaviour, in an effort to maintain a positive social image.

Similar to the static criminal, the main difference between a sociopath and a psychopath is based on the fact that the sociopath will limit his criminality, while the psychopath imposes no such limits on his behaviour. Hence, the psychopath possesses no regard for human life. Moreover, he does not even place value towards his own existence. This character trait, exclusively, enables him to commit the most gruesome and excessively violent crimes. Since the psychopath imposes no kinds of limits on his personal behaviour, this is a key attribute that differentiates him from the sociopath. Only some degree of value towards human life differentiates the sociopath from the psychopath.

In addition, sociopaths may possess some degree of regard, in relation to some moral principle or precept. This kind of social flexibility further distinguishes the sociopath from the psychopath. In actuality, the psychopath is quite stubborn and rigid, in terms of his moral beliefs. He is inflexible because of his lack of moral values. In contrast, the sociopath does place some value towards his existence. This enables him to exhibit some particular common ethical principle, but only during times of his own discretion. Actually, in order to achieve his personal goals, the sociopath will demonstrate some form of culture or socialization. This makes the sociopath more conniving and manipulative, in comparison to the psychopath.

Furthermore, the sociopath and psychopath also differ with respect to their personal imperfections. Within his frame of mind, the psychopath directs his self-hatred and self-intolerance towards his spiritual identity. Therefore, psychopaths that lack material forms of wealth may hold the view that they are incompetent and thus, useless to their society. Those who lack meaningful social relationships may hold the view that they have been rejected by their society. On the other hand, sociopaths direct their self-intolerance towards their physical appearances. Those who lack material wealth may hold the belief that they are a second-class citizen. Likewise, those who lack social relationships may hold the belief that they are lacking, in terms of physical beauty.

In both cases, the sociopath and psychopath's antisocial behaviour will stem from their self-intolerance, towards these specific aspects of their personal identity. Subsequently, this illustrates a kind of obsessive compulsive disorder, where these individuals will also primarily focus on these particular imperfections that may be found in other persons within their community. Sociopaths and psychopaths will hold the belief that these particular imperfections are a naturally inherited part of their identity, both in them and in other persons who share the same characteristics. Similarly, they also develop an obsessive focus towards persons who have mastered these particular weaknesses, essentially because they feel threatened by these individuals, hierarchically. Therefore, the sociopath and psychopath develop a mindset similar to an obsessive compulsive disorder, in relation to their particular faults or imperfections.

Therefore, since sociopaths are unhappy with their physical appearances, they will focus on a lack of physical beauty in other persons, and they will also envy those who do possess physical forms of beauty. In contrast, psychopaths mainly detest their spiritual aspects. These individuals will focus on the character imperfections in other persons, and they will also envy those persons who possess an abundance of the human spirit. In both cases, these individuals will constantly contemplate about their personal imperfections, and this leads to the development of a mindset based on inferiority and loathing.

Psychopaths do possess the understanding that their antisocial behaviour is wrong. Nonetheless, they will always rely on some kind of irrational motive, which justifies their criminal behaviour. These reasons are never objectively sound, though they may be subjectively sound within the mind of the psychopath. This subjective justification provides the psychopath with a good enough reason to continue his antisocial and criminal ways.

Moreover, most psychopaths do not fear incarceration. Furthermore, some psychopaths may actually look forward towards incarceration. These kinds of psychopaths hold the belief that they may find peers, within the jail setting, who will share a similar kind of belief system. If he does find a peer, this will alleviate his state of boredom. Equally, other psychopaths may welcome incarceration, as this may be the only setting where it is possible that they will gain any forms of social authority. These psychopaths will then purposely leave clues pertaining to their criminal acts, because they possess some desire to both be caught and punished. Theoretically, this desire could also represent a miniscule thought of remorse, which merely provides the psychopath with some kind of final connection to the rest of humanity.

Yet, in truth, no psychopaths ever feel truly remorseful about their crimes, and it follows that these individuals also do not fear our justice system. However, within the jail setting, other psychopaths may fear possible altercations with other criminals. Under these specific circumstances, these psychopaths always contemplate about possible future altercations, and this prepares them for any forms of confrontations with other prisoners.

Thus, what some psychopaths do fear are forms of retribution from other persons. While they do not fear forms of social justice that may be associated with their transgressions, they do fear possible instances of physical revenge. This may be due to the fact that while forms of justice are limited by principles of ethics, acts of revenge are not restricted by any such limitations. In general, acts of revenge are only undertaken by other static characters, while the dynamic character usually utilizes social justice as a mode of reciprocity. This facet provides the psychopath with enough reason not to victimize other persons who may be capable of violent acts.

Since psychopaths never demonstrate any forms of remorse, it is also likely that they also do not experience emotions of shame. This also distinguishes the psychopath, to a certain degree, from the average static criminal. Nonetheless, they still do possess specific vulnerabilities based on their particular inferiority complex. As a result, psychopaths contemplate and then prepare themselves for the possible repercussions related to their criminal acts. Yet, their meticulous planning makes them less likely to be caught for their crimes, in comparison to the average static criminal.

There may also be some notable differences between male and female psychopathy. Male psychopaths are more likely to be fascinated with gruesome crimes. In contrast, female psychopaths are not really interested in the method of their criminal acts, but only in the direct consequences that will result due to their criminal acts. This may be due to the differences in nature between men and women. From a plain point of view, men are more action guided entities, while women may be more emotive in nature.

Identifying either male or female psychopathology can be difficult. All psychopaths are guilty of rash, anti-social behaviour. They also demonstrate a lack of concern regarding deviant forms of behaviour. Actions such as animal cruelty, the setting of fires, and the constant destruction of property could be linked to male psychopathology. On the other hand, an inability to maintain personal or intimate relationships, an irrational or excessive focus towards outward appearances, and an inability to deal with, cope with, or recover from experiences of humiliation could mark female psychopathology.

Now, we must ask if there is such a thing as a psychopath who does not commit an appalling murder. In principle, the answer to this question is yes, because there are non-offenders who possess all of the common traits relative to the psychopath's pathology. These persons intend to be responsible for a horrific evil, but they may fail to do so due to poverty or incompetence. Hence, the intention to commit a great evil is a universal trait among all psychopaths, whether or not they are actually successful in this undertaking. Therefore, all psychopaths are similarly guilty of the premeditated aspect behind all horrific crimes.

Regarding religion, the majority of psychopaths do not hold the belief that God exists. Those who do refer to God do so mainly through the notion of self-justification. These individuals may read religious texts, in an effort to justify their criminal tendencies. Therefore, these individuals are not truly religious, but they are also not truly atheists. Rather, these persons seek to justify their antisocial behaviour through religious principles, in an effort to gain forms of acceptance with respect to their criminal acts.

There may also be a second reason why some psychopaths choose to be religious. In effect, entering into a religion will provide the individual with a fairly wide social circle. Thus, the psychopath may choose to follow a religion in an effort to make social contacts. Similar to the static character, the psychopath usually remains in a state of isolation, due to his antisocial behaviour. However, as he adopts the stereotype of a religious follower, this affords the psychopath with an opportunity to establish relationships with other persons. In a similar manner, psychopaths who are atheists will also possess the opportunity to create friendships with other atheists.

Nonetheless, the choice of whether to become either a theist or atheist is usually based on every person's unique belief system. Those who hold the belief that their lives have some kind of purpose will also usually be theists. Correspondingly, individuals who believe that life has no purpose will usually be atheists. Within the psychopath's frame of mind, the choice to become a theist depends solely upon his particular social circumstances. In actuality, psychopaths who manage to find an accomplice for their criminal acts may then, as a consequence, acquire a belief in God. This is due simply to the fact that his own life has had some kind of value to another human being. Those psychopaths who remain in a permanent state of isolation will not adopt any forms of religious beliefs, essentially due to the fact that their own life has had no value to any other persons.

Accordingly, psychopaths who commit their heinous crimes without an accomplice will usually be atheists, because of the fact that they have not found any other persons, in the world, who share any similar goals. Therefore, isolation provides a concrete reason behind atheistic beliefs. The psychopath believes that there is no God and that he has been created merely as a random anomaly, essentially due to the fact that he has no peers. Therefore, his loneliness, seclusion, and solitude makes him more inclined to believe in non-theistic modes of creation.

This is another reason why the psychopath demonstrates no form of remorse for his crimes. Basically, the atheistic psychopath believes that all forms of life are essentially random anomalies, which have no true purpose. Yet, those psychopaths who are theists can be responsible for similar forms of brutality. The theistic psychopath, who believes in a spiritual afterlife, will commit the grandest of atrocities simply because these acts provide him with an enhanced feeling of power, which may be Godlike in nature. Therefore, the theistic psychopath wishes to feel a degree of authority that may be comparable to some form of a deity.

The theistic psychopath will also hold the belief that forms of authority, during the afterlife, may be established through the degree of evil acts that each criminal may be responsible for. Therefore, the atheistic psychopath brutalizes his victim because he does not believe in any forms of justice within the afterlife, while the theistic psychopath will commit the same act due to the fact that there may be some form of hierarchy, among criminals, during the afterlife.

If he does find an accomplice, either within his community or within the jail setting, the psychopath's choice to adopt some set of theistic beliefs may also provide him with a sense of security. Thus, when the psychopath possesses some kind of friendship with a religious individual, he will rely on this element in an effort to avoid any possible forms of aggression or conflict. In other words, the psychopath will rely on the moral principles found within a religion to establish a kind of friendship based on some degree of loyalty and trust.

This is a second example of the paradoxical state of mind that haunts every psychopath. In fact, every psychopath will wrestle with both theistic and atheistic beliefs. On the one hand, if God does exist, the psychopath can then conclude that he will face forms of legitimate justice, pertaining to his crimes within the physical world. On the other hand, if there is no afterlife, then the psychopath may conclude that life has no intrinsic value, and that we were all created due to some random anomaly. In such cases, his antisocial behaviour may be justified, essentially because of his opinion that moral principles have no true bearing within an orderless world.

During his early youth, every psychopath believed in the existence of God. Yet, when he suffers from major transgressions from other persons, he may begin to question these beliefs. Further, after he realizes that his spiritual nature is made up of mainly negative attributes, the psychopath will further develop his atheistic beliefs. The psychopath wishes to have a relationship with God, due mainly to his ambitions for social authority. Yet, if he lacks the ability to communicate with God, this will mark the beginning of his atheistic mind-set. The psychopath may then act in a criminal manner, in an effort to rebel against the spirit of God. However, even though he has transformed his theistic beliefs into an atheistic frame of mind, the psychopath still does not deny the possibility that God, and a spiritual afterlife, may exist.

Consequently, even the atheistic psychopath will fear reprisal during the possible existence of an afterlife. His greatest fears relate to his social isolation, in combination with vengeful spirits. Fundamentally, the psychopath fears acts of revenge from persons that he may have wronged during his physical existence. Furthermore, if he has not been subject to adequate forms of justice for his transgressions within the physical world, the psychopath will fear possible repercussions during the afterlife to an even higher degree. Subsequently, while the psychopath rarely exhibits emotions of fear within his physical existence, he does fear the unknown forms of justice that could transpire within the next world.

In fact, social justice and revenge are two entirely different concepts. While the static character is fixed on forms of revenge whenever he has been wronged, the exact method that he utilizes could take many differing forms. In some cases, the static character will utilize physical violence, while in other cases he will belittle his enemies through more subtle psychological methods. In contrast, the dynamic character relies on more peaceful modes of justice. These peaceful methods may vary from total disregard, where the criminal loses the potential to create any forms of meaningful relationships, to the restriction of physical freedom. In every case, the psychopath will have lost all forms of recognition and membership within his particular community.

With respect to the afterlife, the majority of all static characters do not believe in an immaterial existence. These individuals do not possess any fears related to either heaven or hell. The only fears they do possess are based on forms of justice, within our physical world. With respect to the remaining minority, these individuals also do not necessarily believe in some form of afterlife. However, they do not deny its potential existence, and hence, they will entertain the fact that an afterlife is still conceivably possible. Within their frame of mind, they do fear a possible state of loneliness, during the afterlife. Those who are guilty of criminal behaviour will also fear possible forms of justice within the immaterial world, even though they may have no conception of how social justice will take its form within this environment.

In effect, within the static character's frame of mind, those individuals who have already been punished for their criminal acts, both through vengeance and social justice, will, with all probability, not be subject to any further modes of punishment. If this is true, then they will also have less to fear during the afterlife, since they have already faced both forms of justice. In essence, there will be no other souls who may be seeking any further modes of justice. Contrarily, those psychopaths who have not received any forms of justice for their transgressions may, indeed, have something to fear during the afterlife. Accordingly, another theoretical hierarchy among all static characters may be based on the level of fear that each of them possesses, with respect to the afterlife. The unpunished psychopath will fear possible forms of retribution during the afterlife, and this makes him a lower ranked static character. Those static characters, who have already faced adequate forms of justice within the physical world, will intrinsically possess less fear, and this ranks them higher than the average psychopath. Accordingly, the amount of fear that each criminal possesses could also theoretically determine his rank among the static character's system of hierarchy, during the afterlife.

Thirdly, the psychopath also exhibits a paradoxical state of mind in the sense that he is a purposeful villain. The purposeful villain is any individual who seeks a negative reputation, within his community, based either on his criminal or antisocial behaviour. Individuals who become purposeful villains have, for the most part, lived a life of total isolation. These persons lack the virtue of patience, and likewise, they cannot tolerate boredom. To address their social isolation, these individuals will become attention seekers. Yet, due to the fact that they are wanting of any moral values, they only possess the ability to acquire negative forms of attention. Consequently, the purposeful villain will intentionally seek a criminal form of reputation, in an effort to address his social isolation. Within these individual's frame of mind, some form of attention is better than none. Similarly, the purposeful villain would rather be a social outcast, than some person who receives no forms of regard whatsoever.

The purposeful villain believes that negative forms of attention may grant him with a better life, in comparison to one that is based on total social isolation. He strives to be the object of someone's personal thoughts, even if this means that he will be categorized into a lower social class, and that he may then be potentially exiled from his community. In these cases, concepts of evil then become an object of creativity, within his mind-set. In actuality, the purposeful villain wants to reveal the totality of his evil spiritual nature to the general public. Some of these individuals may also want to be caught and punished for their crimes of malice. In essence, the purposeful villain craves some form of social recognition and attention, even if this means that he will be labelled, by his society, into a lower social class because of his antisocial predisposition and evil deeds.

In the end, every psychopath realizes that his acts of excessive brutality will make him an outcast within his particular community. When he is eventually caught for his crimes, he will then accept his identity as a psychopathological criminal. In fact, it is the psychopath's natural habitat, within a civilized and socialized community, that marks the only difference between himself and the untamed animals that habituate our wilderness. Therefore, the static character who appears as formless poses the most danger to our society. To combat these criminals, dynamic individuals, who possess the ability to become formless, may evolve into a potential keeper, who will protect the innocent from harm and detriment.

In fact, no human being possesses an utter and total grasp over another person's intrinsic spirit. Our first level of perception begins with individual actions, and thus, another person's character. Hence, character is a form of identity that merely epitomizes our spirit. Yet, every individual also possesses the freedom to act in contrary to the true nature of his fundamental spirit. It is these individuals who present the objective characteristic of being formless.

10   Judgment

WHEN WE OBSERVE other persons, we will naturally judge their actions to either be moral or immoral. In fact, human character is wholly determined by each individual's actions. Therefore, when we observe some individual to be violent, we will automatically judge him to possess a poor character. Nevertheless, in many cases, absolute judgments may be susceptible to err. That is, certain actions are never absolutely moral, nor are some actions absolutely immoral. Actually, there do exist some absolutely immoral acts, where their utilization will be immoral under all circumstances. For example, the purposeful torture of another human being can never be morally justified, even during times of war. Likewise, acts of altruism, like protecting our children from undue harm will always be justified, during any era of human existence. Yet, there are actions which may be either morally correct or immoral, depending on the particular circumstances. These are actions that require rational judgement in its evaluation as either an ethical or unethical act.

Since all human beings possess an unbounded will, it is possible that a criminal may demonstrate moral characteristics, while a hero may demonstrate immoral characteristics. It is during these circumstances where we will require a further analysis, if we are to properly determine an action's ethical status. Indeed, it is due simply to the liberty of the will where any person can be guilty of a horrific crime or an honourable act. However, behind every action there is some form of reasoning, and likewise, after every action there is some form of consequence. In order to best determine the moral status of every action, we should more properly focus on the reasons behind an action, as opposed to any other elements that may be associated with a specific action.

Consider the phenomenon of identical twins. How are we supposed differentiate these two individuals? From a physical perspective, it may be difficult to differentiate and properly identify each twin. Indeed, from a physical perspective, many persons may fail in this undertaking. Both twins look the same physically, as their bodily characteristics perfectly match in almost every possible manner. With respect to character, their actions and mannerisms may also be quite similar. Yet, consider the case where one twin exhibits moral characteristics fundamentally, while the other twin merely exhibits the stereotype of a moral character. In other words, from a spiritual perspective, one twin exhibits a dynamic that properly reflects his spiritual nature. The other twin is a static criminal, who perfectly mimics his brother's mannerisms. Perhaps, then, it may be through a spiritual perspective that best enables us to uniquely identify each brother.

Accordingly, while both twins appear to be exactly similar, they are profoundly different with respect to their spiritual nature. Thus, since their character remains similar, the only way that we can differentiate these two individuals may be to analyze the motivations behind their actions. Since both brothers will always possess some facet of a unique spirit, their acts will be motivated by differing reasons, even during occasions where their actions are fundamentally equivalent.

For example, we may differentiate these individuals from the particular circumstances that may be relevant to their analogous acts. Consider this particular scenario. Both twins have shot and killed another human being. Nevertheless, the dynamic twin is a member of his nation's military, while his twin is a member of criminal organization. During times of conflict, the dynamic twin will be justified, whenever his nation is in a state of war. Essentially, the soldier is fulfilling his duty if he shoots and kills an enemy soldier. Therefore, in this particular circumstance, the dynamic twin is morally correct, essentially due to the fact that he is protecting innocent persons through this particular act. Contrarily, his static twin may have similarly shot and killed another citizen, but he is not fulfilling any kinds of a moral duty. This twin is morally wrong, because of the fact that he was avenging a financial loss, which his organization may have suffered. Actually, beyond the reason of self-defence, no person will ever be justified in the act of killing another citizen. Hence, while both twins may be responsible for the same specific act, the reason behind their acts remains entirely different.

Under this particular circumstance, we would not be fair to judge both twins purely through their actions alone. It is the motivations behind their actions which must be judged, if we are to truly evaluate its moral status. When the soldier performs the act of killing, he will be justified in his actions, if he is motivated to fulfill some kind of duty through his acts. Therefore, when the dynamic soldier kills, he is defending his nation. In this case, the soldier is motivated to fulfill the duty to protect his nation-state. In contrast, when the gangster kills another human being, he is not motivated by any rational forms of duty. When the static gangster kills, he is guilty of murder. In actuality, he merely seeks to avenge some particular loss that he has suffered. Therefore, even though both twins have committed the same action, only one is morally justified in his acts. Accordingly, in order to ascertain the ethical nature of a specific act, we must more properly judge the primary reasons or motivations behind the individual's actions.

Therefore, the motivation behind a particular action should determine its ethical status. In actuality, there are two main categories of motivations. These may be commonly known as virtues and vices. Virtues are moral qualities. Persons who are motivated by virtue accomplish some kind of feat in the realm of goodness. In the case of the soldier, the primary virtue that motivates this individual is the quality of courage. In essence, the soldier realizes that he belongs to a particular group within his society, who is capable of fighting wars. Through the virtue of courage, the soldier seeks to protect those individuals in his society who lack the physical means to properly defend their country during times of war.

The realm of goodness is actually quite wide. The scope of a benevolent act determines its effect. Therefore, acts of goodness that affect only a single individual will be small, in terms of its force. On the other hand, acts of benevolence that affect an entire nation will be relatively great in size. Hence, the end effect of a particular benevolent act determines its magnitude.

In contrast, vices are immoral traits. Individuals who are motivated by vices are guilty of crimes against humanity. Crimes against humanity are such offences which suppress the growth of another human being. Therefore, individuals who are motivated by vices are guilty of acts of oppression and persecution. In the case of the gangster, his act of killing is mainly motivated by the vice of vengeance. In essence, he wishes to punish a particular individual who may have wronged him at some earlier time.

The vicious possess a mindset that focuses on what they believe are the negative attributes associated with human existence. Accordingly, they focus more on the difficulties associated with life, as opposed to the many differing forms of wonders. Since they lack the ability to appreciate the many wonders that are perceived through human consciousness, they will also lack the ability to produce any unique forms of benevolent acts. These individuals then commit crimes against humanity in an effort to change their status as a powerless individual, into a being who possesses some degree of influence over another human being.

In fact, the entirely vicious possess a character similar to that of the purposeful villain. Both characters lack a certain degree of respect, within their social circles. Yet, in comparison to the vicious, the purposeful villain merely wishes to be the object of another person's thought. On the other hand, the vicious not only want to be the object of another person's thought; they also want to have some form of influence over this person's actions. Therefore, the degree of impact over an innocent individual's life is the main aspect that differentiates the typical villain from the utterly vicious.

At this point, we must differentiate virtues from principles. Principles are general rules that guide the individual's daily behaviour. Consider the principle of honesty. Persons who have adopted this principle will, in general circumstances, always speak the truth. Nonetheless, when we view such persons, we still lack an understanding regarding the reason why he has chosen to adopt his chosen array of principles. Through the law of hierarchy, we understand that our emotional states have a direct effect over the principles that we adopt. Therefore, those persons who value knowledge will subsequently adopt the principle of honesty. This is due to the fact that true objective knowledge can never be attained without the mutual exchange of honest subjective knowledge.

Nevertheless, we may delve deeper into the individual's psyche and question why he values knowledge in the first place. To answer this question, we must analyze the concept of duty. An individual's duty is realized through the concept of responsibility, in relation to some specific task. The individual will fulfill his duty after he performs a certain set of actions. Consider the duty to acquire scientific knowledge. In order to gain any forms of true scientific knowledge, researchers must first possess the principle of honesty. Individuals who do not possess the principle of honesty will skew their data for personal reasons. These reasons may be based on a bribe or some other mode of profit. Accordingly, persons who lack the principle of honesty do not produce true forms of knowledge, and hence, they lack a significant principle that is necessary to fulfill the duty to acquire scientific knowledge.

For another example, consider the duty of responsible parenthood. In the act of producing offspring, the ethical individual will be mainly motivated to fulfill the duty of responsible parenthood. Those individuals who do not intend to fulfill the duty of responsible parenthood will never be justified in this act, should they do produce offspring. Therefore, only individuals who fulfill a certain duty will be justified with respect to the latter action, while those who do not intend to fulfill any duties will not be justified under a similar circumstance.

In order to become a responsible parent, the individual must maintain a certain set of elements that are associated with parenthood. Therefore, the individual must provide for his children, with respect to food, shelter and clothing. Only those individuals who offer the best possible environment for their children will be fulfilling their duty as a responsible parent. Yet, the responsible parent's duty still requires further elements. These elements will include a definite education on the topic of moral forms of behaviour, and also possibly accepting the duty of serving as a grandparent. Therefore, the duty of becoming a responsible parent requires a combination of many differing elements. When the individual accepts these specific responsibilities, he will be on the right track towards fulfilling his particular duty.

While principles serve to guide the individual's actions, during everyday relations, the act of fulfilling one's duties will require the adoption of a certain set of principles. Therefore, when an individual accepts a specific duty, he will have to fulfill a certain set of responsibilities, and each distinct responsibility can be related to a specific principle. For example, in the responsibility of providing the basic necessities for one's child, the parent must adopt the principle of service. The principle of service is a necessary building block among all forms of cooperative communities. Yet, it is most important when it is directed towards individuals who are categorized as dependents within our society. If the individual does not adopt the principle of service, then he will fail in his responsibility to provide the basic necessities for his child.

Furthermore, the responsibility of educating one's child requires the principle of conscientiousness. Individuals who are conscientious understand the potential effects or ramifications that their actions may have on other persons. Individuals who lack this principle do not comprehend ethical principles and the differences between moral and immoral forms of behaviour. Subsequently, only individuals who possess a certain level of understanding may be potential teachers of a certain kind of knowledge. Those who are ignorant within a specific field cannot be the teachers of any forms of ideals or principles that they may lack. Therefore, those individuals who lack the principle of conscientiousness will fail with respect to the proper education of their child, in the realm of responsible behaviour.

Finally, in fulfilling the responsibility of serving as a grandparent, the individual will require the principle of commitment. The principle of commitment binds two individuals together, for an indefinite period of time. In order to actively sustain and continue his relationship with his children, the individual must also fulfill his potential role as a grandparent. Hence, if he is to truly provide for his children, he must extend a similar form of commitment towards his grandchildren. Within this role, as opposed to providing material necessities, he merely provides a form of spiritual guidance. Therefore, if one is to properly accept the duty of responsible parenthood, he must also possess the principle of commitment towards his grandchildren as well.

In fact, assuming the responsibility of becoming an obligated parent may be the most important duty that exists, in the realm of human life. This responsibility also exemplifies the fact that all duties require a multitude of differing actions, and thus, differing and distinct kinds of principles. Nonetheless, we may further address what motivates the individual to take on a specific duty in the first place. Unfortunately, it is an apparent truth that even though the majority of individuals will accept the duty of responsible parenthood, other persons will not. As a consequence, we must analyze the differences between the former individual and the latter. When we understand the motivations that drive each individual, we may then understand why some persons accept particular duties, while others do not.

Hence, persons must also possess some form of motivation behind their choice to accept a particular duty. In the case of a responsible parent, the individual will take on this particular duty due solely to the fact that he is motivated by virtue. Likewise, persons who do not accept this particular duty will be motivated by some particular vice. Thus, while some set of principles are required to fulfill a particular duty, virtues provide the individual with some reason to take on that particular duty. The individual who takes on a particular duty will be motivated by virtue, while those who shed the concept of duty will be motivated by some form of vice.

Therefore, virtues and vices are firm and unchanging motivational factors behind the individual's choice to act. They provide reason behind forms of action. In contrast, principles represent a certain category of behaviour. As a consequence, virtues may be seen as values, while principles may be seen as the materialization of these values.

Only persons who are motivated by virtue will possess the potential to discover and embrace the many types of wonders that exist within our physical world. Consider the responsible parent. Individuals who accept the duty of responsible parenthood will be motivated by the virtue of integrity. This is due to the fact that they are the sole reason why a new instance of life has been born into our world. As such, the responsible parent realizes that all children require a certain amount of care before they can truly become independents. Likewise, he also realizes the fact that if his child lacks the ability to become an independent, his duty of providing for his child will become a lifelong endeavour. Only persons who are motivated by the virtue of integrity will acknowledge these elements of paternity. Persons who possess integrity have a positive sense of identity, and thus, they will acknowledge the fact that their children also form an important part of their personal identity. As such, persons with integrity cannot be swayed away from their moral obligations, which will most definitely include the duty to provide care for their offspring.

In contrast, those individuals who are responsible for producing offspring, but fail in their duty to become responsible parents will be motivated by the vice of laziness. Actually, laziness is one of the most common forms of vice, but it is most apparent when it is linked to the duty of parenthood. Persons who are predisposed by this vice may enjoy the luxuries that exist within the physical world, but they lack the volition to work towards the production of any such luxuries. In becoming a potential parent, these individuals do recognize the fact that the birth of their child is due to the direct result of their free actions. Yet, they will shed their duty to provide for their children, due to a mindset of inconsequence. While these individuals may care about their own well-being, they do not truly care about the future well-being of their child. As such, they will ignore the fact that all children are born into the world as dependents, and subsequently, they will absolve themselves from any forms of responsibility, in relation to their offspring.

In the majority of cases, the individual will be engaged in an intimate relationship before he enters into the realm of parenthood. Therefore, even before the production of any offspring, the individual will possess a duty towards his partner. In these cases, righteous individuals, who eventually engage in an intimate relationship, will be motivated by the duty to love and support their partner. This duty is exemplified through the act of unconditional love.

The duty of unconditional love requires two principles. First of all, all forms of love are generated through emotions of compassion. Persons who are compassionate will accept the imperfections that may be found in other persons. Individuals who experience compassion will both tolerate and embrace what he believes to be are another person's faults or shortcomings. In most cases, these faults and shortcomings may be mainly based on an individual's character. Within merely carnal relationships, only mutual sexual attraction is necessary to bring two individuals together. However, within all true intimate relationships, acts of compassion are further required, to link both individuals' diverse and distinct souls together. Relationships that lack this spiritual link will only evolve in a negative fashion and compound the problems between two individuals, should they choose to produce offspring. Since these particular individuals cannot produce a spiritual link between each other, it may be that more unlikely that they will ever achieve a spiritual link between themselves and their offspring.

In turn, the individual must also adopt the principle of forgiveness, whenever he enters into an intimate relationship. No persons possess the trait of total perfection, and subsequently an individual's partner may, on some occasion, be responsible for some kind of mistake or error. The principle of forgiveness requires a kind of tolerance directed towards another individual's wrongful behaviour. As a result, the duty of unconditional love requires the acceptance of both another individual's spiritual and characteristic imperfections. On some occasions, this duty requires the act of conceiving another person's imperfections as a form of perfection. Subsequently, to fulfill the duty of unconditional love, the individual must first possess both principles of compassion and forgiveness.

Persons who accept the duty of unconditional love will be motivated by the virtue of devotion. Actually, some friendships are also based on the duty of unconditional love, but the virtue of devotion only surfaces within intimate relationships. This is due to the fact that only intimate relationships require a full and comprehensive understanding, with respect to another person's spiritual identity. In all other friendships, there may be no sense of intimacy, and subsequently, the understanding of another person's general character may suffice. Therefore, intimate relationships may symbolize the highest form of love attainable, where the individual will utilize all of his strengths in an effort to vitalize and nurture the spirit of his partner. When the individual dedicates his life in the defence of his life partner, he can only be motivated by the virtue of devotion. Devotion, then, is a virtue that compels the individual to protect and secure that phenomenon which, in his mind, embodies the highest possible form of beauty that exists within our natural world.

Conversely, some individuals who are involved in intimate relationships may not be motivated by any virtues. Within these individuals' frame of mind, the spiritual attributes of their sexual partner may be irrelevant. What may be of most importance are the mere physical attributes of their sexual partner. Therefore, what drives these individuals to become intimate may be solely based on the elements of physical attraction. Nonetheless, the appreciation of forms of physical beauty, like spiritual beauty, will vary from person to person. In some individuals' frame of mind, wealth or success may represent a kind of physical beauty. In another person's frame of mind, fame or stardom could also represent some form of physical beauty. If this is true, the common element of what is beautiful, within these particular individuals' frame of mind, may be solely material in nature. As such, persons who merely seek sexual experiences are motivated by the vice of greed.

Persons who are greedy place excessive importance on forms of material beauty, all the while placing no importance on any forms of spiritual beauty. Persons who are greedy also do not possess a sense of moderation, in relation to forms of material beauty. They do not place any kinds of limitations on the means that will enable them to gain any forms of material wealth. Therefore, these individuals are not restricted by any forms of moral principles in their quest to acquire forms of material beauty. In the realm of intimate relationships, these individuals will not protect nor defend their sexual partner. They also lack the motivation to tolerate and accept any imperfections that may be found within either their partner's spirit or character. Rather, their motivations of greed force them to focus merely on elements of material beauty instead.

Also within the familial setting, most individuals will possess a natural duty towards either their blood-related or adoptive parents. Whenever someone has experienced a childhood where his parents have both protected him from harm, and provided him with an unreserved amount of care, he will also necessarily possess a duty towards them. This responsibility may be known as the duty of interchange. It is true that all persons are born into this world as dependents. As we age and enter into adulthood, we eventually enter into the phases of independence and then interdependence. Yet, as we mature into our elderly years, many of us will re-enter back into the phase of dependence. This is just the natural human path to seniority. When this occurs, we, as the children of this generation, must accept the duty of interchange. The duty of interchange essentially entails providing of an equivalent amount of care for our parents, similar to what we received during our childhood. It requires the switching of roles from a recipient of care, into becoming a care provider.

The principle of loyalty is of utmost significance to the duty of interchange. If a child possesses no sense of loyalty towards his parents, he will never accept any kinds of duty directed towards them. Yet, every child who grew up in a functional environment may be ethically bound to adopt the principle of loyalty towards his parents. Persons who are loyal will not break any positive bonds that have been established between themselves and another person. In actuality, loyal individuals cannot take for granted the fact that their parents did provide a suitable environment for them during their childhood, which encouraged them to freely mature and develop. In these cases, children who do not develop a sense of loyalty towards their parents may be essentially viewed as misfits, within the familial setting, and in turn possibly as outcasts within the communal setting.

Consequently, the child must also appreciate the childhood that was afforded to him, by his parents, whenever he accepts the duty of interchange. Those children who view their familial environment as one that is mainly dysfunctional will possess no rational reason to accept this duty. Nevertheless, those individuals who cherish their childhood also necessarily possess a duty to protect their parents, should they become dependents at any point during the future. Individuals who possess the principle of appreciation will feel compelled to return some kind of favour, or helping hand, in an effort to express their gratitude and contentment towards one of their intrinsic providers. Accordingly, the duty of interchange is the most palpable mode of action that properly addresses the feelings of appreciation, which naturally arises between a child and his parents.

Individuals who adopt the duty of interchange will be motivated by the virtue of remembrance. Persons who possess this virtue will place value on those individuals who have had a positive influence on their personal life. Similarly, persons who possess this virtue will also shun those individuals who have had a negative influence on their personal life. The virtue of remembrance also requires proper judgment, so that the thinker may properly ascertain which individuals are truly heroic and which individuals are truly villains. Accordingly, whenever we remember the heroic, we will be honouring their spirit. In so doing, persons who are motivated by remembrance will relay a form of respect that is necessary for the duty of interchange. At the very least, the heroes that we remember will be granted a form of admiration and reverence that is consistent with the degree of the positive impact that these persons have had on our personal lives.

On the other hand, those individuals who do not adopt the duty of interchange will be motivated by the vice of hatred. These individuals have mainly compared their childhood to a dysfunctional family environment. They also hold the premise that their parents are mainly responsible for their dysfunctional upbringing. As a result, individuals who are motivated by hatred will wish the worst possible fate, in relation to the object of their negative emotions. Therefore, those who do not acknowledge any forms of duty towards their parents will be mainly holding feelings of hatred towards them. They do not care about the future well-being of their parents. Moreover, they may wish their parents to experience a fate similar to their childhood, within an environment based on the elements of misery and distress.

Similar to his parents, the individual also possesses some form of duty towards his siblings. This is the duty of acceptance and support. When an individual does possess a rational sibling, in most instances, he will have experienced a fairly similar upbringing. Therefore, this shared experience usually serves to unite two siblings, even in cases where they lack any similar forms of personality or character traits. If they experienced similar benefits and hardships during their childhood, they will be bestowed with a deeper understanding of each other, at least in the realm of their spiritual identity. This will usually motivate both individuals to maintain a relationship with each other, and accordingly, they may continue to experience similar rewards and hardships, at the spiritual level. Whenever this occurs, the relationship between two siblings will remain constant throughout their entire lives.

In order to properly maintain a relationship with one's sibling, the individual must first possess the principle of benevolence. Actually, every individual possesses the power to choose his friends, but he lacks the power to choose his siblings. Therefore, there is no observable system of order that determines the characteristic or spiritual makeup of any individual's family members. As a consequence, every individual must possess a certain degree of toleration towards these persons. This degree of toleration is exemplified through the principle of benevolence. Persons who are benevolent will possess a sense of thoughtfulness that is intrinsic to their spirit. In the realm of familial relations, acts of benevolence may be a primary building block, essentially due to the fact that the spiritual nature of one's siblings will vary to some degree. Accordingly, since the spiritual nature of one's siblings may be entirely diverse, only acts of benevolence will serve to universally unite two entirely differing souls. Acts of benevolence will also include a certain degree of toleration, and this is necessary in circumstances where the individual lacks any commonalities in character with another individual. The principle of benevolence demonstrates a primary form of universal toleration directed towards individuals who possess a differing, yet just spiritual nature.

In addition to benevolence, to fulfil the duty of acceptance and support, the individual must also possess the principle of courtesy. Acts of courtesy are necessary during circumstances when an individual's sibling may be suffering from some form of distress. In order to address the primary reasons behind this distress, the individual must offer some form of support that will lessen the impact of his sibling's grief. This may be accomplished when the individual's sibling is shown a certain degree of regard. Acts of courtesy may best demonstrate the level of care and concern that one possesses towards his sibling. Through well mannered-behaviour, the individual demonstrates a candid mode of respect that he possesses towards his sibling. It is through this respect where the sibling, himself, then realizes that what he believes to be are his personal imperfections are merely unique and defining spiritual traits. Therefore, when the sibling becomes a recipient of acts of courtesy, he will eventually come to the understanding that his personal imperfections are not, in fact, imperfect. He may then come to the general understanding that his distinctive spiritual traits may be, in actual fact, significant and definitive. Hence, acts of courtesy demonstrate a form of unconditional regard directed towards another individual's unique spirit. It is through the acts of courtesy from other persons where the individual will, himself, reconceive his personal imperfections as a major element of his spirit. Acts of courtesy and well-mannered behaviour are necessary modes of interactions, during any forms of prolonged relationships between two siblings.

    Persons who accept this duty are motivated by the virtue of empathy. Persons who are empathic demonstrate a form of caring towards another individual's inimitable spiritual nature. Moreover, persons who are motivated by empathy will identify the needs of other individuals, and provide for them. Yet, when individuals become empathic, they usually do so in an effort to remedy another person's anguish and distress. In effect, this virtue is utilized to understand the spiritual nature of another individual, during cases where the latter person is suffering from mistaken beliefs of lowliness. As a consequence, the empathic always direct their feelings of empathy towards those persons who are actual members of their emotional centre. The efforts of the empathic will both nurture and enlighten the spiritual nature of another person. Moreover, when the individual demonstrates empathy, he will be providing a form of spiritual aid that will enable another person to continue to maturate and grow.

Those individuals who do not acquire the duty of acceptance and support will be motivated by the vice of slander. In essence, individuals who are motivated by this vice rely on the belittling of other persons for their own personal acquisition of self-esteem. Persons who are slanderous do realize that they possess major imperfections. However, in an effort to mask their imperfections, the slanderous will continue to identify the imperfections in other persons. As opposed to promoting principles of equality, individuals who are motivated by this vice will continue their efforts to identify what they perceive are another person's personal weaknesses. They will further promote discriminatory thoughts and concepts. As a consequence, through this mode of discrimination, the slanderous will prey on the ignorance of those members of the general public who lack knowledge and experience with respect to the ideals of fairness, tolerance and impartiality.

The majority of non-intimate relationships are based on similarities and compatibilities between two individuals' character. When two individuals meet for the first time, and they recognize that they are compatible with one another, they will naturally become acquaintances.

However, this kind of relationship is quite arbitrary, and it usually lasts only for a temporary amount of time. In his effort to build a mutual and everlasting friendship, the individual must first be motivated to fulfill a duty that is valued by his acquaintance. This obligation is known as the duty of accountability. When the individual accepts this duty, he is essentially offering a gesture of friendship towards his acquaintance. In so doing, the individual will be making his first step towards building a true and lasting friendship with another person. True friendships can only be acquired when the individual has built a greater familiarity with his acquaintance. This degree of familiarity can only be achieved when the individual accepts a form of accountability, in relation to all of his interactions with this other person. Accordingly, whenever the individual meets an active acquaintance, in order to prolong this relationship, he must accept a kind of responsibility. Likewise, he may only cultivate this relationship into a friendship if he actually accepts some form of duty towards this individual.

The duty of accountability requires three principles. First of all, in order to recognize one's compatibilities with other persons, the individual must possess the principle of understanding. It is through the understanding of another person's spirit and character that enables the individual to discover any forms of resemblances or commonalities. Whenever the individual possesses an understanding of another person's persona, he must then make a judgment in relation to this knowledge. If he views this individual as an equally rational human being, he may then develop this relationship into an indefinite friendship. Yet, if he perceives his acquaintance as an irrational human being, he will also, necessarily, lack a definite understanding in relation to this individual's intrinsic spirit and character. Subsequently, in order to build a lasting and permanent friendship, the individual needs to possess an equivalent level of rational thinking with his acquaintance, so that he may grasp an understanding with respect to his acquaintance's motives and intentions. After this degree of understanding is achieved, the individual will then be able to build an unbounded degree of understanding, in relation to his acquaintance's internal spirit and persona.

Next, after this form of understanding is accomplished, the principle of respect will also be required. In essence, persons who possess the principle of respect will direct a form of regard towards both the similarities and the differences within another individual's underlying character. Therefore, the principle of respect is always directed towards another person's behaviour. When an individual behaves wrongly, within the eyes of the perceiver, he does not deserve any forms of respect. Likewise, when the individual acts according to principles of justice, he does deserve forms of respect. In the realm of friendships, the principle of respect is required to serve as a second building block, after the act of understanding is achieved. Likewise, no forms of positive relationships can ever be attained if no forms of respect are ever established between two individuals. Accordingly, in order to establish a true friendship, the individual must hold a certain degree of respect that is directed towards both the dissimilarities and the unique character traits of his acquaintance.

Lastly, the duty of accountability also requires the principle of trust. It is through the principle of trust that enables one individual to depend on another. If there are no forms of dependence present in any given relationship, there are also no forms of trust. This is due to the nature of true and lasting friendships. Among true friendships, the individual must feel free to reveal any of his particular dependencies to his associate. The individual reveals his dependencies in the hopes that his associate will provide some form of aid, directed strictly towards tempering his particular dependency. If the individual suspects that his associate may become devious and successively take advantage of his dependencies, then no forms of trust have ever been established. However, if the individual relies on his associate to provide some form of aid, then he also necessarily trusts this individual. Subsequently, the principle of trust is also necessary among all true friendships.

Persons who adopt the duty of accountability are motivated by the virtue of honour. In essence, persons who are motivated by honour place the utmost importance on the concepts of moral obligation and respect. The honourable always demonstrate respect wherever respect is due, and likewise, they will also refrain from acknowledging those persons who do not deserve any forms of respect. Since those who are honourable are also not hypocritical, they will, in turn, accept accountability for all of their actions and behaviours. In so doing, they mainly demonstrate courtesy and gentleness to other persons. In return for acting with discernment, the honourable will then acquire a positive reputation within their community. This, then, leads to the acquisition of acquaintances. Yet, in order to create lasting friendships, the individual must maintain his duty of accountability throughout all of his relationships. Hence, those who are motivated by honour will always be accountable for their actions, whether their behaviour is based on either goodness or folly. This leads to the formation of true and lifelong friendships.

Friendships are first created through the principles of understanding and respect, and likewise, they are prolonged through the principle of trust. Those persons who do not possess these principles will never be motivated by the virtue of honour. Actually, individuals who do not accept any kinds of duty towards their acquaintances merely wish to temporarily cure their bouts of loneliness. Hence, those individuals who lack the ability to create and maintain any forms of friendships will be mainly motivated by the vice of shamelessness. Individuals who are shameless do not recognize the existence of any kinds of moral principles. Some also do not view certain criminal acts as immoral. Rather, they place higher value on the liberty granted to them through free will. Whenever the shameless are responsible for vicious acts or other transgressions, they will rarely view their acts as immoral. As such, those who are shameless do not experience sorrow if they are responsible for the abuse of another individual. Whenever this occurs, the shameless will have nullified the potential to build any friendly relations with other persons within their community.

In addition to his friendships, every individual will also possess some kind of role in relation to other citizens within his community. In order to become a recognized member of his community, every able bodied person must also uphold the duty to contribute. This is due to the nature of human culture. A community cannot exist without the concept of cooperation, and subsequently, it also cannot exist without any forms of positive relationships amongst its citizens. Furthermore, progress in the fields of medicine, science and technology cannot be achieved if only a fraction of the population accepts the duty to contribute.

Individuals who contribute in a positive manner, within their society, will possess the principles of consideration, determination and dependability. With respect to the principle of consideration, there are many avenues available to the individual, with respect to his liberty to contribute. Everything that exists amidst human society may be, fundamentally, essential for our existence. Obviously, the bare necessities for human existence are food, shelter and clothing. Yet, aspects like technology improve our living conditions, and likewise, forms of art serve to cultivate our spirit. Accordingly, almost everything that any human being has ever created beyond the bare necessities of life is also, to a varying degree, indispensable. When the individual possesses the principle of consideration, he will recognize and become aware of this truth. Subsequently, those who are considerate will analyze the needs of a particular segment within our society, and provide for these persons.

The principle of determination is also necessary in one's duty to contribute. Individuals who are determined will not recognize or be hindered by any forms of obstacles that may impede their personal goals. Accordingly, these individuals will continue to contribute their labour, despite the fact that many hardships still exist before them. Since no forms of labour are undemanding, all forms of contributions require some amount of effort. Therefore, persons who accept the duty to contribute must be determined, because they must employ an appropriate amount of effort to accomplish their personal goals. Thus, in order to truly contribute something positive towards one's community, the individual must first be determined to make a positive difference within his community.

Lastly, the principle of dependability is also necessary in this duty. Persons who possess this principle recognize the fact that every community is built upon the concepts of cooperation and interdependence. As such, these individuals understand the fact that every able bodied person must contribute some form of labour, in order to sustain the interconnected spirit that defines any given community. Likewise, these individuals understand the fact that all forms of development within human civilization cannot exist within an uncooperative, non-communal setting. Therefore, persons who are dependable understand their particular role within their community, and they will fulfill their role even during cases when they lack the volition to contribute. No matter what their part may be, persons who dependably contribute will always have some role in the building of a greater society.

Persons who adopt the duty to contribute will be mainly motivated by the virtue of diligence. This is due to their understanding that all forms of manmade wonders are afforded to us strictly through the efforts of other persons. Instead of merely benefiting from manmade wonders, persons who are diligent also wish to produce some kind of manmade wonder. Persons who are diligent realize the fact that hard work, among many differing individuals, is essential to the creation of any kind of wonder. Subsequently, the diligent view their community as a kind of well-oiled machine, and they will dedicate their labour towards improving a certain facet within it.

Those persons who do not accept the duty to contribute may be motivated by the vice of vanity. Every person who lives within a communal environment must also contribute some form of labour, because of the fact that all societies are founded upon the element of cooperation. Indeed, every individual wishes to fill an important role within his society, and likewise, every person wishes to obtain a well-compensated form of employment. Nevertheless, due to the element of competition, in many cases, obtaining these ideals may be difficult. For these individuals, a lesser role within their society may be unacceptable. Accordingly, these individuals may not contribute any services within their community, due solely to the notion of arrogance. In essence, these individuals place excessive importance on their physical appearance, and consequently, they will refuse to accept any roles that they personally deem are substandard in nature. Those who are motivated by vanity possess a form of arrogance that is directed towards their physical appearances. As a result, personal appearances may impede some individual's duty to contribute, especially during cases where his perceived potential to contribute outweighs his natural means.

For those individuals who are theists, a key duty that is inherently accepted is a duty to God. This duty may be known as the duty of persisting faith. Even for the most dedicated theists, this duty may, at times, be difficult to maintain. This lack of faith may be due to two main reasons. First of all, the element of doubt may impede some person's religious beliefs. Since God does not reveal Himself to us, within the material world, it may be rationally possible to doubt His existence. Yet, the most important element why some persons will abandon their faith in God is due to the prevalence of evil. Throughout our history, mankind has been plagued with so many horrific evils. The most difficult evil to accept is the many occurrences of human suffering. Indeed, within some persons' rationale, the existence of a benevolent God cannot be consistent with a world that is plagued by so much suffering. Therefore, the existence of so many instances of appalling evils could, conceptually, contradict the existence of a caring and compassionate God.

With respect to the concept of doubt, since no individuals have physically perceived God, this may provide some atheists with a reasonable form of doubt, in relation to His existence. Likewise, this form of doubt is liable to affect some theists, especially during times when the theist experiences circumstances of extreme adversity. As a result, those individuals who adopt the duty of persisting faith, despite experiencing forms of adversity, will possess the principle of sensibleness. Individuals who possess this principle have direct access to a wide scope of knowledge and wisdom. Those who are sensible utilize the totality of their knowledge and intelligence during any form of dispute. Accordingly, these individuals possess the ability to analyze every fact that may be relevant within a given dispute. With respect to the existence of God, these individuals understand that the single premise of doubt cannot rationally dissuade any forms of theistic beliefs, essentially due to the fact that there exists so many other premises that may prove the contrary. Therefore, those who possess the principle of sensibleness will weigh all possible relevant facts, and make their judgement according to the totality of their personal knowledge. Within the mind of the sensible, since there are so many other forms of evidence that suggests the existence of God, a single premise, such as doubt, cannot rationally overturn their original judgment.

    Also important to the duty of persisting faith is the principle of objectivity. Instead of concluding that the existence of a benevolent God may be inconsistent with the prevalence of horrific evils, perhaps we should analyze the concept of evil and the most concrete reasons for its particular existence. Life, itself, may be viewed as a kind of wonder, while horrific evils are usually associated with the experience of extreme suffering or the suppression of life. Moreover, life as a human being includes the utilization of a free will. It is through the freedom of our will where it is possible that some persons may hold a reversed outlook on life, on the subject of horrific evils. Therefore, it is conceivably possible that some individuals may view horrific evils as a kind of wonder, all the while associating life with extreme suffering. Correspondingly, it is the utilization of free will, especially in the case of human beings, which provides the birth of horrific and extreme forms of evil. The fact that human beings are afforded with a free will does not excuse the actions of any evil doer. Rather, the scope of our free will merely explains the source of horrific evils. Since our will is unbounded, in the realm of morality, it is possible that any free individual may be responsible for the materialization of evil, just as easily as he may be responsible for acts of goodness.

As a consequence, it is through our free will which enables us to associate life with either happiness or extreme suffering. From an objective perspective, the former individuals may highly value their existence, while the latter individuals may not. Hence, through the power of free will, every human being may either embrace and cherish his existence, or forsake it. Accordingly, from a purely objective perspective, the materialization of evil in our world does not truly come from God. Rather, the most horrific forms of evil are committed by human beings, who are afforded this kind of power solely through their freedom to choose.

It is through the principle of objectivity where we come to realize that we are all moral creatures who possess the will to either live a moral life, or a life inundated with discontent.

The concept of morality possibly demonstrates the outermost limits with respect to the power of our will. Those individuals who value life, also necessarily value their own existence. In contrast, those individuals who do not value other forms of life, conceivably, also do not value their own subjective existence. Accordingly, the power of our will to either accept or reject our own essential existence provides the foundation behind either a moral compass, or a mindset based on downright evil. When the individual rejects his own existence, he will not value any other forms of life, and this leads to the birth and materialization of the most horrific forms of evil. Nevertheless, even during times of extreme hardships, there do exist theists who possess an absolute faith in God's existence. These individuals have accepted the duty of persisting faith, and they demonstrate this through their efforts to quash any forms of reasonable doubt against the existence of God. Subsequently, it is through the principle of objectivity which enables us to remain faithful to God, despite the existence of so many instances of evil.

Impartiality is the final principle necessary for the duty of persisting faith. First of all, in our world there exists many differing kinds of religions, each of which provide a unique definition of God. Since God does not reveal Himself to us within the physical world, no person may either confirm or deny their individual perception of God, in relation to His specific attributes. The duty of persisting faith requires that an individual should continue to believe in His existence during all possible circumstances, but the principle of impartiality allows for a continued faith in God, regardless of His true personal attributes. Therefore, we all have a duty to believe in the same God, despite the fact that we have no actual knowledge of His intrinsic spirit and character.

Secondly, the principle of impartiality also applies to persons of differing kinds of faith. The most important aspect in the duty of persisting faith is the continued faith in God's existence. Even though differing religions stress differing values, all religious persons are united in the fact that they are all theists. The most important aspect of being a theist is having an unwavering faith in God, and not so much how we perceive Him to be. Therefore, in addition to being impartial with respect to the definition of God, those who adopt the duty of persisting faith must also hold an impartial attitude towards all theists who belong to differing and distinct religions. An unconditional form of tolerance must also apply to persons of differing faiths, essentially because of the fact that we all share at least one commonality, in that we have all been created by God. Hence, since all forms of life have been created by God, we must possess an impartial attitude towards each other, especially during cases where there exists real and tangible differences in our religious beliefs.

Those individuals who accept the duty of persisting faith will be mainly motivated by the virtue of peacefulness. The virtue of peace may be exemplified through our spirit, through our character, or through both. Those persons who possess a peaceful spirit continually work towards controlling their negative emotions. All persons experience the emotion of anger, yet only some persons possess the power to negate this emotion through a form of self-discipline. Those individuals who possess a peaceful character freely experience negative emotions, but they possess the discipline to restrain their actions and behaviour, in relation to these emotions. Accordingly, those who are peaceful will repudiate any forms of abuse as a means to an end. With respect to the duty of persisting faith, only those who are peaceful will adopt this duty, because of the fact that they do not succumb to their feelings of anger. Subsequently, these persons will experience happiness on a more frequent basis, in comparison to the angry man. As such, the peaceful will accept the universe as it is, in addition to their particular role within it. Persons who are peaceful will exhibit a particular solidarity, in relation to our natural world. In accepting the unique nature of the universe, the individual will also accept its creator, despite the frequent occurrences of pain and anguish that may exist within it.

Individuals who do not adopt the duty of persisting faith will be motivated by the vice of blasphemy. Those who lack the virtue of peacefulness will always succumb to their feelings of anger. As a response to their negative emotions, these individuals wish to cause extreme pain and suffering in other persons. In particular, denying the sacred beliefs held by the moral individual may be the most direct method that will enable them to accomplish this task. Therefore, in the case of religion, disparaging the existence of a morally supreme God will cause a loss of hope and optimism. Persons who are blasphemous usually seek a form of revenge against not a particular individual, but their entire community altogether. They achieve personal success whenever they are individually responsible for the promotion of gloom and despair.

Individuals who are theists believe that all forms of life have been created by God. In this case, the theist will also inevitably adopt the duty of selfless provision. The duty of selfless provision mainly revolves around the concept of charity. Persons who are charitable possess some form of wealth, and they are willing to provide material aid to other persons through their personal fortune. Within developed nations, no matter what financial circumstances a person may be in, it is usually the case that he possesses more forms of material wealth in comparison to some other person around the world. For example, individuals who are receiving social assistance within a developed country will still possess more wealth than another person who resides within a developing country. As a consequence, individuals become charitable essentially because they possess both the financial means and the desire to carry out this task.

Persons who adopt the duty of selfless provision must possess the principle of equality. Since all forms of life have been created by single creator, it is conceivable to hold the belief that all forms of life also possess an equal right to exist. Consequently, it is through the concept of equality which motivates us to provide some form of aid for persons who may lack material forms of wealth. Ideologically, when we view another human being as a comrade, we will also be motivated to provide for this person, during times of need. Only those who vainly reject concepts of equality will also reject the duty of selfless provision.

Persons who adopt the duty of selfless provision also require the principle of vigour. The act of charity is usually directed towards those individuals who may be less fortunate, in terms of material wealth. However, through the development of goodwill, acts of charity may also be directed towards persons who may be suffering from some form of illness. Individuals who possess the duty of selfless provision may also be motivated to ease the suffering and pain that these persons experience, through acts of charity. Subsequently, those individuals who are vigorous will also provide the source for feelings of optimism in individuals who may be less fortunate. Individuals who adopt the duty of selfless provision must act with vigour so that they may properly address the problems of those who have either been poverty stricken or diagnosed with some form of devastating illness.

The individual who accepts the duty of selfless provision will be motivated by the virtue of resilience. Resilience is a form of courage related to an individual's personal struggles. Those who possess this virtue do not succumb to any forms of adversity. Rather, these individuals will first recognize their personal problems, and then address them through an objective perspective. Subsequently, persons who are resilient possess an innate ability to solve a wide range of problems.

With respect to the duty of selfless provision, only those individuals who possess the capability to solve their own unique problems will possess the ability to recognize and address the problems that may be faced by another individual. Accordingly, the resilient do not merely solve another person's personal problems, but they also pass on the concessions of courage and confidence, and this grants other persons with the capacity to solve any problems that they, themselves, may face at some future time.

Individuals who do not accept the duty of selfless provision are mainly motivated by the vice of jealousy. These persons primarily direct their feelings of jealousy towards the concept of aid. Hence, they become jealous of the fact that some individual, other than themselves, is receiving a form of aid from other persons. Moreover, since these individuals have never been the recipients of any forms of aid, this gives them a rational reason why they should not provide support towards those persons who live in less fortunate circumstances. Subsequently, even though some of these individuals may possess the monetary means to help persons in need, they will refrain from providing aid essentially because of the fact that they have never received any forms of aid themselves. These persons are jealous of the fact that those in need are provided forms of aid, and thus are the recipients of a special form of treatment. As a consequence, this gives them enough reason to abstain from becoming the source of any forms of charity or mutual aid.

The duty of selfless provision is directed towards persons around the world who may be less fortunate than the provider himself. Nevertheless, we must also focus some consideration towards all other forms of life that may exist within our natural environment. This form of benevolence is known as the duty of immutability. The duty of immutability is directed towards both animal and plant species that habituate the wild. Yet, our children will also benefit, if we accept this duty. All forms of life possess an innate right to exist. However, since we have discovered the fact that our environment functions as a kind of interdependent ecosystem, it is in every person's best interest to preserve all forms of functioning ecosystems that may presently exist.

Persons who adopt the duty of immutability need to possess the principle of flexibility. In relation to our environment, there are many aspects in human life which possess the potential to destroy it. For example, our dependence on oil creates forms of pollution. In enough time, this form of pollution will have a detrimental effect on many differing ecosystems. As such, we must shift our entire way of life in order to correct these kinds of potential problems. From an objective perspective, the human race must be flexible, in terms of our oil consumption. In time, our flexibility will be realized, when newer forms of engineering have evolved. For example, if our entire population switches to hybrid technology, this will demonstrate the amount of flexibility needed that will enable us, as an entire species, to fulfill the duty of immutability.

Secondly, persons who adopt the duty of immutability will require the principle of curiosity. In actuality, the only method that enables us to understand the complex intricacies that exist within our environment is through research, and inevitably, environmental science. Yet, those individuals who become environmental scientists must first possess the yearning to gain some form of understanding within this specific field. After the environmental scientist acquires concrete forms of knowledge, it is then up to the common individual to acquire a similar form of awareness, and this will enable both individuals to work towards the goal of ecological conservation. Hence, individuals who adopt the duty of immutability must, necessarily, possess a volition to gain a comprehensive understanding, in relation to the multifarious inner workings of a particular ecosystem.

Those who adopt the duty of immutability will be motivated by the virtue of insight. Insight is a form of knowledge that is not easily attainable. Nevertheless, it is an element that is a defining feature of being human. The individual usually only possesses a form of insight within a particular field or subject matter. Yet, when the individual shares his insight with other persons, this marks the beginning of a form of cooperation among all human beings. With respect to the duty of immutability, all forms of life possess a kind of unique spirit. In the realm of humanity, every person also similarly possesses a unique spirit. When the individual studies nature, he will be granted with a form of insight in relation to some unique spiritual aspect that exists within the wild. As such, when we preserve some element in nature, we are also actively preserving some unique spirit that exists in the wild. Subsequently, individuals who adopt the duty of immutability will gain a boundless form of insight, in relation to the spiritual nature of a given habitat. Those individuals who work to preserve this element in nature do so because they recognize and value the spiritual aspects that may be found within some particular ecosystem.

Individuals who do not adopt the duty of immutability are motivated by the vice of indifference. In essence, these individuals will possess a centre of emotions that is directed merely towards their own existence. Accordingly, persons who are motivated by indifference value little else than the quality of their own lifestyle. These individuals may seek forms of luxury, at the expense of any other living being. Therefore, these persons maintain their selfish lifestyle because they lack a strong ethical stance on most subjects that have some kind of bearing or moral significance. The indifferent are egocentric, and they also lack a sense of communal morality. Accordingly, they do not consider the negative effects that their actions may have on their living environment.

The final duty that an individual may accept is directed towards his neighbour. This obligation is known as the duty of innocuous action. The duty of innocuous action is based on a form of moderation in relation to one's behaviour. Individuals who accept this duty will actively correct and adjust their behaviour, in an effort to maintain peaceful ties with their neighbour. The concept of a neighbour may be defined as any person who possesses the potential to come into contact with a particular individual. Therefore, a neighbour may be any individual who is not currently engaged in some form of friendship or intimate relationship with the agent. In effect, a neighbour is an acquaintance who, infrequently, engages in friendly interactions with the individual. Similar to the entity of a family, one rarely has the power to choose his specific neighbours. A neighbour is just some person who both lives within the same community, and possesses very few elements in common with the individual. Subsequently, in order to maintain friendly interactions with his neighbour, the individual must first accept a form of responsibility directed towards this individual.

Individuals who uphold the duty of innocuous action possess the principle of diversity. In fact, persons from all walks of life may share something in common with any given agent. Persons of a differing gender, ethnicity, religion, or political affiliation may all, in fact, possess the principle of diversity. Actually, it is quite often the case that persons of a differing religion will also possess a differing value system. The same may be true with respect to the individual's political stance. Yet, persons who possess the principle of diversity realize the fact that differing value systems may reveal differing truths, regarding our natural world. Individuals who possess this principle also realize the fact that the value systems that they currently possess could be narrow or mistaken. Therefore, individuals who possess the principle of diversity are entirely open to change, with respect to rigid value systems. As such, they will actively moderate their behaviour whenever they may enter into some form of an ideological conflict, in an effort to demonstrate a form of respect and rational acknowledgement towards an opposing value system.

The principle of obedience is also required in the duty of innocuous action. Primarily, in order to become a dutiful neighbour, one cannot commit any purposeful transgressions against any persons who may reside within his community. Individuals who are responsible for even the minutest of crimes may eventually be deemed as recluses within their neighbourhood. This is due to the fact that all forms of criminal behaviour directly affect some innocent civilian. Accordingly, only those individuals who follow the laws that are established within their society may actually possess the ability to uphold the duty of innocuous action. Criminals who purposefully and continually disregard the laws of their community will be actively neglecting any forms of duty that may be directed towards their neighbour. The individual must also recognize the existence of civil laws, if he is to build some kind of relationship with his communal neighbour.

Those who have adopted the principles of diversity and obedience will then need to acquire the principle of unity. In order to fulfill the duty of innocuous action, the individual must further unite himself with his neighbour, according to some commonality. It is through commonalities in spirit and character where all friendships are made. Yet, there may be few commonalities that exist between two neighbours.

Subsequently, in order to uphold the duty of innocuous action, the individual must first find and recognize the commonalities that do exist between himself and his neighbour. At the most basic level, the principle of unity demonstrates the individual's personal volition to build a relationship with his neighbour, even during cases where there may lack any similarities in spirit or character between these two individuals.

As a result, individuals who adopt the duty of innocuous action will be motivated by the virtue of patience. Persons who possess this virtue understand the fact that imperfections are a common element in human existence. As such, individuals who are patient will naturally accept the mistakes and blunders of other persons. Persons who are patient do not possess either a superiority or inferiority complex. They are extremely tolerant, and this enables them to moderate and temper their negative emotions during difficult situations. Nevertheless, this does not mean that patient individuals should accept immoral forms of behaviour. In actuality, those who are patient possess a strong core of moral values, and it is this attribute that enables them to remain peaceful whenever some other person may be guilty of some kind of error. Persons who are motivated by patience are essentially agents of toleration. Their attitude enables them to remain benevolent during times of conflict. As a consequence, these individuals will rarely offend any strangers, and this enables them to fulfill the duty of innocuous action.

Individuals who do not adopt the duty of innocuous action will be motivated by the vice of despair. Persons who are motivated by this vice usually focus on concepts of negativity, and subsequently, they will also lack many forms of happiness. Their negative attitude may be further responsible for their lack of friendships or acquaintances. In a chain link fashion, this social isolation will compound their feelings of desolation. In order to alleviate these feelings of isolation, their next efforts will be to cause feelings of despair in other persons. As a consequence, individuals who are motivated by despair lack the intrinsic ability to perform any innocuous actions. They may be mainly responsible for insulting their neighbours. These individuals will not treat their neighbours with respect, essentially because they lack a sufficient amount of positive experiences in relation to their own personal esteem.

Therefore, while a certain set of principles are necessary to complete a specific duty, the characteristic of virtue will be the main element that compels the individual to recognize and accept a particular duty. With respect to virtue, individuals acquire these moral qualities through the liberty of the will, in conjunction with the unique spiritual makeup of their soul. Nonetheless, virtue can also be acquired through knowledge. Therefore, as the individual matures through his life, he will also inevitably acquire newer kinds of virtue.

The element of perspective also plays a role in the individual's concept of duty. All human beings possess the power to shift their personal focus from a first person to a third person's perspective. The first person perspective may be known merely as private consciousness. When the individual is present within this mental state, he will be mainly in the process of experiencing his sensory perceptions, and also his emotional states. All living animals possess this level of consciousness. Private consciousness is the most basic form of perception and awareness available to all human beings.

In contrast, a third person's perspective is attained whenever the individual shifts his focus out of a pure consciousness, into a more objective mental state. This mental state may be known as open-minded insight. Whenever the individual enters into this mental state, he will view the physical world through a self-conscious state. Through this perspective, the individual is actually aware of himself as an agent, and he further possesses the ability to analyze the world through another person's perspective. Accordingly, individuals who perceive the world through open-minded insight will shift their focus out of a purely subjective perspective, into a more analytical state. This enables the individual to reflect upon himself, in terms of his actions and overall character.

To illustrate the differences between these mental states, consider the act of breathing. Every person breathes oxygen through a constant and systematic fashion. Nonetheless, even though every person needs to continually breathe to survive, he is not always aware of the fact that he is performing this action. When the individual is not aware of the fact that he is performing this act, he lacks an awareness of his self, and his perspective will be focused mainly onto his physical environment. In this case, he is presently in the state of private consciousness.

In contrast, when the individual actually becomes aware of the fact that he is performing the act of breathing, he will possess an awareness that ranges mainly onto his own being. In these cases, the individual has shifted his perspective out of a state of private consciousness, into the state of open-minded insight. When this occurs, the individual has been granted with a particular wonder, in the form of a second perspective on life. Actually, when in a state of open-minded insight, the individual will not be directly affected by his emotional states. Rather, he is mainly in the process of analyzing his experiences that were gained through a state of private consciousness, and this leads to the acquisition of a form of personal awareness, in the form of intuition. In other words, when the individual possesses the ability to pause, reflect upon, and examine his experiences within a state of private consciousness, he will be entering into the state of open-minded insight. It is this form of intuition that enables each individual to recognize his duties, according to his specific and unique circumstances.

The same thing could be said about the passage of time. Individuals who remain in a state of private consciousness will also lack an inherent awareness of the passage of time. It is only when they enter into a state of open-minded insight where they may shift their focus back onto the phenomenon of time. Accordingly, those who remain in a constant state of private consciousness will always lack an awareness with respect to the passing of time.

Actually, many persons do not utilize their ability to shift their perspective, on a frequent enough basis. These individuals will spend the bulk of their life within the simplistic mental state of private consciousness. Persons who remain in this state view the world strictly through their own emotional states and personal biases. This reflects upon their selfish or egotistical habits, and it is mainly through the mindset and impressions of self-centredness where the elements of corruption and vice are born.

Nevertheless, whenever the static character is guilty of some crime, he will possess the volition to remain out of a state of private consciousness. He does this primarily so that he may plausibly disavow the fact that he is guilty of any immoral act. When he does remain within a state of private consciousness, he will usually centre his awareness on the fact that he is guilty of some form of abuse. This particular awareness then forces him to lower his own perceived social status to that of a criminal. Accordingly, he may then leave a state of private consciousness, while entering into a state of self-denial, in order to deal with these specific feelings. He does this in the hopes that his victims will give him the benefit of the doubt. This feature reflects upon the criminal's static nature, where he will eventually reacquire his quest for social authority.

In fact, the majority of criminals do not recognize the principles of sharing and cooperation. Since they are highly egotistical, they will also usually lack many forms of meaningful relationships. Nonetheless, criminals do seem to cooperate with each other, at least in the task of suppressing the innocent. In this exclusive form of cooperation, static criminals will attack any persons who do not grant them any forms of authority. These forms of attacks also pertain to entire strangers. The motives behind these attacks are based on the premise that their particular acts will weaken their irrepressible victim. Those individuals who do become weakened will then face a high potential to become the victim of another static character. As a result, this is the extent regarding the kinds of cooperation held between two static criminals. The static criminal attacks the robust in the hopes that another static character, who may be unknown to him, will accomplish the goal of achieving the social authority that he, himself, had failed to achieve. This form of cooperation may be analogous to the sole form of duty that exists between two static criminals.

On the contrary, if the dynamic character hurts another individual, he will experience a sense of shame, whenever he returns back into a state of self-consciousness. This sense of realization gives the dynamic character enough reason not to commit any similar mistakes during some future time. As a consequence, this is the major difference between first time offenders and career criminals. The career criminal's lack of self-conscious shame will inevitably lead to more forms of antisocial behaviour. Moreover, when he leaves a state of private consciousness, the static criminal will primarily plead his innocence. Contrarily, when the dynamic character enters into a state of open-minded insight, he will mainly focus on the well-being of other persons.

The dynamic character's natural ability to shift his consciousness gives him a greater ability for introspection. This ability enables him to continually reflect upon his own character, which grants him with a greater understanding of his own spiritual nature. This ability to understand oneself is entirely necessary whenever the individual enters into any true relationships based on friendship or affection.

Subsequently, duties are mainly culminations of action. Those individuals who accept similar duties will also possess common traits, with respect to their character. On the other hand, virtues provide the individual with a reason to take on a particular duty. In these cases, persons who possess similar virtues will possess something in common with respect to their rationale.

In the realm of relationships, when two individuals meet, they will become acquaintances, if they possess a single virtue in common. This relationship will progress into a friendship, if these two acquaintances possess multiple virtues in common. When two friends share similar duties, their friendship will further evolve, and they will subsequently become life partners. Yet, the establishment of a life partner is not something that is easily acquired. In order to share similar duties, these two individuals must both possess similar virtues, in additional to similarities in spirit. Accordingly, it is commonalities among both an individual's personal virtues and his duties which provide the building blocks behind all of his relationships. Minor relationships will evolve into lifetime friendships whenever the two individuals involved have freely chosen to adopt similar duties.

In contrast, familial relationships are established through a converse process. Actually, all persons that belong to a single family will automatically possess lifetime friendships. Familial relationships will only start to deteriorate once a family member has neglected his duties. Therefore, within the familial setting, every individual will possess a lifetime bond with both his parents and his siblings, at birth. Yet, when his parent fails to fulfill the duty of responsible parenthood, this bond will be broken. In a similar circumstance, when the individual's sibling fails to adopt the duty of acceptance and support, this relationship will also spiral in a downward fashion.

Therefore, in the case of acquaintances, these kinds of relationships only have the potential to grow. It is through the recognition of commonalities in virtue and duty which builds a relationship into a lifetime friendship. In contrast, within the familial setting, the individuals involved already, by nature, possess a lifelong relationship. It is only through the abandonment of duty, by any single member, which causes a potential lifelong relationship to decline. Accordingly, the powers of virtue and duty remain clear. Similarities among virtues and duties can turn two strangers into lifelong partners, while the abandonment of virtue and duty can turn family members into adversaries.

Thus, while some duties are associated with free actions, other duties may be associated with specific circumstances or environmental factors. For example, the individual does not possess a duty towards any of his acquaintances, if he does not wish to develop these particular relationships. When the individual accepts a form of duty towards his acquaintances, it is done entirely through his own free will. On the other hand, natural duties are determined by the individual's environment. No individual possesses the power to choose his siblings. These kinds of duties have been placed upon the individual, beyond the power of his will. Thus, natural duties are determined by the individual's specific environmental factors. The adoption of all other duties depends on free lifestyle choices, which are determined entirely through the individual's will.

Furthermore, some individuals are born to fulfill certain duties. For example, in the realm of politics, an individual may possess the innate characteristics related to leadership. These individuals' future contributions may have been determined by birth. In order to fulfill a certain duty, though, one must possess a certain set of principles. Likewise, the volition to complete any duty is also entirely necessary. Therefore, potential duties reflect upon the virtues and principles found within any single individual's spirit.

Indeed, duties are complicated modes of action, in that the individual must possess the relevant attributes to properly uphold any particular duty. As a consequence, there do exist persons who lack the sufficient knowledge to undertake a specific duty. For instance, children should not be compelled to accept the duty to contribute, because they may lack the knowledge that is necessary to properly carry out this task. Another person may lack a specific principle that would enable him to fulfill some duty. The sheltered adult could lack a sufficient principle base required for a particular duty, due to a lack of life experiences.

Accordingly, the most essential aspect of duty is the acquisition of virtue. All individuals must first possess the necessary motivations to carry out their duties. Therefore, the acquisition of virtue is the chief element related to duty. Many individuals do possess virtues, while lacking the inherent ability to carry out their duties. Only cultured adults will have acquired both the sufficient knowledge and the necessary principle base to fulfil their duties. Yet, when an individual upholds the mere intention to accept his obligations and responsibilities, this demonstrates a critical sign that he has matured into a grown adult.

These latter individuals should not be judged by their inaction, but only by their pure motivation to adopt and fulfill their duties. In comparison, persons who are motivated by vice will also be responsible for inaction, in relation to their natural duties. However, these are two extremely differing and contradictory reasons which are the cause of inaction, behind these two individuals.

The virtuous man who fails to fulfil his duties, due to a lack of knowledge, is still virtuous in spirit. In contrast, individuals who lack the volition to fulfill any duties are vicious, since this element reflects upon selfish action. This is due to the fact that all true duties benefit not only the agent himself, but also the individual who is the target of the agent's obligations.

Therefore, the individual may either affirm or deny the actuality that he possesses any duties. Only those persons who accept their duties deserve respect, while conversely, persons who do not deserve respect will mainly abandon their duties. The difference between these two individuals is based on the acquisition of virtue, yet there may also be differences within their specific emotional states. Love and hate are the two most powerful human emotions. Individuals who love other persons will provide for these individuals. In contrast, those persons who are responsible for elements of detriment within their community will be mainly motivated by the emotion of hate.

The limitless nature of the human will enables each individual to experience differing emotions with respect to the same object. Even if no human being possessed the power to direct his emotional centre, the liberty we possess through our will still enables us to make choices that may contradict our inborn spiritual nature. Therefore, individuals who experience emotions of love may be guilty of immoral acts, while individuals who experience emotions of hate may be responsible for highly moral acts. Subsequently, this reflects upon the power that is implicit within a liberated will.

Therefore, all persons possess the power to surpass their inborn nature, and thus, live an entirely liberated life. In contrast, the individual may also fail to achieve his inborn potential, which makes his life susceptible to being determined entirely by his environment. Those persons who are truly free will determine every aspect of their life, while those who are not free will live a life that may be mainly determined by their environment.

In view of that, should we judge morality strictly through the correct utilization of the will? It is an intrinsic part of human nature that we all possess an entirely liberated will. Can we fault any man who merely exercises the freedom possessed within his will? It is through free will where every individual possesses the potential to surpass, live out, or fail to fulfil his inborn nature. However, free will also empowers every person to choose between morality and immorality.

Some persons may be dutiful by nature, while other persons may merely appear to be dutiful. As rational creatures, all human beings exercise the liberty of their will according to their personal rationale. Indeed, freedom is the ability to say yes or no in the same situation, or in essence, the ability to affirm or deny. However, the most important aspect of freedom, or the will, is the reason which compels it to decide. Since two entirely opposite spirits may be responsible for the same action, we must judge, not merely the individual's particular action, but the personal reasons that motivate his actions. Consequently, ethics should not be solely determined by one's behaviour, but also by the specific reasons that motivate each individual to act.

With respect to the will, its capacity to choose remains utterly unbounded. In other words, the immaterial nature of our will is wholly powerful. Through our free will, we possess the capacity to choose strictly according to our own personal volitions. Yet, the set of choices available to all human beings remain finite. This is due to the fact that all human beings are grounded according to a physical existence. The choices available to our will are limited by the physical nature of our universe. I cannot travel to another continent purely through the application of my will. Since I exist as a physical being, I must first obey the laws of physics and build a boat that will carry me to this alternate garden. Subsequently, my will, in this regard, is limited by my physical body. I do not possess the ability to do anything, purely at will, because of my material nature.

All of the limitations placed upon the will create a form of solidarity between all living beings. Our physical nature unites us with other physical forms of life that may be found in the world. In addition, our physical limitations serve to draw some kind of bond between spiritually distinct individuals. Even though the spiritual nature of each person remains entirely unique, since we are grounded by a physical existence, we will, inevitably, share some commonalities in character.

First of all, we all require elements like nourishment and shelter for our continued existence. All animals in the wilderness also require these elements for their survival. Yet, when we analyze its ability to choose, the animal's will is limited by its instincts. When an animal utilizes its will, the choices available to it are limited by its natural impulses, in relation to the concept of survival. Indeed, animals make their choices based on those actions which will further their continued survival. When the bear is foraging for food in the forest and encounters another animal, he is faced with the choice of either getting into an altercation, or he may also flee. This is known as the fight or flight response. In fact, animal instincts may be defined as a form of judgment that lacks the element of reason. Since the common animal cannot make a choice in contrary to his instincts, his spirit will always be compelled by this element of his psyche.

In comparison to animal instincts, human beings possess the faculty of reason. Within our frame of mind, it is reason that mainly determines our judgments. Accordingly, because we possess a faculty of reason, we possess the ability to deliberate between two options before we actually make any final decisions. When we deliberate and finally make a decision, we do so not because of any natural impulses, but mainly through a form of ordered thought. Nevertheless, similar to the fact that the animal's will to choose is limited by his instincts, the choices that are available to us are limited by our faculty of reason.

Therefore, even though we possess an absolute power to affirm or deny, the choices made available to our will are limited by our faculty of reason. Human beings do not choose an action if they have no reason to do so. We cannot apply our will to act according to some option that, in its totality, escapes all forms of reason. Accordingly, no human being possesses the power to choose an act which eludes even the minutest forms of reason. As human beings, we first deliberate and then we choose to act according to some reason. We all possess some degree of rationale that compels us to choose one option over another.

In both cases, the spiritual nature of an entity's existence essentially places a limitation on its choices. It is through our faculty of reason that makes all human beings moral creatures. In contrast, animals in the wild possess no sense of right and wrong. They merely survive. Human beings, on the other hand, possess the ability to deduce. We possess the ability to deliberate between two modes of action, in addition to the possible consequences that may follow should we actually act upon any single option. We possess the understanding that while some of our actions may have positive consequences, other actions may have negative consequences. It is through this mode of understanding, and the power in our will to act or refrain from action, that makes all human beings moral creatures. Through our faculty of reason, we may, then, draw a value system that benefits all individuals. It is this common value system that binds two distinct spirits together.

Indeed, no animal in the wild can be considered to be a moral creature, since it possesses no intrinsic sense of any moral principles. When the animal makes a choice, this decision will either potentially further its existence, or potentially lead to its demise. The animal considers no other elements besides its natural impulses. In contrast, human beings possess a much more powerful intellect. When we make our deliberations, our possible choices do not merely revolve around our continued survival. We also take into consideration how our actions may affect other individuals. In comparison to instinctive behaviour, reason provides us with the intrinsic ability to make these considerations. Reason enables us to make choices according to either some form of virtue or some form of vice. Our ability to understand the complex differences between virtues and vices distinguishes ourselves from the common animal in the wild.

When human beings do act, we are always motivated by some reason that compels us to choose one possible mode of action over another. In principle, human beings make their choices according to what is beneficial to themselves, or what is beneficial to other people. This ideology best represents the differences between vice and virtue. When the individual chooses an action that is merely beneficial to himself, he does not consider any other possible consequences. Accordingly, whenever these choices potentially harm other persons, the motivation behind his choice will be defined as a vice. Contrarily, when the individual chooses a mode of action that is both beneficial to himself and other persons, he will be motivated by a virtue. Therefore, the virtuous consider other persons within their society, while the vicious merely consider themselves.

Thus, when we understand the fact that human beings are rational creatures, we will also understand the fact that reason compels all of our actions. In the realm of morality, we must not merely judge the individual's actions as either moral or immoral, but we must also consider the reasons behind the individual's decision to act. Our will is restricted by our spiritual nature, in the fact that we always act according to some line of reasoning. As rational creatures, the motives present within each individual's psyche will determine his actions. Thereby, with respect to moral judgments, we must consider the individual's reasons, in addition to his actions. For it is entirely possible that a vicious individual may appear to behave morally, due to chance. It is also possible that a virtuous individual may be responsible for some immoral act, entirely by mistake.

Not only can two twins be responsible for the same act for differing reasons, but two twins can also be responsible for entirely opposite actions when faced with the same circumstances. Whenever this occurs, their choices will also be motivated by differing reasons. In fact, regarding our free will, we cannot disunite the link between reason and the choices that we make. Both twins acted differently within the same circumstances because they possessed differing reasons that compelled them to act.

The power of free will enables each individual to either achieve self-pleasure, or affect other persons through a positive manner. This is the main difference between the vicious and the virtuous. Virtue is always directed towards the good for all persons, including the actor himself. In contrast, vice is based merely towards that which benefits the individual. Subsequently, vice could be conceived as a form of self-preservation, while virtue may be conceived as a form of communal preservation. Virtue is always connected with the public good, and this requires the element of knowledge. Yet, true knowledge can only be obtained through the correct utilization of the intellect. Accordingly, virtue is a concept that has been created by the dynamic character for all dynamic characters. In essence, virtue is that quality which motivates all forms of moral action.

Since vice is merely concerned with the good of the individual, more often than not, it tends to have a negative effect on the general public. Forms of vice do not require the utilization of the intellect, because it is derived solely through an individual's private consciousness. Hence, all forms of vice may be more properly related to an individual's emotional centre, as opposed to the intellect, particularly in the realm of personal pleasure.

Therefore, when the vicious do demonstrate forms of moral action, they are merely mimicking the actions of the common citizen. However, when a virtuous individual is guilty of some crime, his psyche has usually been manipulated, in some manner, to commit this act. For example, an otherwise lawfully abiding citizen may commit a crime, such as shoplifting, due solely to the fact that he is battling some instance of a mental illness. Kleptomaniacs do commit unlawful acts, yet they do so through no intrinsic fault of their own. These individuals commit their unlawful acts essentially because they are battling forms of intrusive thoughts that, otherwise, contradict the nature of their true spirit. Consequently, when these individuals are exposed to a different perspective of life, they will undertake a valuable learning process that should enable them to understand the differences between virtue and vice.

Vices differ from virtues in the same manner that tyrants differ from saints, or how abominations differ from the revered. In essence, the tyrant's judgment will always be tainted by his own personal desires, while saints will demonstrate unbiased forms of open-minded insight. As a result, there will be substantial differences in the actions taken by these two classes of individuals, yet there will be even more differences with respect to their particular motivations.

Tyrants may differ from each other with respect to their specific implementation of the will, but they will not differ according to their primary motivations. Their primary motivations will always be egoistic in nature, and thus centred on some form of vice. Yet, due to the fallibility of the intellect, some tyrants will fail to achieve their personal goals, because of their personal ineptitudes and inabilities. The vicious do not possess omniscient abilities, but they are all similar in that they are purely motivated to take actions based on what happens to bring them pleasure or pain.

In a similar fashion, saints may also differ from each other by the specific actions that they take, yet their primary motives will also remain relatively similar. All saints will be primarily motivated by the precept of altruism, and thus they are always motivated by some instance of virtue. Yet, since they may possess dissimilarities in spirit, the specific obligations that they take will ultimately vary. Therefore, it is possible that two saints may possess the same core of virtues, while they differ with respect to the specific duties that they may uphold.

These are the two main classes of individuals that makeup any particular society. Persons who are motivated by virtue will fulfill some particular duty that is required within their community, while persons who are motivated by vice will only consider their own personal needs. Through the liberty of the will, all individuals will possess the capability to choose between two opposing actions. Nevertheless, since we are rational creatures, it is reason that mainly determines our choices. It is the individual's unique rationale that compels him to choose between two actions, and thus it is the individual's unique rationale that subsequently must determine his moral character.

11   Reciprocity

THE UNIQUE INDIVIDUAL will acquire both differing principles and differing virtues throughout his life span. However, there does exist one virtue that is commonly adopted by all persons. This is known as the virtue of justice. Justice may be the most commonly adopted virtue because it fits into a second category of virtues. Those virtues that have been associated with a particular duty belong to the category of personal virtues. Personal virtues are adopted by the individual purely through his own liberty. Moreover, personal virtues require only a single agent to be actualized. They are intrinsic spiritual traits that define an individual.

Every person with a dynamic character possesses some intrinsic personal virtue, or combination of personal virtues, that distinguishes himself from his peers. In contrast, social virtues are adopted when the individual forms some kind of relationship with another person. As such, when two persons form a relationship, this relationship will be based on some particular virtue. This virtue will serve as a basis, or starting point, for all of their future interactions. In essence, social virtues are qualities that define a particular relationship between two persons.

Justice is a social virtue that is held by almost every person in the world. Only those individuals who live out their entire lives in total isolation may actually disregard this virtue. Nevertheless, justice is a difficult concept because many persons will hold entirely different conceptions of this virtue. To truly classify justice as a virtue, it must, necessarily, motivate the individual to fulfill some kind of duty. The particular actions associated with justice, though, will vary quite extensively from individual to individual. Since the concept of justice is vast, it may be prudent to divide its definition into two halves.

Positive justice is a virtue that is established in friendly interactions between two cooperative citizens. It is a virtue that involves the mutual exchange of benevolent acts. All persons that possess a dynamic character will also possess an intrinsic sense of positive justice. This is due to the fact that all persons who are dynamic seek to both acquire, and to be the producer of, forms of affection. Consequently, this is the most basic definition of positive justice. In every relationship between two dynamic characters, the reciprocation of benevolent acts is mainly motivated by each agent's conception of positive justice. Accordingly, these relationships may be entirely based on the ideal of positive justice.

The act of trading within a community setting is also based on the virtue of positive justice. Every individual will specialize into a unique field, and this enables him to contribute a unique service within his community. However, the interactions between two dynamic individuals may also be similar in the fact that every unique individual will be motivated by differing forms of personal virtues. As a consequence, positive justice is not always realized through the exchange of equivalent benevolent acts. Instead, acts of benevolence can take on many differing forms. So the particular kind of act reciprocated through positive justice may not always be entirely equivalent to the original act of kindness, from either a qualitative or quantitative perspective.

In contrast, negative justice may be a much more difficult concept to explain. This is due to the fact that every person's conception of this form of justice will vary, in terms of severity. Within the dynamic character's frame of mind, negative justice is a variation of justice that defines the relationship between a criminal and his community. Yet, many persons with a dynamic character will disagree with respect to the specific exchange of actions that should encompass this virtue. Every individual will agree with the premise that all criminals should be penalized for the transgressions that they commit against their society. Therefore, whenever an individual is guilty of some crime, his community will be righteously implementing some form of punishment. Nonetheless, the penalty associated with negative justice will differ according to each unique individual's sense of justice.

First of all, negative justice may involve the concept of a deterrent. Deterrents are mainly aimed towards reducing criminal forms of behaviour, through stringent consequences. This form of criminal justice requires the application of consistent penalties, whenever similar crimes are committed. Accordingly, whenever our justice system is consistent in imposing the same penalty for like offenses, the criminal will possess a clear idea of his future punishment, before he actually commits any criminal offence. The main element in the concept of a deterrent is based on the fact that the criminal must expect a definitive penalty, whenever he is found to be legally culpable for any specific offence. Therefore, in this case, the sentencing process applied through our courts must be systematic. In order for a penalty to pose as a true deterrent, it must be enforced on a constant and consistent basis whenever criminal acts of a similar nature are committed.

If a specific penalty is lax, within the criminal's frame of mind, it will not serve as a proper deterrent. Likewise, if a single offender is guilty of multiple instances of the same crime, it may also be logical to conclude that the penalty imposed has no deterring effects. Therefore, the kinds of penalties that deter criminal behaviour must be harsh in nature, especially within the mind of those persons who possess the potential to commit a criminal act, at some future time.

Nonetheless, even if a specific deterrent is associated with a harsh sentence, this kind of penalty may still not serve its intended purpose. This is due to the fact that some criminals do not fear even the worst possible penalty related to any specific offence. Thus, individuals who do not fear our justice system will not restrict their actions due to some form of a deterrent. These persons should be known as hardened criminals. Their mental capacity to commit some crime will be entirely free, due to their vicious nature.

Even the most ruthless tyrant's actions may be guided or limited by his core of emotions. In these cases, proper action directed towards the static object of his emotional centre could, conceivably, deter his criminal tendencies. Since all tyrants are motivated to acquire social authority, reducing his scope of power over his society may accomplish this task. However, this requires the proper identification of a potential tyrant, before he actually commits any criminal acts. When this is achieved, instead of imposing any standard penalties for criminal forms of behaviour, our justice system could be modified towards addressing the particular psychological elements that may fuel or motivate a guiltless individual's transformation into a tyrant.

This form of justice will also serve the public's best interest through the concept of crime prevention. Yet, it is a form of anticipatory action that is tailored towards the unique circumstances related to those who are at most risk into becoming a hardened criminal. For example, denying the materialistic criminal's access to material forms of wealth may reduce his inherent capability to commit any instances of a white collar crime. Therefore, if we impose strict fines, particularly in the case of potential white collar criminals, their means to commit any forms of material fraud will essentially be taken away from them. With respect to the blue collar criminal, denying him his physical liberty to commit crimes may remain as the only feasible solution. This is due to the fact that blue collar criminals, in general, do not really rely on any universal tools, except the liberty of their will. In combination with psychological counselling, perhaps the enforcement of a highly restrictive curfew may potentially limit his ability to commit any blue collar crimes.

Therefore, destroying the criminal's means to commit his crimes will effectively reduce the scope of his powers. Conceivably, whenever we reduce the criminal's ability to become fully autonomous, this will create a considerable barrier that prevents him from committing any heinous crimes. However, this form of a deterrent cannot be consistently applied to all of those individuals who may be at risk to commit a criminal offence, essentially because each felon is motivated by differing forms of vice. This kind of deterrent requires a case-by-case analysis regarding the individual's necessary volition to commit a criminal offence. A form of psychoanalysis must, then, be conducted on a case-by-case basis, to determine the individual's potential to commit any criminal acts. In fact, every criminal's emotional state of anger will be fuelled by some other element, namely some form of vice. After we determine this motive, we may then possess enough knowledge to tailor the most effective deterrent.

Nonetheless, the types of penalties afforded to us, as a society, are quite limited. We cannot, for example, use physical torture as a means to deter a potential criminal. However, the hardened criminal may still possess another universal fear, which he shares in common with other offenders. Indeed, some individuals become static criminals, in some part, to gain some form of authority over other persons. Therefore, those individuals who are not deterred into becoming a criminal must then be deterred from becoming a repeat offender. The rebalancing of power could address this issue.

In order to re-establish the most proper balance of power that exists between a criminal and his victim, perhaps we should grant the victims of a specific crime some influence over the justice process. Perhaps the readjustment of social authority granted to the victim of a crime over the guilty perpetrator could serve as a potential deterrent.

Those criminals who are not deterred by their society's sentencing system probably also do not recognize the authority of the courts. Yet, granting the victims of a crime some authority over the offender's future could address this problem. This is due to the unpredictable nature of each criminal's victim. With respect to the concept of a deterrence, within our justice system, the penalties involved must be applied on a consistent basis. Nevertheless, if we grant the victims of a crime some form of authority over this process, the penalty applied will be entirely unknown to the guilty party. The aspect of the unknown could, possibly, serve as a kind of deterrence.

In fact, adding input from the victims of a crime will intrinsically reinforce a balance of power. In essence, through committing his crime, the static criminal has gained some degree of authority over his victim. However, if his victim plays some part in his lawful punishment, the concept of authority has been re-shifted back into the victim's hands. If the static criminal faces losing his last remnants of social authority over his victim, this fate may be more deplorable than the fate that he would have faced had he committed no crime at all. In other words, through the rebalancing of power, the static character faces the possibility of losing any and all forms of social authority that he may have gained through his crime, and this could deter him, in the first place, from developing his criminal habits. In fact, the goal of any static criminal is to abuse another person, in an effort to acquire some form of social authority that he lacked when he was a law-abiding citizen. Ideologically, then, the rebalancing of power could address this issue. If we granted victims some form of influence over the criminal's sentencing process, the active rebalancing of power could serve as a powerful deterrent against those individuals who become criminals, essentially because of the fact that they are motivated to gain higher forms of social authority.

In fact, fear of the unknown may be quite common, especially among those persons who possess a static character. It is entirely possible that the criminal's victim could possess a forgiving spirit. In this case, the victim could actually push for a more lenient sentence than the standard deterrent. However, it may also be possible that the criminal's victim will lack this principle in its entirety. These victims will be naturally filled with anger and rage, because of the fact that they have suffered some form of loss at the hands of an unlawful criminal. In these cases, the victim may wish to impose an even harsher sentence than the standard deterrent. This latter kind of justice may be mainly based on the concept of revenge. In these cases, the penalty sought may be excessive in nature, in comparison to the standard penalty that may be regularly implemented by our justice system.

The differences between victim revenge and the rebalancing of power are based on the conceptual differences between a punishment and a deterrent. Therefore, the main purpose in the concept of revenge is to inflict an equivalent level of harm against any given transgressor, while the main purpose of the rebalancing of power focuses on insuring the possibility that the guilty party will pose no further harm to his society.. Another conceptual relationship between these two modes of justice may be further analogous to the natural relationship between war and peace.

In fact, this kind of sentencing process could act as a powerful deterrent, in cases where the criminal demonstrates no forms of remorse. Hypothetically, the guilty offender will essentially be faced with a game of Russian roulette, in terms of the penalty that he must serve after he is convicted of some crime. Therefore, when a standard deterrent poses no threat to a potential criminal, the addition of victim input could change a constant penalty into something that is defined solely by the impact that the crime has had on its victim.

The rebalancing of power could also better serve the public's best interests, because it is a form of justice that is tailored towards the unique circumstances of each separate criminal act. All victims are distinct human beings who possess a unique spiritual nature. Similarly, all persons will also possess a distinct sense of justice. Therefore, a standard deterrent may merely serve either the common person's interest, or the community's interests. Yet, the rebalancing of power will add a voice for those persons who are the actual victims of abuse. When granted influence over the sentencing process, these individuals, then, will not merely remain as the victims of a crime. In actuality, they are granted with a kind of liberty that was taken away from them through some criminal act. Their involvement within the justice process will then make them, in principle, active pursuers of justice.

Without this mode of justice, our penal system may be mainly defined as a form of communal justice system. It is communal in nature because it associates a specific crime with a standard penalty, even though the unique circumstances of each crime may differ in nature. Therefore, it mainly recognizes the impact of a crime on its community, as whole, rather than the impact that it had on the victim himself. If we were to implement the rebalancing of power, as opposed to a standard form of justice, our justice system will essentially be recognizing, and individualizing, the impact and effects of a given crime on its victim.

By changing our focus away from a mode of communal justice, onto a form of victim's justice, this shift in focus could also potentially serve as mode of education. In actuality, the rebalancing of power could provide a greater awareness for potential at risk youths, who do not think about the ramifications that may be associated a criminal act. Those youths, who are at a high risk to commit criminal acts, may then be granted with the awareness that every crime has some potential victim. In essence, these youth's may then comprehend the fact that no crime is victimless. This may then provide all at risk youths with a considerable reason to walk the line.

Therefore, through the rebalancing of power, the impact of a crime on its victim will be more effectively addressed within our justice system. In many cases, granting the victims of a crime some authority over the length or nature of a penalty could also aid with their healing process. Furthermore, individualizing the penalty process could add more social elements to our justice system, and this could contribute towards the socialization and moral education of a guilty perpetrator. The criminal may then come to some understanding with respect to the social impact that his crime has had upon its victim.

At the very least, the rebalancing of power could provide victims with a sense of negative justice. Victim's justice must essentially be a penalty that is added in addition to a standard penalty, which has subsequently failed as a deterrent. Accordingly, this form of additional negative justice could then force the hardened criminal to rethink his guilty actions, and if this occurs, this will mark the start of his rehabilitation process away from a criminal state of mind. If the individual possesses any degree of a moral fibre, then this mode of negative justice could also potentially deter him from becoming a repeat offender.

Yet, the rebalancing of power should not be utilized in every court proceeding. It is mainly an additional tool that a judge may implement, should a criminal express no forms of true remorse for his crimes.

Likewise, it could also be implemented when the criminal lacks any true regard for the impact that his crime has had on its victim. Indeed, when a criminal demonstrates no forms of remorse, this state of mind reflects upon the possibility that the criminal, himself, may feel justified in his criminal acts. Accordingly, a more severe mode of negative justice may be necessary to address his feelings of self-righteousness.

Nonetheless, we must ask what drives the static character into becoming a static criminal in the first place. The static character is always driven towards the acquisition of power and authority. In his quest for social authority, he may subsequently utilize criminal acts as a means to acquire this power. When the static character commits criminal acts, he will be bounded by few social norms or criminal laws. If he further evolves into a hardened criminal, he will be responsible for repeat offences. These latter individuals will commit criminal offences without a second thought.

Moreover, the majority of criminals commit their crimes due to their overwhelming feelings of anger. When the static character does not achieve the kinds of social acceptance that he needs, he will then enter into a state of rage, and this will motivate him to commit some form of crime against his society. However, when the individual does evolve into a static criminal, his anger must also be fuelled by the element of vice. Accordingly, the criminal commits his crimes as a reaction to some element that exists within his society.

Other static characters become criminals when they feel that they have become victimized by some individual. Their feelings of anger will then fuel their acts of revenge. Yet, this only occurs after the static character enters into a certain breaking point. When the static character feels that he is unfairly victimized, he will seek to victimize that individual who is responsible for the corresponding offence. Thus, when motivated by the concept of revenge, the static character will essentially revert back into a more animalistic state, where instinct replaces any forms of reason. After he has discovered the weaknesses of his enemy, the static character will then utilize a form of revenge, which may be known as the process of exponentiation. In essence, acts of exponentiation occur whenever a static victim recognizes and places an excessive focus towards his abuser's social deficits, and successively compounds them.

Next, through the method of exponentiation, an undetermined war, based on rage and authority, between the static victim and his abuser will ensue. Within the mind of all persons with a static character, those individuals who possess the least amount of personal weaknesses should be granted an authoritative role. However, the definition of what constitutes as a weakness will vary to a large extent. This is due to the fact that the acquisition of more social authority will always be the ultimate goal of the static character. Material forms of wealth may be the most common strength that is recognized or accepted by every static character. Nonetheless, feelings of envy, and then subsequently anger, will cause even more dissention between these two static individuals.

In these cases, a temporally infinite war will transpire, until one individual submits himself to the other person's demands. Neither individual will experience any feelings of peace, because they both suffer from some kind of an inferiority complex, which is the essential focal point of this war. Both individuals will remain in a state of anger, due to a war based on vengeance, and likewise, they will never be able to appreciate any forms of wonders that have been granted to them by nature.

The only sense of justice that exists within the static character's frame of mind is based on this form of negative justice. As a consequence, some static individuals believe that they are acting justly through their acts of exponentiation. In actuality, they are merely materializing a form of revenge. Indeed, all persons with a static character do possess an intrinsic sense of revenge. Within their frame of mind, revenge is the most efficient mode of social justice. Yet, the most effective mode of revenge, within the static character's frame of mind, may be obtained solely through the method exponentiation. In these cases, the static character will never experience any forms of peace, essentially because he will always be engaged in a cycle of abuse with another static character, which is based primarily on the other individual's social deficits.

Due to the fact that the static character is always seeking higher forms of authority, he will also always be lacking some element in life. These deficiencies will fuel his bitterness. Moreover, when the static character views the interactions between two dynamic characters, he will naturally come to the expectation that all of his personal relationships should be based on similar elements. When he does not receive any similar forms of friendly interactions, he will be further consumed with jealousy and fury. This is usually what marks the birth of a hardened criminal.

If our justice system fails to serve as a deterrent, this individual will then evolve into a repeat offender. The hardened criminal, then, may be classified as an unrepentant repeat offender. In these cases, since our standard penalties have no bearing over the hardened criminal, it may be logical to conclude that we must escalate our penalties, so that they will possess the potential effect of a standard deterrent. Therefore, in these specific cases, our justice system must then shift its focus from deterring criminal behaviour, into properly punishing criminal forms of behaviour. This shift in our paradigm towards criminal justice will be necessary to properly penalize those individuals who tenaciously become repeat offenders.

Punishments are mainly directed towards inflicting some kind of harm onto the criminal. If a regular deterrent does not serve its purpose, then a true form of punishment must be more severe than the failed deterrent itself. Indeed, the concept of punishment could be associated with the concept of revenge, while the concept of a deterrent may be associated with the restoration of order. However, whenever a given deterrent fails in its purpose, the concept of a punishment may be the only form of justice that will aid in the reconciliation of order. This is due to the fact that the standard deterrent has essentially failed to serve as a harsh penalty, in itself. When a society's justice system truly punishes an offender, it will, effectively, impose some kind of negative effect onto the criminal himself.

In fact, the hardened criminal does realize that his acts are criminal in nature. Nevertheless, he is able to rationalize the pain that he inflicts on other persons, due to his ever increasing ego. His ego provides him with a slanted justification behind his criminal acts, and this enables him to carry on with his life as if he did nothing wrong. This kind of rationale is mainly utilized by those individuals who evolve into repeat offenders.

Nevertheless, we still must ask if a society is just in inflicting some form of physical pain onto the outlaw or recluse. The answer to this question is most definitely no. That is why incarceration is the main penalty enforced, according to most major forms of criminal behaviour. As a result, the only way we may righteously punish a given offender is to take away his liberty, for period that is longer than the standard deterrent. If our society focuses on the expulsion of freedoms, this may be the most peaceful method that will enable us to justly punish an unremorseful offender.

Firstly, a society may only justly punish those offenders who possess no potential to become rehabilitated. If the individual demonstrates that he may change his character back into a law-abiding citizen, then our society must make an equivalent gesture that will aid in his rehabilitation. Furthermore, our harshest penalties must be applied solely to those persons who become the most callous criminals. These individuals will be guilty of inflicting some kind of physical harm against another living being. In comparison, other hardened criminals may be guilty of lesser offences, like property or monetary crimes, but they will be individuals who are constantly guilty of repeat offences.

Therefore, crimes against living beings are totally different from property crimes. When the individual is guilty of materialistic crimes, his actions are not as serious. These types of criminals may not deserve to be severely punished for their crimes, and comparatively speaking, the need for a deterrent is not immediate. Nonetheless, the phenomenon of criminal evolution will always apply, and thus, some criminals who commit property crimes may pose some further harm against living beings, at some future date. With respect to these individuals, we must clearly focus on crime prevention. Indeed, longer forms of incarceration could potentially deter these individuals from evolving their criminal conducts. In actuality, every callous criminal most definitely committed minor offences before he threatened the physical safety of another living being.

If the criminal pleads himself to be guilty of some offence, he is admitting responsibility for his criminal act. In some cases, a guilty plea could demonstrate some degree of remorse. Yet, in most other cases, the individual does not dispute his criminality mainly so that he will be penalized with a lighter sentence. Modes of justice that serve to truly punish some individual should, necessarily, cause feelings of true guilt within him. Therefore, in the latter case, since the criminal does not really express any true feelings of remorse, it would be pertinent to sentence him with some form of punishment.

In other cases, the individual will only express remorse after he has disputed his charges and lost his battle within a courtroom. Also in these cases, the individual only expresses remorse primarily so that he will be penalized with a lighter sentence. Therefore, under many circumstances, the criminal's expression of remorse will not be genuine. These latter cases should be analogous to those cases where the criminal completely fails to express any feelings of remorse.

This circumstance illustrates two differing instances regarding the concept of an apology. In the case of persons with a dynamic character, the individual will actually experience sorrow because he was responsible for injuring some other living being. In these cases, the dynamic criminal will have committed his crime due solely to ignorance or a lack of understanding with respect to our civilization. Through his expression of regret, he is indicating the fact that he will not become a repeat offender.

On the other hand, the static criminal has hurt another being due precisely to premeditated thoughts of malice, hatred and revenge. In the static criminal's frame of mind, feelings of sorrow will not be directed towards the harm that he may have imposed onto another being. Rather, he will regret committing his previous transgressions mainly due to the consequences that he will face, as a direct result of his criminal actions. When the static character becomes labelled as a hardened criminal, he will have lost any authority that he may have previously possessed within his community. As a consequence, he may also express an apology, merely to regain a degree of authority that he has just lost. These kinds of individuals will only apologize to their victims if they have been publicly labelled as a static criminal, and thus, labelled as a lower class citizen.

Accordingly, this illustrates the difference between genuine and token remorse. The individual who is genuinely remorseful will seek to actively minimize the pain that is suffered by his victim. In so doing, he will always take immediate responsibility for his criminal acts. Those who are genuinely remorseful will also not become repeat offenders, and as a result, they will make every effort to abide by the laws that are established within their community.

Contrarily, persons who express token remorse are merely motivated to minimize the pain that they will experience, as a result of their criminal prosecution. They seek to minimize their physical pains, in relation to incarceration, in addition to their social shame. As a consequence, these individuals do not truly feel dishonourable with respect to their criminal acts. They merely wish to boost their public image and lessen the social shame that they will be subject to from other persons within their community.

In the latter case, the victims of a crime will continue to suffer, due to a criminal's lack of true remorse. Whenever the hardened criminal lacks any feelings of remorse, he will also lack feelings of sympathy or compassion. As a consequence, these types of individuals do not deserve a sense of pity or mercy themselves, with respect to their failure to act according to common moral standards. It is these kinds of individuals who deserve not merely the standard deterrent associated with their particular offence. They deserve to be wholly punished for their offence.

This is another major difference between the criminal who possesses either a static or a dynamic character. Within his relationships, the static character will continue to analyze any possible weaknesses within his peers, mainly in his quest to acquire more social authority. In contrast, the dynamic character will continue to discover new spirits and wonders that exist in our world, during his lifetime. This is what mainly fuels his positive perspective.

As a direct result, the dynamic character's outlook on life will eventually cause feelings of sorrow within him, whenever he has harmed another living being. Individuals who experience true remorse after they have harmed another human being do deserve feelings of pity and mercy from their community, in return. Nonetheless, the hardened criminal rarely experiences any feelings of true remorse for his crimes. Since most of his crimes are premeditated, the hardened criminal will have planned his crimes for some time before he actually commits these acts. As a result, he will further possess enough intellectual insight to foresee the possible repercussions that he may face, due to his criminal behaviour. This prepares him for the potential consequences that he may face, whenever he comes face to face with our justice system.

Inversely, persons with a static character will never experience any feelings of pity towards a genuinely remorseful criminal. Victims who possess a static character will find it necessary to inflict an equivalent form of abuse that they have suffered, from any kind of criminal. In so doing, the static victim will be addressing his inferiority complex, through duplicating his personal feelings of emptiness onto a remorseful criminal. Accordingly, the static victim will always focus on the vice of revenge, simply because this is the easiest mode of action that will relieve his personal suffering.

The static victim will always justify his acts of exponentiation through the sympathy that he receives from his community. Yet, this individual does not merely seek to acquire forms of justice. In fact, he will mainly utilize the method of exponentiation in his effort to acquire new instances of power. Thus, even when this individual is successful in achieving some form of authority over a criminal, he will still never reach a state of internal peace, simply because he will continue his mere quest for authority. Indeed, some forms of authority that he seeks may not even be attainable, within our natural world. As a consequence, the majority of static victims will never achieve a state of peace even when they are granted with a form of negative justice, simply because they must continue their indefinite, yet meagre, quest for power.

In fact, the dynamic character will never utilize the method of exponentiation in his effort to acquire some form of justice. The method of exponentiation will only be employed by persons who possess a static character. As a consequence, a particular fear that is held by every static character may be based on a fear of retribution. The common criminal will only commit his crimes if he believes that he can potentially escape all forms of prosecution. He may also commit those crimes where he does not fear any forms of retribution, in relation to his criminal acts. Hence, the criminal's degree of abuse, whether it is emotional, psychological or physical, depends entirely on his personal sense of fear. If he possesses few fears, then there are potentially no limits with respect to the amount of abuse that he may inflict on another living being. Nonetheless, he knows that if he commits a crime against another person with a static character, forms of retribution will almost always necessarily follow.

Undeniably, fear may be the only concept that limits the static character's actions. Fear restricts some persons with a static character from evolving into a static criminal, and likewise, fear limits some static criminals from evolving into a hardened criminal. Since all static characters are aware of this, their concepts of vengeance will also be mainly focused towards their enemy's personal fears. Conceivably, the greatest common fear held by all persons with a static character may be the permanent reduction of their social authority.

Hence, every criminal possesses some form of weakness. Determining this weakness, however, must be conducted on an individual basis. The individual's crime will also be somewhat relevant to his particular weakness. For example, the tyrant is unfair and unethical with his mode of governance over a particular society. He does not appreciate life, intrinsically. He only loves the power that he possesses over other human beings. However, the fact that he loves social authority makes him a social creature. Therefore, this criminal's particular fear may be based on an absolute loss of all forms of social authority.

Furthermore, the bank robber will view the lives of persons with extreme wealth, and he will then become jealous of their material possessions. The rapist will observe the feelings of love experienced between two persons, and he will commit his crimes because he wants to experience a similar feeling. Equally, the terrorist may view some aspect of the society that he attacks, and then commit his acts of destruction because of his feelings of ill will. The serial murder, who is essentially a domestic terrorist, will also envy some aspect in the lives of his victims. In effect, crimes based on feelings of envy indicate a social motive behind all forms of criminality. This makes all static criminals social creatures, who are mainly angry with the fact that they lack some element in life that other persons freely enjoy.

The static victim, then, will always centre his acts of revenge based on the greatest fear held by his enemy. According to the static victim's rationale, revenge may be the most proper form of justice. As a consequence, when a criminal commits his offence due to the vice of envy, true vengeance entails focusing and compounding the particular fears held by this individual. In other words, the best form of revenge possible may be to further deprave those elements from the static criminal, of which his feelings of envy are based upon. Through this action, the static victim's concept of revenge will be based on the active compounding of the specific fears that may be held by the static criminal. Within the static victim's frame of mind, true justice will be based on the exponentiation of the static criminal's personal fears, which are essentially the fears that primarily motivated his criminal acts.

In actuality, every criminal is partially motivated by his need for social acceptance. Therefore, the static criminal will usually experience fears related to possible instances of negative justice. Indeed, forms of revenge are never formally established, in the same manner that lengths of incarceration are associated with specific categories of crimes. Forms of revenge depend highly upon the moral compass of the criminal's victim, and thus, the static criminal can never really prepare for any forms of revenge that he may potentially face. In fact, forms of retribution, from victims who possess a static character, could also be conducted through some illegal act, but this is a form of punishment that lies well beyond the scope of our society's integrity. In these particular cases, the static criminal may also express feelings of regret, essentially in an effort to gain some form of sympathy from his static victim.

We know that the common bully always chooses victims who, in his mind, are perceived as "easy targets". One conception related to an "easy" target may be based on the otherwise peaceful, or pacifistic, characteristics of another person. Hence, the common bully essentially relies on his victim's pacifistic characteristics, to elude any forms of revenge. The bully never chooses a target who may, in his mind, seek any forms of retribution. If this is the case, then it is also true that the bully will fear those persons who will inevitably seek some form of revenge, due to some abusive act. This is the limited mindset of the bully. In these individuals, fear serves as a main deterrent that limits the targets of his acts of aggression.

If the common bully is similar to all other forms of criminals, then it is conceivable that the majority of criminals will also fear the concept of revenge. This, then, may pose as a definite form of deterrent. Nonetheless, forms of revenge can only be actualized by the victims of a specific crime. In these cases, granting the criminal's victims some form of authority over the specific penalty applied by our justice system could also, then, serve as a mode of revenge. Of course, there will be a limited scope of options that are made available to the victims of a crime, through our justice system.

In most cases, the penalties applied to a given criminal must remain equitable to the crime committed, in terms of victim impact. For example, enforcing the death penalty on a petty thief will not be just, simply because the magnitude of the crime committed does not resemble the magnitude of its penalty. Nonetheless, if we empower the victims of a crime with the choice of a fairly equitable penalty, in relation to the true impact of a crime, the force of this penalty could still be quite severe. Indeed, fining a millionaire will not have as much of an impact in comparison to fining someone who is homeless. Even though both individuals may be guilty of committing the same crime, the resulting impact of the penalty enforced will be entirely different. Hence, by including the victim's input within our justice system, we may be actively addressing the true impact of some crime, and this may result in a higher degree of justice.

Static criminals, then, will be solely deterred due to their personal fears. Nevertheless, penalties based on fear will be primarily based on the concept of vengeance or revenge. In fact, the focal point of a particular criminal's personal fears may be quite extreme in nature. In these cases, it would be impossible to implement a form of punishment, based on each individual criminal's personal fears, because our justice system will then be based on acts of utter immorality. In order to avoid this possibility, we may have to consider the impact of a crime on our society and its impact on the victim, and then determine some kind of middle ground. Perhaps, the best possible deterrent may reside somewhere between these two modes of social justice. We will be guided by the truest sense of social justice if we consider the impacts of each crime, and then implement some form of reciprocal punishment accordingly.

Criminals rely all too much on the peaceful nature of human society. Those persons who do commit crimes either do not fear the potential punishments associated with their crime, or they rely too much on individual instances of appeasement. In the latter case, they may hold the belief that they will not face any heavy repercussions for their transgressions. This is the true essence of the bully, who picks victims that will not retaliate when faced with forms of abuse. Within the mind of the bully, a forceful deterrent may not be in place within our society. Accordingly, those individuals who are not deterred will inevitably continue to abuse other persons, until a more proper deterrent is implemented within our justice system.

However, some individuals in the world do not fear even the most severe lengths of incarceration. The temperament of these individuals may be classified at the most extreme degree of psychopathy. For these individuals, lifetime lengths of incarceration should be mandatory. A lifetime sentence will be wholly necessary for all persons who are psychologically classified as chronic violent offenders. This mode of punishment will not deter those individuals who are characterized as extreme psychopaths. Its only purpose will serve to protect our society from any possible future offences.

The individual who is guilty of inflicting an unruly amount of pain onto another living being should be considered as the most dangerous possible offender. The distinction between whether this individual inflicts pain on another human being, or another form of living being in the wild is not important. Those individuals who are responsible for extreme forms of animal abuse are still, technically, deliverers of torture. Moreover, if these criminals are not punished for their crimes of animal abuse, their criminal tendencies will most definitely evolve, and they will then, at some point in the future, be guilty of causing pain to some other human being.

Every callous criminal who wishes to repeatedly inflict undue harm onto another living being should be categorized as a sordid terrorist. Indeed, those who intend to physically or psychologically torture another living being possess only the utmost of malicious intents. When we differentiate the common criminal from a sordid terrorist, this is where differences in our penal sentencing process must be applied. The common criminal possesses the capacity to be rehabilitated, while the sordid terrorist only possesses the capacity to reoffend. Therefore, while our standard penalty based on the concept of deterrence could be satisfactory in the case of the common criminal, it will not be effective in the case of the sordid terrorist.

To qualify as a kind of common criminal, the individual must possess the personal volition to become rehabilitated from his criminal ways. Even though the sordid terrorist is a social creature, he will still lack this volition. As a consequence, the sordid terrorist lacks an inherent capacity to become an equal and law-abiding citizen. It is in these specific cases where we should escalate our justice process from the standard deterrent, to a lengthier form of incarceration. Indeed, this kind of punishment will essentially shift our idea of justice from the concept of a failed deterrent, to the concept of maximum crime prevention.

In cases where the sordid terrorist is guilty of a pattern of offences, severe lengths of incarceration may be the only proper solution. Since the sordid terrorist demonstrates no potential to become rehabilitated, lifetime lengths of incarceration must always be considered. We can only secure the safety of persons within our communities if we impose this length of punishment towards those individuals who will inevitably continue to reoffend. Nevertheless, we must reserve this length of punishment only for those individuals who will continue to threaten to harm other living beings, if they are granted with the physical liberty to do so. These types of individuals only represent a small percentage of the criminal population. Successively, it would not be just to impose such a penalty on those individuals who demonstrate some ability to become rehabilitated.

Accordingly, only those individuals who will continue to terrorize other persons should be punished with a more severe sentence, in comparison to a standard penalty. Those persons who are classified as a sordid terrorist must not possess the liberty, or the means, to continue their destructive habits. If we take away their liberty, and thus their raw ability to terrorize other persons, we will be taking one more step towards maintaining a peaceful society.

Furthermore, all criminals who share similar intents should be classified into a single category. Consider the differences between first degree murder and attempted murder. There are different penalties associated with both acts. Yet, the rationale within both crimes remains the same. Both individuals possessed the intent to end another person's life. The only difference between these two criminals is based on a lack of success. In one instance, the individual was able to materialize his criminal intents, while in the other case the individual lacked the competence to complete his goal. Conceptually, however, both criminals are guilty of the same crime.

Accordingly, we must categorize persons who will inevitably reoffend into the same category of persons who are actual repeat offenders themselves. In so doing, we will be actively providing a form of security for those individuals who would have been the victim of a liberated, yet intrinsic repeat offender. In fact, within the mind of the psychopath, committing an act of violence may be similar to taking an illicit drug. When committing a violent act, the act itself, or the effects of this act, may be too much of an exhilarating experience to give up. In these specific cases, the psychopath will then continue to commit his crimes, for an indefinite period of time. It is these kinds of un-rehabilitatable criminals who must be incarcerated for their lifetime, in order to protect the general public from any possible future offences. Therefore, through this mode of justice, we will be prioritizing the common civilian's right to live in a peaceful community, over the psychopath's right to freely reoffend.

Hence, we must take every sordid terrorist's freedom away permanently, both as a form of punishment, but also as a means of crime prevention. Similarly, hardened violent criminals, who are not psychopaths, must also be treated like a chronically destructive reoffender. The latter kinds of individuals must be incarcerated for an unspecified length of time, until they can prove to our justice system that they will pose no further threats to the general public.

There would be no security established for other persons within our society, if we grant physical liberties to those criminals who will inevitably reoffend. Therefore, a future victim's right for security should outweigh the sordid terrorist's right for liberty. These latter individuals must be kept secluded from the general public, until they pose no further threat to the innocent civilian. Accordingly, when the convicted terrorist continues to pose as a potential harm to another living being, he should never be granted the potential liberty to carry out his will.

As a peaceful society, our ability to punish the guilty will be limited by the integrity of our spirit. In some person's frame of mind, those who are guilty of extreme forms of torture should, themselves, be subjected to some form of physical torture. However, as a community, we possess the responsibility to maintain a peaceful and ordered society, both for our own sakes and for our children's sake. Through this responsibility, we may either impose strict fines for those who are guilty of minor offences, or we may choose to restrict the freedom of those who are guilty of major offences.

Both forms of punishments are geared towards reducing the capabilities of the common criminal. In addition to the standard deterrent, when we further impose severe economic penalties, we will also be effectively limiting the criminal's communal freedom. The criminal's ability to create fear within his community will be reduced if he lacks the financial means to achieve his goals. For example, all arsonists rely on a specific set of tools, in order to commit their acts of terror. If these kinds of criminals lack the monetary funds to commit their crimes, the additional fines imposed will both punish and disarm these kinds of criminals.

Likewise, the criminal's potential to travel and commit crimes within a foreign country should also be taken away as a mode of punishment. Every culture possesses a unique justice system. Therefore, while a specific deterrent may work in one nation, it may not necessarily work in another nation. As a result, while the criminal may be deterred to commit some crime within his native country, he may not be equally deterred by the justice system of another nation.

Thus, wealthy individuals, who become hardened criminals, will merely continue to commit criminal offences whenever they travel to a foreign country. Through this kind of penalty, we will be limiting the freedom of the individual in a manner that may be analogous to a form of incarceration. In essence, criminals who become identified as a hardened criminal must not be granted the freedom to commit their offences among differing nations around the world. If they are granted this luxury, they will merely threaten the security of citizens within that particular nation. Proper forms of crime prevention will require the further reduction of liberties, in many differing forms, for those persons who will mainly reoffend when granted the freedom to do so.

To best deter the common criminal from evolving into a hardened criminal, we must also utilize some kind of formal monitoring system. A criminal therapist could provide counsel, which may address any underlying psychological issues that affect this type of criminal. In essence, those who demonstrate rehabilitative qualities are the only types of candidates who deserve to be granted parole. The criminal who demonstrates promise may be given the option to serve the rest of his sentence outside of a formal prison, within some kind of rehabilitation program. Nevertheless, a positive psychological evaluation will be necessary whenever we reduce a criminal's punitive sentence. In turn, this additional element may also provide some criminals with the necessary motivation to wilfully complete a full rehabilitation.

At this point, we must ask what is more unacceptable, an injustice regarding a criminal or an injustice regarding a law-abiding citizen? In an ideal world, both forms of injustices are unacceptable. Yet, on many occasions, numerous persons who are responsible for wrongdoing evade punishment within our justice system. Our justice system is tailored towards protecting the innocent, while the victim's right for justice mainly comes in second. Indeed, our justice system follows a certain set of principles that leans towards protecting the wholly innocent from becoming convicted of any wrongdoing.

The principle "innocent until proven guilty" requires concrete evidence for a proper conviction. This makes it more difficult for the innocent to be convicted of some crime. In cases where the accused is truly innocent, there should exist no concrete evidence that proves his guilt. Therefore, our justice system should prevail under the latter circumstances. The drawback to this aspect of our justice system is based on the possibility where there may be a lack of sufficient evidence available, which proves the guilt of the genuine perpetrator of a crime. When this occurs, the victims of crime will not be granted any forms of social justice, and likewise, in these cases our justice system will have failed.

Consider the possibility if we reversed this principle. Thereby, our justice system would revolve around the principle "guilty until proven innocent". In these cases, there is a greater chance to convict a suspected person of interest. As a consequence, our justice system will be favoured towards granting justice to the victims of a crime. Yet, it also results in a greater chance that an innocent person may be convicted for a crime that he did not commit. Within the rational person's frame of mind, this possibility may be a much graver injustice.

Hence, requiring the burden of proof is a just principle. It is geared towards providing a form of communal justice, where no innocent persons should be convicted of a crime that they did not commit. It requires a certain burden of evidence to prove that some civilian is actually guilty of some crime. In turn, implementing the burden of proof in a converse fashion may be equally just. Perhaps, we should further require the burden of proof whenever we examine the common criminal. In these cases, the onus may be on the common criminal to prove that he has fully abandoned his criminal habits. Thereupon, a similar burden of proof may be necessary when, and if, we are to re-classify a hardened criminal as a truly rehabilitated law-abiding civilian. In essence, we must place the onus on every criminal to prove to the state that he can actually return to his community and live cooperatively as an equal and law-abiding citizen.

True social justice must not be merely based on the values of one's society, but also upon the values of the victim as well. We cannot provide a true system of justice if the victims of a crime are disregarded, due to some alternate principle. Proper social justice must deter any possible future instances of a crime, but it must also provide some form of peace for the victims of a crime. In most cases, the victims of a crime need to be granted with an adequate form of justice to begin their personal healing process. Moreover, a society that disregards the principle of victim's justice will detract from the individualistic concerns that serve to develop its culture. To accomplish some form of justice for the victims of a crime, we must shift our focus, as in the tradition of feminism, towards the needs of these individuals. Feminists grant our society with a perspective that can only be envisioned by those who are female in gender. Similarly, our justice system must take into account the victim's perspective of justice, and thus create a system of ideals that takes these individual's personal feelings into account.

As in the case of most other forms of minorities, the most ethical way of life should require input from every citizen, within any given community. The majority must take into account the minority's thoughts on any given subject, to make any kind of system more inclusive. Similar to the political system of democracy, our justice system should provide for the needs of all of its citizens. Only when this occurs will our system then become the most comprehensive system of justice. Every ethical system, whether it be a political or justice system, must include each law-abiding citizen's perspective. In many cases, the minority's stance could potentially be the most ethical.

Deliberate the possibility of entering into a war in order to free a society from an oppressive dictator. Perhaps, we should first ask those, who are native to this particular area, whether or not they would support this kind of war. In this specific case, the minority could best represent the actual victims' viewpoints, who are the actual victims of oppression. Hence, in this case, the opinion of the minority may be the most just, when determining the best possible resolution for this problem.

Therefore, to accomplish a higher sense of justice, our judicial system must weigh the impact of a crime both on our society, and on its victim. In so doing, the victim will essentially be granted with a degree of authority over his abuser. By empowering the victims of a crime, we will also be advancing a more forceful concept of justice. In the latter case, it may be highly ethical to weigh the impact of a crime on its victim, and successively grant the victim with some kind of role within the justice process. If the victim is excessively harmed by some offence, then he should have some influence regarding the weight of the penalties imposed onto a guilty offender.

The debate between implementing a punishment versus a standard deterrent, thus, could include vengeance as a kind of punishment. On the surface, a severe punishment may act as the most logical deterrent. Every deterrent must be harsh to be effective. Therefore, acts of vengeance could, potentially, pose as a major deterrent in themselves. Yet, the differences between modes of revenge and punishment may be vast. The main difference between a punishment and revenge is based on the differences in ideologies between a community and the individual. First of all, forms of revenge are usually highly subjective. Every unique individual may possess a differing concept, regarding the most proper form of revenge. Within the static character's frame of mind, most forms of revenge will involve inflicting some form of equivalent harm onto another person. In contrast, forms of punishment may be more general in nature, simply because those persons who are members of our judicial system must agree upon an ethical mode of justice. Accordingly, forms of punishment are based more on a collective will, while forms of revenge are based more on the will of an individual.

In fact, forms of criminal organizations utilize the concept of vengeance in an effort to maintain their authority, and they are usually successful in this undertaking. Within these individuals' frame of mind, modes of revenge will usually involve physical elements like torture, or other kinds of equivalent emotional or psychological harm. However, true forms of justice, or just forms of punishment, will mainly involve a peaceful means. By incarcerating some individual, we are not technically inflicting any physical harm onto this person. As a result, modes of revenge can only be justified if they are backed by the general will, and thus, reclassified as alternate mode of communal punishment. In effect, when a form of communal punishment includes fair modes of victim's justice, its force will become far greater than any of these latter concepts alone.

Hence, the forms of punishment enforced through our justice system are primarily communal in nature, while most forms of revenge mainly involve personal ego and individual satisfaction. With respect to the dynamic character, every individual's soul will possess a distinct set of personal virtues. As a consequence, each individual will also have distinct concepts, on the subject of security. Similar to revenge, the embodiment of communal security may also be materialized in a vast amount of modes, but some common concept of security must be upheld through a communal justice system. Therefore, even though the concept of justice could be boundlessly subjective, we must all agree upon a single method that is wholly objective. The validity of our justice system must be based on the integrity of our entire society.

Accordingly, when a victim's concept of justice conflicts with the integrity of his character, it cannot be validated by our judicial system. This is due to the fact that, through his feelings of anger, the victim may inevitably develop an angry or chaotic character. When this occurs, the victim's internal turmoil will only serve to disrupt his inner peace. Likewise, order within his society should also be negatively impacted. In order to avoid this potentiality, we must select a form of justice that is compatible with the absence of any forms of vice. In other words, the internal motivations or intent of our justice system must always be based on some form of virtue, if it is to truly represent the will of the general public.

For instance, a victim may be entirely virtuous if he takes the life of a criminal, when this action is conducted through the motive of self-defence. The sordid terrorist will never relinquish his goals to disrupt the establishment of peace, and when a victim comes face to face with this kind of abuser, the act of self-defence may require acts of utter extremity. Nevertheless, if the victim is primarily motivated by the vice of anger, his subsequent actions will be entirely unjustifiable. The integrity of the victim's character may be at risk when his motives change from those based on virtue, to those based on some form of vice. While forms of subjective justice may be wholly moral to the individual, the actualization of some of these conceptions of justice could cause damaging effects against his rectitude and probity. As a consequence, extreme concepts of revenge cannot be upheld within our justice system, because most forms of revenge will be mainly chaotic in nature.

Within the victim's mind, social justice may never be equivalent to victim's justice. Yet, even though there may be an individual victim, all crimes are also, necessarily, committed against the victim's community. As a result, our current justice system is more inclined to focus more on communal forms of justice, over victim's justice. Nevertheless, we can improve our concept of social justice by adding elements of victim's justice, whenever this is appropriate. As a form of communal justice, the penalties invoked through our justice system must seek to deter an individual from becoming a criminal. Nonetheless, when these penalties do not serve to deter the individual, we must address these specific circumstances with something that will effectively deter the criminal from becoming a repeat offender. When harsher forms of penalties serve this sense of victim's justice, we should consider addressing this particular victim's needs.

Therefore, if we focus on the principle of deterrence, as opposed to the principles of either punishment or vengeance, this would, indeed, serve the main interests of most victims. In essence, honourable modes of victim's justice must be primarily directed towards the creation of a newer and a more effective deterrent. Since we are all rational creatures, we must ask ourselves if the reasons behind an instance of criminal justice may better serve the public interest, in comparison to the punishment itself. If we direct our focus purely on punishing a guilty offender, this could benefit some victims. However, if we focus on the most important reason behind criminal justice, the paradigm of deterrence would be the main focal point. In seeking the best possible deterrent, we are actively seeking to eliminate the existence of all possible potential criminal acts, during future generations.

No rational victim wants any other person to become victimized by the same crime. Therefore, a revised form of social justice must take into account this particular need for justice, in cases where this kind of justice may be deficient. Effectual deterrents must both deter guiltless individuals who may be at risk to commit an offence, in addition to criminals who are at risk to commit repeat offences.

Moreover, every victim that suffers a loss from some form of crime will regain a sense of peace, if his society works towards preventing any similar future offences. The only way to accomplish this feat is to focus on finding some form of penalty that will serve as a truly effective deterrent. Some individuals will fear longer terms of incarceration. Those criminals who possess no such fears will inevitably be prone to reoffend. It is in these cases where our justice system should focus on protecting a potential future victim's interest, by utilizing an indefinite length of incarceration, until the criminal, himself, can prove that he will pose no more criminal harm to his society.

Therefore, a true deterrent against criminal acts must result in lesser criminality, and more instances of peace. Theoretically, this goal is far more important than punishing a guilty offender. Accordingly, our justice system must also be cautious whenever it implements a form of punishment that ranges well beyond the scope of an effective deterrent. Deterring forms of crime must be the primary objective of any justice system, while implementing forms of punishment onto a guilty offender must be considered merely as a possible means that will enable us to accomplish this task.

As a consequence, in some cases, a deterrent may only require minute forms of punishment. In these cases, we must ask the question of whether justice is really accomplished when the effects of a crime entirely outweighs the effects of the consequent penalties for it. Perhaps, to answer this question, we must consider the victim's perspective. Within some victim's eyes, true justice will only be accomplished if the effects of a punishment for a crime are equal to the effects that this crime has had on its society, and in particular, its victim. In other words, the punishment for a crime must cause some equivalent form of affliction. Nevertheless, the most important effect of criminal justice will come about if a specific punishment brings peace to both the victim and his community. Therefore, true forms of justice must encourage peace on a universal basis.

Ideally, whenever this is the case, our society will be mainly shifting its focus away from criminal sentences based on a punishment, over to sentences that are aimed towards crime prevention. Thereby, a justice system's key aim should be to protect every member of its society, while individualistic concerns regarding punishment and revenge must be put aside, should it be the case that a grave injustice will result in either case. Therefore, in some cases, a lax penalty may also be warranted, if it serves its true purpose as a solid deterrent.

As a peaceful society, most civilians would prefer a form of justice that is based on the principle of deterrence, as opposed to a form of punishment. As a result, our justice system would not be fulfilling its duty to the general public by releasing chronic violent offenders from incarceration. By implementing harsher kinds of penalties against those individuals who will become repeat violent offenders, our justice system will be upholding the maxim that violence will not be tolerated within our society. This may give potential violent offenders enough reason not to commit any acts of violence in the first place. As such, a forceful deterrent may be wholly necessary to encourage peaceful relationships among those individuals who are at most risk to commit violent offences.

In order to provide our justice system with the necessary means to protect our society, we must grant our judges with the power to implement further modes of justice through two additional clauses. The first clause will be based on a rebalancing of power, through the victim's right for justice. The second clause is also highly related to the first clause, because it will consider the criminal's potential to reoffend. If our justice system is granted with the power to consider these additional factors, then it will incorporate a wider range of justice that is relevant to the establishment of a maximally peaceful society.

Thus, we must apply differing forms of justice according to differing categories of criminals, in addition to their specific criminal misconducts. The common criminal will be mainly guilty of property crimes, but he also possesses the ability to be rehabilitated. Justice for this individual must differ from those individuals who become chronic criminals, essentially due to the fact that the hardened criminal exhibits no promise to become rehabilitated. Moreover, the sordid terrorist's main goal is to abuse an innocent individual, in his effort to gain social authority. Justice for the sordid terrorist must be equally more severe.

The main purpose of any justice system is to maintain a lawful, civil society. To accomplish this task, it must effectively discourage all forms of criminal behaviour. Yet, while one penalty may deter the common criminal, the same penalty may not deter the hardened criminal. As such, when we punish an individual for his criminal behaviour, we must not merely take into account the specific criminal act. In fact, we must also determine the motives behind his acts, and essentially, his capacity to reoffend. In so doing, when we psychologically evaluate an individual to be a hardened criminal, the rights of his potential victims must take precedence over his liberty to reoffend. In other words, the peaceful coexistence that exists within a civil society must be prioritized over the hardened criminal's freedom to commit further criminal acts.

Therefore, in the case of the hardened criminal, we must penalize these individuals through an indefinite length of incarceration. The hardened criminal should only be granted the liberty to re-enter into civil society, when he proves to our justice system that he has become a freely rehabilitated citizen. Likewise, those individuals who do not possess the volition to become rehabilitated from their criminal ways should not be granted the liberty to re-enter their community and victimize other innocent civilians. As a consequence, our justice system must further consider the criminal's potential to reoffend, in order to implement the most righteous mode of justice. The penalties that it applies during the latter circumstances must be flexible enough to either deter the hardened criminal from becoming a repeat offender, or physically prevent him from committing repeat offences through the enforcement of indefinite lengths of incarceration. The most potent justice system should prioritize a potential victim's right to live in peace, over the repeat offender's liberty to abuse this individual.

As a consequence, in our establishment of a communal form of justice, we must additionally balance both the victim's needs, in addition to any potential future victim's needs. Therefore, the highest possible form of justice will not merely restore communal order, but it will also bring peace to the victim's soul. The truest form of social justice must not merely benefit a society, but also the victims of any given crime. This requires a dedicated focus on the concepts of maximal crime prevention, and if necessary, forceful methods of restraints.

Every citizen possesses an innate right to live in peace, without being threatened by any other individual. Yet, when the common citizen becomes a victim, his concept of justice may be entirely subjective. Indeed, the concept of justice can be materialized in an unlimited manner. However, if a community wants to establish a true justice system, the forms of justice implemented by this system must be based on common values. Therefore, although the concept of justice may be boundlessly subjective, it must be applied through an objective perspective. Our justice system must implement a form of justice that will be commonly accepted by every person within its community. It must be based on some form of a collective or collaborative agreement, in order to retain its integrity as an authoritative governing body.

Ideally, every victim must transcend the concept of revenge through a more objective mode of justice. The motive of revenge can never benefit the individual's entire community, simply because it arises strictly through emotions of anger and personal biases. When forms of anger are personified, it will threaten the community's establishment of social order. Therefore, our justice system must draw a fine line between a mode of punishment, and the most effective deterrent. In fact, true communal justice arises through the spirit of sympathy. We must balance a form of criminal punishment that will address both the victim, and his community's need for justice. It is this concept that will strengthen the bond between two common law-abiding citizens.

The second most important social virtue is freedom. It is a social virtue that is inherently linked to justice, because freedom is necessary for all forms of morality. Recall the fact that God is not truly responsible for the grotesque amounts of evil present within our world.

On the contrary, all forms of horrific evils are due to human beings, in conjunction with free will. If it is true that freedom, and not God, is the cause of all evils, then it must also be true that freedom is the sole cause of goodness.

Consider the white oleander. It cannot be said to have an either moral or an immoral spirit. It merely exists. The same could be true with respect to wild life. When we compare human beings to the animal in nature, human beings are afforded with a higher form of freedom. Since animals in the wild merely act according to their instincts, they do not possess the raw capability to commit the kind of evils that some human beings are responsible for. The killer whale hunts the seal purely for its own survival. It is neither a moral nor an immoral creature. It merely chooses according to the natural instincts that have been programmed into its psyche.

Yet, when we view human beings, we do judge persons according to some standard of morality. This is due essentially to the wider scope of our freedom. Human beings do not act according to mere instincts. We act according to some form of reason. Yet, the power of our free will enables us to either act or refrain from acting, in every given situation. Likewise, we also possess the power to either act according to the reasons within our psyche, or in a totally opposite manner. The freedom within our will enables us all to choose between two contradictory modes of action. As a consequence, this feature makes us all moral creatures.

Accordingly, acts of goodness cannot come from a life force that lacked the raw capability to act in a contrariwise fashion. In a similar manner, acts of utter evil cannot be produced by a life force that lacked an intrinsic ability to refrain from producing these kinds of acts. All forms of morality can only come from a form of life that possessed the freedom to choose otherwise. Moral action requires freedom.

When the agent possesses the capacity to act according to either goodness or malice, he will possess the necessary amount of freedom that is necessary for all moral judgments. As a result, we cannot judge forms of goodness or evil, with respect to a life force that lacked the raw capability to act in a contrary manner. Therefore, no person can be the recipient of any acts of goodness, or malice, from any individual who lacks the social virtue of freedom. It is due to the freedom possessed within an individual's will that enables us to judge his moral character. If human beings lacked the social virtue of freedom, concepts of morality and immorality would be trivial and impertinent.

Equality is the third most important social virtue. Similar to freedom, equality is also linked to the social virtue of justice. In the case of positive justice, the virtue of equality provides a foundation for all forms of social interactions. The social virtue of equality is evidently upheld in all forms of peer to peer relationships. This makes equality a kind of guiding principle as well. Yet, even during interactions where there are forms of authority involved, the virtue of equality still remains prevalent. For example, during healthy parental relationships, the child will inevitably obey his parents, and submit himself to their authority. However, in return for the authority that he receives, the parent will provide for his child. Therefore, the concept of positive justice is primarily based on the virtue of equality. In all forms of give and take relationships, the agent involved will possess a moral obligation to provide for his partner, in cases where he has received a similar amount of provisions from that individual. This moral obligation, then, is principally based on the social virtue of equality.

Relationships based on the virtue of equality will never involve any forms of a power struggle. It is true that many relationships may be based on authoritative elements. However, the social virtue of equality maintains a balance of power between two persons, through the concept of mutual regard and the ideal of common interests. Persons who establish a relationship based on the social virtue of equality will recognize the independence and personal autonomy of their partner. Both parties involved will also hold a form of spiritual toleration towards each other. In the end, these kinds of relationships will grant both individuals with equivalent feelings of respect and esteem.

Contrarily, the concept of inequality is mainly based upon the concept of negative justice. When the static character upholds concepts of discrimination, he usually does so due to his feelings of personal incompetence. The static character then evolves into a bigot whenever he holds the personal belief that he has been wronged by some class of individuals. Next, when his feelings of anger escalate, his negative emotions will evolve, and he will hold a form of hatred towards this class of individuals. In essence, the bigot will then discriminate against these persons, due solely to his mindset of incompetence, in combination with his feelings of hatred.

The concept of inequality is usually subconsciously derived through the self-loathing of the bigot, based on his own personal imperfections. When he feels that he has been attacked, by way of his personal imperfections, the bigot will invert his feelings of anger, as a means to cope with and accept his natural imperfections. Accordingly, his discriminatory feelings will then result.

When two persons with a static character first meet, they will inevitably enter into a battle for social authority. The loser of this battle will be faced with two options. He may either submit himself to this other person's authority, or he may continue to engage in this battle. If the static character chooses to continue this spiritual battle, this is where feelings of revenge towards a single individual may evolve into feelings of revenge against an entire class of individuals. Subsequently, the static character's inability to moderate his feelings of anger due to these lost battles, in conjunction with a lack of self-toleration towards his own personal imperfections will, subsequently, cause him to react in a vengeful manner. This latter condition marks the birth of all forms of discrimination and inequality.

A second category of social virtues exist not between two human beings, but between God and man. The social virtue of mercy exists between God and the individual who is driven by vice. This is due to the fact that the concept of mercy is an act of God, which can only be actualized by God. In fact, only God understands the totality of life experiences that drives and motivates the vicious. Likewise, only God has knowledge of the many hardships faced by those who are driven by vice. In a similar fashion, God also comprehends the true impact that the vicious have on their society. Therefore, when the vicious are guilty of some crime, only God comprehends the totality of this act, with respect to the events that preceded this crime, and the subsequent events that may follow this crime. Since God possesses omniscient knowledge, He is the only life force that possesses the inherent powers to be truly merciful.

Only those individuals who both recognize and freely admit their guilt may be the potential receivers of mercy. In all forms of vicious acts, one individual is being wronged by another. If the vicious do not experience emotions of shame in relation to their acts, they cannot be the recipients of any forms of pity. The act of forgiveness can only come about when the offender experiences feelings of true remorse. To express his feelings of regret, the offender must not dispute his guilt, and moreover, he must acknowledge the pain that he has inflicted onto another living being. When the vicious accept total responsibility for their malicious acts, they will openly retain their identity as an offender until they have received utter and complete forgiveness for their misdeeds.

The vicious will sometimes gamble on the peaceful nature of most individuals, in an effort to gain some type of pity or forgiveness for their criminal acts. Yet, those individuals who never accept full responsibility for their criminal behaviour can never be the recipients of any forms of forgiveness. These criminals experience no forms of sorrow in relation to their crimes. They may exhibit some form of emotion, mainly in an effort to gain sympathy from other persons. Yet, these types of criminals are extremely cunning and insincere. As a result, they can never be the recipients of any forms of forgiveness. In these cases, the criminal will be alienated from his community and the only forms of forgiveness or mercy that he may receive, in relation to his vicious acts, can only come from God.

Another virtue that belongs to this category of social virtues is that of unity. Only persons who are motivated by virtue will acquire the social virtue of unity. This is due to the fact that in order to be dutiful to God, the individual must also be dutiful to other persons within his community. In essence, human beings are much simpler life forms, in comparison to God. As a consequence, those individuals who lack the ability to fulfill their duties to other persons will also, necessarily, lack the ability to be dutiful to God. Since God is spiritually limitless, a relationship with Him first requires a comprehensive understanding of the human spirit.

From a spiritual perspective, all forms of life will possess an intrinsically unique life-force. When the individual gains some understanding of another person's spirit, he may then choose to engage in a form of relationship with this person. It is through friendships with other persons that provides the individual with a starting point for a relationship with God. When the individual values another human being, he will demonstrate a love for the human spirit. This love for human life will inevitably grow to encompass his own essential spirit. After the individual comes to value his own existence, his emotions will further expand, and he will naturally come to love the creator of all spirits. It is through this evolution of emotions of love that creates a natural relationship between the individual and God.

After the individual establishes a relationship with God, he will come to realize that God is an entity that is spiritually limitless. This realization creates a higher form of consciousness within the individual. As a consequence, when the individual establishes a unity with God, he will be then blessed with the capacity to unite with all other kinds of spirits. Since God is spiritually infinite, when the individual creates a unity with God, he will then possess the inherent ability to unite with all other kinds of spirits that may exist within our natural world.

Therefore, the social virtue of unity brings two unique spirits together. It is a necessary element among all kinds of relationships. Those who lack this virtue will be isolated, estranged and eventually forgotten. This virtue is also responsible for all forms of cooperation that exist within our physical world. It is a virtue that ties two free individuals together, in order to accomplish some task that cannot be achieved, or efficiently achieved, through an independent manner.

Accordingly, the virtue of unity binds two distinct spirits together. After the individual forms a relationship with another person, he may then embark on a similar relationship with God. When the individual acquires a unity with God, he will then possess enough knowledge that enables him to unite with all of God's creations. Therefore, after the individual unites with God, he will possess a degree of awareness that will enable him to unite with all other kinds of spirits. For some persons, a relationship with God may suffice. Yet for other persons, a unity with God will merely serve as a starting point for a unity with all other distinct and unique forms of life.

As a result, differing kinds of relationships will be based on differing social virtues. In effect, every human being possesses a unique set of principles and personal virtues. Yet, when the individual enters into some form of a relationship, this bond will be based on some connecting virtue. When two individuals interact with each other according to a common virtue, this relationship will then possess the capacity to maturate and grow. Therefore, the adoption of a social virtue will enable two entirely unlike souls, based on their principle base and personal virtues, to form some kind of a connection with each other. Likewise, when a social virtue becomes neglected or abandoned by a single party within a relationship, this will inevitably lead to the dissolution of that friendship.

Therefore, while personal virtues determine individuality, social virtues determine sociability. Persons who possess more personal virtues should, ideally, receive more recognition within any given relationship. On the other hand, persons who possess more social virtues will, naturally, possess a wider range of friendships. Social virtues are reciprocated within all true relationships. Accordingly, both individuals who engage in a relationship will share the same social virtues. The mutuality of social virtues creates a foundation behind every kind of friendship. It may also determine the individual's collective respectability and social class.

In theory, God granted human beings with a free will mainly because He values liberty itself. In fact, the main element that primarily differentiates species of life, within our planet, is based on an increasing degree of freedom. In comparison to forms of vegetation, animals possess more liberty, in relation to their physical bodies. When compared to the wild animal, human beings are granted with a higher form of intelligence, and thus, more spiritual freedom. However, one element that is common among all forms of life is based on the fact that the freedom within our immaterial souls is grounded, and limited, by our physical bodies.

Correspondingly, the human soul can be corrupted, but never corrected. This is due to the essence of goodness and evil. Innocence is an intrinsic quality of goodness which entails pureness of thought. It is a quality that may only be found in persons who possess a dynamic character. Corruption, on the other hand, is the main effect behind an individual's incessant quest for social authority. It originates strictly through persons who possess a static character. Therefore, evil doers will lack the personal volition to act according to principles of morality. Likewise, individuals who are motivated by vice will never accept any forms of duty. When these individuals do act with some form of restraint, they do so mainly to camouflage their true intents. As a consequence, their evil tendencies will still remain, whenever they are granted with the proper opportunity to commit their acts of malevolence.

Contrarily, persons with a moral spirit may commit criminal acts whenever their innocence has been corrupted by some form of evil. This demonstrates the elements of ignorance possessed by those persons who inherently retain an innocent nature. Yet, it also demonstrates an absence of rational thinking within these individuals. Accordingly, whenever these individuals become rehabilitated from their criminal ways, their soul is not being corrected, as so much as it is being reset back into its original position, into a more dynamic frame of mind.

The individual's direct reactions to feelings of pain directly relates to his moral character. Persons who inflict pain on others to address their own suffering demonstrate a highly immoral character. Contrarily, those who work towards alleviating another person's adversities, due to their own hardships, demonstrate a highly moral character. Therefore, according the principle of positive justice, the most giving individual should also receive the most, within any given friendship. All friendships will be based on some social virtue, in conjunction with positive justice. Nevertheless, some individuals may also fail to acquire any forms of social virtues. The totality of these individuals' relationships will be based merely on the rudiments of negative justice.

12   The Newborn State

THE NEWBORN STATE is built upon the sharing of common ideals amongst all law-abiding citizens. It first begins with a newborn city, and it ends with a newborn world. At present, there are two major political systems that govern the majority of nation-states. The systems of democracy and communism reflect upon two differing roles that a legitimate government may take in order to serve the basic needs of its citizens.

In an equal fashion, the newborn city will also be founded through the spirit of cooperation. It is a close-knit community because all of its inhabitants will share a similar kind of lifestyle. It is based both on manmade creations and natural environmental features, such as mountains and beaches. Yet, even though each civilian may share the same manmade and natural luxuries, each civilian may also be affected by the same social problems. Accordingly, a newborn city will be based on the ideal of sharing, with respect to both resources and potential difficulties.

From an objective perspective, the individual must, necessarily, adopt the principle of cooperation if he wishes to enter into and gain membership within a community based environment. By gaining membership within a specific community, the individual may then expect that his essential needs, related to civilized living, will be addressed and met. Yet, the price for this gift requires that the individual, himself, must contribute and provide a kind of service within his community.

Within every established community, there exists some level of dependence between each citizen. With respect to the principle of contribution, every person specializes into a chosen field of interest. What every person contributes will vary on an individual basis. One person may specialize in farming and provide food for his community, while another may specialize in building shelters, and another individual will be responsible for the creation of clothing. Accordingly, within all communities, there exists a level of cooperation between all individuals, based on the element of specialization. The main aim of any community is to secure every person's basic needs, within the realm of survival.

Before the establishment of human civilization, there was only anarchy. Individuals would have probably created a collective, based on a common blood line. Next, separate collectives would have grouped into a lone collective, based on the sharing of common values. Eventually, this collective would grow to the point where a unified form of order would be needed, and this is accomplished through the vision of a leader.

A leader will be nominated, by the people, to lead and manage the best interests of his community. In a just state, a leader will be appointed based on the element of respect. However, if this individual turns out to be an unjust leader, then in time, he will be responsible for the creation of immoral laws, and possible crimes against humanity.

This is due to the fact that all unjust leaders will be marked by the character trait of aggression. In the unjust state, the most vicious leader will retain his power mainly through the element of fear. As a consequence, within an authoritarian regime, every individual's human rights will eventually be disregarded and abandoned. By its definition, human rights are the fundamental prerequisites that will provide a minimally good life, for every law-abiding citizen. Yet, within tyrannical states, crimes against humanity will mainly evolve, due to the elements of corruption and poor leadership.

Conceptually, this is a type of government whose authority will be based upon a certain degree of absolute power. Its complete opposite may be based on the concept of anarchy, where there are no forms of governmental authority. Yet, if given the choice, most rational persons would rather live in a state of anarchy, in comparison to an authoritarian regime. Within a state of anarchy, no person will ever be subject to any unjust laws.

Nonetheless, no rational individuals will reject the rule of just laws. Hence, most persons would prefer to live under the rule of just laws, over a state of anarchy. In comparison to a state of anarchy, a governing body will create laws to manage the general public's interest, which essentially safeguards every citizen's human rights. Therefore, the ideologies of morality and ethics will be the main focal point of any just governing body, and those bodies which lack these constitutional elements will never acquire a legitimate form of authority.

After every state around the world is governed by a legitimate authoritative body, the next step towards the progress of human civilization will be based on the creation of a community among nations. In essence, resource rich nation-states must assume a leadership role and supply their resources in an effort to aid poorer states. In the end, the differentiation gap between developed states and developing states will be inherently minimal, and this will mark the beginning of a newborn world.

Within a community of nations, there will be states that follow either democratic or Marxist principles. However, these differences in political policy merely reflect upon a more diverse world community. The main purpose of every governmental body is to create some system of order. First of all, governments collect taxes so that they may complete projects that benefit their entire community. For instance, services such as an education system and a health care system will be commonly valued by all individuals within a developed society. Secondly, governments are also granted the powers to create laws that will either punish or deter criminal forms of behaviour. Therefore, the primary role of all governmental bodies is to create a functioning society.

Civil laws reflect upon the values of peaceful persons. Tort and contract laws have been created because our society values the principles of honesty and social responsibility. Other civil laws may represent additional values, based on concepts of virtue. Yet, if the individual does not agree with the laws established within his community, either criminal or civil, he still possesses the freedom to consider living a life either within another nation, or within an environment that is outside of all forms of civilized society.

Therefore, individuals who do not value the spirit of cooperative living still possess the right to live somewhere away from their community, in nature, or in other words, within the wilderness. Individuals who reject all forms of criminal or civil laws will, indeed, possess this option. The individual who rejects his society's established laws will also, subsequently, devalue the virtue of positive justice. Conceivably, persons who do not value any forms of social order will prefer a more chaotic lifestyle.

From the opposite perspective, persons who openly contest and reject the laws that are established within their community should have their membership rejected on a permanent basis. In actuality, the individual should not possess the right to reap the benefits established within a cooperative community, if he callously rejects the laws that constitute it. Therefore, the individual's membership within his community must be circumstantial, and based on the element of social justice. In essence, the most callous criminals do not respect the laws that guide moral behaviour within a communal setting. As a consequence, this demonstrates the fact that these individuals also do not hold any forms of respect towards any other members of their community.

All human beings possess a free will, and this grants us with the ability to act according to our own free choice. Yet, the kind of freedom granted to human beings can also potentially result in some form of abuse or transgression against another person, through some mode of criminal behaviour. The main difference between the common criminal and the law-abiding citizen resides in the fact that the average citizen guides his actions according to some moral system of thought, where he intends to act in manner that will not produce any forms of transgressions against another person. In contrast, the common criminal lacks such a moral system of thought. As a consequence, criminal laws have been drafted to deter lawless forms of behaviour.

For the lawbreaker, then, the ideal environment may be based either within the wilderness, or some kind of chaotic habitat, that is comprised merely of his peers. In these settings, no true communal laws will be established, and subsequently, the callous criminal may habituate an environment where he will not be subject to any forms of criminal law. Nevertheless, within the wilderness, instead of human beings, nature will serve as the sole governor. Therefore, the lawbreaker's lifestyle will still be governed, just by a differing body. Even so, within this particular environment, he may not be deemed as a heinous outsider or delinquent.

Every nation-state creates similar laws that regulate criminal behaviour. In the just state, laws have been created to protect the innocent from all forms of abuse. In these states, individuals will only be punished if they violate the laws that are established within their society.

Nonetheless, the protection granted to us by our laws is limited merely at a physical level. Criminal laws will merely prevent forms of physical harm to other persons.

Hence, in most cases, forms of psychological or emotional abuse are usually not punishable, as a criminal offence. Since all persons possess an innate right for thought, this right naturally extends to their innate right to express their thoughts. Therefore, in the just state, the citizen should not be criminally liable with respect to the expression of his thoughts. It is only in the unjust state where laws have been created explicitly to regulate the expression of an individual's thoughts. This kind of censorship solely serves to further the interests of those who are in power.

Since laws have been created to dissuade physical forms of criminal behaviour, there will inevitably exist further laws that secure the individual's possessions and property. When an individual is guilty of theft or vandalism, he will be subject to some form of criminal law. Subsequently, criminal laws are also aimed towards preventing rogue individuals from destroying any forms of private or public property. In fact, the nature and scope of all criminal laws remains quite similar across differing nations. They were created to maintain peace and order within a cooperative society. Only the nature of civil laws will vary, according to each nation's governing body. Therefore, the materialization of civil laws may vary according to diverse nation-states across the world, and it is this element that mainly differentiates one culture from another.

Every community will be fundamentally based on the principles of either personal autonomy, or communal welfare. In fact, the only just political systems currently utilized around the world are founded on one of these two principles. Democratic societies focus on upholding the personal liberties of each of its members. Among democratic societies, individualistic independency may be the most valued principle. Accordingly, a democracy forms a right-wing type of government, because it is a system that is based on lesser forms of governmental intervention. This concept supports and encourages individual sovereignty. From an individual's standpoint, a democracy may be the more superior political system because it is based on the virtue of freedom. Therefore, citizens who reside within a democracy will possess more power to govern their own personal lifestyle, and thus benefit through the ideologies of personal autonomy and self-determination.

In contrast, communist societies focus more on the well-being of its citizens, on a communal level. Communism is a left-wing political system in that it is system based on many differing forms of governmental interventions. These kinds of governmental systems will have high rates of taxation, in order to provide more services for all of the citizens who reside within its jurisdiction. As a consequence, within these societies, the wellbeing of all persons, in the form of an equal distribution of wealth may be the most valued principle. From a spiritual perspective, communism may be the better political system because it upholds the virtue of equality, in the form of a materially classless society. Moreover, from a social perspective, it may be the more superior political system because it is based on the emotion of compassion.

Therefore, communism encourages communal prosperity, while a democracy encourages individual prosperity. Nonetheless, the concept of a community, otherwise, remains fairly consistent among both systems of government. The main difference between democratic and communist states is the reallocation of wealth. Within democratic states, the individual possesses more freedom to determine his own wealth, and this benefits those persons who possess a natural capacity to acquire huge sums of capital. However, within communist states, the reallocation of wealth will benefit those persons who may lack the natural or inherent capability to acquire large sums of material wealth.

Indeed, material possessions are a creation of man. No kinds of complex human innovations or creations exist in the wild. All kinds of inventions are due to the higher intellect that man possesses, in comparison to the animals that habituate the wilderness. In essence, the creation of material possessions may naturally lead to the creation of capitalism, which serves as our main system of trade. The invention of currency then provides the basis for an economic system, which facilitates trade between two working-class citizens. Furthermore, markets exist around the entire world to facilitate the trading of resources between nations. Therefore, an international market is another ideological invention that is born through the natural development of human society.

Within a free market, the acquisition of money encourages competition, and this, in turn, stimulates the creation of a higher quality of goods. Hence, in theory, capitalistic systems may better encourage the development of a society, because individuals who contribute the most to their society will be rewarded through a higher class of wealth. Yet, the problem of poverty also remains relevant within the capitalistic system. Thus, in order to cure the problems associated with the marketplace, we must find some kind of moderate ground between the two extremes of capitalism and socialism.

A non-capitalistic, or moneyless society, could encourage nobility. Within the most ideal environment, poverty does not exist. Therefore, both higher classes of wealth, and money itself, should not exist within this environment. Fundamentally, goods and services would be exchanged through an honour system, based on the virtue of reciprocity. Nonetheless, we do not live in a perfect habitat, simply because some persons will not recognize any forms of an honour system.

Therefore, within an imperfect habitat, money is required as form of trade. Yet, as a direct consequence, the problem of poverty will still remain. Persons who lack the intrinsic ability to contribute something positive to their society will be plagued by a lack of wealth. Moreover, where there is poverty, there also exists greed. Thus, a further problem associated with the capitalistic system may come about through a predominant focus on the acquisition of material wealth. Greed leads to the excessive consumption of material possessions. Those persons who oppose greed will possess the virtue of moderation. Within a grand marketplace, moderation will be the only mindset that is fit to battle the evils that are linked to greed. Individuals who possess this virtue will possess the ability to differentiate their wants from their needs.

Within capitalist societies, there exists a large gap, with respect to the distribution of wealth. Accordingly, the problems associated with capitalism should be effectively addressed in states that endorse principles of socialism. On the surface, the solution to the problems of capitalism seems to be addressed through the political system of communism. Democratic nations that adopt socialist principles will equalize wealth, so that those who lack the raw ability to contribute will be given aid, and essentially a higher quality of life. When these societies implement principles of socialism, they will guarantee a minimum standard of life, for all law-abiding citizens, who may lack the capability to provide for themselves.

Undeniably, human civilization is, necessarily, defined by our progress within both our culture and our scientific knowledge. Through science, we possess the ability to cure diseases, and through technology we can increase the efficiency of our daily activities. We also enrich our spiritual existence through fine art. These elements of progress truly define the cultural nature of our species.

With respect to the nature of being human, we possess both an immaterial soul and a material body. In retrospect, it is conceivable that both systems of democracy and communism will also mainly focus on one of these two aspects of our existence. Communism may seem to focus on the cultivation of an individual's soul, through the virtue of equality. On the other hand, within a democracy, persons may acquire large fortunes, and this leads to the purchase of material objects that serve to please the individual's bodily sensory experiences. Therefore, while communism may serve to cultivate the human soul, democracies may serve to cultivate the human body. Both political systems seem to focus on a single aspect of humanity. If this is true, then it may be difficult to determine which system will be more just.

In actuality, we cannot ignore one aspect of our nature over the other. The freedom that we possess over our bodies was never meant to be governed by some other individual, or collective of individuals. Yet, we also require forms of spiritual enlightenment, which recognizes our neighbours as equally significant beings. The best possible life will be based on fulfilling every need of the individual, through all aspects of his humanity. Indeed, a life that lacks this form of moderation will result in an unbalanced way of life.

Proponents against the concept of a democracy could believe that there may be too many freedoms that are associated within this kind of political system. In contrast, proponents against communism may believe that there exists too much governmental control within this system. In a tyrannical state, there may be a form of subjugation, in the form of a lack of human rights. Therefore, the main difference between all three political systems is based on the degree of control that a government possesses over the lives of its citizens. Indeed, the ability to live freely is essential to our being. Therefore, no forms of tyranny can ever be categorized as a just political system. Yet, providing aid to those who are in need, through our own personal wealth, does seem to be a worthy goal for all of humanity.

Therefore, perhaps the best political system may be comprised of the finest qualities that define both a democracy and communism. The concepts of both freedom and equality must be carefully managed into a single political system, in order to provide the best possible life for all of its inhabitants. The most legitimate form of government will serve the needs of all of its citizens, and not merely those who belong to a small minority. When it is successful in this undertaking, it will become a just system of politics. Therefore, when a nation secures the basic needs for each of its citizens, it will rightly evolve into a legitimate form of administration. Subsequently, the model society should be governed by both democratic and communist ideologies. Both ideological systems will have a firm place in the newborn world.

At current times, no nation state is based absolutely on democratic or communist ideals. Every nation state that exists adopts, to some degree, principles from both political systems. However, the most important principles upheld in distinct nation states will differ. Therefore, in order to reconcile the differences between communist and democratic states, we must first build a political system that is based on some kind of common ground, which unites all human beings together. This common ground is based on the ideology of innate rights.

Innate rights are fundamental qualities that are intrinsic to life as a human being. These rights are granted to us as living beings, through the culmination of our material body and our immaterial soul. As a result, they are rights that define the nature of our existence, as human beings. When we reflect upon these rights, we will then come to a greater understanding with respect to our true inherent nature. Furthermore, the mutual recognition of these rights will enable two individuals to realize the fact that they are both members of the same race. Therefore, innate rights define the core nature of human existence.

First, the intrinsic right to exist is the most basic innate right. This right is basic to all forms of life. Thus, if something is a form of life, it by nature, also exists. Moreover, all beings that do exist within our material world will possess the innate right to persist and survive. When applied to human beings, the innate right to exist encompasses not merely our physical existence, but also our spiritual existence. Therefore, through his innate right to exist, the individual necessarily possesses the right to develop and mature in a manner that is free from any forms of intimidation or coercion. The innate right to exist grants every human being with the liberty to grow and maturate according to his own will, autonomy, and volitions. Furthermore, this right supersedes any other rights which may, potentially, violate this right. For example, a nation's government cannot create laws that will oppress or threaten the growth of some subpopulation, even if such laws may be viewed as just. Such policies will essentially be infringing on these citizens' most basic right. Hence, no forms of governmental laws can be esteemed over the individual's right to exist.

Closely connected to the first innate right, the second innate right is for security. The innate right for security upholds an individual's right to live free from the abuse of another individual, whether this abuse is conducted through a mental, physical, or emotional means. This right is essentially an extension of an individual's innate right to exist, since it safeguards all persons from forthcoming or impending dangers. Therefore, if something possesses the right to exist, it also possesses the right to exist free from any forms of potential harm. Moreover, like all other rights, the individual's innate right for security is granted to him at birth. For example, babies are born into the physical world as fully dependent beings. They rely on their parents for their security, until they become strong enough to live as independents. Yet, the security that they receive is not conditional. Therefore, parents are fully obligated to provide security for their children. Those who fail to do so will have violated their child's most basic innate right. Accordingly, these individuals will be as guilty as any other persons who may be guilty of some form of abuse. Those who violate another person's innate right for security will be guilty of a major transgression.

The innate right for thought is the third innate right. This right frees all individuals from any forms of interference with respect to their personal belief systems and rationale, whether some form of suppression is conducted through a government, religion, or other organization of persons. Human beings are granted with a complex intellect by nature, and the utilization of our intellect necessarily requires freedom of thought. Accordingly, no forms of thought should ever be subject to any forms of restrictions. Without freedom of thought, there would be no forms of cultural, scientific, or technological growth. Indeed, the human intellect is the main element that differentiates us from all other species of life. Through the application of thought, human beings possess a qualitative ability that is absent within all other forms of life that may be found in nature. Therefore, the power of our intellect is an intrinsic aspect of our nature that fundamentally differentiates us from all other forms of life.

Expression is a kind of extension of one's thoughts. Similar to the individual's thought processes, forms of expression should also not be regulated, or suppressed. The innate right for expression is a necessary element that is directly related to our innate right for thought. Through language, we are granted with a unique capability to communicate our often unique and complicated thoughts. Likewise, similar to our rational thought process, complex modes of language are also absent among all other forms of life within our natural world. The innate right for expression enables two individuals to share and embrace their personal conceptions and ideologies, and this provides the primary basis for our spiritual growth. Moreover, all forms of true and lasting relationships are based on the free exchange of each individual's distinct personal ideas. Those individuals who promote some form of censorship will remain biased, discriminatory, and wholly ignorant.

The fifth innate right is for choice. The innate right for choice reflects upon the individual's free will. Nonetheless, it is bounded by all other persons' right for security. Therefore, every individual possesses the right to choose, so long as he does not violate or abuse some other being's right for security. Every sentient form of life possesses an innate right for choice, because it possesses a will that is powerful enough to enable it to elect one alternative over another. In human beings, the innate right for choice grants each person with the right to live a fully autonomous way of life. Hence, the innate right for choice is merely an exercise of our will. Nonetheless, the individual's innate right for choice must be restricted in cases where his choices will pose some form of harm to another living being.

The individual's innate right for peace is the final innate right. It serves as an end goal for almost all instances of life. Moreover, this right is intrinsic to all forms of life that exhibit some form of consciousness. Even the lowest animals within an ecosystem deserve peace, which is a socially harmonious life that is devoid of all forms of undue pain. While the innate right for security reflects upon physical forms of pain, the innate right for peace reflects more upon spiritual forms of pain. Hence, the innate right for peace grants every individual with the freedom to pursue and acquire spiritual fulfillment, which may be free from all forms of oppression, suppression, and tyrannical subjugation. Since every individual will possess a differing concept of the most fulfilling life, the true realm of peace may be infinite. Nonetheless, the individual is only free to seek personal fulfillment, so long as his actions do not trump another individual's innate right for peace. For example, some individual may choose to abuse alcohol as a means of achieving a state of peace. However, if he possesses a social circle that depends on him, such as a spouse or children, then his quest for peace may lead to a form of neglect. When this occurs, the individual's quest for peace will conflict with the established peace of his family members. Thus, his concept of peace will be purely flagrant, and it cannot be justified either ethically, or rationally. All in all, peace emanates solely wherever there are no forms of transgressions passed on by one individual over to another.

Successively, individuals who violate the innate rights of other persons will be actively forfeiting any claims towards their own innate rights. Therefore, persons who violate another person's right for security cannot, themselves, claim this right for themselves. Indeed, those individuals who choose to abuse another person's rights cannot expect to be protected by those same and exact rights. For those individuals who seek to destroy any forms of human existence will also abandon their own humanity. In principle, individuals who violate another person's right for security will be living a kind of life that is comparable to any lawless animal in the wild. It would be extremely hypocritical to violate another person's right for security, while seeking self-protection under the same right. As a consequence, individuals who do not acknowledge another person's innate rights will have lost any and all claims, with respect to the benefits that these rights will have provided for themselves. Individuals who continue to violate the rights of others cannot, simultaneously, benefit from those exact rights.

In actuality, persons with a static character do not acknowledge the existence of innate rights, simply because they gain social authority through the primary method of exploitation. Their quest for authority also entails the fact that they do not recognize the virtue of equality. As a consequence, the static character is guilty of violating the most basic innate right. Every person's innate right to exist, in a spiritual sense, will be violated by individuals who suppress the growth, autonomy and development of another person. If the latter persons gain political authority, the individual's right to exist, in a physical sense, may also be in jeopardy.

Alike, the individual's innate right for peace may also be potentially violated whenever a static character gains political authority. This results whenever the static character imposes some form of cruelty or tyrannical persecution towards some subpopulation, which becomes the target of his authoritative whims. In turn, whenever an individual's innate right for peace is violated, it will also often be the case that any or all of his other innate rights will coincidentally be violated. Since the static character is narrowly driven by envy and rage, the targets of his anger will often become victimized in the form of a firm denial, with respect to one or all of their innate rights. In these cases, forms of negative justice, based on the objective of re-establishing a sense of peace, will be wholly justified. Yet, in addition to negative justice, forms of positive justice directed towards the victims of abuse and oppression may also effectively re-establish a state of peace.

Subsequently, when a person with a dynamic character gains political authority, he will both advocate for and grant innate rights to all of his constituents, because he is motivated through feelings of affection. Undeniably, every human being possesses uncertainties. However, the main difference between the static and dynamic character remains in the fact that while the static character will attack another person's insecurities, the dynamic character will seek to positively address and shelter another person's insecurities. As a consequence, while the dynamic political leader demonstrates the characteristics of caring and support towards his populace, the static political leader will mainly demonstrate egoism and malice.

In addition, the elected dynamic political leader will always remain true to his word, because he has acquired the principles of honesty and trust. In contrast, the elected static political leader does not retain his principles of honesty, mainly because his quest for political authority will have been achieved. Hence, the latter types of leaders will not concentrate their efforts towards the maintenance of their moral integrity.

Social class is a cultural construction that mainly denotes leadership capabilities. Within the dynamic character's frame of mind, those individuals who possess more personal virtues will belong to a higher social class. Contrariwise, those persons who possess more vices will belong to a lower social class. Individuals who possess more personal virtues will naturally belong to a higher social class simply because these individuals tend to put the needs of other persons above their own needs, and this attribute is what defines them as just leaders. In truth, personal virtues are intrinsic to ethical codes of behaviour. These attributes provide the individual with a firm reason to uphold forms of goodness. This is why individuals of a higher social class will be granted with the responsibility to lead their social network. Moreover, persons who possess more vices will belong to a lower social class simply because they will always prioritize their own needs over the needs of their peers, and this makes these individuals poor leaders.

  Indeed, there are many differing social classes within our civilization. This may be best illustrated through the topic of athletics. Indeed, there exists a class of citizens who are not athletic, another class of citizens who compete at an amateur level, and a final class of citizens who compete at a professional level. Yet, social class does not merely represent pure capability. Persons who belong to the highest social class will understand the general spirit of all persons who may belong to a lower social class. It is through this kind of understanding where the competent professional possesses the capability to lead. Furthermore, this type of leader also possesses the power to amalgamate differing classes of values, held by differing classes of civilians, into a single and lone system. Only persons who possess a dynamic character will place an onus upon themselves to ensure that each individual, who belongs to their social network, is both acknowledged and spoken for. It is this characteristic that reflects the highest possible class of a potential political leader.

Hence, in addition to the innate rights of man, there are also innate leaders for man. Natural leaders are both chosen and valued by the totality of the general public. However, natural leaders do not necessarily possess skills, exclusively, within the realm of politics. True innate leaders will choose to contribute according to a wide range of possible fields. Correspondingly, these individuals are leaders because they possess the ability to inspire every person that they meet. They also possess the capability to understand and empathize with persons of an endlessly wide variety of spiritual natures. Therefore, innate leaders possess an intrinsic capability to acquire a multitude of friendships. They develop new relationships with relative ease. Moreover, since gaining friendships are a primary goal of all social creatures, innate leaders will also subsequently acquire higher degrees of respect. It is the sociability within their unique spirit that makes these individuals natural leaders.

In theory, innate leaders will gain political power whenever they possess an abundance of relationships, based on social virtues. These individuals will usually be engaged in numerous amounts of friendships and other relationships, which ultimately transforms into forms of political support. First of all, individuals who justly gain political power will demonstrate their personal virtues on a consistent basis. In so doing, these individuals will demonstrate some form of duty directed not merely towards persons within their social sphere, but also towards other forms of acquaintances who may reside within their community. After the innate leader acquires more acquaintances, he must then demonstrate some form of true regard towards these persons, and develop further relationships based on some distinct social virtue. When the individual demonstrates that he is an agent of virtue, his actions will deserve reciprocation. It is at this point where he will receive esteem from the general public, and subsequently become elected as a true communal leader.

The best political leader will possess not a stubborn or rigid standpoint, but an outlook based on a more collective philosophy. Only persons with a dynamic character will become adaptable to changing environments, and this makes them the best possible representative for a dynamic community. Accordingly, the best possible political leader will always represent the totality of his people's will. The best politicians, then, serve as moral guides. They are students who belong to the highest possible social class, simply because they possess a firm understanding with respect to their community's essential needs.

As a consequence, the best possible leader will acquire more virtues after he gains some form of social authority. The most important political virtue is that of responsibility. When an individual assumes some form of lawful authority over another person, he has not been granted this power to fulfill his own ego. The general public has granted these individuals with some degree of authority so that they will possess the capacity to implement common goals and values, into the real world.

In fact, the virtue of responsibility is necessary for any forms of true agency. In the political realm, agents will represent and advocate for the needs of their populace. Nonetheless, all true agents also possess the ability to distinguish between right and wrong. After these kinds of distinctions have been made, a true agent will then act upon ideals of righteousness and morality. Next, the true agent will then accept accountability for his actions. If he makes a mistake, he will do everything in his power to rectify his errors. It is this kind of accountability that, necessarily, must be acquired by any individuals who seek legitimate forms of political authority.

Civic society cannot exist without political agents who accept full accountability, in relation to their leadership role. Without political agency, an ordered society could never exist. Humankind would then lack any forms of a civil society. Indeed, a thriving community can only exist when our political leaders possess the virtue of responsibility, with respect to every decision that they make. Individuals who do not take responsibility for their decisions and actions will essentially be denying their agency. When these individuals do not accept responsibility for their choices and actions, the needs of their community will inevitably be marginalized and lost.

Sincerity is the second most important political virtue. Individuals become elected into office because they possess a firm vision of how their society ought to be. Subsequently, when the individual does gain political power, he must materialize all of the promises that he has made to his constituents. Politicians who renege on their proposals are dishonest, and mainly insincere. Contrarily, politicians who possess the virtue of sincerity appreciate the power that has been granted to them by the general public, and they will, in turn, work towards completing the ideals that they had set forth, before they attained any degrees of official political authority.

Forbearance is the final political virtue that is based on a form of self-control. In order to properly serve the interests of his society, an elected politician must balance the needs of his populace between two extremes. Therefore, the virtuous politician must create an existing equilibrium between citizens that value either left or right wing policies. This is due to the fact that a just politician must recognize the needs of each and every individual citizen. The politician who merely values one extreme within this equilibrium places value only on a specific sector within his society, while he neglects to place any forms of consideration or value towards other legitimate points of view.

The political virtue of forbearance differentiates good political leaders from the common citizen. Good leadership involves the recognition of values possessed by all persons who may belong to a given social circle. In order to accomplish this, the just politician must tolerate viewpoints that may potentially contradict his own, and prioritize the needs of his community according to those policies that will benefit the greatest possible majority, within the general public. Therefore, when a potential conflict arises, the just politician must, potentially, possess enough dignity and reverence to his substitute his own ideals, with the will of the general public.

The main problem with corrupt politicians is based on the fact that they merely appear to possess some set of personal virtues. Therefore, corrupt politicians build their social relationships essentially through a misconception. When this becomes known, their social virtues will slowly deteriorate. In other cases, the corrupt politician may have possessed a minimal sense of duty. However, after he becomes corrupted with power, he will choose to pursue his own self-interests over the needs of his society. Consequently, both kinds of individuals will be guilty of abandoning their particular social duties.

The unjust leader will become corrupt after he has acquired a certain degree of authority. He will then, at some point, neglect the principle of trust that has been established between himself and some other person, or persons, within the general public. Whenever dishonesty surfaces within any relationship, the friendship established will usually be irrevocably broken. Animosity will then become the defining feature in any future relations between these two individuals.

Furthermore, the unjust politician also possesses the vice of cowardice, simply because he will always succumb to his personal fears.

In effect, he feels that his authority may be threatened, whenever a law-abiding citizen experiences any forms of positive emotions. This is the primary reason why he utilizes oppression as the main method to control the populace that he governs.

In a subsequent fashion, the concept of martyrdom will then reign supreme whenever some state is governed by a tyrannical leader. Whenever a person with a static character commits crimes against the state, he is usually motivated by some form of material gain or revenge. However, a person with a dynamic character only commits such crimes in cases where he is subject to some form of oppression. Hence, the dynamic character will be motivated, by the concept of rebellion, whenever he has been subject to the abuse of individuals who unjustly utilize their political power. He becomes a martyr because of the fact that he will take on the relentless task to overthrow his society's corrupt dictatorship, before he gains any forms of true political power.

In these cases, the dynamic character will view his political environment mainly as barbaric, and that it is also driven by a narrow viewpoint. He will then organize an active rebellion against those who are in power, mainly because he is motivated to overthrow an unjust governing body. In actuality, he risks his own security in the hopes that his actions will draw some form of attention towards the injustices that exist within his society. He will achieve success when other persons within his community recognize the same faults.

In time, the general public will renege and then withdraw their support towards a tyrannical dictator. After this occurs, a revolution may then be inevitable. This revolution will then lead to the eventual overthrow of an unjust political leader. The people will then follow a new leader, because of the fact that he is just, and that he will also change his nation's governing body into a just institution. After the people successfully overthrow an unjust regime, the just leader will then create new laws to prevent similar forms of injustices from happening at future times. This is how most tyrannies dissolve. The creation of newer laws reflects upon a kind of communal justice, in relation to the wrongdoings that an unjust leader has inflicted upon his community. Consequently, the concepts of reciprocity and justice will eventually evolve from a dissolved tyrannical regime.

The latter event marks the creation of a newborn state. The leader of the newborn state will surface after the unjust politician loses the last remnants of his political power. In so doing, the newborn political leader will further recognize all of the innate rights that are intrinsic to human existence. After these universal rights are established, the state may then possess the potential to develop into a culturally advanced society.

Indeed, human beings require more than basic material necessities for a peaceful coexistence. Animals require nourishment and sustenance for daily life, yet, human beings require more than this due to our innate intelligence. While we require an ordered civilization for daily living, animals require nothing more than the wilderness of nature. The additional attribute of our intelligence marks a way of life that makes human beings the most complex form of life that exists in our natural world. Accordingly, human beings may only flourish after we establish legitimate governing bodies which institute a form of order, within our societies, that supports a co-existence based on peace and the safeguarding of our innate rights.

The level of governmental intervention, within a society's affairs, depends entirely on the needs of any given community. Societies with many social problems may require more government interventions, while societies that have fewer social problems may not require a similar degree of intervention. Likewise, some social problems may be directly linked with a large population, while other problems may be connected to a smaller population. Social problems may pose as some kind of threat to an individual's security, or it may threaten the existence of peace within an entire nation. As such, the newborn state will not necessarily be based on either a communist or democratic system. In effect, the newborn state will be governed in a dynamic fashion, which utilizes either left or right wing principles, based on social necessity. Accordingly, a unique cultural identity may be a key defining element of the newborn state, since its level of governmental intervention will vary, essentially, on a case-by-case basis.

The recognition of human and innate rights is the most essential constitutional building block behind all newborn states. If our civilization did not recognize the existence of human rights, it could not be truly defined as a cultivated society. In the latter case, human existence would be downgraded into living within a purely lawless habitat. In a similar fashion, a nation without a government would be reduced into a geographical area that is comprised merely of independent tribes. The concept of anarchy then implicates a lack of social order between these tribes, because there will be no formal connection established between them.

Within a tribally oriented world, there would be no exterior forms of cooperation. Each original tribe would be led by a single leader, and it is this individual who will organize a simplistic system of social order. In reality, it is this person's job to prioritize the basic necessities for his tribe, and subsequently, the discrete needs of each tribal member. However, within this simplistic system of order, there would be no complex forms of essential services, such as education or health care. The establishment of essential services can only be accomplished when independent tribes join together to form a nation. After this is accomplished, independent tribes will then possess the capability to pool their resources together with other tribes, and then create something that never could have been created in an independent fashion.

Hence, within a tribally oriented world, there would be no elements such as technological or scientific progress. A formal education system will be needed for any kinds of this progress. Yet, this kind of system must be further based on the cooperative efforts between distinct colleges and universities. Therefore, in order to build the most powerful educational system, the unity of many different research facilities, among many differing nations, will be necessary. As a result, scientific and technological progress, on its grandest scale, can only be realized through the elements of unity, on a world-wide basis.

A formal education system will require enough resources to teach both children and adults. It is the fundamental element behind a developed nation. Yet, this kind of system requires a universalized standard that is common among every school that exists within a nation-state. This standard will impose a minimum level of formal knowledge held by all graduating students. Students who have met this educational standard will then, formally, possess the necessary pre-requisites for unique forms of complicated employment. However, this standard can only be universalized by some body that possesses true authority over every possible school. The kind of authority that is necessary for producing a universal standard among differing levels of schooling, then, must be based within a political system. Hence, a functioning political system is necessary to lay out a universalized standard of order within the education industry, and this may then efficiently encourage further progress within our civilization.

Consequently, an official kind of connection will be necessary for the ideal of cooperation, and cooperation is the most essential attribute that defines a true community. Through the creation of an education system, a nation will be further strengthening the establishment of human rights for its peoples. Indeed, a minimally good life can only be produced in societies that provide essential services for its populace. Therefore, when an independent nation possesses the capability to provide essential services for its citizens, it will provide not merely the most basic necessities of life, but also the most complex necessities that are required for a prosperous life.

In turn, the creation of the newborn world can be comparable to the creation of a newborn state. In this paradise, tribes may be analogous to entire nation-states, while a nation-state may be analogous to the entire sphere. The birth of a newborn world occurs for the same reason that stimulates the birth of a newborn state. It is through the concept of cooperation that best benefits our civilization, as an entire species. Likewise, it is through the concept of cooperation where the problems of a single nation-state may be addressed and fixed by another nation-state. The condition of poverty mainly differentiates rich nations from undeveloped nations. At present, this is the major problem that our civilization, as a whole, must address if we are to continue to build a newborn world.

The limits of the newborn world can only be defined by the limits of the most developed nation. In the newborn world, a health care system will be fundamental in every nation. Yet, a self-supporting medical system first requires an education system, and a standardized education system requires both a resource rich and a fully operational political system. Indeed, some undeveloped nations cannot even provide the basic necessities of living for their civilian population, such as food, shelter and clothing. As a result, our first goal must be to provide forms of material aid, if we are to accept the duty to develop a globalized health-care system.

Since the most basic elements necessary for human life are lacking within the undeveloped world, those nations that are developed do possess a moral responsibility to provide aid to these countries. After solving the problem of poverty, the next project that must be completed, within an undeveloped nation, should be the creation of a functioning political system. Yet, the type of political system implemented within an undeveloped nation must remain entirely representative of those persons who will be subject to its rule. Since there exists a wide range of feasible political systems that successfully govern developed nations, the political system that these peoples do adopt must also be similarly autonomous. Therefore, the project of globalization, accepted by richer countries, should only address the intrinsic problems that affect undeveloped nations, which is mainly poverty. After this problem is addressed, a developed nation may also aid an undeveloped nation with the establishment of essential services, like education and health care, all the while leaving the type of political system implemented entirely in the hands of the nation itself. This is the ethical limit regarding the creation of a newborn world. The key goal of globalization is not, strictly speaking, to develop undeveloped nations, but to utilize our material wealth to aid developing nations with the preservation of human life.

Hence, the newborn world is built upon a limited concept of globalization, where all of the richer nations focus on the reduction and abolition of human suffering, within poorer nations. Yet, the possible development of a tyrannical government, within poorer nations, could pose as a fundamental problem in the creation of a newborn world. It is only within these specific circumstances where we will possess the duty to intervene, and aid such nations with the development of a more righteous mode of government. In fact, within the newborn world, there can exist no instances of tyranny. The existence of all forms of authoritarian governments must be actively abolished in its creation. When this is accomplished, all nations will then possess the potential to enter into a single community. Indeed, only relationships based on cooperation will potentially solve and address any kinds of worldly concerns. On a global scale, the most important issue is the loss of human life. However, modes of cooperation, necessary to address this problem, will be rarely embraced by those nations which are governed by an authoritarian regime.

To solve these worldly issues, entire nations need to cooperate with each other, in the same manner that individuals depend on each other within a community. Each nation must accept some kind of role, within a community based setting, and contribute according to its potential resources. For example, one nation may offer building materials, while another nation may provide labour, to address issues of homelessness within poverty stricken nations. Similarly, another nation may provide food, and another may provide clothing, to those same undeveloped nations.

In comparison to charities, nation-states possess more economic stability. Therefore, while charities do provide some form of short-term relief within impoverished nations, entire nation-states may be best suited to provide a form of long-term relief. The best possible solution, regarding the problem of poverty, will come from a higher organization of individuals, mainly through some nation-state. The continuing development of an undeveloped nation will further require some form of coordination between differing developed nation-states.

After the creation of a functioning political system within a developing nation, the next concern should be the creation and implementation of a world-class health care system. Conceivably, to accomplish this goal, developed nations must first continue to provide both material and medical aid to poverty stricken nations, for an indefinite period of time. The creation of a nationally independent health care system will require many resources, and a substantial amount of time. Actually, this eventual development of impoverished nations could take many generations. Nonetheless, as long as we are focusing our efforts towards resolving these issues, we will continue to make substantial progress both towards our cultural existence, and also towards the intrinsic advancement of our species.

An international government will be needed within the newborn world, whose authority may be used to organize and direct the sharing of resources between nations. Its powers will include the conceptual powers of taxation and spending. Most importantly, though, it will coordinate the relief effort between a contributing nation and a developing nation. In the same manner that a national government will address the needs of its citizens, a world-class governmental body will identify and manage the needs of those nations, who may be most in need. The best possible outcome will come about when developing nations are granted enough aid to transform from a dependent nation into an independent nation.

The scope of an international governing body should not be limited by any kinds of territorial boundaries. As such, environmental concerns may also be more effectively addressed through a world-class government. Potentially, this government may also more efficiently tackle other kinds of world issues such as astronomical exploration, and other possible types of joint projects. Accordingly, it should possess enough authority to effectually address all kinds of global concerns. An international government will be primarily constituted towards the protection and conservation of life, on a worldwide scale. It should possess the ultimate power to preserve our planet, in its entirety.

The birth of the newborn world will also involve the creation of a universal constitution of rights. A universal constitution will differentiate human civilization from all other species of life. It will be based on the concepts of ethics and reason. In the making of a universal constitution, we must first identify all of the values and ideals that every person has in common. We must then base a universal constitution on these ideals, and further discover the most peaceful method that will enable us to realize these morals. We must unite towards a similar goal, and then work out our differences through some common ground.

Similar to human rights, the establishment of innate rights can only exist within a united, and not a divided, people. A world-class government will be founded through a set of rights that links all human beings together, regardless of their geographical location. Nevertheless, other universal principles must be built upon the principle of a compromise, so that they will be based on elements that are common among all forms of just political systems. Indeed, all communities are based on the free and cooperative actions of those individuals who comprise it. If one nation does not agree on a specific policy, then a compromise could be the only solution. Yet, if a nation's leader is truly a man of integrity, he will be motivated to establish a form of compromise that is acceptable on a world-wide scale. This kind of mindset, amongst our politicians, is necessary to establish the existence of a newborn world.

Accordingly, a universal constitution must address the unique needs of every participating nation. It must be built through a unanimous consensus among nations, who will be the primary contributors within this form of government. All member nations must also be dedicated towards the main mandate of an international government, which is based on the preservation of all forms of life. Since every human being possesses an innate right to exist, the first responsibility of this government will be the redistribution of wealth towards those persons who are most in need. Essentially, nations that contribute an abundance of resources within this coalition should be granted more authority within it. These contributing nations should make kinds of decisions, within the international union, as to which nations need their support the most.

Entry into an international coalition will always be voluntary. Nations who do opt out in participating within this coalition will have no forms of input, pertaining neither to its decisions, nor can they be prioritized over participating nations, in terms of resource sharing and resource allocations. Consequently, those nations who are in need of resources must first submit themselves to a global constitution, which will uphold a charter of fundamental human and innate rights.

Moreover, it is possible that a single nation may irrationally withdraw its support towards an otherwise universally accepted policy. However, if it is a nation that is not contributing any forms of resources towards poverty stricken nations, its membership will not be of utmost importance. National governments who do not subscribe to the goal of the preservation of life should also be denied entry.

Consequently, a highly intricate and cooperative global community will be created through the establishment of an international government. Its first mission will be to provide a permanent solution towards solving the problem of poverty, on a global scale. After this goal is accomplished, we may then focus on the creation of other necessities, such as a world-class health-care system and an education system, within these impoverished nations.

Undeniably, a globalized government will be compulsory to address all forms of global issues. Yet, we must still cherish and value all of the differing cultures that comprise our current civilization. Therefore, every nation-state must still possess the intrinsic freedom to govern its citizens, according to either a left-wing or right-wing system. A world-class government will only improve the efficiency of diplomatic interactions between sovereign nations. Its main effect should produce a globalized community that will reap all of the benefits secured through the concept of a highly cooperative and peaceful community.

An international government will principally collect resources from resource rich nations, and reallocate these resources towards those nations who are most in need. Practically, it may also work towards the preservation of human life, through the abolition of war. In order to maintain a state of peace between all nations, this government must focus on the principle of cooperation, mainly through trade. Indeed, it will cost contributing nations much lesser resources to provide aid to some country, in comparison to going to war with it. Yet, those undeveloped nations who seek forms of aid must first acquire membership within the international government. In so doing, they are making a gesture towards upholding the ideals of cooperation and peace.

Thus, relevant to an international government is the method of diplomacy. Nations who are members of an international government should mainly resolve their disputes through communication, negotiation, and if necessary, mediation. Easier channels of diplomacy between nations will become a secondary effect, in the creation of a globalized government. However, we must also consider conflicts between member and non-member nations.

In the latter case, there is a possibility that a tyrannical regime may possess extreme values that do not agree with any established international laws. When this occurs, we must decide whether such nations actually deserve membership within an international government. Any nation that seeks membership for any other ulterior motives, such as gaining some form of international authority, should be denied entry. The goal of the preservation of life can only be accomplished through the spirit of cooperation, and a degree of compliance between distinct nations.

For the resolution of disputes between member and non-member nations, we must ask if the method of war will be inevitable. In fact, the unjust leader will view war as a means for the acquisition of power. Furthermore, it is these individuals who view peace as a mainly anomalous condition. In other words, within the tyrant's frame of mind, peace may be an unobtainable goal that is fundamentally extrinsic to human nature.

Nonetheless, within the dynamic character's frame of mind, war, and not peace, is the anomalous condition of man. In truth, the concept of peace cannot be anomalous because war is a distinct creation of the human species. Indeed, amongst all forms of living creatures that exist in our world, war is an idea that only afflicts human beings. It is a concept that does not exist anywhere else in nature. As such, persons with a dynamic character will always view war as a last resort, to address the loss of innocent lives, whenever diplomatic channels have failed.

Therefore, war may not always be justifiable whenever there is oppression with no loss of life, because diplomatic channels may still be utilized to achieve some degree of peace. The declaration of war made by a dynamic character will always be utilized as a final resort, whose sole purpose will be to end the persecution of the innocent. It mainly begins with a lack of acknowledgement, in terms of equality, where one person will seek total sovereignty over another. For instance, war is sometimes utilized during land disputes. When two nations use war to solve this form of dispute, the value of land skyrockets over the value of human life. This war will, then, be motivated by the vices of vanity and conceit. Nonetheless, if these two governments utilize the method of diplomacy, their mutual agreement will actively decrease the value of property, while it simultaneously increases the value of human life.

This is why whenever one nation makes a declaration of war, it is a mode of action that must always be utilized as a final option. The taking of lives can only be justified whenever its purpose is to save other innocent lives, who may be facing forms of injustice and oppression. As a consequence, the mere consideration of war will be solely directed towards tyrannical regimes. Tyrants form an unjust government because they do not carry out the will of their peoples. Within the unjust government, taxes are not collected for the benefit of its community. Rather, taxes merely benefit those persons who are in power. Within these regimes, the definition of criminal behaviour may also be flawed. For the most part, only persons who pose as a threat to the authority of a tyrannical regime will be deemed as criminals. Thus, whenever a government does not address the needs of its citizens, its exercise of power will merely promote its own welfare. Acts of oppression, then, will necessarily follow.

Wars can exist between tribes, nations, or alliances of nations. In the latter two instances, war will usually be initiated by the leader of an authoritarian regime. This is due to the fact that all tyrants will possess a psychopathic temperament, and thus, their pursuit for higher degrees of social authority will be lifelong. Indeed, within the tyrant's frame of mind, a life without power is not a life that is worth living. Therefore, the most basic declaration of war will be initiated after a tyrannical leader physically harms a group of innocent civilians. In theory, this war will not end until the tyrant's authority over the innocent is weakened and then destabilized by the force of a liberating army.

Comparatively, civil wars are engaged between alliances of tribes, within a single nation. Yet, this type of war will also be engaged towards some form of tyranny. In these cases, a specific group of tribes will similarly face oppression from a tyrannical leader. Subsequently, both civil and international wars will usually be fought for the same ideological factors of self-governance and freedom from subjugation.

By its constitution, an international government must actively seek to maintain peaceful relationships between independent nations, on a world-wide scale. It will be primarily founded on the spirit of assistance and collaboration. Membership within an international government requires all nations to resolve their disputes solely through the method of diplomacy, and not through war. If this holds true, no member nation may declare war against another nation who is also a member of this coalition. Such policies, based on comradery, could serve as the ultimate principle that will deter any kinds of future wars, either big or small. Indeed, any rogue nation who carries out a pre-emptive strike against a member nation will risk waging war against all other members of the international coalition. It is in these specific cases, where an international government will be justified in engaging in a war. Yet, its use of force must be utilized solely to prevent potential future occurrences of undue harm.

When every nation gains membership, an international government will inevitably possess the necessary authority to prevent any potential for future wars. Accordingly, the constitutive element of peace among all members of an international coalition will provide other non-member nations with a considerable reason to seek membership. The sharing of resources and moral principles, based on diplomatic relations, will provide the majority of nations around the world with a valid and substantial reason to join an international coalition. Therefore, those nations that do seek peaceful relations with their neighbouring countries will also, necessarily, seek membership within this organization as well. Nations that do not seek membership within an international government will not subscribe to the values of peace and cooperation, of which all communities, small or large, are built upon.

It is a world-class government's mandate to maintain peaceful relations between all peoples, based on the social virtues of justice, freedom and equality. Therefore, diplomatic relations will always be the sole method of interaction between two member nations. If modes of diplomacy do fail, then the nations in dispute will risk having their membership revoked. In these cases, sanctions could serve as the main penalty against an offending nation. In this event, our governing body will redirect any resources granted to warring nations towards some other member nation.

In actuality, the United Nations is a global organization that does possess the basic framework for an international government. An international coalition will establish a universal constitution that will unite every existing political system together. This means reconciling the fundamental differences between democratic and communist governments, into a single and cooperative community. At current times, the United Nations has successfully maintained its mandate, in that it has actively maintained diplomatic relations amongst all of its member nations.

Yet, this is the limit of the United Nation's powers. Its foundation is primarily based on the concept of diplomacy. Its role does not include the duties of taxation and spending. In order to tackle world issues such as poverty, a universal health care system, and other concerns such as environmental problems, the United Nations must be granted with higher forms of authority over sovereign nations. These kinds of worldly issues will only be most efficiently addressed through an international governing body.

At present, there are two possible solutions that will solve the problem of loss of life in developing nations. First of all, an international government may be granted with enough authority to manage the flow of aid between richer and poorer nations. If this solution is not feasible, then the latter responsibility must be freely adopted by some member nation. During the latter circumstance, developed nations must abide by a kind of honour system, where they will carry out their duty to provide aid, purely through the liberty and will of their constituents.

In essence, the creation of a universal constitution should not be difficult to create, if each participating nation focuses mainly on its similarities with other nations. Common values will be upheld, while unique and distinct values, based on a left or right wing system, may be debated. Indeed, every political system possesses flaws, which could be potentially addressed by the opposing wing. Therefore, democratic principles may address problems within a communist government, and likewise, communist principles may solve problems within a democratic government.

Criminal laws will more or less overlap between all distinct sovereign nations. Therefore, secondary to innate and human rights, a universal constitution may also have its basis in criminal law. In a similar fashion, a universal constitution should also focus on abolishing modes of governance espoused within tyrannical regimes. Criminal laws within these systems may be largely viewed as unjust, and thus, they may contradict forms of criminal laws that are established within legitimate political systems. To establish a rights based constitution through the basis of criminal law, we must focus on the immoral consequences of a crime, and the specific human values which have been violated. Moreover, we must further consider the criminal's main motive and objective behind his acts of criminality. Through this inverse perspective, we may then rightfully establish the most fundamental human rights that have been violated through acts of criminality. Indeed, every citizen possesses some right that has been taken away by some form of criminal activity.

Nonetheless, civil values may only be established when each member of the international government agrees to its content. A universal constitution must be based solely on the common needs among all citizens, who may belong to a diverse set of nations. On the other hand, the establishment of specific civil laws may be unnecessary, unless we want to build a global community that is unified under a single international political system.

With respect to political interactions, in some cases a compromise may be difficult to achieve, especially when both sides of a dispute are labelled as extreme. Perhaps in these situations, it may be more pertinent to develop a system of laws where each position is utilized according to each individual and specific scenario. For example, an extreme right-wing law may be most fitting when applied to one circumstance, while an extreme left-wing law may be best applied in some other circumstance. This is not a maxim against the ideal of universalism. Rather, it may be viewed as maxim that is based on the principle of relative ethics. According to the principle of relative ethics, while one ethical principle may apply under one situation or circumstance, it may not necessarily apply under another.

The most dynamic political leader will encourage and increase forms of political participation amongst all law-abiding citizens, through the method of consultation. Yet, the greatest leader will reserve this mode of participation only for the most controversial issues. For example, how is it possible for a political leader to understand the needs of persons with disabilities, if he himself has never faced this predicament? When creating policies for those constituents who are affected by some form of disability, it may be prudent for a political leader to query this specific class of citizens. By understanding the most essential needs of a specific interest group, the just leader will more properly implement political solutions with the greatest possible outcome, related to each particular issue. This is an example of the utilization of the principle of relative ethics.

In fact, the dynamic leader gains power not merely because he possesses an ideal vision of the perfect state, but upon the fact that he also considers his constituent's vision of the perfect state. Only a dynamic leader will possess enough insight to properly envision the specific needs of future generations. This makes him, not merely a governor of his people, but also a speaker for his people.

However, one possible criticism that may be related to the principle of relative ethics pertains to the element of judgment. If ethical principles are indeed relative, then how is one supposed to know when a specific principle is applicable, and when it is not? In effect, individuals who use the principle of relative ethics may be guilty of tremendous inconsistencies, whenever they utilize an ethical principle in one circumstance, but not another. As a result, we must ask if this principle enables the individual to "cherry-pick" his righteous beliefs, according to his own personal whims. The answer to this question remains in the fact that all human beings must constantly and continually utilize their faculty of reason, whenever they perform any kinds of judgment. In so doing, relative ethics will be justified whenever there is a rational consensus established among knowledgeable individuals, who may be viewed as experts within some chosen domain. If all of these experts concede the fact that their current mannerisms are out-dated, then it is their moral obligation to adopt a newer moral principle. In turn, whenever the latter considerations occur, cultural progress has been made.

For instance, in many cases, even within democratic societies, politicians will make decisions that contradict a universally recognized virtue, such as freedom. For example, the freedom to bear arms may be righteously rejected to encourage the preservation of all corporeal forms of life. In some cases, these kinds of decisions may not be well understood within the general public. Indeed, at some point in our history, the right to bear arms may have been necessary, for the purpose of self-defence. Yet, at current times, the majority of individuals will, instead, principally rely on policing authorities for their physical safety. Thus, if there is rational consensus established, among other politicians regarding this policy, then it may be justified simply because these individuals are experts within the subject of civil society. The true value of a consensus demonstrates a shift in thinking, with respect to universal principles, into a universal mindset. Therefore, instead of valuing a single concept or principle, we are placing more value on rational and dynamic human judgment.

The principle of relative ethics does not dissolve or abolish all instances of universal principles. In cases like human and innate rights, the universal application of these rights will be entirely justified. As a consequence, the principle of relative ethics may also be applied to itself. Hence, the principle of relative ethics will never be an absolute principle in itself. In some cases, the application of newer ethical principles will be necessary, while in other cases, the application of older universal principles will be most suitable.

In fact, the utilization of the principle of relative ethics may be quantitatively rare. This is due to the fact that it is a principle that may only be applied by experts within any given field. These individuals include judges, who are experts in justice, and politicians, who are experts in governance. True experts possess forms of knowledge based not merely on ideals, but also through experience. Within the justice system, judges should make ideal rulings according to their own conception of justice, in addition to established forms of communal justice, and the victim's sense of justice. On the other hand, politicians should create policies based both on their own ideas of virtue, in conjunction with known policies that are effectively applied among other nations. Therefore, relative ethics requires the use of both rational universal knowledge, and subjective empirical knowledge. All virtues are, from a universal perspective, rational ideals. Nonetheless, the correct application of each unique virtue will vary according to each unique circumstance, and the spiritual nature of those individuals who will be affected by its application.

Subsequently, the principle of relative ethics reflects upon the unique spiritual nature of each and every individual, particularly when analyzed against the similar experiences of another human being. All persons possess a unique state of mind, and therefore they will come to value unique elements in life. Accordingly, the principle of relative ethics addresses the potential problem of general, yet out-dated principles, due to the fact that each individual possesses distinct concepts regarding justice and peace.

Relative ethics will become more significant within a continuing scientific and culturally progressive world. This is due to the fact that we will possess further forms of advanced technologies, which, in turn, will grant us with far greater abilities through the cycle of each generation. Yet, with the greater abilities granted to us through science, there is also the possibility that newer forms of crimes will also evolve. The most damning criminal we may face are the ones who have discovered some flaw within our justice system. Through their criminal ingenuity, the most abysmal criminals will use this flaw to escape and evade prosecution. When we discover any of these kinds of exploits within our justice system, the most peaceful resolution may be to make a form of amendment, which is driven by the principle of relative ethics. Subsequently, the utilization of relative ethics will enable systems, like our justice system, to address dynamic circumstances that may be new to our civilization, of which past generations may have never faced.

Ethical principles, by definition, will serve to preserve life, and thus all of God's creations. In contrast, immorality only serves to destroy instances of life, and this acts in contradiction to the spirit of God. In our world, if God's role is the creation of all life, then our role, as the next authoritative species of life, is to serve as its caretaker. Indeed, it is due to our heightened intelligence that will enable us to complete the duty to strengthen and secure the lives of all of God's creations.

In view of that, the universal responsibilities of a globalized government will primarily include the provision of all of the basic and essential necessities of life for all of its citizens, but also secondarily, the preservation of all other forms of life that habituate the natural environment. For persons, the most basic necessities in life are food, shelter and clothing. Nonetheless, a fully up-to-date health care system is also an essential necessity, and the creation of which necessarily includes a formal education system. The creation and implementation of these more complex necessities, within developing worlds, will take much more time to realize. The completion of a newborn world will only occur after every nation possesses the resources of both basic and complex necessities.

A formal education system will not only provide the building blocks for a health care system, but it will also be responsible for the creation of inventions and technology that will further increase our quality of life. Therefore, formal education systems are necessary for a higher quality of life. What is more, creativity is a rare character trait. As a result, at current times, the scope of human creativity has yet to reach its peak. The human species can only reach its maximum level of productivity when there is a formal education system established in every possible nation. Indeed, it is possible that, at some point in the future, a potential researcher from an undeveloped nation may find the cure for a disease, like cancer, if he were granted a world-class education. Thereby, the quality of our lives can only reach its maximum potential when every individual around the world possesses access to a formal education system. If some person from a developing world does make a scientific breakthrough, then our investment within these nations will be wholly vindicated. Nonetheless, at current times, since some nations still do not possess a world-class education system, the element of human creativity will continue to be an underused resource.

On the whole, we could not create a newborn world if we did not have the existing forms of technology that we possess at present times. Considering the amount of time that is necessary in the development of science and technology, future generations will be the main beneficiaries of our generation's ingenuity. For instance, in the development of a cure for any illness, it will take many years of research and testing to produce an end product. If this cure takes fifteen years to develop, then the main beneficiaries will not be the scientist's generation, but, by in large, his children's generation of life. This indicates that it is in our nature to be giving, especially in the realm of improving our children's quality of life.

As a consequence, developed nations should possess two main duties. First of all, developed nations must provide leadership within a world-class government. This form of leadership will be directed towards solving social problems, on a global scale. Their second duty is to continue progress within the fields of science and engineering. Taken together, both duties will require a substantial amount of resources.

Yet, as long as we focus our efforts towards the most efficient use of our resources, both goals can be accomplished. In turn, a more humanistic world will be born. World-class leadership will be the primary foundation behind a newborn world.

At current times, since the United Nations possesses very limited powers over each nation, we live in a nationally sovereign world where, intrinsically, there is no higher power than each citizen's national government. In other words, our world is currently based on the philosophy of national sovereignty. Yet, in a fully globalized world, the United Nations, or a similar body, will act as a unified governing body, and thus, it will possess a more significant amount of political authority over each nation.

Therefore, the newborn world will be founded through the continuous development of our culture. It is in human nature to value and feel compassion for another living being. Accordingly, the expression of one's emotions always comes from within, deep inside an individual's spiritual makeup. As emotional creatures, we possess the power to identify our values through our inward emotional states. As a result, social intolerance originates through self-intolerance, whether this form of hate is directed towards that individual's intellectual or corporeal characteristics. In a similar manner, acts of altruism originate through a love of life. From a political perspective, nations which elect governments that uphold cooperative principles will, by nature, live the highest possible quality of life, while those nations that are governed by tyrannical regimes will suffer from inequality and oppression, and thus will be lacking many qualities of life.

The newborn world will also be a world where both human civilization and the natural environment will subsist in a harmonious fashion with one another. Humans will not solely rule the Earth, but we will also form a peaceful coexistence with all other forms of life. When we place an unprecedented value on our natural environment, it is at this point where we may truly acknowledge all of the possible fruits that are inherently present within our physical world. In the best possible world, there will be no true borders between human civilization and the natural world.

Paradise is a community that is comprised of persons with like wills, who are mainly motivated by peace and affection. War is the only thing that can turn paradise into pandemonium. Therefore, a world where there exists war can never be utopian. The abolition of war can only occur in a world where there are no forms of injustice. Even so, a utopian world will further depend on the leadership capabilities of persons with a dynamic character. Consequently, within this world, care and empathy will replace wars of all kinds.

In contrast, the worst possible world will be comprised of feuding wills that revolve mainly around hardships and the continuous endurance of these hardships. This world would be comprised mainly of persons with a static character, where anarchy replaces any forms of social order. In this realm, there would be an endless strife between tyrannical leaders, and there would be no forms of laws honoured which could keep the peace between independent nations. Acts of revenge would be the main mode of justice, where an escalating cycle of abuse would ensue between two individuals. In this world, every person would be subject to another individual's abusive behaviour, and any relationships established would be merely based on superficial elements.

The world we currently live in possesses both elements of paradise and social disorder. Cooperative communities represent the most ideal environment, but these environments are plagued with criminal activity and other kinds of social chaos. Terrorism serves as an international threat to any forms of national paradises. Yet, forms of domestic terrorism may still exist, whenever a tyrant utilizes fear in an effort to control his populace. Likewise, similar acts of terrorism may also exist within some peer to peer relationships. In our history, the only solution to terrorism may be based on the phenomenon of war.

In actuality, a terrorist can only be neutralized when his control over some innocent being is either broken or undermined. Terrorism exists as a criminal ideology, and as a rational form of action whenever persons believe that their anger can empower themselves over nonviolent or nonaggressive individuals. Therefore, all acts of terrorism are premeditated, yet they also depend on the static character's private calculations, with respect to his chance for success. The terrorist, therefore, relies on physical threats and forms of destruction because the fear that he produces is the sole means that will grant him his desired social recognition and authority.

Every terrorist has tried to acquire his personal needs through a non-violent means, but has failed in this undertaking. In a similar fashion, there are other types of individuals who will also use the tool of fear in an effort to gain social recognition and authority. Nonetheless, these types of individuals may not necessarily utilize any forms of a physical threat. These persons will mainly use forms of emotional or psychological abuse to achieve their personal goals. According to policing bodies, these individuals are not truly classified as terrorists. Yet, these persons will follow the same methodology to achieve their personal goals. These kinds of individuals will have many similarities in common with the average terrorist. As a consequence, acts of terrorism will continue to exist until there are no more denials of innate rights, against any single citizen. Only when a nation achieves a state of internal peace and security, will it evolve into a newborn state. Likewise, a newborn world cannot be achieved until every nation evolves into a newborn state.

The physical world is further based on the central elements of space and time. In contrast, our political world may be mainly based on the concepts of freedom and equality. The system of democracy empowers each individual citizen through the establishment of personal freedoms. Moreover, the virtue of freedom places value on individual choice and personal autonomy. Individuals who live by this virtue will not subscribe to any forms of denial, with respect to another individual's human and innate rights.

In contrast, the concept of communism strives towards the ideal of socialism, through the establishment of material equality. The virtue of equality essentially recognizes an equivalent level of value for all human beings. Individuals who live by this virtue will not discriminate against persons who are of a differing race, gender, or nationality.

One of the worst possible political systems will be based on a dictatorship, where one individual possesses a certain degree of absolute power over each citizen. Levels of absolute power are a key attribute that is commonly upheld among all unjust states. The second worst possible political condition is based on the concept of anarchy, where no forms of order will be established.

All citizens around the world can only live a prosperous life if their governing body adheres to principles of morality and a higher code of justice. The virtue of moderation entails some form of balance between both ends of the political spectrum. Criminal laws evolve through the virtue of justice. Indeed, the virtue of justice will be universally upheld by every individual. However, its materialization can be subjective and circumstantial. This is due to the fact that every human being possesses a unique spirit that is defined by a unique set of principles and virtues.

If the latter statement is true, then every kind of relationship will also be unique. This is the main reason why differing nations possess differing cultures. Moreover, if it is true that every human being possesses faults, then it may also be true that the foundations of every nation also possess faults. For example, during our history, previous empires have utilized the method of war merely to acquire land and, essentially, sovereignty over that area of land. In so doing, these empires may be guilty of many injustices incurred towards the original owners of that disputed land. Persons who are indigenous to this land will have then been subjected to foreign laws and government, without any forms of explicit consent.

Since every governing body will possess imperfections, the laws that they implement may also be flawed. For instance, at some point in human history, the public's right to bear arms would have been a necessity. Nonetheless, at current times, in our era of peace, the right to bear arms is no longer a necessity. This right was created during a specific time in our history, where the persons who created it have essentially failed to identify the specific needs of the same populace, at some future date. Subsequently, every body of laws should be open to revision, specifically to deal with the possibility of flawed, unjust, or out-dated principles.

At current times, only domestic terrorists will possess some reason to support the right to bear arms. Therefore, some laws that may have been vital within our history have no bearing today, and thus, they cannot be relevant to our way of life at modern times. At current times, the right to bear arms merely carries a high potential to infringe on another person's innate right for security. As a consequence, civil laws need to be constantly reviewed and corrected. Only the models of human and innate rights may remain absolute. Likewise, when a governing body is motivated by virtue, it will adopt a characteristic similar to that which defines the dynamic character.

When a government adopts the characteristic of being dynamic, it will always be in a constant state of evolution. In addition to developments in science, technology and medicine, we must also make every effort to further develop our culture and way of life. Nevertheless, forms of political revisions are only necessary in cases where a change in law will address some current social problem. If a specific law or principle remains just, or if there are no kinds of problems that are associated with a specific political policy, then no revision will be necessary. Accordingly, there will still exist a large body of laws that will continue to maintain a just form of order among all sovereign nation-states.

No person is capable of time travel to the future, and thus, we may still lack insight with respect to potential problems that we may face at forthcoming times. Each generation will be responsible for a slight change in our culture, due both to the evolution of our ideas and scientific knowledge. As a consequence, every possible charter must be flexible enough to consider the needs of future generations, whenever possible conflicts of interest may arise. On the other hand, the denial of certain preposterous, outlandish or invalid ancestral rights may also be needed, if they no longer apply, according to the current norms of a developed culture. Therefore, the revision of our laws must continue to be dynamic, only when such laws contradict positive forms of change and reform. The laws which guide us must always be based on some personal, social, or political virtue.

Every kind of community will be founded on the principles of cooperation and interdependence. The particular contribution chosen by each individual essentially reflects upon his personal will. In general, persons with a dynamic character will be motivated to contribute more services within their community, in comparison to what they receive. This is due to the fact that dynamic persons will both love their existence, and the interdependent aspects that make up an ordered and civilized community. In contrast, persons with a static character will usually wish to receive more services from their community, in comparison to what they contribute. This is mainly due to their faulty belief that they are, or should be, a privileged member within their community. It is these types of individuals who, when they gain political power, will inevitably evolve into a tyrannical ruler. In the end, only leaders who acquire the political virtue of responsibility should be elected into power. These individuals will further possess the social virtues of equality, freedom, and justice, and thus, they will uphold these virtues within their society. It is these social virtues, in addition to political virtues, that will define the true nature of a newborn world.

13 Beauty

THERE ARE TWO MAIN FORMS of beauty that exist within our universe. The first category consists of man's idea of beauty. All works of art are the sole creation of man. Yet, the content in all forms of art merely reflect upon forms of beauty that may be found in nature. For example, a scenic painting could represent some environmental wonder that exists within our natural world. Sculptures are three dimensional figures that illustrate some object of importance. Likewise, works of literature reflect upon the power of human language to describe our natural world. In a similar manner, forms of music may be comparable to the pleasant sounds made by birds in the wild, while modes of dance may express their movements of happiness. Theatre is a form of three-dimensional story telling that reflects upon the unique experiences of some individual. Finally, forms of fashion may represent a form of visual beauty that also reflects upon some form of physical beauty that may be found in our world.

Nonetheless, while the latter forms of art serve to cultivate human civilization, the spirit of art may also be observable within the realm of human productivity. For example, all human beings require some form of shelter for their daily living. However, the current effects that many forms of architecture have on persons may be comparable to other more traditional works of art. Likewise, many forms of engineering, especially in the automotive industry, could also be viewed as a work of art. Furthermore, through the evolving computing industry, the power of visual graphics may also be considered as a work of art. In actuality, all forms of art are designed to invoke some form of emotion within the individual. Yet, the ability to produce art is exclusive to human beings, essentially because of our greater intellect. The most effective works of art will cause intrigue and curiosity within the individual.

Some works of art may invoke emotions that were not intended by its author. In addition, two individuals may discover unique forms of beauty in the same work of art. One person may discover beauty through reading a creation of Tolstoy, while another person may discover a form of passion after he has viewed this work of art within the cinema. Yet, even when a single work of art invokes differing emotions in distinct individuals, it still possesses the potential to initiate some form of connection between these persons.

On a general level, the most powerful works of art are those that reach and affect the quantitatively greatest audience. However, on an individual level, the most powerful works of art are those which are observationally repeatable. Therefore, individuals who continue to examine a particular piece of art enjoy the emotions that they experience as a direct result, and they also wish to relive their particular emotional experiences. In particular, the genre of music may demonstrate the greatest power over the individual, essentially because of its repeatability. The invention of karaoke reflects upon the repeatability of music.

In comparison, while the general individual may read a book or watch a particular film for only a single time, music has become a particular source of pleasure that is highly repeatable. The power of music, over the individual, may be the greatest simply because it engages the imagination of the perceiver to a much greater extent, in comparison to other genres of art. For example, a movie may re-enact some individual's personal story, while a book may provide knowledge within some specific subject matter. However, within the genre of music, the perceiver possesses a higher freedom to link his own experiences with a particular instance of art. Therefore, the genre of music encourages the individual to release his thought processes, while he is simultaneously enjoying a piece of art. In addition to encouraging certain emotions, the genre of music further encourages the individual to imagine, and this makes it the most powerful kind of art that has ever been invented by our civilization.

Even the sporting industry may be considered to be a kind of art. It may be equivalent to a kind of dance, in that the athlete's physical ability, within the realm of hand-eye coordination, demonstrates a form of skillful movement. Furthermore, professional sports encourage athletic activity at the amateur level. Therefore, professional sports may be directly correlated with the physical health of some individuals. Yet, professional sports become a form of art when the spectator recognizes the fact that the skill of those who are engaged within some athletic activity surpasses his own. Hence, the professional sporting world may be comparable to a kind of physical art, in the same manner that the genre of dance is considered to be a form of art.

During the history of our civilization, genres of art may have been limited to poetry and drawings. As we have evolved, we have invented musical instruments, paint, and other forms of artistic tools. During recent years, we have included beautiful human movement, through the core of events exhibited at the Olympic Games, the culinary arts, and photographic forms of art. All of these inventions seem to indicate that human evolution, within the arts, may be just as important as advancements within the fields of science, engineering and medicine. Similar to science, art is a conceptual invention of man, but it is based on the human faculty of imagination. Indeed, creativity is the main foundation that drives all forms of art. As a consequence, the value of arts, to human civilization, cannot be less than the value of science because it is in human nature to be imaginative, in the same manner that it is in human nature to be rational. Moreover, beauty and the emotion of happiness must be included as two of the most basic and indispensible elements that are linked to the human spirit.

Differing forms of art will be pleasing to differing human senses. Other works of art will be pleasing to an individual's spirit. Furthermore, some works of art may additionally require our faculty of cognition. For example, instrumental music may be pleasing to the individual's spirit, while musical pieces with lyrics may require forms of cognition. Likewise, some works of art may require the element of human experience, to qualify as a form of beauty. As a consequence, some works of art may be directly targeted towards a specific subgroup of persons, within a large society. In essence, non-universal forms of beauty will always be uniquely judged by each individual. This actually makes non-universal forms of beauty rarer than universal forms of beauty. In fact, there may be more universally recognized forms of beauty, in comparison to instances that belong to an exclusive and unique class of beauty. As such, the power of unique forms of beauty enables it to create sub-cultures, and sub-cultures create diversity within a large community. Accordingly, since all forms of beauty possess the power to cause emotions of happiness within the individual, this makes non-universal forms of beauty just as important as universal forms of beauty.

In every genre of art, there will exist many differing forms. Consequently, this exemplifies the unique nature of every artist, and essentially, his spirit. Since each form of art contains some form of beauty, it is the concept of beauty that essentially unites two human beings together. It is a universal love for music that enables me to enjoy it with other persons. However, it is through my unique life experiences that will enable me to enjoy something that possesses a unique form of beauty. The differing kinds of unique beauty exemplify the fact that each person has chosen a way of life, which is primarily based on a distinct path. Yet, when a form of universal beauty is commonly recognized, this serves to unite all human beings together again. Accordingly, this makes the concept of beauty a social virtue.

On an individual level, the most beautiful works of art will evoke a positive emotion in the individual, which is predominantly the emotion of happiness. However, it is clear that some elements in nature may also invoke this emotion within an individual. Hence, some elements in nature may possess an equal degree of beauty, because they also evoke emotions of happiness within the individual. Moreover, similar to art, some forms of natural phenomena will be recognized as a universal form of beauty, while other forms of natural phenomena may only be beautiful from a subjective perspective. In comparison to man's work of art, God's work of art is comprised of all of the forms of natural beauty that exists within our universe. Natural objects with a form of universal beauty possess the potential to foster the individual's soul. Yet, forms of unique natural beauty will have an impact on the individual's distinctive character.

The differences between the natural environment and our cities mark the main differentiation between the two primary categories of beauty. While nature is the habitat of the wild animal, cities are the most prevalent habitat of man. Both environments will possess distinct elements of beauty. Accordingly, while nature is the materialization of God's idea of beauty, cities are the materialization of man's idea of beauty.

Thus, man is responsible for the concept of art, while God is responsible for all of the natural forms of beauty that are present in nature. God is a creator, and man has successfully emulated this trait through the establishment of industries and technology. Yet, the human invention of industry does have a negative effect on our planet's natural habitat. When greenhouse gases negatively affect the natural environment, manmade cities possess the power to destroy nature. In a similar fashion, when a bear forages for food within human communities, nature possesses a similar potential to destroy man. In both cases, the conceptual boundary between our cities and nature has essentially been ignored.

Nevertheless, the abolition of this boundary is important to both man and all of the animals that may be found in nature. Through the elements of pollution and overhunting, a complete harmony has yet to be established between our cities and nature. A complete harmony can only be accomplished when there is a compatibility established to the point where one environment does not take precedence over the other. When this occurs, any conceptual boundary would then dissolve and this, in turn, would abolish a theoretical forbidden zone. Thus, when a balanced form of coexistence is established, both environments will subsist in a harmonious fashion with the other. Without this equilibrium, some element of beauty will be predictably lost.

Within the dynamic character's mind, all other forms of life that exist in nature also possess the potential to represent some form of intrinsic beauty. In these cases, the dynamic character will also experience many differing degrees of happiness, as a direct result. In essence, within the dynamic character's frame of mind, existence itself is beautiful. Only natural or manmade objects, which evoke emotions of indifference, will have very little value to the individual. Moreover, that which consistently evokes emotions of wrath possesses no true forms of beauty.

Within the static character's frame of mind, existence is only beautiful whenever he possesses some kind of power or authority over another form of life. Therefore, since the static character only places value on some specific way of life, he possesses a narrow view with respect to the nature of existence itself. Individuals with a narrow view of the "good life" will undoubtedly face many more difficulties in life, in comparison to those persons who possess a wider view of the "good life". Indeed, the ability to recognize and appreciate many differing kinds of beauty in our universe depends entirely on the subjective mindset of the individual.

Inspiration is a social virtue that is directly related to beauty. Persons who possess the ability to recognize and appreciate some specific instance of beauty will, as a reaction, experience a form of inspiration. This makes inspiration a natural effect of beauty. Indeed, all forms of beauty possess the potential power to inspire some individual. Those persons who do become inspired will be motivated to prolong that specific instance of beauty. For example, a painter may be motivated to outline a portrait of Helen of Troy, so that other persons may be equally astonished by her beauty. Therefore, people who become inspired wish to extend the conceptual life of some instance of beauty, for an indefinite period of time.

    Yet, while forms of inspiration may take many differing shapes, it does not change in essence. For example, some person who views a portrait of a woman may then be motivated to write a poem about her. A cycle of inspiration may then ensue. In essence, the latter work of poetry may then inspire some musician, whose music will inspire some doctor, who, in turn, inspires some child that inevitably maturates into a world leader. This world leader may then inspire some common citizen, and the cycle of inspiration may continue, without any forms of restrictions or limitations. Thus, while the spirit of inspiration remains the same, only its essential materialization will vary from person to person. The specific manifestation of all forms of inspiration depends entirely on the spirit of the producer.

    In addition to beauty, greatness is another social virtue that possesses the power to inspire. However, the definition of greatness will also vary from person to person. I may perceive a courageous soldier as great, and this inspires me to adopt the virtue of resilience. My child may then be inspired by my resilience, and this motivates him to adopt the virtue of integrity. As a result, the core essence behind all forms of inspiration will continue to exist as long as there continues to exist persons who both perceive it, and agree that it is something that is valuable to all of humankind.

Indispensible to the concept of greatness is the principle of humility. Humility may be one of the most beautiful principles. Indeed, no human being is omniscient. Yet, those persons who demonstrate humility essentially transform their personal achievements into a form of beauty. This is due to the fact that acts of humility promote forms of equality, within all social networks. Persons with humility openly accept the personal imperfections of another person by promoting forms of equality through their most often grand and highly difficult accomplishments. Therefore, acts of humility will distinguish champions from the conceited. By acting with humility, the champion will continue to maintain a form of mutual respect between himself and the common citizen. Therefore, the principle of humility is beautiful because it is a quality that promotes impartiality within a diverse achievement oriented community.

All forms of greatness will originate through the element of intelligence. Man possesses the capability to transcend his natural abilities, essentially because we possess a higher form of intelligence. For example, only birds possess the ability to fly, while only marine species possess the ability to habituate the oceans. However, through our intelligence, we have created inventions that grant us with the capability to both fly within the atmosphere, and explore the depths of the ocean. Man was never granted these abilities by nature, but it is through our nature where we possess the capacity to acquire these abilities. It is through our intelligence where we are granted with the capacity to surpass our natural capabilities. Hence, if intelligence is a necessary pre-requisite related to our ability to observe and understand the universe, then from a logical perspective, some form of intelligence must also be mandatory in its creation.

Everything that is beautiful and great originates through a creation of God. For example, the painter who is inspired by a woman of great beauty is, most definitely, inspired by a work of God. God is the creator of both all other forms of life, and women with great beauty. The same is true regarding all other original sources of inspiration. Since everything in our universe is created by God, everything that inspires the artist, at the core, is fundamentally a work of God. Moreover, since God is spiritually limitless, the kinds of beauty and greatness that could exist will potentially be infinite.

Yet, in addition to art, war is also a creation of man. Although every man possesses the capacity to inspire, he also possesses the capacity to destroy. Those who are constructive are motivated to create a higher quality of life, for all of humankind. The inventions of science, technology, and medicine necessarily pave the way for a higher quality of life, with respect to our physical existence. In contrast, the invention of the arts will pave the way for a higher quality of life, with respect to our spiritual existence. When taken together, the human potential to be constructive reflects upon our volition to establish a peaceful coexistence with all other forms of life that live in our natural world.

On the contrary, individuals who are not constructive will essentially be destructive. While individuals who are destructive possess the volition to experience subjective forms of pleasure, they do so without any regard towards any other instances of life. In time, when these individuals lose the ability to achieve any forms of self-pleasure through a peaceful manner, they will resort to some form of abuse, in an effort to achieve further forms of self-pleasure. These individuals become destructive because they do not value any forms of peace or order that may be established within their society. As a result, those individuals who become increasingly more destructive will place increasingly less value towards any forms of a peaceful coexistence.

It may be argued that some forms of art will actually promote violence or unethical modes of behaviour. For example, horror movies tell the story of persons who possess an irrationally violent disposition. Gory video games may also be thought to encourage violent modes of behaviour, within our youth. Similarly, combat based sports, like boxing, may also promote the acceptance of violence within our communities. Nonetheless, these elements of our civilization are merely constructs that reflect the class of individuals, who are solely destructive in nature. Therefore, in a sense, these elements merely represent the most unfortunate elements linked to human existence. Indeed, within the immature mind, these kinds of art could promote ideas that have yet to be conceived. Nonetheless, ideas will always remain immaterial in nature, and thus, they are entirely different from modes of behaviour. Thus, while some kinds of art may educate an innocent child within the realm of violence, they do not possess the power to compel that child to act in such a manner. The individual's innate right for thought is a sacred right, considering the fact that human beings possess a kind of intelligence that is unmatched within our physical world. Accordingly, the introduction of ideas can never be outlawed or regulated in the same manner that irrational and destructive modes of behaviour are at current times.

This leads to the necessary distinction between freedom of thought and freedom of action. All forms of sentient life possess an intellect that enables them to think freely. Yet, while some thoughts are intelligent, other kinds of thoughts may not be equally as intelligent. Indeed, thought, by itself, poses no real harm to any human being. Therefore, even if it were possible to do so, it would be immoral to restrict any individual's thought processes. Nonetheless, in some cases the expression of thought could hurt another individual, in the form of hate speech, while in other cases acting upon one's thoughts will lead to the physical harm of another living being. In these specific cases, when thought leads to acts that will harm another living being, this is where the open utilization of one's freedom cannot be tolerated. Therefore, from a universal perspective, while it may be morally wrong to constrain the individual's freedom for thought, in many cases, it will be morally right to constrain his freedom to act upon his thoughts.

Therefore, while freedom of thought is valuable to all persons, the restriction of certain free acts will be of equal value to all persons. Yet, God could not create any forms of creatures that possessed a free intellect, where they simultaneously lacked a free will. If the individual lacked a free will, then he will, necessarily, also lack the ability to think in a fully autonomous fashion. For free will does not merely reflect upon the choice to act, but also upon the ability to freely contemplate about one's choices. If human beings were not moral creatures, then it would not be necessary to criminalize certain forms of behaviour. Yet, we are moral creatures, due to the fact that we all value the virtue of justice. Accordingly, since God has made it in our nature to be moral creatures, our freedom to act must always be evaluated through the freedom in our intellect. Since intelligence is the main element that differentiates us from all other species of life, our freedom for thought must be set at a higher precedence, and be of a higher value, in comparison to our freedom to act. Subsequently, it is the freedom of our thoughts that must always govern the freedom behind our choices to act.

God has granted every sentient form of life with the power of free choice. Nonetheless, considering the amount of evil that exists within our world, we must question the true value of this freedom to our lives. In the case of an individual's ability to commit evil, freedom cannot be viewed as a valuable human attribute. Yet, if God is omniscient, He would have known that the freedom that He granted to human beings may inevitably lead to the rise of evil. Perhaps God granted freedom to conscious beings because He wanted to create forms of life that possess the same features that exist in Him. Behind acts of constructive behaviour lies a kind of freedom that enables the individual to have chosen otherwise. The same is true with respect to destructive behaviour. Therefore, since God has granted every human with this power of choice, it is possible that He may place more importance on an individual's freedom to choose, over the choice itself. If this is the case, then the reason behind any choice will be of more significance than the actual action itself.

As such, the difference in motives behind constructive and destructive behaviour personifies the difference between peace and war. Forms of violence will involve any form of premeditated harm to another living being. Since modes of violence are essentially antisocial in nature, the reasons behind violent behaviour will also always be of this categorical nature. In comparison, persons with a peaceful temperament do not resort to any modes of violence, whenever they interact with other individuals. These individuals will mainly solve their disputes with other persons through the elements of rationality and goodwill. In the end, peaceful modes of interaction promote friendships, brotherhood, and a thriving civilization.

With respect to the beauty of our entire universe as a whole, God's creation, as a totality, may be intrinsically viewed as harmonious.

Harmony exists in everything where there exists a form of unity among diverse and differing elements. For example, natural wonders such as a rainbow may be perceived to be harmonious, because it is a single object that is comprised of differing colours that accentuate one another. Since every living being needs water for its continued existence, other persons may view waterfalls as harmonious. In essence, water symbolizes vitality, while the fall itself symbolizes an endless continuation of this vitality. Other persons may also view rainforests as harmonious. This is due to the fact that there exists so many species of life that interact, and likewise, depend on each other for their own survival. Oceans represent a similar thriving and peaceful coexistence among differing species of life, within a distinct kind of habitat that differs from our own. Similarly, mountains could symbolize a kind of greater splendour that exists within our natural world.

The star filled universe seems to implicate the existence of an infinite amount of diverse spirits, even though at current times we lack the capability to confirm this hypothesis. Yet, we may still possess the capability to scientifically confirm the latter hypothesis when we view our own physical world. In fact, when we consider each distinct human being, we will recognize the fact that each individual possesses an entirely special and unique spiritual makeup. Even in the case of identical twins, both individuals will possess a kind of spirit that differentiates himself, to some degree, from his sibling. Therefore, the physical world that every human being perceives could provide us with a substantial reason to infer that there could exist an infinite amount of diverse and differing spirits, within the entire cosmos.

When we analyze the distinct spirit of some individual person, we will view an entirely unique form of beauty. The beautiful individual may be said to possess a giving spirit, essentially because the makeup of human civilization is primarily based on a community of persons who contribute some kind of service within their community. Therefore, the individual who contributes is beautiful because he is working towards a progressive society. The beauty of human civilization, as a whole, may be based on the fact that even though each person possesses a differing spiritual makeup, we are all still working towards a single cause, which will always be the creation of a better world. Therefore, human civilization is beautiful, because it is built upon a form of harmony that exists between entirely unique spiritual beings.

To individually perceive is to exist as a fully autonomous creature. Accordingly, distinct forms of beauty will always be recognized through a subjective perspective. Nonetheless, from a universal perspective, if there were no forms of harmony, could there exist any forms of beauty? It is the harmony present within God's work of art that provides the main basis for the beauty present within our universe. Imagine a differing possible kind of human existence. Consider the possibility that the power of our vision may have been, by nature, increased so that it would be comparable to the power of a microscope. With this kind of vision, we could not view the basic physical structure of any elephant, palm tree, or brook. Instead, persons with microscopic vision would simply perceive the basic morphological structure of some plant or animal cell.

In reality, no person can physically visualize the basic structure of a cell, but our lack of visual power in this sense does not entail the proposition that cells do not exist. Our senses are limited, and so is our intellect. Accordingly, if we merely perceived the world through this kind of microscopic power, would there still exist any forms of beauty? Perhaps, some persons would enjoy seeing the differing kinds of cell membranes. However, because of the power of our vision, we would lack the ability to view any natural wonders in our world, as we see them through our current standard of vision. In fact, many other persons would agree with the statement that within this condition, we would have lost the power to view many forms of beauty. As a consequence, these individuals would then further agree with the premise that in our present condition, there does exist a kind of harmony between the power of our vision and all of the visual wonders that exist within our natural world.

Therefore, in addition to the creation of an ordered universe, God has further created a harmonious universe. If no intelligent being created our universe, and our universe was created by some kind of random anomaly, how is it possible that there exists so many instances of harmony? The interdependent kind of harmony that all life forms depend upon is synchronized to a point that enables the continued and prolonged existence of all life on Earth. Is it really possible that something without intelligence could have created the complex synchronization of independent entities that subsists within our universe? Indeed, it is through our faculties of reason and cognition that enable us to create a kind of ordered civilization that is unrivalled, with respect to all other species of life. Subsequently, this implicates that the creation of an ordered universe, itself, must also require some kind of intelligence, albeit to a much higher degree.

In fact, human existence is merely one possible mode of existence. The power of our eyesight faces limitations, and the same is true regarding all of our other senses. In a similar fashion, the power of our intellect also plays a major role, with respect to our personal experiences. In one instance, a child may experience some kind of fascination with a cardboard box. However, as he ages, his idea of beauty will continue to develop. Therefore, the power of our senses, in combination with our intellect, will cause differing perspectives with respect to what we judge is beautiful.

Since all persons view the world through a subjective point of view, most instances of beauty will be judged through a subjective perspective. Therefore, whenever a universal form of beauty is recognized, every human being must, necessarily, share a similar kind of judgment. It is through our similarities, regarding forms of beauty, which enables one individual to form some kind of bond or brotherhood with another.

A shared concept of beauty marks the creation of all forms of lasting friendships.

In the case of the static character, these individuals will always focus on material forms of beauty. However, physical beauty is rarely universal. I may adore the latest supermodel, while my closest friend may adore his high school sweetheart. The existence of the formless character will also be relevant in this respect. The true nature of the formless character's soul is essentially distorted through his actions. Therefore, while his spirit is representative of one identity, his character illustrates the complete opposite. In cases like these, it may be difficult to ascertain whether an individual's physical beauty is truly representative of his soul. The possibility of misconception forces the common citizen to mainly judge beauty not from a physical standpoint, but always through a spiritual standpoint. Since it is entirely possible that an individual's physical looks may be a deception, this element forces us to define true forms of beauty through some other manner. Therefore, beauty can never be merely physical, but it is always spiritual. As a consequence, forms of spiritual beauty may be the only universally recognized form of beauty.

This is why persons with a dynamic character always focus on elements of spiritual beauty. Examine the world through a horticultural perspective. In fact, there may be no significant biological differences between a flower and a weed. Yet, the differences between a purple iris and a yellow dandelion may be vast, at least from a cultural perspective.

The iris must be planted and cultivated, while the dandelion grows solely through a random and sporadic fashion. Indeed, flowers are universally deemed as a form of beauty. In contrast, the majority of weeds remain unwanted in comparison.

Nevertheless, now compare the purple iris to the yellow tulip. Which flower is more beautiful? It may be the impossible feat to generate a complete consensus, within our society, as to which flower possesses more beauty. One individual may prefer the colour purple, while another individual may find that the blooms of the tulip will have more natural beauty. Thus, the differences between two instances of flowers will remain entirely based on their physical beauty.

At first, the differences between a flower and a weed may not be easy to discern. Physically, both instances of life are a member of the same categorical species. The most denotable differences are primarily defined through a spiritual basis. It is the human spirit which determines the difference between a beautiful flower, and a common weed. It is the cultural element of our society that mainly categorizes one plant species as a flower, and another species as a weed. Therefore, while beauty is subjective, it is also a cultural construct. The flower does represent a universally recognized form of spiritual beauty. However, the particular instances of physical beauty, within this category of life, will be subject to the individual's unique tastes.

Some persons may hold the view that all forms of beauty are defined primarily through the element of constants. In other words, standard conceptions of proportion may define what is physically beautiful, while concepts related to rhythm may define beautiful forms of sound. Nonetheless, these universal constants seem to put some kind of limit on what we deem is beautiful. If one individual goes against the status quo and argues that some newer quality is beautiful, it may not be recognized as a form of true beauty because it is not a universally recognized form of beauty. In order to solve the debate as to what qualities truly represent some form of beauty, we must acknowledge the fact that beauty is always subjective.

For example, all forms of popular music possess a constant, in the form of rhythm. However, what if we consider a collection of random musical notes? Is it really possible to exclude a collection of random sounds, with no rhythm whatsoever, as a form of beauty? Many persons could argue the notion that a random collection of noises or sounds cannot be classified as a form of music, simply because it lacks the uniform standard of rhythm. Nevertheless, regardless of this latter fact, it is still entirely possible that a collection of random sounds could possess some form of beauty.

In fact, some individuals may find that the chatter of the golden-breasted woodpecker, or the babbling starling, does contain some form of beauty. Hence, this may be one example of a beautiful collection of sounds, which inherently lacks any kind of rhythm. What one individual deems is beautiful may not be deemed as equally beautiful by another individual. This makes the subjective element of beauty the only constant characteristic behind its definition. If the latter case is true, it may be impossible to impose any forms of limitations on what we define is music. In fact, any limitation we may apply towards the concept of music will create some kind of common standard, yet this standard itself serves no true purpose. For if it is possible that some individual may enjoy a collection of sounds that does not meet some concrete standard, then it should also be evident that beauty itself cannot be limited by any pre-defined constituting elements.

Even though we cannot place any clear limitations on our definition of beauty, there are some elements of beauty that should be universal features, within every perceiver's frame of mind. One of these elements is timelessness. Any entity that is timeless possesses the ability to travel both to the past and to the future. This kind of ability is not physical, but merely conceptual. For no person possesses the physical ability to travel to some other time period, either in the past or the future. It is only the ideas of man that possesses this power. For example, consider a book written by Plato. This book was written over 2000 years ago. At present, it is still being studied by modern day academics, and it will continue to be studied by future academics for an indefinite period of time. In reality, Plato, himself, did not possess the ability to travel into the future. It is only his ideas that continue to be relevant during present times. His ideas have transcended time in a manner that his physical existence could have never achieved. Likewise, since some of his ideas were inspired by his teacher, the ideas that we conceive in his writings existed even before he had actually put pen to paper. Therefore, the ideas that Plato addressed existed before he created his works, they existed during his own physical lifespan, and they continue to exist at current times. As a consequence, even though Plato himself lacked the ability to travel through time, his ideas have, essentially, transcended time.

As a result, even though physical individuals may be forgotten, their ideas may continue to exist for some period of time, during their future. This makes time travel possible, at least ideologically. Likewise, this further illustrates the intrinsic importance of our freedom for thought.

The primary definition of dynamic indicates that individuals, who possess this characteristic, will continue to live an active and vigorous life. Persons with a dynamic character will study the history of human civilization, in an effort to learn from past mistakes that may have been made during previous generations. Similarly, the dynamic character will also continue to make plans for his future. All persons with a dynamic character will consider ideas that have existed within their past, and moreover, they will also create potential ideas that may continue to exist within their future.

In contrast, persons with a static character are always bent on forms of revenge. This marks a further difference between the dynamic character and the static character. Individuals with a static character possess a single-faceted mindset that is obsessively focused towards any wrongdoings that they may have endured during their past. Subsequently, the static character will focus all of his efforts to acquire some form of revenge, or essentially, some form of negative justice. In fact, these individuals do not concern themselves with any future achievements. The only achievements that they do strive for will merely grant them with the capacity to fulfill some form of negative justice. Hence, the static character's present demeanour always remains entirely focused on his personal history. His mindset will always be focused on his past, and this makes him incapable of any other modes of conceptual time travel. Likewise, the static character demonstrates a limited potential with respect to his capacity to develop a progressive mindset. Since the static character does not possess the capacity for future conceptual time travel, he will eventually be disregarded and forgotten.

In a corresponding fashion, a further element related to beauty is the concept of readiness. Readiness is a beautiful virtue that is directly related to future times. The science of medicine was created through this virtue. Institutions like our education system and policing forces were also established through this virtue. In essence, the virtue of readiness reflects upon the human will to protect, and provide aid for another human being. Therefore, the fundamental core of our civilization depends on the realization of this virtue. In adopting this virtue, the individual will prepare for a wide range of possible scenarios that may be relevant within his social network. Yet, it may be truly impossible to prepare for all possible contingencies, simply because no person possesses the quality of omniscience. Therefore, through the application of this virtue, the individual will simply demonstrate attentiveness, in relation to the most significant objects that belong to his emotional centre.

The individual essentially travels to the past whenever he analyzes life during a previous era, and he travels to the future when he passes on all of his knowledge to the following generations. With respect to the virtue of readiness, individuals who possess this virtue are capable of conceptual time travel because they possess the ability to prepare themselves for a multitude of possible scenarios, during forthcoming times. The most common preparation that all persons with a dynamic character make will always be based on an optimistic future.

Persons who direct their focus towards future times will also recognize beauty as an end, and never as a means. For example, some individuals will seek to preserve forms of unique beauty, so that other persons will possess the capability to perceive these forms of beauty for themselves. In effect, the existence of museums of art essentially serves the latter task. Contrarily, those who merely focus on the present day will only be concerned with the material ends that are acquired through forms of beauty. These kinds of individuals will actively seek to utilize forms of beauty, in an effort to acquire their own personal goals. For example, the common bully will actively seek to abuse the innocent in an effort to acquire some form of self-esteem. Likewise, the con artist will manipulate and then take advantage of the kindness of other persons, in his effort to plunder their material wealth.

Accordingly, this type of active utilization of beauty should never be confused with the individual's quest to perceive forms of beauty. Indeed, there exists a clear division between those individuals who wish to perceive beauty, and those who wish to exploit it. For the most part, individuals who direct their entire focus towards present times will usually be using beauty as a means to an end, while those who attend to and contemplate future times will embrace beauty both as an integral and an inherent end.

Hence, the static character does not possess the ability of conceptual time travel. Since revenge is a main motivational factor behind the majority of the static character's actions, he will lack the inherent capability to travel forward through time. Without a doubt, the static character will always remain within the past, simply because he focuses all of his mental energy towards all of the trespasses and transgressions that he has faced throughout his lifespan. Thus, the static character mainly focuses his habits of preparedness towards possible future altercations. Since these individuals focus their entire mindset on forms of revenge, the only forms of measures that they do make will revolve around potential future struggles. Therefore, these individuals merely possess the ability to prepare themselves for the negative experiences, or suffering, that they have endured at some point during their lives.

Persons who adopt the virtue of readiness will seek to increase and cultivate the longevity of, not their own spirit, but another person's internal spirit. These individuals possess a high capability, in relation to their analytical skills. Indeed, scientists travel to the future through their experimentations and observations, while artists travel to the past through their memories of beauty. Yet, conceptual time travel requires the additional ability of rational self-awareness. Individuals who possess this capability will demonstrate a high level of maturity, and this enables them to differentiate and isolate an aging body from an aging mind. When the mind develops at a faster rate in comparison to one's body, this is what enables the individual to travel through time.

Yet, if we all possessed an infinite lifespan, we must question whether or not the concept of time would actually exist. In fact, the concept of time only has bearing on our material existence. Within our finite lifespans, we are affected by two kinds of time. Constant time is the continual and methodical dimension that measures standardized intervals between two events. Introspective time is the unsystematic measurement of a subjective experience. Therefore, conceivably, during the passage of one hour of constant time, one individual could hold the belief that he has experienced seventy minutes of introspective time, while another individual may hold the belief that he has experienced merely fifty minutes of introspective time. This latter subjective measurement of experience defines the phenomenon of introspective time.

In both categories, time merely measures a single experience. Yet, constant time always remains objective, while introspective time always remains subjective. Indeed, from all subjective perspectives, time is always relative. This may be evident in each individual's unique physical lifespan. It is possible that two individuals may live a life that spans a differing amount of constant time, even though they experience a mainly similar period of introspective time. In this case, constant time is only relevant to our physical existence, while it has no true bearing on our actual experiencing of time. If this is the case, within an infinite immaterial world, the element of time should not have a similar importance. In an infinite world, only spirits would exist, and likewise, the concept of death would not exist. As a consequence, constant time only serves as an important marker within the material world. Our physical world is constituted on the element of dimensions, yet these dimensions may not exist within the immaterial world. Consequently, the true makeup of the immaterial world may not just be beyond the realm of human perception, but also beyond the realm of our imaginations.

Thus, constant time will only be an important dimension within a finite world. Persons who focus their awareness towards the dimension of time will shift their focus towards the phenomenon of constant time. In contrast, persons who focus on ideologies, or the sublime, will lose their awareness of constant time. As a consequence, the passing of introspective time always remains subjective, and thus, largely inconsistent with the passage of constant time.

The latter fact is due to the difference between simple and complex ideas. A simple idea is a concept that possesses only a single attribute. When the individual shifts his focus towards a ticking stopwatch, this may be categorized as a simple idea, because the continuous movement within this object is merely a single and finite idea. In contrast, when the individual focuses his attention towards the sublime, he will be focusing his attention towards a complex idea. A complex idea possesses more than one attribute. For example, when the individual focuses his attention towards a chronograph, he is focusing his attention towards the passing of seconds, minutes and hours.

When the individual is in the process of examining a complex idea, he will be examining many differing properties that may be associated with a multifaceted idea. Nevertheless, when the individual focuses on the properties within a complex idea, each property will take differing intervals of constant time to examine. In other words, the amount of constant time that passes, in relation to the examination of each attribute, will not be equivalent to each other. Some properties may be clear and easily understood, while other properties may take further amounts of deliberation. Thus, the examination of a clear and plain attribute will take less constant time, in comparison to the examination of a more complicated attribute. As a consequence, the individual misjudges the passage of constant time simply because the examination of each attribute, within a complex idea, will not take equivalent intervals of constant time to complete.

Thus, when the individual misjudges constant time in relation to a clear and plain attribute, he will hold the belief that the amount of introspective time that has passed is actually greater than the amount of constant time that has passed. Contrariwise, when he misjudges constant time in relation to a complicated attribute, he will hold the belief that the amount of introspective time that has passed is lesser than the actual amount of constant time that has passed. Therefore, introspective time exists only in beings that possess a consciousness. Introspective time always measures the length of one's experiences, but constant time is always utilized to make comparisons, regarding our experiences. When I look at the ticking of my watch, I am currently conceiving constant time. However, when I examine the sublime, I will lose my objective awareness regarding the passage constant time.

The experiencing of introspective time will always be completely relative and dependent on the unique spiritual nature of each individual. During an equivalent lifespan, it is possible that some individual from Chile may experience forty years of introspective time, while another individual from Finland may experience eighty years of introspective time. It is also possible that during a corresponding amount of introspective time, some individual from Chile may age to an equivalent of one hundred years of constant time, while an individual from Finland may age merely to an equivalent of fifty years of constant time. In both cases, the experiencing of introspective time will be of more significance, in comparison to the experiencing of constant time. Accordingly, introspective time does not merely measure the length of an individual's unique experiences, but it is also relevant to the subjective importance of his experiences.

It is only in the case of a doppelgänger twin where the experiencing of more constant time may be more valuable in comparison to introspective time. In this case, both the individual and his doppelgänger will, by definition, experience the same experiences, and thus, they will also experience an equivalent amount of introspective time. Yet, in this specific case, the twin who experiences more constant time will, chiefly, possess a longer physical lifespan. Accordingly, it is in this specific circumstance, alone, where some individual will value the experiencing of longer lengths of constant time, in comparison to his peer.

Thus, constant time will only be relevant within the material world. This is due to the fact that the material world is primarily based on the concept of the finite. All forms of life within the physical world possess a finite lifespan. Furthermore, the individual will only experience constant time whenever he is missing some element of beauty in his life. In contrast, introspective time may be mainly relevant within an immaterial world. Since the immaterial world is built upon the concept of the infinite, there will also exist an infinite amount of beauty within this world. As a result, since the individual will never be lacking any forms of beauty within the immaterial world, he will be mainly experiencing differing lengths of introspective time for his entire lifetime.

A possible reason why God does not choose to reveal Himself to us within the material world could be due to the principle of faith. Faith is another beautiful principle where the individual possesses a subjective belief in something, even though he may lack any clear or concrete forms of evidence. Nevertheless, all kinds of faith do require some kind of basis or justification, within the individual's subjective frame of mind. Hence, persons who have faith in God's existence may hold the original belief that all forms of life possess some form of meaning.

If some person has had a positive influence on your life, then his life will also ultimately have some kind of meaning to your own. Likewise, if you cherish this person's existence, then you will also cherish your own. This is due to the fact that this individual's positive influence will invoke some kind of a positive emotion within you. From a contrary perspective, if your life has had a positive influence on someone else, then your life will also be meaningful to this person. Therefore, a meaningful life is one that is valued by another person.

Moreover, if life is meaningful, then it also has some form of purpose. Hence, if some person has had a positive influence on your life, he will also fulfill some kind of purpose within it. Yet, due to the individual's unique centre of emotions, faculty of judgment, and free will, what he deems is significant to his life will essentially be comprised of a finite set of entities. As a direct consequence, any entities that do possess some kind of meaning to an individual must have been carefully designed to serve that particular purpose. Likewise, those entities which were never designed to fulfill any purpose can never have any meaning to the individual.

Reconsider the concept of art. Forms of music are designed to please the individual's sense of audition. Likewise, forms of paintings are designed to please the individual's sense of sight. Yet, the particular instances of art that every person finds beauty in will vary on an individual basis. One individual may prefer the genre of rhythm and blues, while another individual may find beauty within the category of opera. In a similar fashion, one individual may prefer a distinct set of paintings, while another individual may find value in an entirely different set of paintings. Thus, whenever some work of art invokes a positive emotion within the individual, it must have been designed specifically to fulfill that purpose. Likewise, since only distinct and particular instances of beauty will ever actually have a positive impact on any single individual, the individual will essentially value only a finite set of instances of beauty. Accordingly, what the individual deems is meaningful to his life will always be comprised of a finite set of entities.

Only forms of beauty can ever have meaning to the individual. Therefore, due to his subjective definition of beauty, only a limited set of entities will actually serve some kind of purpose within his life. Furthermore, what the individual finds is significant to his life will also, intrinsically, possess some kind of purpose. Likewise, anything that is significant to the individual will also possess a form of beauty.

On the other hand, if some entity lacks significance, then it also serves no purpose. Consider some randomly created entity. Some randomly created entity was never designed to fulfill any purpose. It merely exists, or it does not exist. Moreover, there is an equivalent chance that some randomly created entity exists, in comparison to the chance that it does not exist. Likewise, the chance that it may come into existence, at some point in our future, is equivalent to the chance that it may never come into existence. Therefore, since it is entirely possible that a randomly created entity may have never come into existence, it cannot fulfill any tangible purpose.

This is due solely to its conceptual essence. The conceptual essence of any entity is defined by all of the qualities or elements that it possesses ideologically, or in other words, its entire abstract nature. When some individual perceives a material object, or theoretical idea, he will automatically store that particular perception within his memory. When he later re-examines that particular perception, that immaterial idea will be the object's conceptual essence. All of the properties that define a distinct material object will be included within its conceptual essence. Therefore, the conceptual essence of any material object will be its exact immaterial representation, or in the case of an idea, its precise ideological reflection.

Anything that has a purpose must possess a conceptual essence that will actually serve this purpose. Therefore, if some entity did serve some kind of purpose, in the case that it does not exist within the material world, its basic conceptual essence would still serve that particular purpose. Yet, in the case of a randomly created entity, this is both illogical and impossible. For a conceptual essence must first exist in order to serve any kind of a purpose. Since it is entirely possible that a randomly created entity may have never come into existence, it is equally possible that its conceptual essence may have also never existed. Therefore, due directly to the arbitrary nature of its existence, that conceptual essence lacks any forms of a true and inherent significance.

Since there is an equal chance that a randomly created entity may have never existed, even if it did exist, it does so by mere chance. Accordingly, because its conceptual essence also exists due solely and merely to chance, it lacks immanent meaning. Any conceptual essence that is insignificant can never have meaning, or be meaningful to any person. Likewise, any object that is insignificant will never serve any kind of a reliable or tangible purpose. Hence, no randomly created entity can ever serve any kind of a purpose.

Contemplate Greek mythology. This religious ideology has evolved through hundreds of years of storytelling, and at current times, it is still passed on from generation to generation. In actuality, the Olympians embodied a possible metaphysical or material nature, regarding the essence of God. Nonetheless, these deities never truly existed within our physical world. The characters of Zeus, Athena, and Apollo merely exist within our thoughts and imaginations, and thus, they solely possess an immaterial existence. Yet, regardless of this fact, the conceptual essence of Greek mythology, as a specious definition of a group of deities, does serve a purpose. This purpose enables the individual to envision a possible mode of existence, related to God.

Now compare Greek mythology to the modern day cult. The leader of this cult invented a fictional system of religious beliefs, merely in an effort to acquire wealth and some form of social authority. However, consider the possibility that this same individual was born into a highly affluent family. This individual would most probably gain some form of employment within his family's enterprise, or he may simply choose to live on the avails of his family's capital. In the latter case, he would have no need to invent an imaginary religious ideology, simply because his need for some mode of employment would not be immediate. Accordingly, due to the latter possibility, there is a considerable chance that this particular cult will have never been born.

In addition, if this particular individual possessed the capability to find alternative modes of lucrative employment, he may have never chosen to invent a religious ideology. In fact, there are many other factors, such as the individual's sociability, intellectual prowess, and his ability to maintain authority, which will determine his raw capability to create a successful cult. Likewise, the particular details that define an effective ideological system will be highly dependent on the individual's creativity, and the scope of his imagination. Therefore, there exists a reasonable and practical chance that some particular cult may have never come into existence.

Correspondingly, if some cult were never materialized into the physical world, its basic conceptual essence alone, as a fictitious religious belief system, would never serve any kind of a purpose. The primary objective of any cult is to provide its leader with an abundance of material wealth, in addition to providing its followers with a sense of belonging. Yet, consider the possibility that a successful cult never existed. If a highly successful cult was never actually materialized into the physical world, then its conceptual essence, alone, would never serve any of its objectives. In other words, the conceptual essence of a successful cult, on its own, does not provide any persons with a sense of belonging. The success of any cult depends wholly and entirely on its material existence, or its materialization within the physical world. Without any forms of a physical or material existence, the particular conceptual essence of any cult would never accomplish any of its objectives. If this is true, then this conceptual essence lacks intrinsic significance and inherent meaning.

If some cult did serve a purpose, then its conceptual essence would continue to serve that purpose, even after the death of its leader. Indeed, all true religions continue to flourish through each passing generation. Nevertheless, every religious cult dies with the death of its leader. As a consequence, one of the major differences between a true religion and a religious cult is based on the fact that while true religions continue to gather followers during succeeding generations, the future of a radical cult will always be tentative. While the conceptual essence of a true religion continues to exist after the death of its leader, the conceptual essence of a radical cult will cease to exist, after the death of its leaders. As a consequence, this indicates the fact that while the conceptual essence of a true religion does possess meaning and significance, the conceptual essence of any radical cult possesses no true meaning or significance.

Therefore, due to its haphazard existence, the conceptual essence of any cult fundamentally serves no true or proper purpose. Both the birth and the death of any cult will be determined strictly by chance. As a direct result, its conceptual essence does not possess any forms of true meaning or significance. Some cult may have existed, or it may have never existed. Yet, because its fictitious ideology lacks significance, its conceptual essence will also lack purpose. In the case that some cult never existed, then its conceptual essence would also not exist. In the case that some cult did exist, then its conceptual essence was devised, and mainly dependent upon the whims of its leader. Accordingly, the conceptual essence of a cult was never truly designed to serve any kinds of an actual or meaningful purpose. Since its conceptual essence was never designed to fulfill any kinds of a meaningful purpose, no cult can ever serve a proper purpose. Any entity that lacks purpose will further lack any forms of beauty.

Comparatively, Greek mythology does serve a purpose. From a material perspective, no Greek God has ever existed within our material world. However, whether or not any Greek God has ever existed, the conceptual essence of Greek mythology still remains. This indicates the fact that the conceptual essence of Greek mythology does possess significance. The main purpose of Greek mythology grants the individual with a conception related to the possible materialization of a deity. Therefore, even though no characters within Greek mythology have ever existed in a physical manner, its ideology, or conceptual essence, still continues to subsist. Since it was designed to serve a purpose, the conceptual essence of Greek mythology will possess the innate potential to fulfill that particular purpose. Therefore, if Greek mythology does serve a purpose, its conceptual essence will possess the further attributes of beauty, meaning and significance.

Therefore, the conceptual essence of Greek mythology does possess significance, while the conceptual essence of any random cult possesses no significance. Moreover, since Greek mythology was designed to serve a purpose, its conceptual essence will possess the potential to fulfil that particular purpose. On the other hand, if a fanatical religious cult lacks a physical presence within the material world, then its conceptual essence would never accomplish any of its objectives; one of which would alleviate the loneliness of its members. Therefore, this conceptual essence, on its own, lacks intrinsic meaning and significance. Since the fictitious religious ideology espoused within a cult lacks meaning and significance, it also can never serve any true or proper purpose.

The conceptual essence of Greek mythology was designed to serve a purpose within our physical world. In comparison, the surfacing of a radical cult is both random and arbitrary, and thus, its conceptual essence lacks any kinds of an inherent meaning. When a conceptual essence does possess significance, it will then serve some form of purpose. Yet, in order for something to serve a purpose, it must have been designed specifically to fulfill that purpose. With respect to any randomly created entity, its conceptual essence merely exists, or it may never exist. This indicates the fact that this conceptual essence is wholly insignificant. Furthermore, the conceptual essence of any randomly created entity was never designed to fulfill any kind of a purpose. Since it was never designed to serve any purpose, its conceptual essence will also lack the potential to fulfill any kind of a purpose.

When an entity does serve a purpose, it must have been designed specifically to serve that purpose. This is due to the fact that only something that was explicitly designed to serve a purpose can actually possess the potential to fulfill that particular purpose. Thus, to have purpose is not an easily acquired attribute. Consider a large university building complex. Only persons who wish to further their educational pursuits may actually find some kind of purpose, regarding this particular infrastructure. For individuals who do not pursue a higher education, the concept of a university will, from a personal standpoint, lack significance, and thus it will also serve no meaningful purpose. Furthermore, after a student graduates from his studies, in his frame of mind, that particular institution will have lost some of its characteristic or qualitative purpose. Therefore, even though some entity may have been designed specifically to fulfill some kind of purpose, it may not, necessarily, serve any purpose to the distinctive or lone individual.

Anything that lacks purpose cannot have meaning or be meaningful to any individual. On the other hand, everything that has meaning to the individual will also serve some kind of purpose. Thus, if life does have some form of meaning, then it must have been designed specifically to serve a unique purpose. In turn, if life does have purpose, this implicates a theory of creation based on a form of intelligent design, and also that God exists.

Contrarily, it may be possible that some randomly created entity could possess some form of beauty, within some individual's frame of mind. Nonetheless, this kind of beauty will always be extrinsic in nature. This is due to the fact that even if that entity never came into existence, the individual would still, conceivably, find some kind of significance in its conceptual essence. Hence, the individual will be finding meaning and purpose in some conceptual essence that may have never existed.

Consider Plato's ideological invention known as the ring of Gyges. The ring of Gyges permits its owner to turn invisible purely at will. In theory, this would enable its owner to both act immorally, and evade any forms of a consequent punishment. Conceptually, this ring may then additionally grant its owner with a form of absolute power. Indeed, the concept of absolute power will represent a kind of beauty to some individuals. Yet, even though the ring of Gyges exists only conceptually, many individuals will still dedicate their lives towards obtaining the goal of absolute power. Therefore, these individuals mainly value a possible effect that the ring of Gyges may produce, should it exist within the material world.

Nevertheless, the concept of absolute power does not exist within our societies, simply because our civilization is built upon the social virtues of freedom and equality. As a consequence, the conceptual essence of absolute power was never designed to fulfill any kind of purpose. It is merely a by-product of random thought. In a consequent fashion, the conceptual essence of absolute power serves no true or proper purpose, within our material world. Any persons who do find beauty in the concept of absolute power will be, primarily, valuing some conceptual essence that is wholly insignificant to our civilization. This individual, then, would be finding meaning and significance in essentially nothing. Yet, the latter case represents an irrational scenario, for if the individual valued nothing, then he would not even value his own existence. Within this individual's frame of mind, nothing would be meaningful, significant, nor would anything serve any kind of a purpose.

In the case of the individual who is totally isolated, if he cherishes existence itself, then his life will possess some form of meaning, at least, albeit, to himself. Both this individual, and the individual who holds the belief that all forms of life have meaning, will hold the further belief that the creation of our universe does also have some kind of meaning. However, in the latter case, it is still logically possible that God does not exist. In essence, if we were to randomly pick some person, who contributes in a positive manner within his community, his life will undoubtedly have some kind of value to another person, regardless of whether God does or does not exist.

Contrarily, persons who hold no kinds of faith in God's existence will also hold the belief that all forms of life are an anomalous and random creation. These individuals may, then, hold the further belief that life has no purpose. Yet, these individuals still adopt the vices of selfishness and vanity, in an effort to treat their own particular existence as an ultimate end. When the atheist denies the idea that life has meaning, he does not objectively apply this belief towards his own personal existence. In his quest for social authority, the atheist can still hold the contradictory belief that his life, alone, does have significance or meaning. Nonetheless, due to his incessant need for social authority, the atheist will be destined to live a fate based on solitude and loneliness.

Therefore, in a universe that lacks a physical God, the individual may still eventually find some kind of meaning in life, either in his own life or in another person's life. As a result, a universal belief that is held by every human being, at the very least, is the premise that one's own life has some kind of significance or importance. Yet, when the individual matures and finds significance in other persons' lives, his mindset will further evolve, and he will eventually find some kind of significance in all other kinds of beauty. Since the latter individual will not merely classify beauty according to physical characteristics, he may further discover that the forms of spiritual beauty that he does recognize may be the original source behind all forms of physical beauty.

Since every person with a dynamic character possesses the ability to recognize forms of spiritual beauty, rationally, he must then accept the possibility that there could exist a non-material, spiritual world. This is where the principle of faith fits in. The theist does not truly possess any concrete evidence that will prove the existence of God, with total certainty. Yet, the multitude of spiritual beauty that exists within our universe does implicate, in his frame of mind, some form of rational design. Beauty invokes emotions of happiness within the sentient being. As a consequence, forms of spiritual beauty do possess meaning to an individual's life. When the individual finds beauty in his own spiritual nature, he cannot but conclude that all other forms of beauty that exist, in the totality of our universe, will also possess some form of meaning. Since the totality of both spiritual and physical forms of beauty may essentially be infinite, our universe must additionally possess some form of meaning to a creature that possesses the raw capability to comprehend infinite amounts of beauty. This creature can only be God.

In fact, our universe, in its totality, is expanding, and thus, it will always be giving birth to new kinds of spirits. Since every sentient being possesses a unique spirit, there lies a potential for the existence of an infinite amount of spirits within our universe. Likewise, an infinite amount of spirits implicates an infinite amount of beauty. Correspondingly, the universe, as an entire system, could also be viewed as a single and harmonious instance of beauty. We have faith in God because we believe that the universe, as an instance of beauty, must have meaning to some entity that possesses the natural ability to recognize the totality of beauty that may be found within it. Without a doubt, the infinite forms of beauty that may exist within our universe can only be truly comprehended by a being that possesses the characteristic of omniscience.

In actuality, all forms of beauty require a perceiver, but more importantly, all forms of beauty are unique. Since the universe contains distinct instances of beauty, these instances must have been designed specifically to please the perceiver of beauty. Moreover, if the entire universe is full of beauty, then the entire universe will also be full of meaning. Yet, instances of beauty can never be arbitrary or random, because this would mean that every random object in the universe is also meaningful. Without a doubt, we know that the latter notion is false. If every object in the world is beautiful, we would then be living in a paradise. Within paradise, every object possesses meaning, and when an object is born into paradise, this leads to the birth of a new kind of valuable spirit. Yet, the world we currently live in is comprised of elements of paradise, through the birth of new spirits, in addition to elements of war, which is the destruction of these spirits.

The principle of faith does revolve around the concept of beauty. Faith is a higher category of belief, which may be analogous to the relationship between that which possesses some form of universal beauty, and that which possesses a unique form of beauty. Persons who possess faith do not require an indubitable proof regarding the existence of God, simply because they possess the ability to perceive unique forms of beauty. Persons who possess the capability to perceive brilliant forms of beauty will not require a universal consensus among all persons, who will agree with their particular assessment of beauty. These individuals realize that there does exist brilliant forms of beauty, despite the fact that other persons will lack the capability to recognize or perceive it. Beauty exists due to the individual's distinct ability to perceive. Faith, on the other hand, originates through the perception of a magnificent form of beauty.

In a similar fashion, individuals who possess the ability to perceive the immaterial do not need concrete forms of evidence to conclude that an immaterial world does, indeed, exist. Hence, all persons who possess faith do possess a rational reason to believe in the existence of God. These individuals perceive forms of beauty that exist within the immaterial spirit, and this enables them to further perceive all other forms of spiritual beauty that may exist within our universe. The beauty of our universe, in its totality, lies in the complicated, yet harmonious relationship that exists amongst all of its parts. From a logical perspective, a complex, but interconnected system of independent elements can only be designed by a highly rational and intelligent creator.

The concept of faith does not merely entail a belief in the existence of an immaterial world. Rather, individuals who do possess faith will also possess the volition to exist within this immaterial world. Hence, persons who lack faith, both, will not believe that an immaterial world exists, nor do they possess any volition to exist within it.

Thus, those who have faith in God will naturally believe in both a spiritual existence and an immaterial world. The most common conception of this immaterial world may be known as heaven. In heaven, no forms of pain will exist, as it is a world based purely on the concept of beauty. To possess faith in a world that is founded on the concept of beauty, the individual must first value instances of beauty that may be found within the material world, and he must also characterize his own life as a potential source of beauty. Therefore, the individual must characterize his own life as something that is equally as beautiful as the other kinds of beauty that exist within either the material or the immaterial worlds.

Persons who believe in heaven will also value life over non-existence. Many conceptions of heaven are based on utopian principles, because the concept of the material has been associated with the concept of the finite. Subsequently, because the physical world is finite, the immaterial must be defined without any kinds of limitations. The concept of limitlessness, in conjunction with natural liberty, indicates a form of existence that may be unparalleled, within our physical universe. It also implicates the possibility that there exists many other differing kinds of wonders that cannot be embodied or perceived within a material world. Similarly, there may also be many concepts that are unknown to the individual, simply because these concepts are not accessible within a purely material world.

God may have granted human beings with the faculty of imagination so that we may have input with respect to our concept of utopia. If this is true, our physical world could be mainly a product of God's imagination, while heaven could be a product of the human imagination. Therefore, God could have created an immaterial world, not based on His own idea of utopia, but primarily based on our own concepts of utopia. It is rationally possible that the creation of heaven could be based mainly on the human idea of what paradise should be.

If the material world is finite, then logically, the immaterial world must be infinite. Likewise, if the material world is comprised of physical bodies, then the immaterial world must be comprised of immaterial spirits. Yet, within the immaterial world, is there any kind of division that distinguishes unlike souls? According to the concept of beauty, there does exist a division between differing and unique spirits. Those who cherish the physical beauty present on Earth will also cherish the differing kinds of beauty that exist within the immaterial spirit. Likewise, since the theist holds the belief that God is a supremely moral spirit, He must have created an immaterial world that is also full of a similar degree of beauty.

The human intellect and will emanates from God's ability to both create and destroy life. As a supremely moral being, God may have created creatures with a similar power because He values the virtue of justice. Every person possesses the freedom to either value or detest his own subjective existence. God may exercise His own conception of justice by granting human beings with the capability to value either existence or non-existence. If this is true, then human beings may possess a finite physical lifespan so that every person may conceive a possible end, with respect to his own existence. Accordingly, human beings may possess this kind of freedom so that those individuals who do not cherish their existence may be granted their wish, and in a subsequent fashion, their immaterial spirit may then perish with their physical existence. The human ability to either value or detest life makes justice the most important social virtue within our civilization.

Thus, while the concept of heaven may be comprised of an infinite amount of immaterial spirits, the concept of hell may not truly exist. The concept of hell could merely represent the end of the totality of some individual's existence. Indeed, the existence of hell does seem to be problematic. Persons who freely act in immoral ways demonstrate a high disregard for life. It would not make much rational sense to create an environment, like hell, for those individuals who possess a disdain for life. From a conventional perspective, the concept of hell represents a form of lifelong punishment for those who are evil and wicked. Yet, from an objective perspective, non-existence seems to be a more fitting end for those souls who possess some form of hatred towards their own existence. Therefore, since God empowered human beings with freedom, from a rational perspective, the latter possibility may be a more appropriate form of justice.

From a moral perspective, God must possess the qualities of mercy and compassion. Therefore, since God is morally supreme, those spirits who discover happiness within their physical existence should be granted a further form of existence, in terms of an immaterial existence.

In actuality, God must have created the physical universe because of His love for life. Yet, because He is morally supreme, He has granted human beings with the will to either embrace life or forsake it. Our unbounded will proves the fact that our creator did not create us primarily to serve as slaves to His rule. The individual may choose to serve God, but this entirely reflects upon his innate right for choice. Further, because He is morally perfect, it is reasonable to believe that God has created an immaterial world for those beings who share a common love for life, and ultimately, existence. Hence, if God is supremely moral, this gives us a reason to believe in the existence of some kind of immaterial world, and that heaven does truly exist.

Indeed, the nature of human beings, regarding our immaterial soul, does provide a reasonable faith behind the existence of angels. In turn, the concepts of angels and demons seem to implicate the possibility that God is responsible for some kinds of interventions during our daily lives. The diverse nature of spiritual beliefs also makes it possible that God does speak to select individuals, but this may be impossible to prove. Yet, the capacity of the human will, and our autonomous exercise of the will, may indicate the possibility that He is a passive being. Nevertheless, if there does exist such a thing as a divine revelation, and if the individual uses this revelation towards the production of goodness, then he should be looked upon as a kind of angel.

Even though God has granted every sentient being with a unique spirit, by granting freedom of thought He has encouraged the free development of every individual's spirit. One major consequence of this freedom marks a division between a beautiful spirit, and a kind of spirit which lacks any forms of beauty. Indeed, selfishness cannot be beautiful, because those who are selfish only treat their own lives as some kind of an end. Contrarily, selflessness may be beautiful because such actions entail generosity, and subsequently, a kind of gift. Therefore, the equilibrium between selfishness and selflessness may be comparable to the equilibrium between a vain spirit and a beautiful spirit.

The opposite of a beautiful spirit can only be known as a monstrosity. Nonetheless, only human beings possess the potential to become the most destructive monsters, or savages, within our physical world. No animals in nature possess the potential to become monsters, because their instances of violent behaviour are always motivated by their instincts to survive. Yet, human beings do possess the capacity to become exceedingly violent, whenever the motives behind these acts are irrelevant to their basic survival.

Therefore, regarding evil, it does exist in our world. Concepts of evil are born through the free flowing thoughts of the demon. Mental states such as anger, hatred, intolerance and inequality are all born due to the distinct mindset of the demon. Subsequently, those individuals who continually prey on the confusion and indecisiveness of other persons should be looked upon as demons. Moreover, true demons will encourage doubt regarding all forms of established knowledge. Yet, evil triumphs only when there are no forms of goodness in our world, who will actively oppose it.

Indeed, a supremely moral God loves the universe that He created. However, we must ask if it is possible to understand the concept of love without understanding feelings of hate? If God is truly morally perfect, it is conceivable that no forms of evil should exist in any kind of world. Nevertheless, God may have created free will to illustrate the true powers that may be associated with an act of love. The negation of love is the concept of hate, and hatred is the root of all forms of evil. Furthermore, evil may be defined not merely as a lack of love, but also as the materialization of feelings of hate.

Therefore, emotions and acts of love and hate will always be due to the free utilization of the will, both on the part of the perceiver and on the part of the actor. The actor's behaviour, in the latter respect, serves to differentiate the angel from the demon. As such, the concept of love will always be associated with existence, while the concept of evil will always be associated with the concept of death. While angels demonstrate a preoccupation with life, demons demonstrate a preoccupation with death. Furthermore, while angels will be motivated to act through their faith in God, demons may be responsible for the reinforcement of doubt, in relation to any moral creator.

A life fulfilled with beauty comes from man's independent ability to focus on whatever he chooses to perceive. In our natural world, there does exist many forms of pain that are not human inflicted. Forms of disease and our finite life span inflict a form of pain that cannot be averted. Natural disasters may provide another source for uncontrollable human suffering. Thus, if an omnipotent being did create our universe, grief and suffering seem to be natural properties belonging to our very nature and existence.

Clearly, feelings of happiness may be universally important for a well-lived life. However, may we say the same about our emotions of sadness? There does exist many differing kinds of beauty in our world. It is these instances of beauty which provide the main source behind our emotions of happiness. Correspondingly, we will experience emotions of sadness during the absence of these instances of beauty. If the latter statement is true, then our emotions of sadness will be just as important as our emotions of happiness.

Consider the phenomenon of rare gems. Rare gemstones, like opals, do represent a source of beauty. Yet, is it possible for the individual to live happily if he did not possess any kinds of gemstones? In actuality, many persons do live a fulfilling life, despite the fact that they do not own any gemstones. Furthermore, the majority of these individuals do not experience feelings of sadness, directly because of the fact that they do not own any gemstones. Accordingly, under this circumstance, it is still possible to live a well-lived life.

Now consider a two thousand year old elm tree, situated in the middle of a rainforest. Would this rainforest retain its unique beauty if this tree were to suddenly fall? Most persons would reply no. Nonetheless, would these same persons experience emotions of sadness due directly to the fact that this forest has lost some element of its beauty? Most rational persons understand the fact that death is a natural element of life within our physical world. As a consequence, most persons will not experience emotions of sadness under this circumstance.

Yet, persons do experience feelings of sadness in the absence of other forms of beauty. The main source of this beauty comes from live, sentient beings. When a child loses a pet, he will inevitably experience emotions of sadness. Likewise, if an adult loses his friend, he will also experience feelings of sadness. The finite nature of the physical world only serves to reinforce the importance of each and every individual to his community. When one individual ceases to function properly, due to illness, this does pose an impact on our civilization as a whole. Therefore, people do experience emotions of sadness, when they have lost particular sources of beauty. Sadness is a natural reaction whenever the individual loses a form of beauty that is a fundamental cause behind his emotions of happiness.

No rational individual welcomes feelings of sadness into his life. Yet, this emotion is important because it represents the particular and distinct sources of beauty that are important to the individual. Some sources of beauty are valuable to the individual, while other sources may be of a lesser importance. When the individual loses a valued source of beauty, he also loses a source of intrinsic happiness. Emotions of sadness may just be the natural progression of sentiments whenever an individual is missing an extremely cherished and valued object of beauty.

Undeniably, emotions themselves are beautiful. If no human being possessed emotions, we could not truly recognize any forms of beauty. Likewise, without emotions, we also could not experience any feelings of love. Emotions of love depend on each unique individual's perception of beauty. Acts of love will always be directed towards the most significant kinds of beauty that are perceived by the individual. Therefore, another element that may be universally associated with true beauty is the virtue of love.

In general, the gender differences between man and woman will attract one individual to another. This type of association may also be evident in a parent's relationship with his child, and also in some forms of friendships. In essence, the gender of a man may be stereotypically linked with the concept of a protector, while the gender of a woman may be stereotypically associated with the concept of a life-force. The female sex possesses the capacity to bear children, and this places the responsibility on males to become the general provider. From this deduction, another distinction that we may make may be based on the concepts of innocence and confidence.

If a further universal element may be linked with beauty, it is the element of innocence. This is due to the fact that all children are born into the world with this defining characteristic. Innocence may be defined as a form of purity that involves the absence of vice. Yet, in order to empathize with her child, a mother must also possess the characteristic of innocence. Females who do not possess this attribute may not be able to relate with their child, and this will negatively affect the parenting process.

Those who are innocent will truly understand the virtue of love, because they possess an unbounded principle of sympathy. In actuality, the innocent lack concrete knowledge with respect to any riches that may be achievable through the concept of vice. As a consequence, they do not truly comprehend concepts like hatred and intolerance, due simply to a lack of life experiences.

The opposite of innocence is insecurity. Insecurity should never be confused with innocence. The insecure do understand concepts related to malice and disregard. They mainly experience problems when distinguishing moral character traits from immoral character traits. Hence, their perspective of right and wrong may be more or less obscure. Insecurity leads to a form of self-doubt relative to acts that may either be accepted or shunned by the general public. Therefore, those who are insecure will always cast doubt related to all of their personal mannerisms.

On the other hand, those who are confident possess a firm understanding of evil and goodness. Likewise, those who are confident are highly aware of the fact that they possess knowledge of the virtues. With this knowledge, their actions may be, then, mainly characterised as vigilant. Having the knowledge that their acts are motivated by virtue enables the confident to assert their character, in all kinds of circumstances, without any fears of repercussion. For example, to properly provide for his children, the individual must first have confidence in his raw capability to protect them.

Confidence is a form of beauty, but it should not be confused with conceit. Conceit involves the mindset of superiority and inequality, while confidence is mainly founded upon the knowledge and expert utilization of the virtues. The conceited individual believes in his own righteousness, even when he is faced with a decidedly firm and rational opposition. As a consequence, this individual will continue his static ways without any form of regard towards other individuals. Since the conceited are self-centred, they will also, necessarily, lack the intrinsic ability to learn.

The attribute of conceit may be partially gained through forms of social approval. When the individual gains some form of approval, he may acquire a higher degree of buoyancy, with respect to his immoral ways. Through his lack of concern and empathy, the static character may then feel justified in his relentless pursuit for social authority. Even the smallest degree of social approval may provide the conceited with a level of sureness, and this enables them to personally justify their selfish rationale. Yet, when the static character loses his self-assurance, he will, subsequently, lack the raw ability to implement his true will. Accordingly, when the conceited lose all forms of social approval, they will also lose the righteous justification that they have assimilated, in accordance with their selfish mindset.

In contrast, when the dynamic character gains confidence, he will never act merely in his own best interests. In effect, he will naturally acquire a greater perspective, with respect to the best interests of his community. The dynamic character may then accept the role as an advocate. However, in cases where he loses confidence, the dynamic character may also lose forms of objectivity that he may have previously possessed. Hence, the element of confidence will always be positively associated with the element of leadership.

In the interactions between the confident dynamic character and the conceited static character, hostility may be the truest defining element. Through his conceit, the static character will purposely seek to shatter the confidence attained by a dynamic character, simply to experience feelings of social authority. For a similar reason, individuals who are insecure will purposely target and harm those who are innocent.

When the dynamic character battles his enemies, there exists a great potential for two of the following results. First of all, those who are innocent may lose some of their confidence. In a converse fashion, those who are confident may lose some of their innocence. Nevertheless, as a direct result, this phenomenon will serve to actively enhance feelings of intimacy between an individual who is confident and an individual who is innocent.

When the static character fails to achieve victory within his battles, he will then come to the understanding that it will be a daunting task to wage war against all that is beautiful. The personal failures of the static character may then motivate him to join a collective of his peers. Yet, the static character will only join a collective if he possesses a similar goal with its leader. As a stronger grouping, they will then choose to participate in a similar, yet futile battle.

The static character's loyalty will never be permanent. Moreover, it is entirely possible that the static character will create enemies who are members of the same collective. When the individual makes a personal nemesis, this will usually lead to strife within that collective. It is rarely the case that the two individuals involved will put their differences aside, and discover some form of a compromise. Nonetheless, these persons will continue to obey their collective's leader, simply because they have been unsuccessful in achieving some form of authority, when acting alone. In time, the animosity between two unsympathetic members will resurface, and the relationship between them will revert back into one that is based on hostility.

In actuality, the static leader may have never established a true and positive relationship with all of the members of his collective. As a consequence, if this leader fails to accomplish the goals of the collective, the members of that collective will simply renege their obedience to him, and some may seek leadership within this collective for themselves. However, when these individuals fail to destroy some element of beauty that exists in our world, it is at this point where the collective will eventually disband. These individuals will then face the permanent condition of loneliness and solitude.

Within intimate relationships between two persons with a static character, the elements of insecurity and conceit may essentially be traded or swapped. In the female, when levels of conceit replace levels of insecurity, her natural maturation process will have been disturbed. Subsequently, her anxiety, in combination with a false sense of self-assurance, will essentially transform her demeanour into a frame of mind based on guiltlessness. In the male, when levels of insecurity replace levels of conceit, his natural maturation process will regress. In these cases, his self-assurance, in combination with a degree of anxiety, will transform his demeanour into a mindset based on the concept of condemnation.

In our physical world, man could not exist without the existence of women. Yet, the same may be said about women. Both genders represent a differing category of the human spirit. At the most rudimentary level, the male gender could symbolize courage, while the female gender could symbolize splendour. Therefore, customary forms of male beauty may be mainly spiritual in nature, while customary forms of female beauty may be mainly physical in nature. Indeed, the concept of opposites creates distinction and uniqueness. When two unique spirits do achieve a unity, the resulting spirit that they produce will be based entirely on emotions of love. In these cases, both individuals, from a subjective perspective, will then experience personal fulfillment. In effect, the totality of human civilization could not subsist without the virtue of love that exists between two unique spirits.

When both innocence and confidence may be found in a single individual, this combined quality should be known as worldliness, or grace. In fact, when the individual bases his character towards the middle point between the two extremes of innocence and confidence, his actions could be viewed as an intentional act of love. The individual then naturally acquires grace because he has established some form of an interconnection with the contrasting attributes of his partner's soul. In time, this individual will develop the further traits of gentleness, sensitivity, and incorruptibility.

From a subjective perspective, then, emotions of love will provide both spiritual and physical completion. Yet, from every other perspective, love is a form of beauty. The virtue of love is beautiful because it has the power to transform uniqueness into likeness. For example, the virtue of love can alter feelings of anger into feelings of happiness. Likewise, love can also alter feelings of loneliness into feelings of wholeness. The virtue of love is also beautiful because it directly opposes the concept of hate. Hatred is a vice that reinforces feelings of anger and dissent.

In actuality, love may be the only general quality among all of the elements in the human soul. First of all, from a subjective perspective, love may be an act of the intellect. Those persons who possess an extremely giving nature are essentially agents of love. Secondly, love is an emotion that is felt between life-partners. Individuals who become life-partners take this step in their lives essentially because they recognize the intrinsic beauty that exists within their partner. Thirdly, love is also a principle. When the individual becomes an advocate within his society, he essentially becomes a practitioner of love. Individuals who are practitioners of love provide the fundamental building blocks that turn distinct tribes into functioning communities. As a consequence, the boundless nature of love also makes it the most powerful virtue.

Without a doubt, maternal instincts lead to unbridled compassion, while paternal instincts lead to unfettered justice. These kinds of principles make all responsible parents agents of love. The act of parental love is motivated through the creation of beauty. Consider the most rudimentary form of life. Kinds of vegetation, like old growth trees, mainly reproduce through seeds. This indicates the fact that something that is infinitesimally small may transform into something that possesses boundless amounts of beauty. All individuals will share a similar thought whenever they enter into a state of parenthood. Accordingly, wherever there is beauty and happiness, there will also be love.

In fact, numerous species of animals in the wild would become extinct, if there were no forms of motherly love. Therefore, animals in the wild also possess parental instincts. The relationship between a parent and child illustrates the fact that the virtue of responsibility may also be a quality that is found within all of nature. Acts of affection provide the most important link between two generations of life. As a result, love may also be the most rudimentary virtue that exists in the totality of our natural world.

With respect to the dynamic character, the virtue of love that exists between two persons will always be mutual. Every individual possesses a wholly unique perspective of our world. Yet, it is the voluntary sharing of our experiences which adds beauty to an already beautiful world. Accordingly, love also serves to compound the feelings of happiness experienced by every human being.

On the other hand, forms of respect can often be one-sided. While love is mainly directed towards the spiritual nature of some individual, respect is usually directed towards the actions and achievements of another individual. When forms of respect become reciprocated within some relationship, it transforms into a kind of love that is directed towards the character of an individual's companion. Nonetheless, while love is always directed towards family members and close friends, forms of respect may be directed towards a more general social target. It is an important form of love that may be directed towards acquaintances and other persons who may not be actual members within an individual's social network. Indeed, every constructive member within a community deserves respect. Therefore, the act of respect is reserved for persons who possess some kind of significance, not necessarily on a personal level, but on a communal level as a whole.

What about the concept of unconditional love. Is unconditional love idealistic? In actuality, all agents of love do hold faith in this concept. Therefore, all acts of true love are unconditional. However, feelings of love are conditional. For every individual experiences emotions of love on a conditional basis. This is the main reason why persons possess a limited number of lifetime partners. The individual acquires a lifetime partner on the condition that he experiences emotions of love, whenever this individual is within his presence. However, a further condition requires that the individual's partner must also experience a similar degree of love.

Accordingly, the concept of unconditional love does remain idealistic in some sense. Love is a form of beauty, but it is also directed towards that which is beautiful. Therefore, if there were no forms of beauty present within our physical universe, there would also be no forms of love. Unconditional love remains idealistic in the sense that it must be reciprocated, in order for it to truly exist. Single dimensional forms of love may exist in some relationships. In these cases, the agent of love may mistakenly perceive that his feelings are reciprocated by his partner. Nonetheless, this latter judgement will be wrong whenever there are forms of negative afflictions that exist in condition with an act of love. Hence, forms of unconditional love may be illusionary within the individual, especially whenever there is a lack of beauty that plagues his partner's frame of mind.

The dynamic character is prone, by nature, to love that which is beautiful. Theists believe that all of nature is beautiful, mainly because nature is the creation of God. The universe is God's idea of paradise, at least on a material level. The atheist may still perceive some forms of beauty within the universe, but he claims that the creation of this beauty is not due to any forms of intelligence. Moreover, other individuals may entirely deny the existence of any forms of beauty within our universe. Due to their feelings of jealousy, these individuals will then be motivated to destroy all of the forms of beauty that exist within the theist's frame of mind. Such individuals who seek to destroy culturally recognized forms of beauty act in opposition to the work of God, and thus, they cannot be a part of God's idea of beauty. Indeed, individuals who are motivated to destroy the concept of beauty will also lack the ability to find any forms of beauty in themselves. Yet, they are still fundamental creations of God, nonetheless. It is this subjective judgment of beauty that marks the dissent between persons with a static character and persons who possess a dynamic character.

Those individuals who continually destroy God's idea of beauty will also constantly live in a state of war and aggression. Since these individuals do not wish to establish a peaceful coexistence with nature, they also lack the ability to produce any forms of love. In these individual's frame of mind, the concept of love remains entirely conditional. The specific conditions established, though, will vary. The most central condition will revolve around the notion of social authority. Hence, these individuals will remain in a warring state with other persons until they are actually granted some form of social authority over them. Yet, even when this authority is achieved, the individual may continue to utilize the concept of conditional love, in his effort to acquire higher degrees of authority. In the end, the static character's acquisition of social authority will merely enable him to view some form of beauty within his own inner spirit.

Therefore, there is a major difference between unconditional and conditional love. Persons who are agents of unconditional love will live in a state of peace with all other forms of spirits that may exist within nature. Individuals who become sources of conditional forms of love will only uphold an armistice with other forms of life, when they have been granted the utmost degree of social authority.

Indeed, to truly appreciate life is to further appreciate all of God's creations. We must, on a whole, appreciate the totality of nature. Only those individuals who accomplish this feat will possess the capability to live in a state of peace, within our physical paradise. Those who do not accomplish this feat will actively ignore the fruits of nature, and subsequently, they will also deny the existence of God. Such individuals may place little value on anything else, except for their irrational and ridiculous need to be treated like a deity. These individuals may be viewed as spiritually lifeless, since they lack the ability to appreciate all of the other kinds of spirits that exist within our natural world.

On the other hand, persons who value their own existence will also value the other spiritual aspects that may be discovered within our physical world. Subsequently, persons who possess an appreciation for all of the spirits that exist in nature will live the most fulfilling life possible, as opposed to those who view everything in nature as irrelevant, and thus, insubstantial. This is due to the fact that existence, itself, is both a wonder and a gift.

Ponder the distinction between a tree and a rock. Both entities possess the attribute of a physical existence. Yet, when we view a tree, we perceive that this entity also possesses a spiritual existence as well. In actuality, a tree possesses the capability to grow, while no rocks possess this capacity. In the same manner, the differences between those who value their spiritual existence and those who do not may be eerily similar. Persons with a static character will always remain firm in their subjective frame of mind. Therefore, individuals with a static character will mainly live a physical existence, without any forms of spiritual growth. In comparison, the rock exists physically, and it also does not demonstrate any forms of growth. The rock, moreover, merely demonstrates the potential to deteriorate.

The static character will only achieve happiness if his want for power and authority is granted by some individual. In fact, his entire existence will revolve around this persistent need. He does not truly appreciate the phenomenon of existence. Thus, since existence is a wonder in itself, the static character mainly takes life for granted. He possesses an all or nothing approach, with respect to the acquisition of social authority. As a consequence, he will never find happiness in the wonder of existence itself. Either he achieves a minimal degree of social authority, or he will continue his pursuit towards accomplishing this irrational goal.

By his very nature, the dynamic character will always continue his constant search for the truth. As a direct consequence, he will also continue to accept and understand new forms of spirits. The latter action enables him to develop spiritually throughout his entire life. Therefore, the element of spiritual growth also distinguishes persons with a dynamic character from persons with a static character.

Perhaps, God does not take up a physical form, within our universe, because He values faith over conformity. As opposed to conformity, it is possible that God may place more value on freedom and personal autonomy. Through the freedom of the will, every individual possesses an unconstrained autonomous ability to develop his own spiritual being. Yet, persons who have faith in God will simultaneously need His leadership, in this respect. These individuals want to understand His wisdom, related to both morality and immorality. In some decisions that persons face, there may be no clear cut answer as to whether some choice may be moral or immoral. Therefore, persons who possess faith also freely seek His guidance, with respect to their spiritual development.

On the other hand, individuals who lack faith will essentially possess the attribute of disobedience. Such individuals will not require any similar forms of guidance from an almighty creator. As a consequence, it is only in the case if God does reveal Himself to us physically, where the egotistical individual may then change his faith regarding His existence. Yet, because He values freedom, God may not value slavery, or other kinds of individuals who follow Him merely because of their personal fears. Through the social virtue of freedom, God may seek followers who choose to obey Him, through a wholly independent and autonomous manner. Therefore, the difference between autonomous followers and the fearful slave could be a substantial moral reason why God does not reveal Himself to us within our physical world.

Due to the individual's innate right for thought, the entire realm of religious beliefs that exist in our world should be protected by the state. Indeed, religion encompasses a set of beliefs that, in theory, should be directed towards the betterment of human culture. It provides spiritual enlightenment, and it also defines concrete forms of moral behaviour. Nonetheless, in many cases, acts of violence may be justified through religious beliefs. Whenever this occurs, the true purpose of religion will have been grossly misused.

Conflicts in duty are the most direct causes behind any holy wars, yet the motivation behind following a religion remains similar on a universal basis. All persons who are truly religious believe in the existence of a supremely moral being. In a subsequent fashion, the true conceptual essence within any religion mainly promotes peaceful modes of conduct. Therefore, religion mainly serves as a form of education, in relation to the realms of morality and immorality. Yet, the existence of doubt and agnosticism paves the way for differing conceptions of God. As such, persons who carry out holy wars probably do not possess a true faith in God. These individuals should, in fact, be looked upon as demons. In fact, no individual possesses the right to start a holy war, due solely to conflicting religious beliefs. Since, no person possesses a certain form of knowledge in relation to the true nature of God, no person will be justified in the creation of an act of war, based purely on his subjective beliefs regarding his duties to God.

Indeed, the moral duties of man will differ according to each unique religion. Differing religions will each provide a unique conception of God, and similarly, a unique concept of morality. Therefore, the proper separation of religion from political philosophy is morally correct, due to the existence of many differing kinds of religion. As a consequence, no individual should possess the political authority to favour one religion over another. Freedom of thought is an innate right, which subsequently empowers the individual to analyze and compare one belief system with another. The existence of many different religions simply entails the fact that there also exists many differing ethical ways of life. To be truly fair, a political system must embrace differing modes of thought, whenever these belief systems both abhor criminality and define morality. Yet, it is the politician's job to serve the interests of every citizen within his society, and subsequently, not to promote his own particular religious beliefs. Political systems were mainly created to govern our material existence, while religions mainly serve to govern our immaterial spirit. The separation of the material from the immaterial marks the main differences between political philosophy and religion.

If we change our focus away from the ideological duties defined within a certain religion, we will then maintain a necessary similarity based on why we actually believe in some higher power. When the individual's primary motivation for following a religion is acknowledged, then all persons of a differing faith will establish a true unity with each other. Religious persons all believe in the existence of a supreme being. Therefore, all those who are religious must also possess a firm system of beliefs within the realm of morality.

Due to every individual's innate right for thought, true religious beauty could be best represented through an amalgamation of differing forms of religion. Indeed, the duties of man will differ according to each unique religion. Yet, these differences exist merely because of each individual's differing conception of God. The one commonality among all religions is based on the fact that they are all moral systems of thought. The concept of morality, then, must be the main starting point that unites differing kinds of religions together. If we focus less on the duties that each religion demands upon us, and more upon why we actually believe in a higher power, then the motives behind each person's faith can serve to unite all distinct religions together.

Therefore, if we all believe in God, and we adopt a particular religion due to our ideologies of morality, this can then serve as a foundation that will unite all persons of a differing faith together. The concept of morality may be common, whenever it places value not merely on one's own life, but on all other kinds of life as well. Therefore, according to this principle of morality, the individual must further value persons of all other faiths, even if there are no commonalities that exist between his religion and other systems of faith.

The existence of God entails the premise that we should all live a principled life, based on the concepts of morality and cooperation. It is through this unity that will enable us to work out the major differences that exist between distinct religions. The main principle of cooperation should prevent any forms of potential for any holy wars.

Indeed, due to the power of free will, there may be no single path to glory. One religion defines a specific way of life, while another religion defines another. To solve these potential conflicts, an interwoven religion would, ideally, combine both the positive and the compatible elements among all religions into a single system of thought. Any incompatibilities, then, may be omitted from this general system of thought, and this grants the individual with the personal liberty to abide by a commonly established principle, freely through the power of his will.

All religions possess the same focus. In essence, God is a supreme and infinitely moral creator of all forms of life. Likewise, all religions teach moral forms of behaviour, while condemning all forms of immorality. All religions define a particular way of life, which centres on God as the ultimate role model. This includes adopting the principle of love, while simultaneously denouncing forms of hatred. Moreover, the embracing of God may be necessary for the best possible life, while those who do not believe in His existence may be prone to sin. The further differences that distinguish each unique religion could be viewed as less consequential. For example, each religion teaches a unique concept of the afterlife. Yet, the commonalities that exist between unique religions should make a general system of thought, based on a form of universal consensus, also the most rational.

Incompatible principles may also, seemingly, exist within a single religion. This is largely due to misinterpretations, and misunderstandings regarding specific readings within a certain religious text. As a result, conflicts of opinion will also lead to the recognition of incompatible principles within a single religion. Misinterpretations may also lead to the possible endorsement of unethical principles. Indeed, if a religion promoted forms of evil, it could not be truly categorized as a religion. Immoral systems of thought, related to a single religion, may be mainly supported by groups of religious extremists.

Therefore, misinterpretations may inevitably lead to the promotion of forms of evil, within any single religion. For example, in one religion, homosexuals may be depicted as evil persons. However, within the mind of most rational persons, homosexuality, by itself, constitutes no true form of evil. In another religion, non-believers may be targeted for violence. Nonetheless, holding a differing system of beliefs also constitutes no form of evil. These kinds of immoral judgments will be due to the misinterpretation of some verse, simply because of the fact that another verse written within the same religious text will essentially promote a contradictory moral principle.

Indeed, differing religions will define differing kinds of sins. They also focus on differing central ideologies. Selflessness, or self-sacrifice, may be relevant to the values that all human beings currently possess. This may be evident in our parental instincts. Those individuals, who adopt the duty of responsible parenthood, will inherently sacrifice their lives and personal wealth to provide for their children. The active submission to God's will is also relevant within human civilization. Individuals who adopt the duty of persisting faith will essentially become His agents. Agents of God do not only possess a faith in His existence, but they will also recognize His moral values and confine their actions according to these principles. Accordingly, agents of God will never succumb to acts of violence, simply because all forms of violence will be commonly categorized as immoral acts.

Personal enlightenment is also relevant at current times. Persons who possess this kind of awareness will turn their inward focus towards the spiritual world. Personal enlightenment also pertains to a form of self-consciousness that centres on the subject's own spiritual nature. This type of self-consciousness leads to a kind of acceptance and resilience that is directed towards one's own imperfections. Individuals who accept their personal imperfections will also accept the imperfections in other persons. Moreover, personal enlightenment is necessary for all forms of positive relationships that exist within any given society.

Personal autonomy, in the form of individual growth and development, is also highly valued within our society. For this to occur, the individual must recognize the fact that there are many differing paths that will lead to both a fulfilling life and happiness. This form of recognition can only be acquired by those persons who adopt a certain type of responsibility over their actions and behaviour. In fact, the truest kinds of personal growth can only be achieved after the individual takes personal responsibility for all of his actions. It is only after the individual becomes accountable where he may actually learn from his personal mistakes, and acquire some degree of spiritual growth.

The fulfillment of an individual's duty to his community is also relevant within our civilization. In actuality, the duty to contribute must be adopted by all able bodies, essentially due to the fact that the existence of any community depends entirely upon the principle of cooperation. On a similar note, the individual must not merely draw a connection between himself and his community, but he must also unite with all of nature. In order to unite himself with everything that exists in nature, he must adopt the duty of immutability. After he acquires this duty, he will then possess a connection not merely with his peers, but also with God as a whole, and thus, all of His other creations which habituate the natural world.

Differing religions do layout unique systems of thought. Hence, they will also focus on differing conceptions regarding our spiritual existence. The belief in heaven centres around an immaterial existence within an environment filled with bliss. Nevertheless, along with the concept of heaven, the environment of hell may also exist. The concept of hell implicates a similar immaterial existence, but it is an environment that is reserved exclusively for demons. Therefore, the concept of heaven and hell provides for two immaterial worlds, which are based on the division of persons who are moral and those persons who lack any forms of morality.

Contrarily, the belief in reincarnation negates any kind of a spiritual existence within an immaterial world. For the most part, within the concept of reincarnation, after death, merely the physical nature of each individual changes. Therefore, after one's passing, life merely takes on a differing physical form, within our natural world. The concept of karma is also related to reincarnation. Karma is a kind of justice that is based on the ideology of cause and effect. In essence, the individual's actions, related to morality, will determine the next form of his physical existence. Yet, beyond the realm of reincarnation lies the concept of nirvana. Individuals who reach this type of existence will be freed from the cycle of karma, related to death and rebirth. Within this concept, life merely takes on a differing form or shape. In some schools of thought, nirvana may be attained before death, while in other schools of thought nirvana may only be attained after one's physical death.

Indeed, even within a single religion, there exists differing schools of thought that interpret many fundamental teachings in extremely diverse manners. These types of factions do not surface due to any forms of misinterpretations or misunderstandings. Factions within a single religion may be largely due to the individual's own rationale and belief system, regarding a characteristically vague principle within a single religious text. Therefore, the existence of divisions within a single religion is due in large part to the individual's unique upbringing, within the realm of morality and ethical codes of behaviour.

The static character mainly views religion as a kind of farce, since the existence of God can be disputed and thus, since His existence relies merely upon the concept of faith. Persons with a static character will take the view that since no person can prove the existence of God, He does not exist. Therefore, atheism mainly originates from persons who lack the principle of faith. Yet, in rejecting the existence of God, the atheist may be guilty of a huge fallacy. Intrinsically, the atheist believes that since God's existence is improvable, He does not exist. Nonetheless, since it may also be impossible to prove that God does not exist, the atheist's main premise lacks true validity. Hence, the proof behind the atheist's denial of God's existence cannot logically justify his belief towards a random form of creation.

Yet, the rational premises behind atheism do possess the power to turn persons who were once believers into atheists. As a consequence, personal belief systems are fundamental to the definition of an individual's identity. Since all beliefs are doubtable, every individual's system of beliefs will be entirely unique.

This leaves us back to the beginning, where the belief in God's existence is entirely based on each individual's will, and not on any kinds of certain evidence. Individuals on both sides of the debate may have an equivalent basis behind their particular system of beliefs. In every case, the individual will be faced with the choice of either believing in God or becoming an atheist. Indeed, only his personal and subjective beliefs will serve as the main source behind his faith. Regarding his choice, the individual can neither prove that his beliefs are true, nor can he prove the contrary. Every individual's faith, or lack of faith, appears to be entirely rational, according to his own subjective frame of mind. Yet, both the theist and the atheist must agree with the fact that even if some premise cannot be proved on a universal basis, this does not entail the fact that it is not true. Therefore, both individuals must agree with the fact that each belief set is warranted, despite the fact that it may be false.

In a subsequent fashion, any forms of debate on the subject of the existence of God will usually be useless and nonsensical. In a similar fashion, determining a single definition of God should also face complications. Any single religion's definition may be true, but it is equally possible that God could possess every quality that may be found within all possible religions. Differing attributes will mainly symbolize differing personal values related to our material and immaterial existence.

Thus, the individual can choose to follow the most important principles stressed within each religion, or he may remain loyal to a single faith. The most important aspect, however, is based on the effects that a religion has over the individual's character. If some religious belief grants peace to the individual, then it may be a belief that is entirely inseparable from his existence. Likewise, when a religious belief promotes the well-being of an entire community, it may be equally inseparable from human culture. Yet, on the same note, a religious belief that causes feelings of dissension or strife within the individual may serve no true purpose, whatsoever.

Agnosticism, in actuality, has contributed towards the beauty of human civilization. The agnostic belief system reflects upon the individual's power of choice. However, agnosticism is not the same as atheism. By definition, agnostics believe that it is impossible to know whether or not God exists. Atheists, on the other hand, hold the firm belief that God does not exist.

The agnostic belief system serves humanity because it forces the individual to focus on his material existence. In a subsequent fashion, this will empower him with a greater ability to recognize and embrace all of the forms of natural beauty that exists within our physical world. In a corresponding fashion, it also forces the individual to direct his focus towards that which is knowable within our natural world. It is impossible to prove, with absolute certainty, that God does exist because He has never revealed Himself to us within our material world. In a similar fashion, persons may deny the existence of an immaterial world simply because no human being can prove, without some degree of doubt, that an immaterial world does indeed exist. Since agnosticism places doubt on the existence of an afterlife, this encourages the individual to direct his focus towards his present day, physical life.

With respect to material objects, it may be absolutely possible to prove, for example, that this particular piece of paper exists. I can see and feel this physical object, through my sensory perceptions, and I can also be confident in the fact that if I showed this object to my friend, he will experience an equivalent perception. Nonetheless, the immaterial world, due to its metaphysical nature, can only be perceived by my mind. I do not view anything that is immaterial through my five senses. The immaterial is perceived strictly through my intellect. On the one hand, I do possess the ability to communicate my personal conceptions, but I do not possess the capability to know, with absolute conviction, that my partner will view an exact replication of my thought. This provides the foundation behind a rational doubt against the existence of an immaterial world, while it simultaneously proves the fact that the physical world is concrete and that it does exist. The doubt that exists against the existence of God has similar difficulties, based on the imprecise sharing and exchange of one's thoughts. Consequently, it is this degree of doubt that forces all persons to direct their focus more towards the concrete material world, and less towards the immaterial world. This latter aspect further extends to both qualitative and quantitative forms of beauty that may exist within our physical world.

Every theist's belief in the immaterial world will be entirely based on subjective reasoning. Again, there exists no clear and objective material evidence that will prove, beyond a reasonable doubt that God exists. Theists will promote the principle of faith, while the atheist will promote the concept of doubt. Since God does not take on a material form, and since He does not choose to reveal Himself to us within the physical world, the individual's doubt will always be justified, at least within his own point of view. Nonetheless, we must conclude the possibility that since He has not revealed Himself to us, if He does exist, this is explicably what He wanted. Hence, if God does exist, then He may have wanted human beings to possess some degree of doubt regarding His existence. In turn, the atheist may then ask the question why?

To answer this question, we must examine whether the concepts of faith and doubt are important to human civilization. The answer to this question may inevitably be yes. The limitations within the human intellect will always produce subjective beliefs, based either on faith or doubt. Faith may be categorized as a positive subjective belief, while doubt may be categorized as a negative subjective belief.

In fact, we have created indubitable knowledge through the ideology of science, and through science we have increased our quality of life. The creation of medicine may be the most formidable invention of man. Instead of merely relying on divine forms of healing, we have created medicines, cures and other forms of treatments for those who are affected by illness. Similarly, instead of relying on God for justice, we have created a system that punishes evil doers. Subsequently, because we lack the ability to prove God's existence, we have, in turn, improved and cultivated our own material existence. Since we cannot prove the existence of an immaterial afterlife, this further compels us to focus on our physical existence. Through this focus, human civilization has evolved, not merely through a material perspective, but also culturally.

Persons who hold doubts regarding our physical universe will, thus, motivate our quest to gain knowledge of it. It is impossible to know whether or not there is life in Antarctica, if no person has actually explored that territory. Knowledge of the Antarctic can only be accomplished after some researcher has actually physically explored it. Therefore, we cannot hold a concrete belief that there are forms of life in Antarctica, until some individual has actually confirmed this hypothesis. Doubt motivates persons to confirm their particular beliefs, and this leads to the acquisition of concrete knowledge.

The limitations of the human intellect may make total knowledge of the universe an impossible feat. Yet, it is the concept of doubt that encourages us to explore our world, and in time, the entire physical universe. In this case, the concept of doubt is important to our civilization, because it motivates the individual to acquire concrete forms of knowledge. Since knowledge leads to all of the accomplishments found within the realm of human society, it may be the most important property that defines the true driving force behind our civilization.

After we have acquired total knowledge of our own physical world, we may then question whether or not there are any other forms of life that exist within the entire universe. Persons with faith will hold the belief that there are other forms of life that exist within our universe, while persons with doubts will hold the belief that the only forms of life, within the entire universe, merely exist on Earth. From a scientific perspective, it would be entirely narrow-minded to conclude that the only forms of life that exist in the universe may only be found within our own material world. If it is illogical to conclude the latter notion, it may also be, consistently, similarly illogical to deny the possible existence of another kind of world, based on the concepts of the spiritual or immaterial.

Thus, persons who possess a faith in the existence of God will also believe in the existence of an immaterial world. Yet, since these individuals lack knowledge regarding the immaterial world, their concept of it may be entirely based on their imaginations. As a consequence, we may now draw a direct correlation between faith and the individual's imagination. In actuality, all forms of creativity are first born through an individual's imagination.

Therefore, while faith stimulates our imagination, doubt motivates us to acquire actual forms of knowledge. Nonetheless, both faith and doubt possesses a further role within human civilization. In essence, our imagination is required for all forms of creativity. In addition, knowledge is also necessary for our ability to create. Accordingly, both our imagination and forms of concrete knowledge are central to our creative process.

Consider the subject of architecture. First of all, the individual must imagine an appropriate and aesthetically pleasing physical structure. The latter form of creativity is entirely dependent on the architect's imagination. Nevertheless, the actual creation of the building itself requires further knowledge within the fields of mathematics and engineering. Hence, the architect's ability to create also depends entirely on technical forms of knowledge. As such, all human creations are dependent first upon our imagination, and then upon the knowledge that we have gained, pertaining to our material world. Thus, both elements of faith and doubt are crucial for our ability to create.

When we imagine, we are responsible for the creation of an immaterial idea. Likewise, when we investigate, we may discover some kind of a material fact. With respect to faith, the individual's journey will first be motivated by his will to believe. Yet, the element of doubt may also stimulate our imagination. After we utilize our imagination, this will then motivate us towards exploration and after we have completed our explorations, we will then be granted with concrete forms of knowledge.

Subsequently, perhaps the journey of exploration, through both our faith and our doubts, may be equally important to us, in comparison to the actual ideas and knowledge that we gain because of these mental processes. Between our will, and our adoption of a certain belief, there exists some length of experience. With respect to faith, between the individual's will to believe and his imagined thoughts, the journey that he takes may be essentially marked by the spirit of acceptance. In a similar fashion, with respect to doubt, in between the individual's will to disbelieve and the concrete knowledge that he gains, his fundamental experience will be characterized by the concept of rational judgment. These two paths of experience may be the two most significant aspects related to all of our beliefs.

Therefore, in a journey marked by the spirit of acceptance, the individual will be open to embrace a multitude of differing kinds of possibilities. On the other hand, persons whose experiences are characterized by the concept of rational judgment will possess discipline. When a faithful individual meets a doubtful person, their particular experiences will be the main focal point, with respect to their exchange of knowledge. If these two types of individuals form an intimate relationship with each other, the experiences of one individual will, then, shape the experiences of the other. In the end, these two individuals will form a kind of bond where each person will mould his character according to the experiences of the other. Through this solidarity, the resulting spirit that is produced, in both individuals, will be based on the principle of mutual respect.

On a further note, those individuals who possess little faith will have their experiences marked by a lack of acceptance. These individuals will not embrace unique and differing kinds of spirits. Likewise, individuals who possess little doubts will lack important forms of discretion. These individuals may be exceedingly lax or careless, especially towards any instances of maladaptive behaviours. When these two types of individuals join together, the resulting character that results will be based mainly on the vice of discrimination.

Therefore, the concept of agnosticism has served to improve human culture, because it is a principle based on realism, and this encourages us to gain knowledge of our natural world. Likewise, it also forces human culture to place a higher value over our physical existence. Furthermore, agnostics may actually increase the theist's faith in God. Within the theist's frame of mind, to believe in God, one is not required to prove His existence. The only kind of proof required to have faith remains solely in his subjective beliefs. Since his faith does not depend on his ability to prove his beliefs to other persons, the concept of agnosticism should have no bearing against his faith. Therefore, since the agnostic's view is irrelevant to the theist, this provides him with another reason to increase his faith in God's existence.

This additional premise enables the theist to cherish his own distinct, unique and independent rationale. Yet, agnosticism further affects us spiritually, since it paves the way for the existence of multiple forms of religion. Within every religion, loyalty may be paramount. Therefore, the theist will usually remain loyal to a single religion, or system of belief. However, because of the agnostic's point of view, there may be no form of hierarchy that ranks one religion over another. Accordingly, no religion may be deemed as a more superior faith. The agnostic, thus, inadvertently creates a form of equality among all distinct faiths. In turn, from a political perspective, every faith should be equal under the rule of law.

Theoretically, some atheists may hold a specific definition in relation to the attributes that God should possess, if He truly existed. The individual may then become a disbeliever due of the fact that there does not exist a specific entity that possesses the particular attributes, which are laid out by the atheist. In actuality, the atheist mainly holds his beliefs due to the problem of evil. Within the atheist's frame of mind, the existence of a supremely moral, omniscient, and omnipotent God may be wholly incompatible with the existence of evil in our physical world. Indeed, if God did possess the latter three attributes, then He could have created a world without any forms of suffering. Hence, the concept of evil could form the primary foundation behind the atheist's beliefs. Within his frame of mind, the existence of God is incompatible with the existence of pain and distress in our world. Therefore, the atheist concludes that there is no God simply because there exists too many instances of misery and suffering within our natural world. The atheist may hold the further belief that if God did exist, then no persons would ever suffer from any degrees of hardships, during their entire lifetime.

In addition, while some persons may possess a relationship with God, other persons will lack an integral ability to communicate with

Him. These latter individuals may hold the further belief that since God does not respond to their wishes, He does not exist. As a result, these individuals will then lose faith in His existence. Other individuals will become atheists due to the premise that since God neither acknowledges nor is concerned about them, He does not exist. Indeed, these persons will place expectations on the attributes or properties that should belong to God. They may also hold the belief that they possess an inborn right to place forms of personal expectations on Him, even though He is an intrinsically free being. Therefore, some individuals will deny the existence of God, simply because His spiritual makeup does not conform to their personal expectations.

The element of slavery may also be relevant to the atheist's mind-set. Individuals who believe in the existence of a supremely moral being may, as a consequence, adopt the role to serve God and His interests. Yet, some persons will perceive this kind of dedication, essentially, as a form of slavery. Therefore, the latter individuals may become atheists, simply because they do not wish to become a servant of God. What these individuals do not realize is the true power of free will, which if He exists, was granted to us by Him through our very nature. Therefore, any individual who wishes to serve God does so entirely through his free will, and likewise, any individual, who so desires, may refrain from accepting this particular duty.

The atheist's problem of evil may refute the existence of a supremely moral and omnipotent creator of our universe. Nonetheless, this also seems to indicate that every person's idea of God will differ. In actuality, no theist will dispute the fact that there does exist evil and suffering within our world. The theist maintains his faith despite the fact that there do exist instances of evil within our material world. However, within the theist's mind, evil is not necessarily a product of God's will, but it is mainly the product a sentient being's free will.

As a consequence, the theist and the atheist may be similar to each other in the fact that they both believe in a specific definition, regarding the true essence of God. Therefore, in addition to the agnostic belief system, the atheistic belief system should be granted with a form of political equality, when compared to any single religion. The equality established between differing religious beliefs, including agnosticism and atheism, enables a nation's government to create general policies, which are independent of any single religion. Instead of defining a set spiritual way of life, political policies are mainly directed towards the physical existence of human beings, whose primary aim is to promote the greatest possible way of life. The absence of religious principles, therefore, enables a governing body to focus entirely on our material nature, which is the most direct method that will effectually improve our quality of life.

The theist will be open to accept the existence of God, no matter what properties He may possess. Faith is always dependent on the rationale of the individual. Yet, the individual's conception of God will be entirely based on his knowledge of the physical world. The individual's knowledge of the physical world always leads to a universal undertaking, pertaining to one's conception of God. It is reasonable to assume that all of the properties in the universe also exist in its creator, if the individual believes in the law of reproduction. Pertaining to the law of hierarchy, it may be equally reasonable to assume that some entity governs the entire physical universe. If the latter two laws are true, then God may be conceived as being who possesses an unlimited, intelligent free spirit. However the individual perceives God, His most universally accepted attribute will be based on the premise that He is the fundamental creator of our world. As the first cause of all possible causes in our world, every person who is a theist will share the same conception that God is the absolute father of all forms of life within our universe.

On a further note, agnosticism also builds the foundation behind both innocence and insecurity. Religious persons do acknowledge that some form of doubt does subsist against the existence of God. Yet, they also realize that an equivalent form of doubt may be present against the atheist's particular system of beliefs. Since these two instances of doubt may be equivalent to each other, this provides the theist with a logical reason to disregard all forms of doubt that may exist against his particular beliefs. Therefore, the theist demonstrates innocence whenever he disregards any kinds of a logical doubt. On the other hand, the atheist demonstrates insecurity when he realizes that the forms of doubt that exist against theism may be equally applied to the ideology of atheism.

For the most part, theists will not consider the kinds of doubt that exist against their system of beliefs, in the same manner that the atheist does not consider the kinds of doubt that may exist against his particular system of beliefs. As a consequence, by omitting forms of doubt in relation to his religious beliefs, the theist's faith in God will be further strengthened, and fortified. Indeed, agnosticism does pave the way for a form of equality between theistic and atheistic modes of belief. It also provides a level ground regarding forms of doubt that exist against each particular system of belief. As a consequence, this enables the theist to direct his focus solely on the rational foundation behind his beliefs, which subsequently serves to reinforce his own subjective faith. The individual should experience an even stronger form of faith that would not exist without the presence of the agnostic belief system. By acknowledging the existence of both forms of doubt, those individuals who maintain their beliefs can exhibit a higher degree of faith, essentially due to the fact that they cannot be persuaded to change their system of beliefs, due solely to the element of doubt. As a result, doubt should never be a factor that will dissuade the individual's distinct system of beliefs. The act of negating doubt enables the individual to place a higher value upon his own unique and distinct system of faith.

Within an infinite universe, all kinds of worlds are possible. Therefore, when we consider our total knowledge of the physical world, both theories of creation do remain plausible. Whether or not God exists, there may be more evidence that supports His existence, as opposed to against. If we possess an immaterial mind, then God may be the only intrinsic source behind the phenomenon of the immaterial. In actuality, the individual's inclinations towards his beliefs on creation will essentially be based on forms of subjective elements that will lack any forms of a universal proof or justification.

Perhaps the existence of beauty may provide the theist with the best reason to justify his rationale. All that is beautiful will invoke a high positive emotion in the individual, like joy or serenity. Both joy and serenity are high emotions because they are rarely experienced, during the totality of one's life. Elements that do cause feelings of joy and serenity essentially add meaning and significance to one's own existence. Therefore, our ability to both recognize and appreciate forms of beauty creates a kind of harmony between the individual and the natural world. Every instance of beauty in our world is important because of its power over the individual's emotional state.

In contrast, negative emotions only detract elements from the individual's life, since these types of emotions will mainly draw our focus away from forms of beauty, on to that which intrinsically lacks any forms of beauty. In a similar fashion, when any forms of beauty are lost, our entire civilization will also experience a loss. In essence, our civilization has lost something that brings delight to our soul. The perception of beauty, indeed, is an important part of our sensory experiences, and sensory experiences are a valuable part of human existence.

When we lose some form of physical beauty, we have essentially lost something that is precious to our sense of sight. Furthermore, if we were to lose all correlative forms of physical beauty, this could be comparable to losing our sense of sight. Without any forms of physical beauty, our sense of sight would be less significant to our existence. All the same, if there still existed music, our sense of audition would be more important than our sense of sight. Nevertheless, within our material world, there exists many unique and differing kinds of beauty. This makes all five of our senses important elements of our existence. So if there were no forms of beauty present within our universe, our sensory experiences would have less meaning to our material existence.

If everything were beautiful, then nothing would be meaningless. Correspondingly, if everything was meaningless, there would be no forms of beauty. In actuality, the purely innocent may take the view that almost everything in the world is beautiful, while the purely insecure may take the alternate view that almost everything in the world lacks beauty.

A beautiful life is one that has meaning. Meaning signifies importance, and importance signifies a necessity. This form of necessity indicates that the individual is an integral component within some other person's life. From an objective perspective, a life has value when its course has had a positive effect on some other form of life. Therefore, the beautiful life is one that has an immanent value to another living being. In a similar fashion, the life that has a continuously negative effect on another living being can never be beautiful. All that which lacks beauty can neither be meaningful, nor valuable to the innocent human being. Beauty represents only the highest ideals, and this is what makes it rare.

Hence, beauty transcends both space and time. It exists conceptually, mainly within the individual's mind. More specifically, it is a conceptual reaction to some phenomenon that causes rapture within the individual's soul. On the other hand, the material world is defined, necessarily, through the elements of space and time. As a consequence, instances of beauty will additionally create a unity between the material and the immaterial components that exist in nature. Our ability to perceive beauty enables us to perceive all of the meaningful and significant immaterial spirits that exist in our natural world. Nonetheless, the original source of all forms of beauty in our world must also possess the attribute of beauty. Therefore, when the individual possesses the ability to perceive differing forms of beauty in our world, he will also possess the ability to perceive the intrinsic spirit of God.

In a universe with God, life is a meaningful creation, and thus, life has some type of purpose. Moreover, existence, itself, may be viewed as a wonder. Since existence is a wonder, it is also a gift. Nonetheless, a gift cannot be granted by something that lacks intelligence. Only an intelligent being may be the primary cause behind a gift. Consequently, existence, itself, must be something that is valued and appreciated by both the theist and God Himself.

Within this universe, every form of life possesses some unique purpose. Therefore, from a fair and open-minded perspective, the element of death may also serve some sort of purpose. Nevertheless, the nature of this purpose will be beyond the scope of human understanding. Indeed, existence will always be associated with a physical end, but it may not necessarily be associated with an immaterial end. If this holds true, then death within our material world would be the element of human existence that merely marks a new kind of birth into the spiritual world.

Death mainly occurs during the absence of beauty. The beauty in question, though, is never based on physical forms of beauty. Death only occurs during the absence of spiritual beauty. This is due to the fact that physical beauty will always be entirely subjective and dependent on each observer's point of view. In contrast, spiritual forms of beauty are not subjective. They are universal. The nature and makeup of spiritual beauty never changes, with respect to all living beings. Yet, physical appearances do change, simply due to the characteristic of age. Therefore, spiritual forms of beauty never change, while physical forms of beauty do change. As a consequence, all forms of spiritual beauty remain unchanging, resolute, and timeless.

Within an intelligent creator's mind, death may be as significant as life itself. In the case of a spiritual afterlife, God's reasons behind our physical deaths may then be grasped. However, our emotional states tend to blind our intellect, in these cases. Our emotional experiences are simply a natural part of existing as a human being. What we do know is that death marks the end of our physical existence. Yet, we do not know much more beyond the latter fact. We do not know if death is a permanent end, or whether we will continue to subsist in some other manner. It is possible that we may be reborn, in some manner, back into our physical world. It may be equally possible that we will be destined to continue living within some form of immaterial or spiritual world. Yet, it is this lack of knowledge that causes pain and sorrow whenever we lose the company of a loved one.

If we were able to answer these questions, without any forms of doubt, it may be possible that our culture may then come to terms with the phenomenon of death. Correspondingly, if we possessed the ability to comprehend God's reason for death within our physical world, it may be possible that we will then accept this phenomenon. All we know is that death within the material world is permanent. If we experience emotions whenever an individual has passed away, then it is in human nature to question the value of death, and its ultimate role within our existence. Our doubts lead to anguish, and the inevitable continuation of our emotional responses makes the concept of death both intolerable, and conceivably, without any kinds of worth. Indeed, we value our material existence so much that we view its end without any kinds of a rational acceptance. If existence is a gift, then death cannot be valuable. Within the individual's frame of mind, the wonder of existence, itself, makes the concept of death entirely illogical. Yet within God's mind, there is some rational reason behind its origin.

Indeed, our vision of utopia may be limited to what we perceive, both through our senses and through our imagination. Yet, our concept of utopia excludes the phenomenon of death, especially when it happens to our loved ones. In these cases, since we are blinded by our emotions, we may then question the value of death, in accordance with our physical existence. We may also question if God is truly an infinitely moral and omnipotent being. If He does possess these qualities, then it should be the case that He will sustain our existence in some other manner, due to our love for existence. Nonetheless, our concept of utopia cannot equal God's concept of utopia, simply because the scope of our intellect is limited, while He possesses the quality of omniscience. We do know that if God does exist, He does so merely within the immaterial world. The existence of this immaterial world implicates the possibility that we will, additionally, experience some form of reality within it.

Every person possesses a unique imagination, with differing concepts of a utopian world. If God were to create a utopian world based on the totality of ideas produced by the human imagination, this world could possess an infinite amount of spiritual qualities. Yet, there may also be many elements that would not exist within our concept of a utopian world. For example, in every person's conception of utopia, no forms of violence would exist. Similarly, no individuals would ever be subject to any forms of abuse. In a consistent fashion, no kinds of wars would exist within our concept of utopia. Therefore, in our concept of a utopian world, there would be an absence of pain, in the form of grave injustices. Absolute authority would not exist within our concept of utopia, at least in the form of an unjust totalitarian regime. Similarly, the granting of all possible innate rights would be a primary foundation behind this world. A universal conception of utopia would comprise a world where the individual will be granted every right to a beautiful life.

On the other hand, if God is neither omniscient nor omnipotent, then it may be possible that the concept of death may reflect upon His own limitations. This is a possibility that provides all human beings with a substantial reason to value the gift of existence, to the utmost degree. Our increased value towards existence will naturally extend towards our family members and friends, and this makes death a kind of concept that we will never come to terms with. Hence, even though limitations are a natural part of our existence, some of these limitations may be impossible to accept.

Our knowledge of the essence of God can only come from the truths that are established within our physical universe. As the almighty creator, we can only understand His intrinsic spirit through the kinds of unique and differing spirits that exist within all other forms of life. Whatever properties that exist in one form of life must also exist in Him, since all of His creations should essentially be a physical extension of His immaterial ideas. Hence, increased knowledge of our universe will translate into more knowledge regarding the true essence of God.

Nonetheless, we may also know Him through the non-living entities that are present within the universe. For example, the moon could signify His love for His creations. Similarly, comets could symbolize the presence of other kinds of wonders that may exist beyond our own solar system. Likewise, shooting stars could represent the power and authority that God possesses over the entire cosmos. Whether or not these interpretations are true depends solely on the truths of His existence. If God does exist, then every property within the universe must also be found in Him, while if He does not exist, nothing in the world will symbolize anything.

In both theories of creation, the birth of our universe will be due to a single cause. Either God created our universe, or a few particles of matter have evolved into our universe. If the latter case is true, it may be equally reasonable to question how the origin of these molecules, themselves, came into existence. Through the model of infinite regression, we could postulate that some entity A is responsible for the creation of some entity B, which is responsible for the creation of some entity C, and that entity C is the direct cause of our universe. However, we are still left with the question of how entity A came into existence. Indeed, there is no problem of infinite regression if are to attribute God as the sole cause of our universe. This is due to the fact that even though we know very little about Him, our knowledge of Him does implicate an infinite amount of power. Our lack of knowledge regarding the infinite, thus, can be extended with respect to a lack of knowledge regarding the cause of His existence. Therefore, due this lack of knowledge, the problem of infinite regression does not apply, if we do consider God to be the sole cause of our universe. In this case, our ignorance regarding the total nature of God serves us in that it grants us with a less problematic theory of creation.

The individual cannot rationally deny the existence of God, if he cannot provide another reasonable account for the creation of our universe. The atheist denies the existence of God; however his alternative simply assumes another theory of creation, which at current times remains similarly problematic. The atheist merely provides another alternative to God, without providing any substantial evidence that would make his beliefs any more likely than the theist's beliefs.

Accordingly, the problem of infinite regression does provide a similar degree of doubt against the theory of evolution, in the same manner that the problem of evil provides a form of doubt against the theory of an intelligent design. The theist holds that God is the first and prime cause of our universe, while the atheist holds a form of material creation that lacks both intelligence and any forms of morality. This division within our communities will be entirely based on the individual's personal system of beliefs. Opposing beliefs will lead to differing consequences.

Perhaps, to solve the problem regarding the origins of our universe, the individual must examine the particular reasons that lead to his distinct beliefs. The reasons behind his chosen belief system will be just as important as its conclusion. This makes both the theist and the atheist's system of beliefs entirely subjective, where the reasons behind their beliefs may depend mainly upon their diverse outlooks on life itself. Within the theist's frame of mind, the atheist may be irrational, while within the atheist's frame of mind, the theist may be equally without reason. Accordingly, the existence of God can only be proven to individuals who hold a similar outlook on life. Persons who believe that all forms of life on Earth have meaning will ultimately believe in an intelligent and moral creator, while those persons who possess a trivial attitude towards other forms of life on Earth will ultimately believe in a form of random or anomalous creation. Accordingly, the kinds of values upheld within both the theist's and the atheist's rationale will wholly justify their differing systems of belief.

Objectively, opposites bolster our will to choose. In fact, the human intellect may grasp a clearer comprehension of some ideas, due essentially to the existence of opposing concepts. Accordingly, God may have materialized the idea of death, so that we could grasp a higher understanding of life. The same may be true of love. He may have created the capacity to hate, so that we could acquire a concrete definition of love. Likewise, human beings may be finite creatures simply so that we could discover some degree of understanding, regarding the infinite.

Actually, in many cases, we fundamentally desire opposites. For example, when it is cold outside, we desire warmth. Likewise, when it is dark outside, we will then desire light. Nonetheless, at other times, persons tend to stay away from opposites. For instance, persons who experience happiness do not want to associate with those who continually experience anger. Similarly, persons who are selfless do not become friends with those who are mainly selfish. Opposites, then, are concepts that contrast one thing from another.

The static and dynamic characters could also be conceived as opposites, due to the fact that the emotions of anger and happiness will share a similar relationship. Both anger and happiness are powerful emotions. Both emotions can permanently mould the individual into a fixed perspective of life. As such, the good life can never be more than one of happiness. Since happiness is an immaterial emotion, it is a concept that essentially transcends the material world. In essence, spiritual life forces will provide the main source behind feelings of happiness, and likewise, some forms of material entities may not necessarily provide any feelings of happiness. In addition, happiness leads to peace, simply because the emotion of happiness creates a harmonious feeling within the individual's soul.

In contrast, emotions of anger originate through a disordered soul. Since happiness is responsible for a form of internal harmony, the absence of happiness may be equally responsible for a lack of internal order. In turn, the disordered soul then leads to the development of an angry soul. In fact, disorder is the main cause of a warring state. A community that possesses no order cannot be truly categorized as a cooperative social network. Thus, an inability to establish a cooperative social network will inevitably lead to war. This makes tolerance and intolerance polar opposites of one another, which respectively reflect the truest essences of a nation state and civil unrest. On an individual level, tolerance leads to a flourishing life, while intolerance leads to a life that is lacking. Similarly, the opposites of benevolence and deceit also vanquish the individual's soul into either companionship or lonesomeness.

Happiness may be the most beautiful emotion, while anger is that emotion which lacks the most beauty. This also makes kindness one of the most beautiful principles, while in a simultaneous fashion it makes egoism the most monstrous category of action. Similarly, respect reflects upon the most beautiful intellect, while disrespect relates solely to the most ignorant of all intellects.

On the contrary, pleasure is mainly derived through material objects, like food and drink. Therefore, those who possess material forms of wealth may potentially experience a lifetime full of physical pleasures. Yet, happiness is not equivalent to pleasure because it is an emotion that is entirely related to the individual's spiritual being. Therefore, within the immaterial world, it may be possible that we will not experience any forms of pleasure, but, on the same note, we may still experience the emotion of happiness. Pleasure does belong to the same class of emotions as happiness, although it should be categorized as a lower emotion. It is a lower emotion because of the fact that it is an emotion that is dependent on the material world. Moreover, feelings of pleasure are lower in intensity when compared to the emotional states of joy or serenity. Hence, the distinction between pleasure and happiness illustrates the main difference between feelings derived through the material, from feelings derived through the immaterial.

Therefore, happiness will always be associated with the immaterial, while pleasure will always be associated with the material. Immaterial sources of beauty will naturally cause feelings of happiness, while material sources of beauty will cause feelings of pleasure. Yet, the concept of death has only been linked to our material existence. No individual can correlate death with our spiritual existence. As a consequence, since death is merely associated with our material existence, it is a concept that can only be correlated with an absence of pleasure. Likewise, since the concept of death cannot be associated with our spiritual existence, it is only the absence of our immaterial spirit that can truly cause a lack of happiness. Thus, while the absence of some person's material existence may cause a deficiency within our sources of pleasure, it is only the absence of an individual's immaterial spirit that will cause a deficiency within our sources of happiness.

Why all forms of life die may be beyond anybody's comprehension. If God is truly omnipotent, then He could have created a world where nobody dies. Correspondingly, it is conceivable that within this world, there would also be no forms of evil. Nonetheless, the concept of opposites may be a key principle behind His creativity. The opposite of man is woman, and likewise the opposite of freedom is slavery. It is highly probable that God created opposites to grant sentient beings with the power of complete personal autonomy. Indeed, in the creation of our physical universe, God still possessed the freedom not to create any forms of life. He created all sentient beings with the power to either embrace or disregard forms of beauty. He created forms of life that could choose to procreate or abstain from creating anything. Indeed, if all sentient forms of life refused to procreate, then the natural world would contain less forms of beauty. More importantly, though, the continued existence of any species of sentient beings depends entirely on the free will of those who currently exist.

Therefore, if every sentient species refused to procreate, all that would exist in our universe would be forms of vegetation, and non-conscious physical objects. Yet, non-conscious material objects have no influence with respect to their physical existence. Contrariwise, forms of vegetation do possess the power to reproduce, yet they lack the freedom to refrain from committing the latter action. Therefore, to differentiate physical objects from autonomous beings, God granted a conscious will to some species of life, fundamentally to grant these beings with the necessary power to either embrace existence, or reject it.

When we examine the concept of the infinite, instead of human beings, it is possible that God could have created an Earth with some other kind of ruling species. Similarly, there are an infinite amount of possible worlds that He could have created, instead of the Earth. From a rational perspective, God created reproducing forms of life because this is a part of His own spiritual nature. He also granted forms of life with an incrementally increasing amount of freedom because He possesses a similar form of autonomy. Hence, God may have created a universe based on opposites to heighten the powers of freedom and choice within every sentient being.

In the creation of a finite world, God has granted us with the potential to grasp some idea of the infinite. In actuality, no person possesses a concrete conception of the infinite, due simply to the limits of his intellect. Nonetheless, because we are exposed to the concept of the finite on a daily basis, we do, in a subsequent fashion, possess some inkling with respect to the infinite. In effect, most persons do possess a concrete understanding regarding the concept of opposites, and it is this comprehension, alone, that enables us to imagine some phenomenon that may be infinite in nature. Therefore, in the creation of opposites, God has graced human beings with a limited potential to conceive the true nature of both the universe, and His existence.

Indeed, there are a multitude of other phenomena in the world that grants human beings with the power to conceive the concept of opposites. Examine the phenomenon of black and white. From the laymen's point of view, black and white are colours that contrast each other to such a degree that they are considered as opposites. Technically, black and white are not truly categorized as colours. Black reflects no forms of light, and thus it may be defined merely as the absence of colour. On the other hand, white is a reflection of all colours, and thus it may be defined as a mixture of all colours. However, this technical definition of black and white also reflects upon the fact that they are opposites.

Consider the scenario that no forms of light have ever existed. For example, if an individual were born deep within a cave, everything that he sees would be black. In this particular situation, we must question whether this person would be able to imagine the many colours of a rainbow, if he has never perceived any forms of light. If he left this cave, he would be able to see the many differing colours that exist within our natural world, essentially because he will have been exposed to some degree of light. Yet, if he remained within that cave for the totality of his life, he would probably lack the ability to either imagine or understand the concept of a colour, due essentially to a lack of light.

Therefore, light is necessary for our perception of colour. In a corresponding manner, individual consciousness is necessary for our perception of the spirit. All forms of life embody some kind of spirit. Yet, in order to perceive these spirits, the individual first requires a consciousness. Compare sentient beings to forms of plant life. Since forms of vegetation lack the perception of sight, it is this reason why they will also lack the ability to perceive any forms of colour. In an equivalent manner, since they also lack a consciousness, they will further lack the ability to perceive other kinds of immaterial spirits.

Accordingly, individual consciousness is necessary for the perception of spirit, in the same manner that light is necessary for our perception of colour. For instance, differing flowers may symbolize differing aspects of love. Yet, without any forms of a consciousness, no entity would possess the raw ability to fathom these concepts. To exist, then, may be simply to possess a form of spirit, while to exist with some form of individual consciousness may be to live a life with the added ability to perceive the immaterial spirit.

In a corresponding fashion, one may further question which concept best describes the opposite of existence. Indeed, we cannot compare human existence to the existence of an inanimate object, simply because these are merely two differing classes of physical phenomena. In the same manner, it may not be rational to compare our existence with the lowest form of life, which is plant life. In the latter case, we are essentially comparing a form of existence without any forms of consciousness, to a form of existence with some form of individual consciousness. Therefore, the opposite of human existence also cannot be a non-sentient form of life. In some sense, to exist as a human may be to possess a unique soul, while the opposite of this may intrinsically be nothingness.

Any spirit that possesses some form of consciousness should be said to possess a soul. The human mind may be conceived to be comprised of the individual's intellect, centre of emotions and array of principles. Yet, when we include his unique experiences, this immaterial phenomenon should be defined as his soul. Every person does possess a unique physical body. Therefore, to exist as a human may be to exist as the culmination of a unique immaterial soul with a unique physical body. Nonetheless, our soul is the most intrinsic part of our identity. Without it, our bodies would merely be lifeless physical objects. Accordingly, it is this latter entity that would be comparable to any other inanimate object that exists within our natural world.

Hence, even though the opposite of existence is non-existence, how can we conceive the concept of non-existence? In fact, non-existence, itself, must be defined as nothingness, because something that lacks a unique physical body and soul cannot be defined as anything. Indeed, life as a human being may be properly defined as the totality of one's experiences, or the totality of one's existence within the material world. As such, the concept that best defines the entire opposite of human existence must be defined as a totality without any forms of a spirit, experience, or a material body. Therefore, the true opposite of existence must be non-existence, or in other words, nothingness.

The concepts of randomness and order may also be conceived as opposites. Therefore, in a sense, the big bang theory may be the complete opposite of the theory of intelligent creation. According to the big bang theory, our universe would have been mainly created through a sporadic fashion. Within this universe, it is entirely possible that another world could have evolved, instead of the Earth. Likewise, it is further possible that no human beings would have ever been created, and that something else could have come into existence in our place. Therefore, it is entirely possible that the Earth could have been created without any human beings. This marks a possible universe without human beings.

Similarly, it is further possible that everything that exists within the entire universe may have never come into existence. Hence, there is also a real possibility that no forms of life would have ever come into being within our universe. This entails the notion that all forms of life were created by mere chance. Since the entire universe would have been born in a random and sporadic fashion, it is also possible that another kind of Earth, with totally differing characteristics, may have come into existence by the exact same cause. This would make all forms of life on Earth equally as purposeless, and hence, highly comparable to any non-living material object. If this is true, then everything that exists within our universe will have no significance, whatsoever. Within this universe, no single instances of life will have any meaning, because it was entirely possible that no forms of life would have ever come into existence. Indeed, within this universe, nothing will have any meaning, because there was a necessary and compulsory chance that it may have never come into existence.

Hence, both life and death would have no meaning, simply because everything in the universe was created merely by accident, without any meaningful cause. This cause is not meaningful because human existence would not be a necessary element in the design of the universe, and thus, something else could have come into existence in our place. Human life, then, would be no more valuable than some other lifeless object, simply because it is highly possible that we may have never existed at all. The random and accidental creation of our universe will, thus, make death equally as inconsequential, in comparison to life itself. As such, the concept of death could be viewed both without any kinds of significance, and as merely an unfortunate element linked to life.

If all forms of life may have easily never come into existence, this makes every form of life a randomly created anomaly, with no known future. Since all forms of life are merely a random creation, the future of status of our civilization will be equally determined at random. Human beings could exist forever, or we may become extinct. Both possibilities will remain equally as likely. Likewise, all of our accomplishments would lack meaning, simply because the future status of our civilization would always be questionable and uncertain.

Yet, we must ask the question that if all forms of life are merely a random creation, how is it possible for life to subsist within our universe? In actuality, if our universe was created purely at random, then the evolution of life will further possess no kinds of regularity, and the chance that all forms of life will continue to subsist should also be determined arbitrarily. Therefore, if the universe is evolving in a strictly random fashion, there is a real possibility that no forms of life will continue to survive. This is due to the fact that a strictly randomly evolving entity should not, intrinsically, be governed by anything that possesses the characteristic of universality. Nevertheless, through our observations, we do know that the Earth is governed by some universal laws, such as the laws of physics. In effect, the laws of physics represent a kind of constant, in that it regulates all of the material phenomena that exist on our planet.

All forms of life also require constants, for their continued survival. This constant comes in the form of nourishment. Therefore, if there were no constant supply of elements like oxygen, water, and nutrients, every form of life on Earth would eventually face extinction. Yet, there does exist a constant supply of life sustaining elements, within our natural world.

Accordingly, within a randomly evolving universe, the birth of any form of a constant does seem to be inconsistent and problematic. From a purely logical perspective, it may seem to be impossible for something that is random, by nature, to produce some form of a constant. If something is random, by definition, then how can it change its intrinsic essence, with respect to transforming into some kind of a constant? Ideologically, randomness and constants denote to two fundamentally diverging concepts. For instance, consider the act of gambling. It is an activity that would lose the characteristic of randomness, if it constantly produced a winner, or equally, if it constantly produced a loser.

Therefore, a random cause should always be directly correlated with a random end result. By its primary definition, a random result will never yield a constant outcome. Accordingly, the theory that something random can sustain something that is constant does require further explanation. Something that is random should always remain random, because that is its inherent nature. If this premise is logically sound, something that possesses a random nature can never produce any forms of a constant. Thus, if life was created purely at random, then the continued existence of all forms of life on Earth should also be determined at random. By this premise, it may be highly improbable that our world will continue to exist as it is, without experiencing any forms of major changes.

Yet, in actuality, there does exist many kinds of order that do govern our planet. Universal laws like the laws of physics seem to indicate that, at the very least, our world is governed by this particular constant. The existence of all other forms of science also seems to indicate that our natural world is governed by other kinds of laws, and thus other kinds of constants. In fact, the concept of science is based on the creation of laws, through experimentation and observation, and this necessarily entails the characteristic of universality. Many other laws, such as the laws of hierarchy and reproduction, remain entirely constant within our physical world.

Ecosystems illustrate a further kind of physical order within our natural world. Likewise, there exists a similar form of physical order, which governs the human body. In the same manner that the human body is lacking when one of its parts is malfunctioning, the same is true of all ecosystems. For example, due to its systematic nature, if the heart ceases to function, the human body will also cease to function. The same may be true regarding the most important components in any given ecosystem. Therefore, similar to the human body, an ecosystem will cease to function if enough of its components are not functioning, according to their proper nature. Indeed, any ecosystem that lacks some component, due to the extinction of some species of life, will lack completeness. As a consequence, without some system of order, every ecosystem would eventually disintegrate.

The philosophy of reason, furthermore, indicates a form of conceptual order present within our intellect. Reason is based on the ideology of cause and effect. Therefore, behind every action, we may associate some kind of motive. In a similar fashion, after every action we may associate some kind of outcome. Human emotions also surface as a reaction to some event. Therefore, both the human mind and the human body are governed by some conceptual system of order. When taken together, the property of order seems to be a fundamental element that exemplifies our hereditary nature.

Within most sentient species, the next generation of life will also require forms of constant nurturing, in the form of parenthood. Hence, if the act of parenting, itself, were a random anomaly, then the offspring of many species of life would not continue to survive. Therefore, parental care is another form of constant that is necessary for the survival of most species of life. This further makes the virtue of love an essential and necessary constant within our world. Indeed, the next generation of life cannot continue to subsist if the constants that are necessary for its survival appeared merely at random.

One element in life that remains entirely random, though, is based on the after effects of procreation. When two life forms procreate, the material nature of their offspring will be purely indiscriminate. Elements such as sex and physical looks will always be determined through a random fashion, which is beyond the parent's realm of control. From the child's point of view, the immediate family that he is born into may also be, seemingly, determined at random.

Likewise, the intrinsic spirit of one's child is also not determined on a constant or continual basis. While the only fully determined element of the individual's mind is his intellect, it is only the power of his intellect that will be entirely determined by nature. With respect to his emotions, the individual plays some determinate role through the directing of his emotional centre, and also in the expanding of his emotional equilibrium through experience. Yet, the individual's core of emotions may also be, somewhat, determined at birth. It is only the individual's array of principles that is entirely determined by his own chosen core values. As a result, the individual's soul, as a whole, is never determined by any kinds of constants or universal laws. Both the individual's physical looks and his intrinsic spirit will remain entirely distinct and unique. In this case, there does exist some sort of truth regarding the random creation of life, and this could grant the atheist with some kind of justification regarding his beliefs towards a random theory of creation.

As a result, within our physical world, all forms of constants remain as constants, in the same manner that all instances of randomness remain entirely random. It may not be truly rational to conclude that some constant will somehow lose its essence and transform into something that is random, nor vice versa. In other words, the concepts of constants and randomness contradict each other, and thus, they are utterly incompatible with one another. As such, the massive instances of order present on Earth provide us with a substantial reason to conclude that the universe, itself, is also an ordered phenomenon.

Therefore, we must question how it is possible for something that is purely random in nature to transform into something that is purely constant in nature. Since the concepts of randomness and constants oppose one another, the birth of physical and immaterial forms of order within our universe does require further clarification. Is it feasible for some purely random entity to create another entity that is governed by so many complicated and systematic laws? If the Earth is purely a randomly evolving entity, then all forms of science, including the laws of physics, will possess the inherent potential to become defunct at some point in our future. Yet, the continued existence of all forms of life on Earth does seem to indicate that the universe does possess a constant nature, and if the universe does possess the characteristic of order, this would seem to contradict the big bang theory.

The big bang theory, nevertheless, does implicate the existence of an immaterial world. If it is true that the universe was first born due to a few molecules of matter, then what phenomena existed outside of this distinct and particular substance? In fact, whatever surrounded these molecules, or whatever existed beyond the boundary of these few particles of matter, necessarily, could not be any forms of matter.

Therefore, the surrounding environment that existed in conjunction, and outside of these molecules of matter, must have been immaterial in nature. This, then, implicates the existence of an immaterial world.

Hence, if our material universe is truly in a constant state of growth, then it must be expanding its boundaries over some bordering realm, and this can only be characterized as something that is immaterial in nature. Consider the logic present within the big bang theory. According to this theory of creation, our universe was first born due to the fact that there existed more molecules of matter, in comparison to molecules of antimatter. Since the birth of our universe first began with a few molecules of matter, the expansion of these particles of matter took precedence over the growth of antimatter. Successively, that which bordered those particles of matter cannot be comprised of anything that possessed an equivalent material nature. As a consequence, when a material universe is in a state of expansion, it must, from a logical standpoint, be expanding into the realm of the immaterial. In other words, the growth and development of a physical universe implicates the existence of a bordering environment that lacks any physical properties.

Moreover, the evolution of the universe, that is consistent with the big bang theory, could also implicate the existence of God. This is due to the theory of an external source. If the universe is truly expanding, then its growth necessarily requires some type of fuel, or external source. In the same manner that a flame requires an external source of oxygen for it to expand, the same may be true regarding all ecosystems. For example, consider the oceanic environment. If the polar ice caps were to melt, then the ocean levels would rise, due essentially to an increase in water. A similar concept applies to our liveable habitat. Therefore, if the Earth's atmosphere were to somehow increase and encompass the moon, then our liveable ecosystem would include this particular habitat. Yet, a habitable atmosphere would require higher levels of oxygen. As a consequence, in order to acquire higher levels of oxygen, our atmosphere will require another source of oxygen. Hence, this potential habitable atmosphere would require an external source of oxygen.

Every expanding ecosystem will require additional levels of some life-sustaining element, in the same manner that the growth of a flame requires the element of fuel. The expansion of the human habitat would require an external source of oxygen, in the same manner that an expansion of the oceans would require an external source of water. When we apply this theoretical construct towards the growth of our universe, this would seem to indicate that the physical cosmos also requires some kind of an external source for its continued expansion. If this is true, then the continual growth of our cosmos will necessarily require an external source that exists somewhere beyond the boundaries of our physical universe.

If what borders our material universe is the realm of the immaterial, then an immaterial world does, indeed, exist. Likewise, if the growth of our material universe does require some type of additional element, this external source, necessarily, must come from the realm of the immaterial. As a direct result, that external source which is responsible for the growth and development of our universe can only be known as God. Any external source required for the growth of our universe, that is immaterial in nature, should originate through our concept of God. Hence, both the sustenance and the expansion of our physical universe must be due directly to the existence of God.

In effect, a universe with God as its creator will never disintegrate, simply because life will continue to grow and be sustained by Him. Therefore, if it is true that our universe has existed for billions of years, and that it will also continue to exist for billions of more years, this indicates that it is a thriving ecosystem. On the other hand, in a universe without God, there would be no concrete entity that would serve to sustain life within our universe. In a randomly created universe, there does exist the potential that our universe will disintegrate.

Nonetheless, the conceptual essence of the big bang indicates that our universe is not in a state of disintegration. In actuality, the big bang theory indicates that the universe is truly in a state of expansion. Therefore, the universe is presently giving birth to new instances of stars and planets. If this is true, this further indicates that our universe is also an evolving ecosystem. All forms of growth do require some form of sustenance. Logically, that element which sustains the growth of our material universe must come from something that exists beyond its physical borders. In view of that, that immaterial external source must be known as God. An expanding universe does implicate an external source, and an external source implicates the existence of God.

With respect to theism, we may further ask how a totally rational and mentally healthy person may maintain a concrete idea of God, if He never existed. In the case of one's imagination, purely imagined thoughts exist only within a private mind. Just because I imagined a triple horned unicorn as a child doesn't entail the fact that many other children, around the entire world, also imagined that specific and distinct thought. Nevertheless, with respect to God, many children around the world do possess the idea of an almighty creator, entirely through an independent fashion. In the case of God, there does exist another child, who lives in a differing hemisphere, that also possesses an idea that is similar to my own.

Therefore, in the case of my imagination, I have imagined a triple horned unicorn, while my peer has imagined a kind of Pegasus, with three sets of wings. In this case, we both possess a concrete idea of a horse, albeit with differing properties. Yet, our base idea of a horse remains the same, essentially due to the fact that we were both exposed to the concept of a horse. Therefore, the primary foundation behind our idea of a horse has a basis within the real world. Nevertheless, through our imaginations, we have added properties to that idea of a horse, which, correspondingly, have not come directly through any of our sensory perceptions. Indeed, while I possess an idea of a rhinoceros, my peer has an idea of a bird, and the both of us are combining these unique ideas together, through our imagination. With respect to an almighty creator, every person's idea of God has originated through the same process. While every theist possesses a basic idea of God, every theist also adds subjective properties in relation to this idea.

While my idea of a horse comes directly from my sensory perception of that animal, I cannot imagine a true idea of a horse, if I have never seen one through my own sense of sight. In fact, the individual who lives within the Arctic does not possess an accurate idea of a horse, if he has never seen one through his own two eyes. Likewise, I cannot possess an accurate idea of a penguin, if I have never perceived a picture of this animal, at some point during my lifetime. Indeed, an individual from the Arctic cannot purely imagine a true and exact idea of a horse, any more than I could purely imagine a true and exact idea of a penguin. Yet, while I possess some idea of God, my neighbour within the Arctic does possess a similar idea. In a subsequent fashion, we must question how is this possible? How can so many persons around the world, who have never met, still possess an independent concept of God, even though He, essentially, does not reveal Himself to us through a physical manner? Could one's idea of God be a sole product of the imagination, despite the fact that a multitude of other persons around the world share a similar idea?

In response, from the atheist's viewpoint, the theist's idea of God would be comparable to the phenomenon of a phantom limb. The phantom limb is a sensation where the individual experiences a feeling that a missing limb is still attached to his body. Many individuals around the world experience this feeling, which grants them, at least on a personal level, some reason to hold a false belief. Therefore, the atheist will counter-argue that the theist holds and maintains a false belief regarding the existence of God, due directly to the fact that a concrete material connection with Him does not truly exist.

Even if God does not exist, man's idea of God could still serve some kind of purpose. Within the theist's mind, God exists, at least in spirit. It is the spirit of God which drives the theist towards moral systems of thought. Persons from differing communities around the world will also possess a moral system of beliefs, due essentially to their faith in God. Therefore, in actuality, He does possess an immaterial existence within our world, even if this existence is limited solely within the mindset of the theist.

Those who have faith in His existence possess the idea of a morally superior being. Hence, the individual's idea of God, alone, will motivate him to act according to ethical codes of behaviour. Moreover, since all communities are built upon ethical principles like cooperation, man's sole idea of God will still serve to improve our quality of life. The idea of some morally perfect being provides the common citizen with a substantial reason to act in accordance with the virtues of honour and justice. Since morality is a necessary element among all forms of positive social relationships, man's idea of God, alone, does serve to cultivate the human spirit.

Our faith in God reflects upon the values that we place on life itself. In believing in a highly moral creator, we have faith in the fact that whatever created us also values all forms of life. This reinforces the moral values that we have in place within our communities. Yet, the existence of concepts of morality leads to a deity paradox. In essence, our idea of a morally perfect being motivates us to act according to virtue. Regarding human beings, and most other animals in the wild, forms of offspring will initially depend upon their parents for their primary survival. As a result, most sentient beings possess a sense of cooperation, because this is necessary for the continued survival of their species. Yet, where does this sense of morality and cooperation come from? A simple answer may be based on our love for existence. The fact that our communities represent the spirit of altruism over selfishness demonstrates our natural tendencies towards our love for existence. This leads us to ask the next question. If all forms of life were created by something other than God, where do the universal concepts of love and morality come from? When we view our world, we see that most sentient species of life also follow the principle of cooperation, similar to the spirit that all human communities are built upon.

Likewise, we must further question the fact that if our universe was created by a non-sentient entity, how can sentience be created? According to the law of reproduction, a generation of life can only possess the properties of its parent, and nothing more. Therefore, if the law of reproduction holds true, some being with an infinite amount of spirit must be the cause of our universe. This is due to the fact that the cause of an infinite amount of spirits must also, itself, possess this quality. For even if we just consider the planet Earth, every sentient being that has ever existed possesses an entirely unique soul. Since every spirit is unique, the cause of our universe must be an unlimited kind of being, at least in the realm of spirituality.

Hence, if God does not exist, we must ask what drives the constant spirit of cooperation, within an essentially random and chaotic amalgamation of differing categories of life. Moral kinds of cooperation, observable within human communities, remain prevalent among the majority of species of life that exist in our natural world. Therefore, if the big bang theory is true, is it truly possible for something that is purely material in nature to produce something that is purely immaterial in nature, such as the concept of love? If this is possible, then the immaterial realm should, indeed, be infinite and limitless. Moreover, if intelligent and emotional forms of life can evolve from a few particles of matter, then the evolution of all forms of life, itself, must also be boundless in nature.

Correspondingly, since the evolution of the universe may, necessarily, be limitless both materially and spiritually, this paves the way for the possible birth of a Godlike entity within our future. In other words, if the big bang theory is true, and God does not exist, then it is still possible that He will come into existence, at some future time. Since the concept of evolution may be truly defined without any kinds of limits, the birth of an entity, who possesses the powers we attribute to God, could potentially come about during our future.

Without a doubt, if complex intelligent, emotional and spiritual beings could evolve from a few particles of matter, then why couldn't God evolve from the mere existence of human beings? If the nature of the immaterial spirit is truly without limits, then it is wholly possible that the birth of God could come about during our future. Accordingly, it is rationally possible that God could evolve from the simplistic nature of a human being, essentially because of the miraculous evolution of human beings from a mere few particles of matter.

Even if the big bang theory is true, there still remains the possibility that the two main theories of creation may remain compatible. First of all, it is possible that God could have created the molecules that eventually evolved into our physical universe. Nevertheless, even if God is not the sole cause of these molecules, there still remains the fact that our ever so great and evolving physical universe originated through merely a few particles of matter. In the latter case, the concept of evolution should be sweeping, and not confined by any kinds of restrictions or limitations. In effect, the extreme power correlated with the concept evolution makes it conceivably possible for a Godlike entity to evolve at some future time. In turn, God may either be the author and creator of our entire physical universe, or a creature that could evolve at some point during the future of human civilization.

Bibliography

"Being and Nothingness." Sparknotes. Jun. 2011

    <http://www.sparknotes.com/philosophy/sartre/section4.rhtml>.

Descartes. Selected Philosophical Writings. Cambridge, UK: Cambridge University Press, 1988.

Dowden, Bradley. "Time". Aug. 2001. Internet Encyclopedia of Philosophy. June 2011

    <http://www.iep.utm.edu/time/#H1>.

Fagan, Andrew. "Human Rights". Jan. 2003. Internet Encyclopedia of Philosophy. June 2011

    <http://www.iep.utm.edu/hum-rts/>.

Hawking, Stephen. Into the Universe with Stephen Hawking: The Story of Everything. Dir. Iain

    Riddick. 2010. Television. Discovery.

Hawking, Stephen. Into the Universe with Stephen Hawking: Time Travel. Dir. Nathan Willams. 2010.
>Television. Discovery.

Howard-Snyder, Daniel. The Evidential Argument from Evil. Bloomington, Indiana: Indiana University
>Press, 1996.

Martinich, A. P. The Philosophy of Language. 4th ed. New York: Oxford University Press, 2001.

Moseley, Alexander. "Pacifism." Aug. 2001. Internet Encyclopedia of Philosophy. Jun. 2011
><http://www.iep.utm.edu/pacifism/>.

Murtagh, Kevin. "Punishment." Jul. 2005. Internet Encyclopedia of Philosophy. Jun. 2011
><http://www.iep.utm.edu/punishme/>.

Plato. Five Dialogues: Euthyphro, Apology, Crito, Meno, Phaedo. 2nd ed. Indiana, Indianapolis:
>Hackett, 2002.

Plato. Gorgias. New Jersey: Prentice Hall, 1997.

Plato. Protagoras. Indiana, Indianapolis: Hackett, 1992.

Plato. The Republic. 2nd ed. London: Penguin Group, 1987.

"The Universal Declaration of Human Rights". United Nations. Jun. 2011 <http://www.un.org/en/documents/udhr/>.

Walzer, Micheal. Just and Unjust Wars. 3rd ed. New York: Basic Books, 2000.

"What different flowers symbolize." HudsonValleyWeddings.com. Jun. 2011
<http://www.hudsonvalleyweddings.com/guide/flowers.htm>.

"What do trees symbolize?" Answers. Jun. 2011
<http://wiki.answers.com/Q/What_do_trees_symbolize>.

www.ingramcontent.com/pod-product-compliance
Lightning Source LLC
Chambersburg PA
CBHW071849290426
44110CB00013B/1079